WIGGY!

By Gareth Rogers

Edited by Tony McDonald

Published November 2005 by
Retro Speedway
Tel: 01708 734 502
www.retro-speedway.com

Printed by Biddles Ltd, King's Lynn, Norfolk

Distributed by Retro Speedway
103 Douglas Road, Hornchurch, Essex, RM11 1AW, England
Email: editorial@retro-speedway.com

Set in Sans

ISBN 0 9548336-7-8

Cover photography by Alan Whale, Ken Carpenter& Mike Patrick

PHOTOGRAPHIC ACKNOWLEDGEMENTS
A number of the photographs published in this book have been kindly donated by the Wigg family, and every attempt has been made to correctly identify the individual source. In this respect, we would like to thank the following: Ken Carpenter, Mike Patrick, Alan Whale, Alf Weedon, Hans Fock, Russell Groom, John Hipkiss, John Bollé, Chris Convine, the late Don Ringrow, the late Bruce Grainger, Trevor Meeks, Preben Knudsen, Johann Huber, Wolfgang Radszuweit, Frank Czichon, Debbie Mauger, RobMac Photo, Paul Hornsby, Margit Roessler, Willen Hospice and anybody else whose pictures we have unfortunately not been able to credit.

TO ABIGAIL AND RICKI

In memory of the late Simon Wigg.
A very proud father and international motorcycle racing legend.

Sadly missed.

Never forgotten.

Contents

Acknowledgements

Author Gareth Rogers and publishers, Tony McDonald and Susie Muir of Retro Speedway, would particularly like to thank the following for their special help and enthusiasm in making this tribute to Simon Wigg possible:

Julian and Lynne Wigg
Charlie and Pat Booden
Abigail, Ricki and Alexz Wigg
And everybody else who gave up their valuable time to contribute to the extensive Tributes section.

Mike Patrick, Ken Carpenter, Alan Whale and Alf Weedon for their photographic brilliance.

Dickie Staff
Martin Neal
Nigel Wagstaff
Glynn Shailes
The Willen Hospice

Marios Flourentzou for cover design.

Foreword

By Julian Wigg ('Big Wigg')

SIMON was a very happy little boy, mischievous with an outgoing personality. Our parents, Tony and Rosemary, who were both in their forties at the time my little brother was born, could just about manage him.

The age difference between us was 11 years, so he was more like a son to me in many ways. In fact, I was the one who named him.

I was unhappy with my Christian name – when I was a child nobody was called Julian and I received a lot of stick because of it. So I said to my parents,'let's call the baby something normal, shall we?' I came up with Simon and thought that sounded alright. (Incidentally, I'm happy with Julian these days, to be honest. My son, Alexz, has a 'z' on the end of the name so he can't be confused with Alec.)

I was always interested in anything on two wheels. The only activities that I ever managed to be better at than my school mates were riding a pushbike and eventually riding motorbikes.

When we were based outside Aylesbury – my father, Tony, had a business there – and Simon was three, we used to put him on a pushbike and let him loose down the yard. He used to turn it so hard that he would take the tyres off the rims! Simon was magic on a bike by the time he was four. Funnily enough, Alexz, was riding a pushbike at 18 months, so I could see the same sparkle in him, too. I've also spotted natural talent in other youngsters and it's fair to say that the ones who show flair as children invariably go on to achieve success in motor sport.

Our family moved away to Ipswich and although I went there for a little while, I couldn't make a go of things and came back to live in Buckinghamshire. Eventually my parents also returned to Bucks and Simon was able to gain some attention and influence from me. I suppose he thought that I was some sort of superstar at the time but I wasn't – I never reached the heights that he did.

As Simon mentions in his contribution to this book, there was a local guy, Tony Ward from Whitchurch, who had a Triumph Tiger Cub bike that I think we bought from him for £48. Simon was about 13 at the time and we had started going to local meetings. He was quick and once he learned to change gear, it was obvious that he was would go places in the sport. Even then he had this dream of becoming World Longtrack Champion, an ambition he focused on from a very early age.

We did quite a few meetings together, with Simon riding in the schoolboy section and myself in the seniors. He would work on his bike and then bring it around to ask me what I thought of it? I'd then pull it to bits for him.

One day we went to Braintree, Essex for pre-season practice. He had altered his footrest and asked if it was in the correct position on the bike. I said that it looked alright but Simon insisted that I tried it out for him. So out I went on his bike and all was well until the footrest snapped and I hit my nuts on the crossbar! I wasn't impressed by the welding performed on the frame, I can tell you! Simon was pretty

Julian on the grass at Lydden, 1971.

disgruntled, too, because the damage to his bike meant he couldn't ride for the rest of the day.

A lot of things went wrong on the bike because of our shortage of money. It was an invaluable learning experience for Simon, though, as he had to accept the disappointments as well as the good times. To be a champion you have got to face challenges and meet them. We also realised fairly soon the need to have equipment that is as good as, or better than, everybody else's.

However, we did have a lot of fun, for Simon was quite a comedian. We used to get on really well despite our age gap. Simon was able to learn from my mistakes. By the time I realised what I should be doing, my time had come and gone, but he was ready to push on. Nobody had shown any interest in me and it was a tough learning curve. It takes a long time to make it and if you don't have somebody involved around you with any kind of motorcycling knowledge, then it is difficult. For Simon, he could skip five years' worth of learning, maybe more, because of my experiences. You can't beat the whole context of second or third generation family racers. Look at the Lampkins in trials, the Crumps or Richardsons in speedway, and the Nichols or Nunns in moto-cross. When I take Alexz to national trials events today, I notice how many others haven't got a clue. We are so well organised in comparison. When I started racing I thought: big track, big engine sprocket, open throttle . . . go fast! It's all you know. It takes you a little while – or somebody you respect – to open your eyes and say: 'Try this.'

One guy who did help me was Freddie Watts, who was British 250cc champion at the time. Freddie was unfortunately killed in a racing incident in France in 1969 and just a week before his accident, I beat him on his own bike. He was as pleased as I was. Freddie was a big help and the only rider who bothered to talk to me.

There was an insular hierarchy in the sport back then. Unless you actually beat somebody of note, they wouldn't talk to you. Simon had me to chat to and thankfully that old attitude has gone from the sport now. Today's grasstrack stars seem to have more time for the up and coming youngsters.

Sometimes we got it wrong but I had some ability on a bike and could communicate easily with Simon. By the time I realised how to manage and develop my racing skills, it was too late for me. I had also got bashed about too much. Helping with Simon's career was a case of second time around for me but all of a sudden his progress and success became more important to me than my own. When you see someone who has that special gift and you can help them achieve their goals, it is as satisfying as achieving them yourself. In my mind, it felt as if I was on the bike riding the race with him.

Then there is the other factor of two heads being better than one. All the way home from meetings, if things hadn't gone to plan, we would analyse what had gone wrong. And that happened all the way through Simon's career, not just in the early days. I go through the same post-meeting analysis with Alexz now. What went right? What went wrong? Why did this happen? What's the problem? How can we sort it?

It's difficult unless you have a mentor and, I suppose, I became Simon's mentor. But when the ace German engine tuner, Hans Zierk, came along, it was brilliant. He just took Simon under his wing as if he were his own son. He stated: 'I will sponsor you until you stop riding' – and he bloody well meant it.

Julian tussling with Aussie John Langfield at Salty Creek, Newcastle, NSW, 1973. Simon liked Langy's crowd appeal.

Our father never showed any interest in his sons' motorcycling interests and dreams. He always thought that I was going to grow out of it and I believe he thought the same about Simon. When we started doing well he started slapping everybody on the back and treated it as good news!

Funnily enough, I went back to Waddesdon, Bucks – the village where I was born – at the beginning of 2005. I was looking for a bloke who made exhausts and had worked for motorcycling legend Kenny Roberts. I found the house but the guy wasn't there at the time. His father asked me my name and when I told him, he said: 'When I was a kid in this village, your dad was a god. He was the fastest man anybody had ever seen on a motorbike. He was fantastic.'

Simon giving Julian a lift at Maryborough, Australia, 1986.

Well, my father never told us that! He was always playing the whole motorcycle scene down. He always made out that he didn't understand anything about what Simon and I were doing and certainly couldn't fix any of our mechanical problems. But this recent revelation is really uncanny. I suppose that's where our taste for speed came from.

Simon had so much enthusiasm and my son, Alexz, is the same. If there is an engine running plus fuel and daylight, he'll be away. If I said to Alexz now: 'We've got to go and practice,' he would reply: 'Yes! OK.' Simon's burning desire to race was there from a very young age and it remained with him throughout his career – from schoolkid to World Champion. It wasn't to do with money. It was his pure love of motorcycle racing, or just the thrill he got from riding the bike. There are not many people who can get such a buzz. What is better than to race motorcycles as a sport? I can't think of anything.

As I said, Simon was good as a youngster and he went straight into the adult grasstrack category at 16. Then came the crucial episode with Windsor Comp. They initially wanted to sponsor me but I said to them that they should look instead at Simon, as he really needed some help. I told them that I thought he could go a long way. Pete Webb, who owned Windsor Comp, was brilliant, along with Jeff Bing who used to run Norman Reeves Ford. Simon received a new car from them, while Pete paid for two bikes, leathers and quite a lot of equipment. That was after George Watts had helped Simon in the schoolboys.

It made a dramatic difference, for now we could say forget everything else, this is what we are going for. From that time onwards things moved forward quite a bit because other people had belief in Simon as well as me. I could see the potential in him and Pete took my word for it, which was brilliant.

Simon was totally focused. If a businessman has the self-belief and determination to state that he is going to be a millionaire by the time he is 40, he will probably do it. If anything else gets in the way that they don't need, then they will kick it into touch. Making the decision and meeting it is the hard bit. Once you have decided on your career path, then all the decisions you have to make in life are made for you.

Talent may not matter that much, especially as one gets older. I always say that there are a number of riders who have won a World Championship without having great natural ability. Ivan Mauger was not a natural motorcyclist whereas Barry Briggs was, but Ivan achieved phenomenal success through sheer determination, hard work and by using his brain. Briggo's riding ability on a speedway bike grew with his success. Hans Nielsen had the same qualities possessed by both Ivan and Briggo and he too certainly grew in stature after winning his first World Final, in 1986.

With Simon, there was an awful lot of planning but this follows once you have made the decision to go for it. I think he realised very early on that once he had made his decision to reach the top, he could bat everything else out of the way. It was tunnel vision for him from then on.

Speedway started as simply something for Simon to do between longtrack meetings – a chance to get in some practice and extra time on a bike, to make a few starts on a Tuesday night at Weymouth. He began to be successful at speedway because he did it without

Made it to the top! Julian embraces Simon seconds after his first World Longtrack Final win, at Korskro in 1985.

feeling pressure. I was always keener on grasstrack and longtrack compared to speedway, so if I was asked the question about Simon's priority once he became so busy, it was the longtrack scene. That's where his heart was. I feel sure that Simon is now riding around some longtrack in the sky doing wheelies at 100mph!

In speedway terms, his happiest team days were during the 1983 season he spent at Cradley Heath. They were a fantastic bunch of guys and a hell of a team – so strong, they even had Danish internationals Peter Ravn and Jan O Pedersen at reserve at one time. Erik Gundersen is such a lovely man, more off the cuff than his big rival Hans Nielsen. Erik would have a smoke or get wasted occasionally but Hans never would. They are completely different personalities.

We had lots of scrapes and adventures in the early days of racing abroad. When we got tied up with the Lantenhammer-Weslakes, what Otto liked was for us to bring a load of stuff over for him. In reality, we were his UK exporters. On one particular trip, we had obtained 12 sets of mudguards from Starline, 10 gearboxes and clutches from George Bewdley, 20 Interspan ignitions and, including other bits and pieces, our Citroen Safari was eventually full up. We had a bike without an engine – the engine was obviously in Germany – and we threw that on top of the heap.

In an earlier telephone conversation, Otto's wife, Ingrid, had asked us to also bring over 50 carburettors. We phoned Barry Johnson, who was running Amal at the time, and told him that we needed 50 carburettors by Friday night. Barry said he would do what he could, as he had to get all the staff in urgently. You might think that they had them in stock but the carburettors actually had to be hand-built. They worked throughout day and night to get them all ready. That meant yet another box found its way under the bike in the car that was now jammed full.

Anyway, I was just driving out of the docks in France when a lady driver came across in front of me. I let her in and, as I did, there was suddenly a customs officer alongside me. He saw the mudguards glittering in the back, and stopped us to ask for our paperwork. We had to take everything out of the car, which resembled Aladdin's Cave. The customs official kept challenging us for the paperwork for the consignment but it was anything but straightforward. Some bits were incorrectly invoiced by the suppliers. Some parts we had brought across to offset against the cost of the engine Lantenhammer had tuned for Simon, while we had intended to chase up the money for other parts later.

So we thought: 'We're in the s*** here.' The official then looked at the bike and asked where the engine was. Ironically, the only item we had a carnet for was this bike without its engine!

Inevitably, they eventually locked us both in a room until they decided to fine us £260 and send us back to England. On immediate return to Dover, we headed straight across the port and bought a ticket to . . . Ostend!

Eventually we made it to our destination in Germany, where there was another twist to the tale awaiting us. When we presented the box of carburettors, Otto said: 'Carb rubbers! We asked for carb rubbers, not carburettors!'

We had misheard the accent over the phone, so had to take all 50 carburettors back to Amal, where we also had some explaining to do!

Travel on boats could be bloody hilarious in those early days. Because we were all on tight budgets to race abroad, we would do anything we could to save money. All the riders did. We used to go loaded with the support team in the back of the van but after the Zeebrugge tragedy in 1987, the shipping companies introduced stricter controls – boarding passes and that sort of stuff. We used to travel in hordes but you'd tell the port authorities there was only you and a co-driver in the vehicle. Then you would board the boat and all of your 'secret passengers' would all get out again.

Funnily enough, I went to Sweden one year with Grubby Sharpe, Ian Barclay's former right-hand man in the old Ace of Aces meeting and one-time mechanic to John Davis. Anyway, I was so used to there being more blokes than tickets that I hid him under the bikes. I was asked by a female official how many I had in the van and I told her that there was just myself. She replied: 'That's strange, it says TWO on the ticket.'

What happened was that the BSPA had bought the tickets in advance of a Test series and allocated two people to each vehicle. I was so used to buying a ticket for one that I had gone and hidden Grubby, even though, unbeknown to me, he was legally allowed to travel in the van with me. I could hear Grubby giggling in the background as the lady asked me questions!

When we were overloaded – as was usually the case – the boys would spill out and look for an empty cabin. Sometimes, in the middle of the night, some poor bloke would try and get into bed and find a hell of a shock awaiting him!

In those days we would buy day-return tickets and alter the date on the way back, or spill coffee on them, to disguise the fact they had gone out of date. The tickets were handwritten then, in the days before computerisation. We pulled these little strokes because if you tried to do everything correctly by the book, you couldn't afford to race.

From Day One there were always going to be areas of disagreement between Simon and me over mechanical aspects. The problem is that of having a rider, whoever it is, with some mechanical knowledge of engines and setting them up. As a mechanic or tuner, it is very nice to have a rider who gives you feedback but he doesn't need to know how it is working.

With my son, he doesn't want to know anything – I prepare the bike and he rides it. With Simon, I used to change things without telling him, or there were occasions when he would tell me to change something and I didn't.

Simon tinkered too much and it is a family trait. Even today in my work for the Ministry of Defence, I'll try out different methods and then say to myself: 'Why can't I bloody leave that alone because it is working well enough as it is?' But you are always trying to make something better. If I had a criticism of Simon – that would be the major one. He wanted to change bikes and parts, even when he was winning races.

I remember a longtrack qualifier at Harsewinkel, Germany. We always ran about 16 to 18 pounds on the back tyre. Go under that pressure and you faced the prospect of a puncture. Simon had been dieting to get lighter but he wasn't making starts, so I had to do something about it. I dropped the tyre pressures to 14 or 15 pounds – and then Simon started winning everything.

Team Wigg before the World Longtrack Final at Muhldorf, 1993. Grubby Sharpe, Julian, Mick Day and Steve Brandon.

The next season, he was off at a meeting somewhere when he phoned me at home saying: 'I can't make the starts, what's happening?'

I told him: 'Your tyre is too hard, put 15 pounds in.'

Simon piped up: 'It will puncture.'

'It didn't last year, Wiggy!' I informed him – I should say that I always called him Wiggy and he called me Big Wigg.

'You b******!' he shouted.

My philosophy was: would you rather be second 10 times or first five times? Me? I'd rather win five races and break down in the rest.

I also defend my decision not to tell him all the facts, because it meant he wasn't riding around worrying about the possibility of having a puncture.

I did get frustrated, though, about one mechanic Simon engaged, known as 'Go-Go', who came over from America for a while. I didn't get on with him. He had this really big hang-up about the bike looking good with plastic bits all over everything.

It all brewed up at the 1992 World Longtrack Final at Pfarrkirchen. 'Go-Go' had all this plastic crap and stickers everywhere and I couldn't get at the throttle cable properly. As we went to push the bike out for a race, the cable jumped out of the top of the carburettor. It wouldn't start because the throttle was open too far. And we couldn't get the throttle cable back in for all the stickers.

I was saying to Simon: 'I can't get this back in. What are we doing? Is the sticker more important? You win your races, then everything else will follow. The primary issue is that the throttle works properly. Without that, nothing else happens in your career.'

At other times Simon would be thinking about matching team suits or how speedway should be run. I would say to him: 'Do that in 10 years' time when you are a promoter or you want to be involved in the sport in some way.' Then again, to be fair to him, he was his own man.

When it came to disagreements, we had very few. I think there were times when, out of respect, he wouldn't say something to me and I kept my mouth shut, too. If it came to a confrontation with someone else, I would state my views but with Simon, sometimes I wouldn't. Our relationship held together well – especially as I had been involved in the same grasstrack scene as Simon before he came along. Once you have helped to get someone to the high level that he reached, where he had won World Championships, I obviously had to have respect for his views as well. If you are with someone who starts winning everything, how do you then tell them how to win titles?

When I'm asked which of Simon's five World Longtrack titles meant the most to him, I have to say the first – at Korskro in 1985. You reach a stage where, after all those years of hard work, you wonder if it will ever happen. And then to eventually crack it, it's a wonderful feeling.

At times I was doing everything and Simon would pay for my input, because he didn't always want the responsibility on his shoulders. It's the same now with Alexz – the time and finances I have invested in him applies extra pressure. When Alexz won the European Trials Championship in Spain in 2004, I noticed the difference in how relaxed he was afterwards. Chatting on the way back, he told me: 'That was a weight off my shoulders and I'm glad I've done it. I didn't want to let you down.'

Simon was very upbeat after winning his first world title and Erik Gundersen, with whom we got on really well, was one of the greatest guys on that feel-good factor theme. Erik wanted others to experience what it was like to win a World Final. After he'd won the speedway World Championship for the first time in 1984, he'd say: 'I wish you could feel this, Wiggy. I like you so much as a bloke that I'd love you to do this but I have to try to beat you.'

I thought Simon was so good that he was owed a few World Finals. If you are at the top of your profession, it should drop into place for you.

At the Herxheim World Longtrack Final in 1990, I sat in the pits and said: 'What we could do with, Wiggy, is Karl Maier blowing an engine.' We had suffered a few blow-ups over the years and thought that it was time we benefited from somebody else's misfortune.

As the words left my lips, I heard a big roar – Karl's engine had exploded out of the frame. All Simon now had to do was stay on his bike to win the title, which he did.

Karl and Simon were big rivals but they had great respect for each other on and off the track, too. During that era they were both really at their peak.

After the 1989 speedway World Final at Munich, where Simon was runner-up to his Oxford team-mate Hans Nielsen, we were all wasted but we had to be at a big grasstrack meeting at Berghaupton the next day. At five o'clock in the morning I had to get everybody up at the hotel. Simon had got the promoter to arrange a driver to take him to the Black Forest, so we weren't worried about him. However, we had to get his bikes there and warmed up.

We were running an old transit, which I just drove flat out from Munich through pouring rain. We went all the way through the Black Forest at 100mph and by the time that we reached the track, Simon had scrounged a bike off a junior to do his first heat. In the rush, we just threw the bikes out of the vehicle.

Just before the final, Simon said to Karl: 'I had such a great day yesterday. This is yours today.' Karl did about three laps and just dropped on his backside, leaving Wiggy to take victory. I had

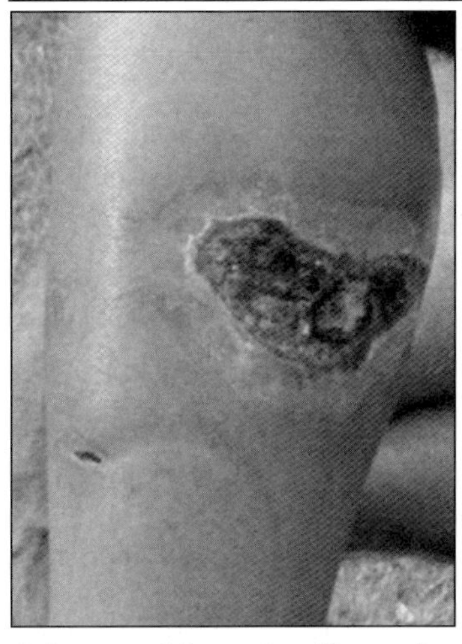

A close-up of the nasty calf wound Simon suffered. Julian didn't always approve of the remedial treatment.

never previously seen Karl fall off, so perhaps he relaxed a bit before the race.

There is the other side of the coin. At a Muhldorf final, Simon ran fifth in his first heat and then won every other heat and broke the track record. He won the semi-final and the final but lost the title by a point. I didn't know what to do, so I went and sulked for days. You go to so many World Finals and absorb so many pressures that eventually you sit around watching other riders suffering their own panic situations. Over time and through experience, you become pretty cool about the balance of luck.

Simon was very tense until he had got a world title under his belt. To be honest, until 1985 it was bloody awful at times. We were trying to go forward and the pressure was enormous. Once the first one is in the bag, you tend to get on a roll.

Simon's preparation was meticulous in many areas. For example, he could be generally overweight, so he had to be very careful what he ate. In the build up to a World Longtrack Final, he would live on salads and coffee.

Ironically for someone who took a strong line against the drugs culture in speedway in the 80s, Simon found himself surrounded by controversy over the amount of caffeine in his system after a blood test at a World Longtrack Final at Muhldorf.

Simon consumed around 10 cups of very strong German coffee before and during the meeting. After the caffeine levels showed up in his post-meeting dope test, there was a big fuss and it was even suggested that he would be stripped of his title. It would have been grossly unfair to such a dedicated sportsman and, thankfully, commonsense prevailed in the end.

As he got older, Simon realised that if he could be as fit at 40 as he was when he was 17, then he would remain competitive. I believe that if Simon had lived, he would have carried on at the top well into his forties.

Once he became a world-beater I did have issues with my brother about trusting everybody who came along. I would say: 'Is this guy for real? Is he a real mate or not? Is he there because you are famous?' I do form opinions of people very quickly. Once you achieve some success, it can be very hard to weigh up situations. People love being with the successful ones and I did try to protect him from hangers-on. However, if you do trust everybody it's quite nice really. And if people you trust then do you a disservice – well, what goes around comes around, doesn't it? They'll do the wrong thing to someone else and that person will bite them a lot harder than you would. I tend to walk away from it. If you don't do the right things to people it'll come back and haunt you. If you make the right moves in life, success will come through and Simon knew this.

We did, though, have a particular problem with Simon over the question of his health. Many times medical 'gurus' were creaming money out of him and I would think: 'Just get to hospital, mate.' I remember incidents with both a very nasty calf injury sustained while longtracking in Germany and the broken neck he suffered at Lonigo, Italy.

With the calf muscle problem, instead of having water injected into it while eating garlic, he needed to be getting air to it. Simon told me that it was getting better but I pointed out that it would be healing anyway. I would tell Simon that the guy treating him was a quack.

What influenced my outlook was that we were raised on osteopaths, herbalists and homeopaths. I feel that you will get a placebo effect from dealing with a problem but if you have something seriously wrong with you, then you should go to a hospital. So it proved for Simon, who became quite ill after one course of treatment.

"They gained his confidence on the pretence of putting together an article based on a Week in the life of Simon Wigg"

When Simon came back after crashing on his back at Lonigo, he drove from the airport and his neck was giving him jip. So he went to see Don Gatherer, who was the England rugby union osteopath at the time. After being pulled around at that session, my brother returned home and commented that his hands felt tingly. I couldn't believe that this guy, without having taken any X-rays, had pulled Simon around in the condition he was in.

My views are borne out of personal experience, too. Before my hip replacement, I went to all these sorts of guys and they would always tell me that I'd soon feel better. What they needed to tell me was that I required a big operation – and only that would get rid of the pain.

So I said to my brother: 'Bloody hell! I think you've got something really wrong with you. Don't let this guy pull you about. Get down the hospital – now!'

The X-rays showed extensive damage to the vertebrae in his neck and within hours Simon was in an operating theatre.

It took him quite a long time to come back from that bad injury. He would go into the first corner and not be right. He would be looking at other riders, watching what they were doing, instead of just looking ahead.

It was some years later before I found out more about the clutch problem that caused his injury at Lonigo. I wanted an old clutch to stick on one of my British bikes, so I pulled out this Bellini clutch and you should have seen the state of the bloody thing – he should have sued them because there was a big mechanical fault with it.

Two bits had locked together and the tolerance was not right. Once Simon had dropped the clutch, it totally locked up and couldn't be controlled by the lever, so it put him flat on his back.

As I said, it took him a while to get over it. Serious injuries do get to you psychologically if they happen often enough. When others whom you are close to are seriously injured or killed, like Erik Gundersen and the late Sepp Betzl, a rider has to control what comes into his head and it's very difficult. The only way to do it is to involve yourself heavily in something else, away from the track.

I know from my own riding days that once you have responsibilities like a wife and children, then you think about them. You have to be very carefree, or very highly motivated and single-minded, to make that first corner and go in with them all without thinking about the worst possible consequences. Guys like Ivan Mauger and Hans Nielsen, who were still at the top in their forties, must have been so good at being able to switch off all those negative thoughts

That said, Simon's pain threshold was legendary. We were at Coventry one Saturday and he had a monster second half crash with Tommy Knudsen which put them both in hospital. Wiggy was out cold on the track and we had a World Longtrack semi-final the next day at Muhldorf. I was saying to him: 'Come on Wiggy, wake up, we've got to go. We've got to go!'

All we could see were the whites of his eyes – I couldn't see his pupils. Eventually he responded by waking up in a semi-conscious state and muttering: 'Right. OK.'

Although Simon was taken to hospital, and was actually passing blood when he arrived there, he discharged himself – even though he was in a mess and didn't know what day of the week it was.

To get to Muhldorf, we had to first travel with Ole Olsen from East Midlands airport to Belgium. After staying at an hotel near the airport, we went flat out to get to the circuit in time. At the track, Simon somehow managed to get through his medical and then qualified.

It was on days like that when Simon showed tremendous courage and character.

The time that he somehow managed to recognise me on the track at Coventry came back to me years later, when he became ill and was out cold after suffering a fit. I talked to him and got a response while nobody else did. He started to move his mouth and then smiled – it was just like one of those other days when I'd be saying: 'Get up, Wiggy, we've got to go to another meeting tomorrow.'

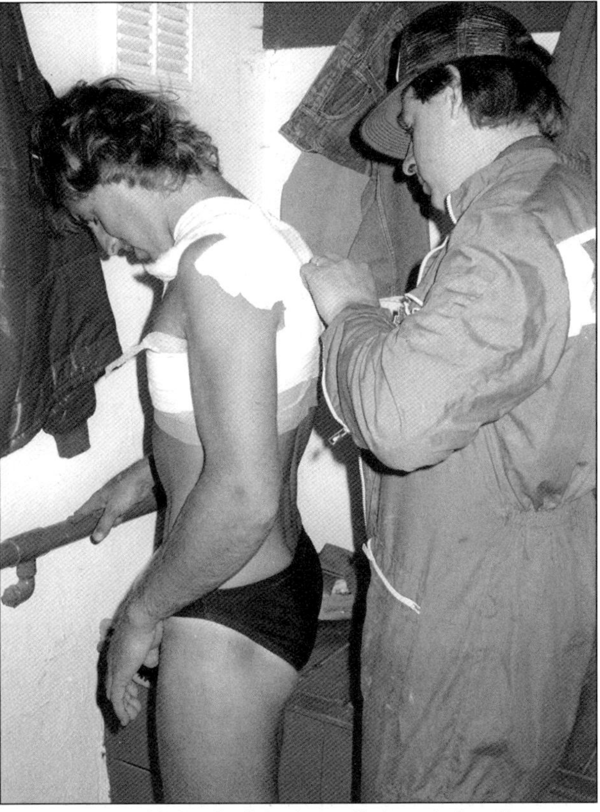

Julian straps up his brother's broken collarbone before the controversial British semi-final at Oxford in 1984.

The chain of events that resulted in Simon's FIM international speedway ban in 1985 started when Malcolm Simmons spoke to us prior to him contesting the 1984 British Final of the World Championship, a meeting for which Simon was only due to line up as standby reserve having suffered a broken collar bone in a longtrack meeting five days before the British semi-final at Oxford. Although he rode at Oxford with the aid of lots of shoulder padding and hundreds of pain-killers, he was devastated to narrowly miss the qualifying cut.

The veteran Simmo, who was among the top eight qualifiers, conceded that he was not going to get anywhere in that season's world title race – he had been world number two in 1976 but was by now in the twilight of his illustrious career – while Simon was an up and coming young English international.

So Malcolm said to us: 'I'm going to give you the opportunity to go further this year.'

He produced a doctor's note to say he had 'flu and withdrew from the British Final at Coventry, allowing Simon to take his place.

Not only did Wiggy battle through the British Final, he was the only Englishman to make it all the way to the World Final itself, held that September in Gothenburg, Sweden.

The national Sunday tabloid hacks from *The People* who subsequently made their allegations against my brother, claiming he 'bought' his place from Simmo, had wheedled their way in with Wiggy. They gained his confidence on the pretence of putting together an article based on a 'week in the life of Simon Wigg'.

What those reporters wanted desperately was for Simon to win the world title or to at least get on the rostrum, to add weight to the claims. Then they could've turned around and wrote how corrupt the sport was, while enjoying a bigger scoop the week after the World Final at Gothenburg. They didn't only accuse Simon and Malcolm – other riders were also forced to answer charges brought by the Speedway Control Board.

A defiant and wily Simmo did not concede anything to the press while Simon's first reaction was that the end of the world had come. Eventually, though, he put things in perspective, accepted the FIM's one-year ban from international speedway for 'bringing the sport into

Simon back home at The Old Stables, Middle Claydon, Bucks after recovering from his first fit in 1998.

disrepute' and started planning his diary around the racing that would still be available to him.

We didn't see it in the scandalous way *The People* did. In reality, an elder statesman of the sport had given up his booking to help a younger rider. It wasn't race-fixing. It wasn't White City, 1982, where four American riders contrived a result to suit their country's desire for more qualifiers for the USA-staged World Final. It wasn't east Europeans getting out of the way of each other in World Finals to help a fellow countryman. It wasn't a top German rider trying, unsuccessfully, to buy off Simon in a World Longtrack Final.

It was simply one rider replacing another in a British round.

Simon was disappointed at what those reporters had done to get their sensational story, which was splashed across two or three issues of one red-top paper at the end of the '84 season. However, I had warned him for a long time that not everybody is your mate, but he always remained very trusting. I don't think a person can change his or her basic character.

Oxford Speedway had its moments, too. To be fair to Simon, the track could be patchy and inconsistent, which he found hard to ride. He didn't want to take the risks that some riders would take on an inconsistent surface.

There was only one opinion I could give him at that time and I offer the same one to Alexz now when necessary. When he goes to events where he doesn't like the place, or the competition is not to his liking, my attitude is: 'Somebody has to take those points. And if someone has to win the event, it might as well be you. You are going there to ride, so let's shut up whinging about the track and get on with it.'

The only time a rider should whinge is to try and unsettle other riders – a form of gamesmanship, if you like. Quite often, Simon would deliberately say to others: 'Isn't the track s*** tonight?' He would even say it to Hans Nielsen occasionally. This psychological ploy was especially useful to Simon if he actually liked the track and thought to himself: 'It's bloody great and I'm going to get on with the job.'

It happened in reverse, of course. After Simon broke his neck at Lonigo, Peter Collins was helping somebody out at a World Final and came up and asked Simon how his neck was feeling. How I interpreted that apparently innocent enquiry from PC was that he was attempting to introduce an element of self-doubt into Simon's thoughts. Simon said: 'That was nice of Peter,' I replied that PC was simply playing the same sort of game that they played with each other.

Simon was an asset to various speedway promotions in various ways. It was him who brought over Roland Danno from Sweden for Hackney, where he was going well before the bad accident that put him in a wheelchair. Previously, Simon had recruited Australian teenager Troy Butler and Germany's Klaus Lausch to Oxford, both playing their part in championship-winning seasons for the Cheetahs.

Troy arrived as a 17-year-old no-hoper, started at reserve at Oxford but couldn't stop crashing all the time. Then he went back home to Brisbane in the winter and won the Australian Championship, so the British League experience had clearly served him well.

All three of those riders lived with Wiggy at different times. I remember Klaus working on his bike one day and while boiling his chains in 'Link-life', a glue-like substance that they used at the time, he knocked it over and made a right mess everywhere!

Simon spent most of the early part of his speedway career racing Godden machinery, before switching to GM in the late 80s and then, in the 90s, saw out his racing days on Jawa.

We had a lot of differences of opinion with Don Godden over speedway engines and I believe that Don would still be making engines today if he had accepted a little more feedback from his runners. The problem was rooted in the fact that despite being a world class longtrack rider, Don never rode speedway. All he thought a rider wanted was something that went a million miles an hour. It's a different issue to understand that, for speedway, what is needed is something that goes forward and makes grip.

The biggest problem, without being too technical, is that we were at the stage where twin carbs were the norm – and they were big carburettors at that, with 40mm ports. When the 34mm carburettor rule was introduced, then the ports of the engine needed to be smaller to provide more flexibility, but Don wouldn't have it. We ended up welding up the heads of the

Spreading the word on national Breakfast TV with Kelvin Tatum.

engine completely, starting from scratch.

I remember Simon going to the last-ever meeting held at the Sydney Showground and cleaning up. Don told us that he knew best, and he'd quote readings from his flowbench to support his argument, but he had never sat on a speedway bike.

So, in 1989, we bought a new GM engine from Trevor Hedge and went on to enjoy a very good year, Simon's best-ever on the shale. We ended up buying three of the Italian-made engines, which proved the best of that era. But had it not been for the issue over port size, Don would still be selling his GR speedway engines like nobody's business.

Of course, to reinforce his views, Don was always telling us how well Hans Nielsen was going on the GR500 'Max'. Well, with all due respect, Hans Nielsen could ride anything! He was like a machine on a speedway bike, he could do it so easily. But Don would turn around and say that Hans was winning this and Hans was winning that, which is not what we wanted to hear in any case.

There is no doubt that, at his best, Hans was magnificent and it was quite a night when Simon finished as runner-up to Hans in the 1989 World Final at the Olympic Stadium in Munich.

Simon's love of the sport shone through in his burning desire to improve everything about it, including the entertainment factor. He saw the value in having a 'Good Cop, Bad Cop' element to meetings. Simon would cite the legend of fiery John Langfield in Australia, a great character who was often more entertaining than the actual speedway! Langfield would punch the referee, or an opponent, at even the slightest perceived injustice. He'd ride the wrong way around the track in protest. Simon recognised what the public liked and how it was all part of the show.

He likened himself to being a supporter and he never thought speedway was all about whether your team wins or loses. He'd say that the racing could be great but the night wasn't complete if, say, the track presenter was rubbish, or the stadium looked dilapidated and strewn with discarded chips and other litter. Some places can be very unprofessional in both outlook and appearance.

Simon was passionate about the sport and had strongly held views. Some of the issues Simon thought should be tackled have been addressed and are now part of the fabric of the sport, so his opinions had to be respected.

I remember that we looked at the programme for the first Grand Prix at Hackney in 1995 containing advertisements for frame-builders and plumbers. Wiggy was dismayed at the lack of prestige for what was the sport's premier event of the year and he'd say: 'They shouldn't be able to buy space in this programme.'

He believed that speedway needed to change itself and become a relevant motorcycle sport, instead of the stock-car racing of the motorcycle world, which it can be at times.

There was Simon trying to raise the profile of the sport and be professionally turned-out, looking after his sponsors as best he could, only for them to turn up at some tinpot stadium with no lights on and dead chips laying about the place, to meet a promoter incapable of holding an adult conversation. I do, however, exempt Nigel Wagstaff at Oxford from those remarks, because he works very hard as a promoter.

The problem we recognised was that the vast majority of promoters are basically speedway fans themselves. They do it for sustained periods without making any money, simply because they love it and the involvement it brings them. I can appreciate the point, as I ran a motorcycle shop for 10 years. Now I've moved on to a new activity that makes me money. I take on work that I don't like doing but I am now always looking at the bottom line.

I think that Simon would have made a position for himself in the sport long-term. He would have batted people out of the way and said: 'I'm going to get hold of British Speedway and these promoters will do what I tell them.'

I thought years ago they should have handed British speedway to Barry Briggs. He is capable of going in anywhere and talking to people at any level. He would have driven speedway forward because he was a household name, and still is. A bloke has to have enough charisma about him to carry it off.

You can be sure that Simon would not have sat still in his retirement from racing. Impossible! He had too much energy, a millions ideas to nourish.

As well as doing the best he could for speedway's sake, Simon also wanted to raise his own profile within the sport, and in many ways the two ideals went hand in hand. He went on Breakfast TV in a great challenge with Kelvin Tatum. Film star Patrick Swayze was the judge as viewers voted for silly items like whether they preferred the green leathers to the blue leathers, etc. Simon would stick his nose in wherever he could – and it was quite a nose!

Simon would have taken his natural initiative, energy and enthusiasm into a promotional or ambassadorial role for speedway and grasstrack racing in this country.

He was so ahead of the game in terms of technical development, too, although the streamlined stuff was originally my idea. What works on a pushbike, will also work on a longtrack bike. I thought, there's another 10bhp here for nothing. You don't necessarily need to play with the engine, you may just need a better shape. I taped a television programme about Chris Boardman, the Olympic Cycling Champion, before rushing around to Simon and saying: 'Look at this. What are we going to do about it?'

Once he got his teeth into the concept, then he started thinking about all sorts of items that could be modified to produce improvement to the aerodynamics. We started with the the seat, which we reshaped to also house the rear mudguard and number. It looked like a road racing back end and, to be honest, at first we thought the FIM wouldn't allow it. But they did and now it's commonplace in longtrack racing.

We also changed Simon's leathers, filling the gap between the bottom of his helmet and his shoulders.

Incidentally, Simon got the idea of wearing green from Glenn Armstrong, a very good friend of mine from our days competing with and against each other on the grass. Glenn, a thatcher by trade, bought a pair of bright, lime green leathers when he started racing – basically, because they were the ones left on the peg that nobody else wanted. In those days no-one wore anything with green on it because it was – still is – considered to be unlucky.

But neither Simon nor I were superstitious and when Wiggy actually used Glenn's green leathers once – to race, incognito, in his name as a 15-year-old – it was the start of Simon's love for green racing leathers and livery, which continued throughout his career and became his trademark. In tribute to his late uncle, Alexz now wears a green crash helmet.

Simon would appreciate that gesture, as I'm sure he would've smiled when myself and a number of the other men turned up for his funeral dressed in the brightest green shirts we could buy!

As I said, Simon and I got on very well and it wasn't until about six months before his first fit that his mood began to change. The only time Simon started to impose himself on me was when I now realise the illness was taking over him.

I went around his house one night and we had a massive argument over a stupid issue concerning our taste in films. I like British-made films like *The Full Monty*, not ones that rely on special effects. Anyway, on this occasion Simon was insistent that I watched a particular type of movie that he favoured, so I repeated my preference and then he really started on me. I tried to make the case that he had to respect what I liked and I would do the same for him but it all got out of hand.

Julian and the eldest Wigg brother, Christopher, carrying Simon's coffin at the most upbeat funeral service.

I came back and said to my wife Lynne: 'I don't like him anymore.'

I was really upset at the time but I now think that this was the first sign of that bloody cancerous monster on the move. If you look at the photographs of him at that time, his eyes have changed and he looks gaunt. There must have been something going on at the time.

Looking back to that night, as I expressed my feelings about Simon to my wife, Lynn, I became really p***** off with myself. I thought: 'How can I say that? We have been such bloody good mates.'

It was a heat of the moment situation but now I look back and understand that it was the beginning of the end for my younger brother. Six months after that unusual and unnecessary row he had his first fit. The diagnosis at the time was wrong. He probably should have had a scan there and then – but the outcome would have been the same.

Once Simon came home from the hospital following his first fit, he was OK again in a sense. He began to plan to emigrate to Australia, where he and Charlie had bought a house at Paradise Point on Queensland's beautiful Gold Coast.

His benefit meeting at Oxford, in March 1999, actually upset a few people because he did such a good job of it – particularly when you consider that he was very ill at the time. Simon made a cracking job of the event, which featured an all-star cast headed by six speedway World Champions. To be fair, and before anyone from the BSPA says so, it's all right running a special one-off event but it takes much more to put on a fixture every week like a conventional promoter.

Simon eventually had two operations to his brain but it was the second one that took away so much of him as a person. He treated his operations as if he'd merely gone in for treatment to a broken leg. His attitude was, 'get them over with and let's go back to racing.'

Until the second operation he was still the same old Simon. The surgeon explained in simple terms there are red and pink areas of the tumour that are operated on, and it is how much of the pink that is taken away that really affects the patient's personality. If they remove the lot, then there is no life to appreciate.

"It was a heat of the moment situation but now I look back and understand that it was the beginning of the end for my younger brother. Six months after that unusual and unnecessary row he had his first fit"

The invasion into the pink areas eroded a lot of Simon's true personality, although he didn't realise that there had been a massive character change in him. It did, however, leave the 'happy' bit still there while the rational part of the brain had been removed.

A constant phrase of Simon's was: 'I like! I like!' For example, when Briggo and his son, Tony, or Ivan and Raye Mauger walked in to see him at the Willen Hospice near Milton Keynes, that's the phrase Simon would use to greet them.

Barry and Tony loved to take Simon out for Indian meals and, it has to be said, the hospice was smashing like that during his last two months alive.

I recall my last days with him. We had lost our two-year-old daughter, Louise, a couple of years earlier, so I knew when the time had come for Simon to go. He died on Wednesday, November 15, 2000.

His funeral and thanksgiving service, held at The Church of Christ the Cornerstone in Milton Keynes and attended by around 1,500 mourners, was a very upbeat affair – just as he had insisted to Charlie and myself that it should be. They played happy music, including a favourite of his by Blur called *Song 2*. Simon wanted to go out with a bit of a party. It was a most extraordinary funeral but it was also a terrific occasion, one that Simon himself would have enjoyed.

It was a very difficult time for all the family and Simon's friends, but I must say how much I admired Charlie for the way in which she showed such extraordinary strength of character and coped with everything so well. Simon dated some very good looking women in his time but he never met anybody he loved and respected as much Charlie.

I think that Charlie felt a little bit awkward when she first got together with Pat, concerned about what others might think so soon after Simon had passed away, but we are all delighted that she has met and married such a lovely bloke. I'm sure, too, that Simon would feel equally pleased and relieved that his family have found happiness again. Pat clearly cares deeply for Charlie and he's also a mega-Dad to the kids, so it's great that things have worked out well.

In my final analysis, I cared as much for Simon as he did about himself, and I know he did appreciate that and my efforts to help him throughout his career. We got on great but, then again, it would've been difficult for anyone not to have got on well with Simon.

Introduction

By Tony McDonald

IT was almost five years ago that the sports of speedway, grasstrack and longtrack racing lost one of its most successful and colourful characters when Simon Wigg died of a brain tumour, just four weeks past his 40th birthday. He left behind his devoted wife, Charlie, and two lovely children, daughter Abigail, then aged six, and son Ricki (3), as well as a legion of admirers from all corners of the globe.

The charismatic Wiggy also left millions of happy memories for us to cherish from his glittering international motorcycling career spanning two decades.

It was soon after winning the last of his five World Longtrack Championships, in 1994, that Simon first conducted a series of interviews about his life and eventful career with author and broadcaster turned speedway promoter, Gareth Rogers. The plan was for hours of tape recordings to become Simon's autobiography.

But time moved on, circumstances changed and after undergoing two operations and despite showing such incredible courage, Simon succumbed to cancer before the interviews were completed and the publishing project could reach fruition. But for a personality who always had plenty to say, who enjoyed communicating with his massive fan base, it would have been a travesty had his achievements and strongly held views contained in this book not been recorded in print.

Which brings us to what *WIGGY!* is all about.

The section in this book titled *Wiggy's World* is Simon's story, as told to Gareth in the mid-to-late 90s. For reasons that are obvious, we do not claim it to be the full story of Simon's life and racing career, but his words form a fascinating insight into what made him tick, where he came from and where he saw his respective tracksports going, for better or worse. Indeed, it's testimony to his intelligent overview analysis of speedway, grasstrack and longtrack racing, and the credibility he possessed, that many of his opinions aired in this book remain as valid now as they did when he first gave them.

No attempt has been made here to alter the tense of his words or change the context of what Simon actually told Gareth – they were his views at the time and we should respect his right to voice opinions on the burning issues surrounding his three different sporting disciplines.

For Simon Wigg spoke from the heart and he had the talent to back up his words.

Wiggy enjoyed a golden period when he was England's Number One on shale – exalted status he shared with his old grasstrack pal Jeremy Doncaster and Kelvin Tatum – throughout the Danish-dominated second half of the 80s. In fact, the record books show that Simon was England's top scorer in the World Team Cup Finals of 1984, 1986 and 1987, while he contributed 11 points when his country last won the World Cup, in 1989.

During the same period, he was also England's leading points man in the individual World Finals of 1984, 1988 and 1989, in the last of which he finished second to his Oxford team-mate Hans Nielsen at Munich, Germany, a country Wiggy loved and where he was probably a bigger favourite than he was in England. Who knows, if Simon had chosen to compromise his annual assault on the longtrack crown and instead put all his efforts into being speedway's No.1, maybe he could have gone one step further and become only the sixth English individual World Champion on shale?

Add in two consecutive British Championship wins – when the title carried so much more prestige than it does today – and many other prestigious victories throughout Europe and

Australasia, and it's fair to say that Simon was a genuine speedway superstar of his era. Not bad for a man whose desire for speedway's top prize never quite matched his almost obsessive pursuit of the much coveted World Longtrack crown.

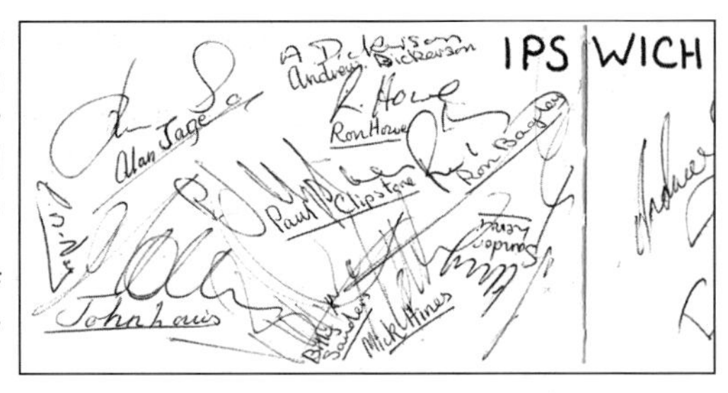

Two pages from Simon's autograph book showing the signatures of his Ipswich favourites in 1972.

On the super-fast 1,000 metre circuits of Europe he was in a class of his own for many years, probably the greatest-ever longtrack racer whose five world titles are a record he now shares jointly with Germany's current top longtracker, Gerd Riss.

Simon set about making fame and fortune on the longtracks after having first established himself as England's undisputed No.1 grasstracker in his youth. Doubtless there are still some grasstracks promoters and administrators from Simon's time who believe that Wiggy became bigger than the sport itself – and perhaps he did. A strong character, he was never afraid to challenge authority – a rebel with a cause.

"Sadly, we can only now try to imagine what he would have achieved for his beloved sport given encouragement and opportunity"

What cannot be argued, though, even by his strongest critics, is that he took his first tracksport love to a new level of unprecedented professionalism in Britain, or that he never stopped caring for it even after he'd moved on to conquer new and bigger goals. Indeed, Simon reveals in these pages how, following retirement from racing himself, he had hopes of restoring the once thriving grasstrack scene to its former glory. Sadly, we can only now try to imagine what he would have achieved for his beloved sport given encouragement and opportunity . . .

Speedway, longtrack and grasstrack didn't only lose an outstanding drawcard, who stood out from the rest and not just for his distinctive green leathers. They also lost a massive, irreplaceable personality who, to coin a favourite Wiggy phrase, was guaranteed to put bums on seats.

I was fortunate enough to see Simon's emergence from part-time speedway hopeful at Weymouth to England star at close quarters. When we at the defunct *Speedway Mail* were looking for an exciting and popular English rider to contribute a regular column in the mid-80s, Wiggy was the obvious choice. Everyone who has ever had the pleasure of interviewing Simon will tell you the same – he was always a real pleasure to talk to and, of course, never short of a quote or several hundred! If you had six empty pages to fill, Wiggy would fill them all. I don't think it was the cost of phone calls to *Chez* Wigg that put us out of business some years later but once Simon climbed aboard his soapbox, there was no stopping him!

Always eloquent and interesting, he was a sports reporter's dream, a great credit to his profession. He was also great news for his sponsors, filling thousands of column inches in newspapers and magazines stretching from Aylesbury to Australia. Only Simon, the marketing men's man made in Heaven, could have dominated the front page of *The Times* newspaper, as he did following the caffeine fiasco that followed the 1993 World Longtrack Final.

And Wiggy invariably spoke so much good sense, too. He would articulate what he thought the speedway authorities needed to do to take the sport forward and, not surprisingly, he became frustrated when the promoters didn't share his own ideology, vision and thirst for progress.

In 1985, when Simon was still serving his one-year international speedway ban – and if ever the punishment didn't fit the crime, then this was it – my partner John Bollé and I invited him along as *The Mail's* special guest for a pre-World Final supporters' get-together at the Hilton Hotel, Leeds. Simon, as ebullient as ever, was in his element, taking over the show to conduct a memorable forum in which he seized the opportunity to express many of his forthright views on the running of the sport. Instead of feeling sorry for himself that he had been denied the chance by officialdom to contest a second successive World Final, held at Odsal the next night, he showed a maturity and intelligence way beyond his 24 years. He impressed everyone present that night

Many people are reluctant to admit personal regrets, but I have a couple where Wiggy is concerned. I could kick myself now for never having gone out of my way to follow him to Germany, where he was King, to witness one of his many brilliant, high-speed Sunday afternoon performances that so enraptured the fans in a country where he is still regarded with great reverence as der Weldmeister. I guess I stupidly didn't appreciate back then the skill and daring involved.

What I regret most, however, is losing touch with him for many years, having moved on from *Speedway Mail* into other fields of sports publishing in the 90s. I was so far removed from speedway for a 10-year period that not only was I unaware of his terminal illness, but I only found out about his death when I read about it in a newspaper obituary. It says volumes about him that *The Daily Telegraph* – a broadsheet not exactly renowned for its speedway coverage – devoted a half-page to the Jolly Green Tracksport Giant ... but then there always was so much more to say about the one and only Simon Wigg.

In *WIGGY!* you will read of Simon's childhood days, about his eccentric family background and the ups and downs he experienced before achieving his schoolboy dream.

In speedway terms, he looks back at how initial indifference at Reading in the last 70s turned into fun days at National League Weymouth, before he went on to more serious business with England, Cradley Heath, Oxford, Hackney and Bradford, in a brilliant shale career that also embraced spells with Coventry, Exeter and King's Lynn before his enforced retirement in 1998.

Simon Wigg liked to have fun and his trademark, toothy grin will forever be etched in the minds of all of us who knew him. But while Wiggy liked a laugh and a joke more than most, he also cared passionately about whatever he did and it frustrated him that those responsible for running the sports at which he excelled did not share his own hopes and professional ideology, or possess the inner drive that he did to take them forward.

He never lost the thrill racing gave him but, to his great dismay, all three of his tracksports have failed to fulfil their potential to attract bigger crowds and the media coverage he believed possible. His typically controversial thoughts – and frustrations – on a number of burning issues are also a fundamental part of this book.

From humorous, although at times heart-rending accounts, to poignant, new tributes from close family members, dear friends, team-mates, rivals, promoters, team managers, media, sponsors and fans from all over the world, *WIGGY!* is an emotional rollercoaster journey will make you laugh and it will also make you cry.

Of course, this book would not have been possible without the immense, enthusiastic and invaluable input of the two people who were closest to Simon – his widow Charlie and elder brother and inspiration, Julian. They have played a key part at every stage of the process and for that they have our heartfelt gratitude.

As well as contributing their own very candid, and at times harrowing, accounts of how they struggled to cope with Simon's illness and his ultimate death, Charlie and Julian have been very helpful to us in numerous other ways. Anyone who admired Simon's meticulous attention to detail, in the way he conducted and projected himself, will not be surprised to know that he kept innumerable scrapbooks and photo albums as a permanent record of his career – from his schoolboy debut on the grass in 1976 to his last laps on a bike in 1998.

These – and others albums lovingly maintained by his late mother, Rosemary – have been kindly provided for our use in research and production of this book. Charlie also made available the visitors' book, kept

Simon's school drawing of Julian leading John Louis.

Charlie and Julian at Oxford Speedway's reunion for their glorious 1985-86 team, held in September 2005.

at Simon's bedside to chronicle the daily stream of people who called in to spend time with him during his last few weeks of life in Willen Hospice, along with a book of 'get-well' messages from people in Australia and the Book of Remembrance signed by those who attended his spectacularly unique funeral. Some of the messages left in these books have been reproduced in our comprehensive Tributes section.

Among other personal items were the autograph book Simon took to Ipswich Speedway as a kid. Typical of his organisational skills, he had allocated each visiting team a two-page spread and on the Belle Vue pages for the 1972 season are the signatures of Ivan Mauger and Peter Collins. Wiggy obviously liked local hero John Louis, in particular, because the 'Tiger' had signed on three separate pages!

Simon knew from a young age where he wanted to go in life – and, it seems, so did the teachers who tried to guide him towards a 'better job' than broadsliding a 500cc bike around a grass field! Simon's reports from the John Hampden School in Buckinghamshire, where he lived after the family moved from Suffolk in the mid-70s, made prophetic reading. "Capable but easily distracted," wrote the Physics teacher. "Intelligent ideas," praised the English tutor, while Simon's French master said of him: "He takes too long to get into top gear and, even then, often experiences power failure." *Sacre bleu!* The teacher obviously wasn't to know that Wiggy would go on to blast away all opposition at leading French grasstracks like Rumilly and Marmande!

As well as Simon's school reports, another item that especially caught the eye was his school art folder containing a number of colourful drawings that he'd produced when aged 12 or 13 while attending Woodbridge School, near Ipswich. Simon, who enjoyed art classes above all others and was near the top of his class at this subject, used felt-tip pens to depict his elder brother in several wonderfully detailed shots of him riding speedway, grasstrack and even ice racing. At the top of one page reads the telling inscription: 'Julian Wigg is the Greatest'. As Simon himself said many years later, after he had become a multi world champion, 'Bruv' had always been his real hero and he was genuinely saddened that Julian hadn't enjoyed the same grasstrack success as him.

We wish to make it clear that no member of the Wigg family neither sought nor expected any financial reward for their full co-operation and support in this project. Julian and Charlie are just pleased that Simon's thousands of fans from all over the world will now have the chance to share in their memories of the man who was a loving husband, father and brother.

However, it is our wish that a donation from every copy of the book sold will go to Simon and Charlie's two young children, Abi and Ricki, and we hope that their memories of their 'Daddy Simon' will be enriched by its publication. We hope, too, that the Wigg family will feel as proud of this lasting tribute to Simon as we are to have published it.

In compiling all the many tributes – more than 60, including those from 10 former speedway World Champions, each with his own personal story to recall – it is plainly obvious that Wiggy is still loved and missed as much today as he was when he left this world to go and organise God's new racetrack on November 15, 2000. No-one who was ever fortunate enough to have enjoyed his company will tell you otherwise.

Above all, this book is a permanent tribute to the life and times of a true motorcycling legend. I hope it gives you at least a little of the enormous pleasure Simon Antony Wigg gave to so many.

Tony McDonald
Publisher, Retro Speedway

Wiggy's World

Simon: in his own words

The first of many Wiggy poses – in 1961.

1 Woodbridge Wildcat

I HAD a natural introduction to racing motorcycles through my elder brother, Julian. When I was a lot younger we didn't actually live under the same roof. At the age of 10 I lived with our parents in Woodbridge, a small town north-east of Ipswich, while Julian, who was 21 then, lived in Aylesbury, Buckinghamshire, where I was born.

As a kid, I was aware of him competing on grasstracks but, unfortunately, I didn't get much opportunity to see him race. He did well as a semi-professional on the grass and had a few rides abroad. Grasstrack was Julian's favourite form of motorcycle sport, although he also did a little bit of speedway at Oxford and Peterborough.

He was a really talented guy but he really struggled financially for a number of years because our father, Tony, didn't help him. It was a great shame – it wasn't as if money was a problem in our family. Our father would have been able to help Julian further his career quite quickly but he didn't appreciate the motorcycle scene at all.

Dad was essentially an entrepreneur who wasn't so much a businessman as someone who would have a go at just about anything. When I was six, he built us a massive house on the land that he owned. It was so big, we could've held a longtrack meeting in the back garden!

He had a string of companies under one banner – an engraving business; a sign-writing company, which was his main trade; a perspex business manufacturing shop fronts and things like that; and a massive T-shirt printing press. He also made exhibition stands in expanded polystyrene and hot-wiring shapes for the exhibitions. Very creative and fantastic with his hands, he could sign-write any vehicle. He'd start with two pieces of string and a bit of chalk, then put up a level line. It would be perfectly straight. You'd look at it and wonder: 'How the hell did he do that?'

I like to think that I have inherited some entrepreneurial, creative and promotional touches from my father. Something was bound to rub off from Dad – and also from my grandfather, who never worked a day in his life. Everard Wigg inherited the family business when he was 18 – and sold it. He was a creative inventor, his profession from the day he left school to the day he died. If you have ever seen Dick van Dyke in *Chitty Chitty Bang Bang* . . . well, that's him. He'd create a contraption 15 miles long, just to boil an egg!

Everything in his house was the product of some crazy idea he'd had. His simple theory was that whatever he built could do a job that he never needed to do himself. He swore blind that he invented the radio before Marconi. He also swore blind that he invented the electric light before Edison!

Simon's parents, Tony and Rosemary Wigg.

Grandfather actually built a cinema in Kessingland, a small village near Lowestoft on the Suffolk coast, where the family came from. The Wigg family owned part of Distillers, or Dalgety Franklyn as it was known then. As I said, when grandfather inherited it at 18, he sold it all. He never worked for his money and did what he liked every day until he passed away at the age of 96. I was eight at the time, so I have fond memories of him.

His wife, Gertrude, used to smoke 60 cigarettes a day and drink half a bottle of brandy – but she lived until she was 94, bless her. Our grandparents both smoked like troopers, drank like fish – and

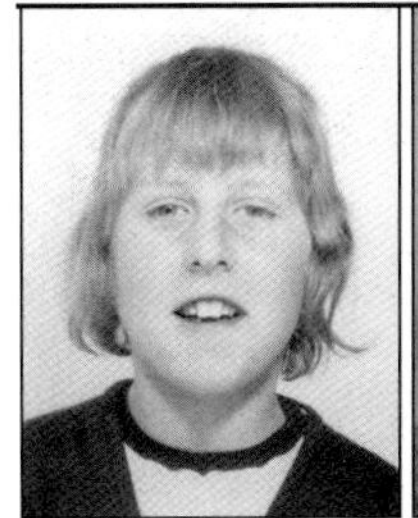
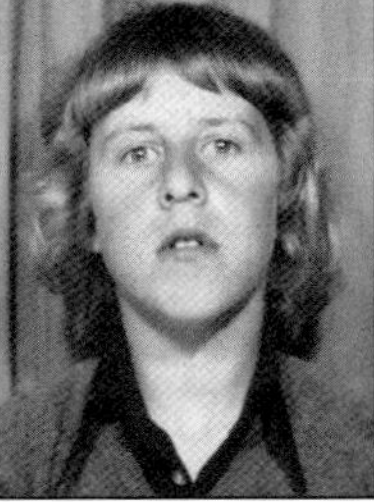

Right: Lynne (Julian's wife-to-be), Julian, Simon and Rosemary.

seemingly lived forever!

On my mother Rosemary's side, my grandfather was an Admiral in the Navy but he died of cancer at 36. My other grandmother was on the West End stage, so there were natural performers on mum's side of the family. Grandmother remarried and my mother enjoyed a wealthy upbringing, waited on by servants and enjoying the luxury of an immense house in Blindley Heath, near the Surrey/Sussex border. When mother and her two sisters and brother reached the age of 21, each of them received the gift of a brand new sports car.

My parents had met during the war in the Air Force at Upper Heyford. Dad was a flight engineer on Sunderland Bombers but ended up in the entertainment corps in Africa. He did the *It Ain't Half Hot Mum* routine, dressing up as a woman and entertaining the troops. Maybe that's where all the speedway fancy dress parties I organised came from!

When I look at my immediate ancestry I come to the conclusion that they were all nuts! They were all eccentric people who enjoyed life.

My Dad's biggest problem was that he trusted everybody – another trait I inherited. That is not always a good thing, though, and he was up and down in business. For every quid he made, he lost one – or even two. Although successful for periods, by the time we moved from Aylesbury to Suffolk, his business had virtually collapsed. The big house that he had owned was gone and we then lived with father's sister, Greta, who once ran the art department at what is now the University of Suffolk. She was a very creative woman and, to us kids, her house was like a funfair, full of paintings, sculptures and lots of other interesting stuff. We lived in one of her houses in Kessingland for a number of years, before moving to Woodbridge in about 1972.

I started watching at Ipswich Speedway around that time but neither of my parents were that keen on me going. I went on the bus with my friends, Nick and Mike Haste, the twins who lived opposite. We weren't necessarily Ipswich Witches fans, but supporters of the speedway. I think that's how 99% of speedway folk are, it's just that the people running speedway tend to forget it.

We certainly made the effort to be at Foxhall Heath when the likes of Ivan Mauger, Ole Olsen and Peter Collins were racing, so we'd probably get to about half a dozen meetings a year. I'd take along my autograph book and try to get the signatures of as many riders as possible. I was really pleased with myself in 1972, when I managed to obtain the autograph of Ivan Mauger, who was World Champion at the time. He dedicated it 'To Simon'. Little did I realise then what an important part he would play in my career many years later.

In the first meeting I ever watched, Malcolm Shakespeare scored about 15 points for Wolverhampton – and I'd never even heard of him! Ole Olsen was the king at Wolves then and although he scored 10 points that night, I couldn't understand how the best rider in the world had been upstaged by a reserve. Anyway, Shakespeare, who stood out as a very tall guy, rode extremely well on that occasion, which was possibly the highlight of his senior league career.

John Louis was the main man at Ipswich Speedway when I was a young fan, although Tony Davey was also very good and Billy Sanders had just come on the scene as a promising kid from Australia. The Witches' line-up also included Ted Howgego, Mike Lanham and Mick Hines.

Although I was impressed by Louis and Davey, and they went about their business very well, they never had the aura of an Ole or an Ivan. When Olsen and Mauger visited Foxhall, they were the famous riders that we'd all read all about. Their style and equipment, their leathers ... everything about them was special and seemed to raise them above the rest.

Simon (third boy from left) lines up for Woodbridge Wildcats cycle speedway team.

Olsen was my favourite rider as a schoolboy – and again, just like my early experience with Ivan, little did I realise that one day Ole would visit my home and try to convince me to sign for his team. I admired him not only because he was a World Champion, but because he could always do something from the back.

It didn't seem that difficult to come from behind if you were prepared to race hard and fast. Ole was great to watch and had everything else going for him. I remember he turned up in a beautiful car and had immaculate Jawa machinery. He was the whole part, the type of rider any kid would've looked up to.

Coming back to Julian, he was very keen on motorcycles right from school age, buying his first moto-cross bike at 14 for no more a couple of quid. Then, being technically minded, he built various items at home in after-school projects. In his first stages on the grasstrack scene, during the early 70s, I think he actually enjoyed riding the bike more than actually winning. At times I thought he sometimes missed the gate deliberately just so that he could really enjoy a more thrilling race.

While I lived with Mum in Suffolk, Julian resided near Aylesbury, Buckinghamshire working for Dad's company. Although father wouldn't stop him from racing on the grass, he made no effort to encourage or help him either. Dad didn't even talk about Julian's racing activities but I was busting a gut to get involved myself. When I went to the speedway, I'd see mascots and other kids with bikes here and there and thought I'd like to do that, too. By that stage I had started to ride a bit of cycle speedway, for Woodbridge Wildcats, which got the ball rolling for me, bike wise.

By aged 12, I'd bought my first motor bike, paying a fiver for an old Suzuki that a few mates and I used to push to the nearby woods and ride around on. We stripped it down and, to make it look more like a grasstrack bike, we made number plates out of paper dinner plates. Julian gave me one of his old crash helmets, a pair of gloves and Doc Marten's boots, and off we went!

I'd stay with Julian during school holidays, for maybe four or five days at a time, and probably went to two or three grasstrack meetings with him before we moved back to Bucks in 1974. It was the biggest thrill of my life to spend some time with him. With me being a kid and him being an adult, it was like – WOW! He was almost my hero as well as my brother. It seemed to me like he lived in another world, some fabulous place where I also wanted to be.

Julian would always take an interest in what I was doing. He had a couple of mini 'monkey' bikes and I can remember him spending the best part of an afternoon teaching me how to ride it. He'd previously taught me a few things in his local field before I'd bought my own bike back in Suffolk. I had every respect for Julian, to the point where if he'd told me to ride into a brick wall at 90 mph, I'd have done it.

He even let me have a couple of rides on his longtrack Jawa when I was still only 13. Once, I had only completed about two laps of a rough 'track' when he came towards me screaming and shouting, because I had gone around flat out in first – and hadn't changed gear. I made myself a little unpopular with him because of that but I did make it around properly on another occasion, after a grass meeting near Aylesbury.

My parents ran an old people's home at Hazlemere, High Wycombe, which meant I was able to go to Julian's place, some 35 miles away, most weekends. Occasionally I'd join him at grasstrack events but he'd started to ride abroad a lot, so I didn't get to go with him as much as I would have liked.

However, quite often I would attend meetings with other riders who lived in the area, such as Mike Garrad and Glenn Armstrong, who were both good friends of Julian's. I was always trying to get to a meeting somehow or other to watch but it was not until the family's move back to Bucks that I had the opportunity to start racing myself.

As my parents weren't keen on me pursuing my interest in motorcycles, and were also unable to help me much financially, I had to raise my own money from a window cleaning round. My brother found a little 200cc Triumph Tiger Cub, which had been manufactured by a guy called Tony Ward. His three sons, Tony, Kevin and Clint, all rode and he had built the bike especially for Clint. But after he'd outgrown it, I bought it from him for £48. Julian organised the purchase and then, to get me started, he gave me a set of his old leathers, a pair of old boots and a crash helmet.

A couple of meetings in which Julian competed also had schoolboy class races, so Dad would usually drop me over at Julian's place on Friday evenings after school. The day before my first meeting, Julian was out practicing with me, teaching me how to slide the bike, when he managed to blow the engine to bits! Because the old motor was by then out of production, it was very difficult for us to get the bits to fix it. Another two months passed before Julian had the time to put the engine back together again for me.

I also had to raise a bit of finance to repair it, which meant more window-cleaning, while Julian negotiated a cheaper deal on the parts needed. The window-cleaning was easy to do and it also kept me fit. And as my parents were wardens of an old people's home with 35 flats, there were plenty of windows to keep me busy! I also did a paper round in the morning to earn a few extra pounds.

My first-ever race was at Gawcott, where the real schoolboy stars of that era were Pip Lamb and Tim Curnock, along with Russell Ing who went on to star in 1,000cc sidecars. All was going well until I fell off. Dickie Staff, who was behind me, promptly ran over my bike. We were to become very close friends.

Although I've said that Dad took very little interest in his sons' grasstrack exploits, I recall that he was with me at my first meeting. He was about as mechanically minded as a fish, so after buckling my front wheel and winding myself in the fall, I took a while to get back to the pits. When I eventually came around the back of the trailer, I found Dad attacking my bike with a mallet he used to erect estate agents' boards in another of his part-time jobs. The handle was about four feet long and there he was swinging this thing at my bike, smashing the wheel to pieces. Horrified at what he was doing to my pride and joy, I just screamed and shouted at him to stop. Fortunately, I managed to borrow a front wheel from someone and eventually finished sixth in the meeting.

It was a bit strange getting used to the amazing adrenalin rush and the pressure I felt in that first competitive meeting. I managed to win my next three events, enjoying some good battles with Dickie Staff, plus a lad called Jem Simpson whose family lived near

Young Simon, just happy to be around his big brother at a grasstrack event.

Dickie, down in Andover. All three of us became very good friends. My father also became friendly with Dicky's dad, Jack, who had previously ridden speedway in the pre-war era and was a terrific character.

Not that they had much choice in the matter, but my parents began to accept that I was going to take up racing and would enjoy it at every possible opportunity. Every time I was asked at school what I thought my future occupation might be, I always replied: 'To be a professional grasstrack rider and compete on the Continent'. The typical reply from the careers officers was: 'Don't be silly!'

While I respect the fact that a school would take that attitude when faced with a starry-eyed pupil like me, it is also true that many of those who express the same strength of commitment I showed early in life, often tend to succeed. In that respect, kids who are very single-minded and know where they are going from an early stage, are normally the ones who have half a chance of getting where they really want to go. A single-minded determination is not only part of the make up of a champion but of other people who know what they want from life. I have always thought that it is important to set targets and goals in life.

I went to a posh public school in Woodbridge, where only three of us qualified for entry places. Everybody else was a boarder and had to pay hefty fees to go there. I was a scholarship pupil and I have to confess that I was top at everything – until, that is, I fell in love with bikes. Although I gave up reading books in order to become a racer, it certainly has been no disadvantage to have had a reasonable education. I eventually lost interest in everything else and, instead of working, I would invariably sit at the back of the class reading Motor Cycle News or drawing pictures of motorbikes.

When my parents and I returned to Bucks, I moved to the John Hampden Grammar School in High Wycombe, which I attended between the ages of 13 to 16. My exam results were mixed – a G.C.E. Grade One in Art, English and Engineering Drawing – but nothing else. I had other things on my mind.

I went on to compete in a lot of meetings around Buckinghamshire in my early days and I find it a great shame that the grasstrack club that was the scene of my first race, run by George and Jean Newsome, who put on up to 12 meetings a year in the South Midlands area, is now no more. I do find it frustrating that the ACU don't spend more time and effort encouraging clubs to run events and offer them the assistance to do so. It does seem the main objective of some people is to make the organisation of activities as difficult as possible. That's not what motorcycle sport is all about. Clubs should be encouraged to come into the sport and run their own meetings, to give local talent a chance.

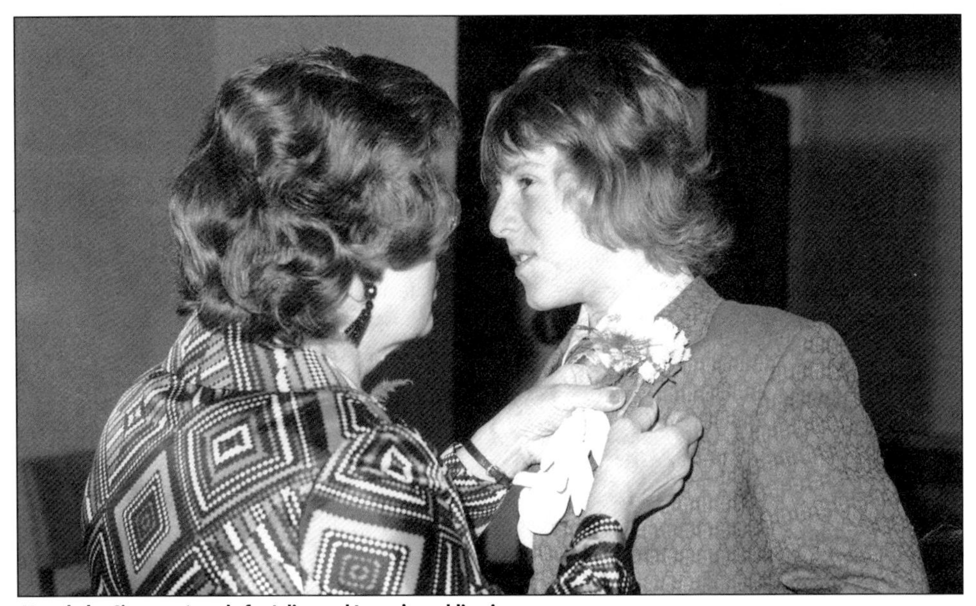

Mum helps Simon get ready for Julian and Lynne's wedding in 1974.

2 Big Wigg and his little brother

THE first job I had was working for my father's silk screen printing company, printing stickers and also doing a little artwork, which I quite enjoyed. Working with Dad wasn't a good idea, though, so after a while we had a talk about it and I decided to go and do something else.

I ended up working for a firm in Homer Green, the next village to where we lived, making hand controls for invalid cars. I felt it was important to branch into the engineering aspect of the world a little bit. I hadn't really enjoyed metalwork at school and didn't relate it to motorcycling until I started to get involved with disabled vehicles. I was only there a few months, because most of the work was repetitious and mundane, like cutting up 300 pieces of tubing, which I didn't enjoy at all.

I probably lasted only six months at the firm, by which time I'd already started to develop my racing. I spent one more year with the schoolboys racing on a BSA, competing in 15 or 16 meetings, before moving up into the adults category.

Just before I left school I sold the Tiger Cub to one of my best friends, Clint Dunn. He also raced at weekends, which gave me another way of getting to those meetings that, quite often, my dad didn't want to go to. Using the money I'd saved, I bought myself a 250cc BSA and it proved to be a fabulously reliable machine that I didn't have to spend another penny on all season.

At the end of the year, George Watts, an Oxfordshire builder, approached my brother, who was very successful on the grass by this stage. A local grasstracker himself, George had some very good machinery but he was retiring and wanted Julian to ride his bikes. Julian was satisfied with his own machinery, so he put George on to me. Julian told him: "My little brother is coming along well. He's got no money but stacks of enthusiasm, so why don't you help him?"

Having the surname Wigg, the younger brother of a prominent and good grasstracker, was a great advantage to 'Julian's little brother', as I was then known. It made life a lot easier for me, there is no doubt about that.

George Watts was a massive help, too. I rode a little Puch moped, that Julian had bought for my birthday, on the road and I'd nip over to George's place at Oxford on weekends. Towards the end of the 1976 season, George would take me to meetings and his influence was more than useful. Chris Baybutt had been 250cc senior champion on a Montessa, prepared by a guy called Colin Saunders, and George managed to talk Colin into lending me Baybutt's bike for the British National Schoolboy final at Lillingstone Lovell in Buckinghamshire. My BSA was a four stroke and very nice and easy to ride, but, suddenly, I had this 250 that flew like a rocketship and much too fast for me.

I rode it at the finals and spent the whole day chasing after the thing. I actually made the start in the final, and should have won it, but Sean Willmott was much more at home on the fast two strokes than me. He whipped past me after a lap or two, leaving me to finish second.

Even so, I was quite happy with that because, in reality, it was still only my first full season of competitive racing. I wasn't able to travel that much because my parents weren't that keen, while Julian was often otherwise engaged on the Continent at weekends.

A few weeks after the National Schoolboy finals we had to give the Montessa back to Chris Baybutt's team, which was disappointing because the BSAs were usually getting thrashed out of sight. Around that time BBC South filmed a feature on Sean Willmott, acclaiming him as a future World Champion. The news crew came to film him at Salisbury, where instead of him stealing the spotlight, I managed to beat him three times on my BSA – even though he had obtained a new engine the night before from the main importer and his sponsor, Brian Goss. Coming just two weeks after he'd beaten me so convincingly in the schoolboy national, it was

Simon gets the better of his main schoolboy grasstrack rival, Sean Willmott.

a great way for me to finish the season.

Again, thanks were due to George Watts, who had lent me another BSA engine for that final meeting. This was something which George had 'breathed' on and, for a BSA, it was very fast and enjoyable to ride.

In the winter George built up a very fast 350 Cole that we managed to obtain from Colin Saunders, although I also started the next season with Baybutt's old Montessa, which George purchased, and a 500 JAP. George had funded the new machinery for me, so we did a deal over the prize money. George had half of it and I would go over and help him with the bikes in the evenings.

The Montessa was such a very different machine to ride compared to the 350, to the extent that I didn't know whether I was coming or going half the time. I was really at home on the 350, which was a nice four stroke. The 250 used to catch me out and it had to be ridden flat out. That made life a little bit difficult for me and I realised later that I'd have been better off without it that year.

Even though I didn't reach any of the British Championships, it was a learning curve while spending time getting used to the different bikes. I'd done quite well in the 350 class and won quite a lot of finals around the country. I also had a few good 500cc rides, reaching most finals where I went but without pulling up any trees.

That was until the end of the season, when we pooled the money we had made, bought a Street-Jawa engine and fitted it into a new bike. I sold the JAP and also got rid of the Montessa as we had everything I needed on the Street-Jawa, including a centre carb. It looked beautiful and was very well prepared by Colin Saunders. I also had a couple of run-outs on my brother's twin-carb Weslake, cleaning up on it at Centre meetings. The Street-Jawa, though, was every bit as good as the bikes the top boys were using – riders like Joe Hughes, Mike Beaumont, Chris Baybutt, John Britcher, Graham Hurry, Mike Garrad and, of course, my brother.

I went up to Shropshire for a big National event and set a new track record in my first event. Not only did I manage to qualify, but I won it by beating blokes like Steve Hartley, Tom Leadbitter and the rest of the top English riders of the day. Then I finished second in the final behind Chris Baybutt, giving him a real run for his money. Suddenly, I thought: 'Bloody hell, I've arrived!'

A week later I competed in another big National down in Kent, where I dropped only a couple of points and again beat some really good guys. Then we went down to Sarne in Wales, where I won the first final. At the time I still had the habit of leg-trailing, which Julian was desperately trying to get me out of because it's a style that is restrictive in terms of your development as a rider. I didn't realise it at the time, because I thought that it looked good – I just wanted to stick my leg out at the back and look stylish, as most kids do.

Anyway, I hit the front in the big final race at Sarne but reached the first corner and then suddenly went a*** over tit!

I had another 10 blokes behind me and although six of them managed to miss me, the back four didn't and one ran over my leg, breaking my ankle quite badly. Not that I realised the problem immediately, because I remember getting up and running through the dust with my ankle pointing the wrong way! I'd previously also picked up a badly broken toe, which I'd hit on a post during the season, and because of the infection discovered in my toe, they couldn't operate on my ankle. I eventually spent a month having treatment in hospital at High Wycombe.

Not only was I ruled out for the end of that season, but my bike was smashed to pieces, including a lot of engine damage. The throttle had jammed while it was grounded – we didn't have cut-outs in 1977. That crash messed me up for a bit but it finished George, who'd invested all the money he had in the world in that bike.

I wasn't the only one to suffer a setback. Julian had been badly hurt in a very bad smash in mid-season, which was a tragedy for him. He'd reached the stage where he had begun to win everything, on a fast bike that was very competitive. He was beating the likes of Ivan Mauger, Scott Autrey, Peter Collins and Phil Crump regularly on the grass. Julian had just got into the big meetings in Germany, competing with the likes of Egon Müller and Georg Hack, when he had a very nasty crash in the Western Winner meeting and badly broke his arm.

At the Clyst St Mary circuit near Exeter, Devon, which used to stage the big Western Winner meeting, Julian went straight through the ropes and hit one of the wooden stakes with his left arm. Such was the impact that he had to have a major operation to have two big plates inserted in the arm. It was just at the stage in life when it was make or break for him and the crash was bad enough to make him think seriously about life after racing.

When Julian recovered from that bad injury, racing was secondary in his thoughts to setting up a business – a shop in Winslow, Northamptonshire selling . . . motorcycles. He was also now married to his childhood sweetheart, Lynne. They still hold hands like they just met last week, which is fabulous.

That accident knocked Julian's career for six. Although he came back after that and was successful again, he was never the same rider as he'd been before the crash.

I feel very sad for Julian, because he was immensely talented on a bike and I believe that, if things had gone his way, he could have been one of the great World Champions. The Continental scene is where he wanted to go and he did get there after a struggle. Good equipment is essential and it was a long, hard slog for him. Julian was slogging away and getting there but injuries ultimately cut short his promising career.

That winter, Julian did a lot of trials riding to keep fit, which led to me buying a trials bike from his sponsor, Windsor Comp Shop, for a couple of hundred quid. I'd actually placed an advertisement in the *MCN's On The Grass* column, appealing for help, at about the time of Julian's accident and Pete Webb, who owned the Windsor Comp Shop, came to my rescue.

Pete agreed to buy me a new Hagon LTR Weslake grasstrack bike and a pair of leathers for the following season, which was like the fairy godmother had just landed for me! Until then I'd earned £17 a week at the age of 17, putting hand controls on disabled people's cars, and then this guy comes up and says: 'I'll buy you a new bike'. To me, it was the greatest thing ever.

In the few months going into 1978, I kept active riding the trials bike I'd bought from Pete, using a little money of my own. Meanwhile, Pete had got in touch with an old acquaintance of his called Jeff Bing, who was sales manager at Norman Reeves (Motors) of High Wycombe, which was run by a smashing character called Tom Pink. They agreed to lend me a Ford Cortina Estate for the year, so I was set up very nicely with a new car, new bike and a new set of green-and-white leathers.

In the middle of the previous season I had my first international ride in the B group of the European Grand Prix held at Hereford Racecourse. Egon Müller and all those guys had come along. At that time they were attracting 25,000 spectators to the major grasstracks, such as the big Shropshire meetings run by Dave Owen and the Hereford event. It was a very exciting scene for a young kid to be a part of, and is the reason why there were so many good youngsters coming through in those days. Those international meetings were fabulous.

At just 16, I didn't do very well at Hereford and spent the whole day wandering the pits drooling over the bikes ridden by Müller and Georg Hack, who were joined there by other German stars like Alois Wiesbock, Willi Duden and Christoph Betzl. They blew away riders like Peter Collins, Ivan Mauger and Briggo – men whom we thought of as gods were made to look like novices by the brilliant Germans.

They had the most beautifully put together motor bikes that I'd ever seen. Egon turned up with a brand new Mercedes full of dolly birds, and so did Georg Hack. I thought, 'this is unbelievable, these guys are like film stars with motorbikes strapped beneath them.' It was very awe-inspiring for a young kid like me.

That was in 1977, and in 1978 I started the season with good backing, good bikes and a good way to get to all my meetings. I'd also trained hard on a moto-cross bike with a good friend of mine called Andy Scott, a top motor crosser himself who lived in High Wycombe, so I felt on top from the first meeting.

Chris Baybutt beat me by a whisker in the national Roger Parker Trophy meeting in Gloucester, a high quality field at Abingdon involving all the top Brits. The next week was the Berks Bonanza, another National event. It had been raining very heavily and halfway through the final I was in fifth place. I managed to rip my goggles down and I went from fifth to win the final on the final lap, passing Tom Leadbitter on the last corner. It was the first National that I had won and my success continued week by week, I was on a roll and enjoyed a fabulous season. Confidence was the key to it all. I began to think I could beat all these blokes – and then I did. I had a very good bike, as quick as anybody else's, although Baybutt had something better than the standard Weslake, which was the machine to be riding in those days.

"They had the most beautifully put together motor bikes that I'd ever seen. Egon turned up with a brand new Mercedes full of dolly birds, and so did Georg Hack. I thought, 'this is unbelievable, these guys are like film stars with motorbikes strapped beneath them.' It was very awe-inspiring for a young kid like me"

Early in the season, the former Crewe speedway star, Barry Meeks, organised a meeting for me in Rumilly, France. I'd been on the way to winning the meeting but managed to knock Joe Hughes off on the last lap. In trying to go past him to win the meeting, I was probably a wee bit desperate as I rushed under him, so they excluded me and re-ran it. Joe won the meeting and I finished third on aggregate. The organisers and spectators must have thought I'd done OK, because they had seen me trying hard and I received another two invitations to race in France later that season.

In the winter of 1977 I got a job working for Dula Engineering, owned and run by Paul Duncombe. Although I had a sponsored Hagon machine from Windsor Comp Shop, I was actually employed by Dula to help make grasstrack bikes. The money wasn't tremendous but Paul taught me a tremendous amount, which enabled me to deal with the fiddly bits on the bike myself.

As soon as I had money coming in from racing on the grass, I packed up work but for several years it was tough making things pay. I was only generating about £20 a week, riding from week to week, and sometimes I'd go to meetings without even enough money in my pocket to get home – unless I managed to win some races. So the pressure was on in a lot of ways, but it was all positive pressure and a lot of fun. At least I was doing what I wanted to do, all day and every day, which was very important to me.

By the end of the season I had managed to buy a spare engine, I progressed very quickly and most weekends I was winning races or actual meetings. I was also getting increased sponsorship, mainly organised by Pete Webb, covering chains, goggles and crash helmets.

First speedway portrait – at Reading, 1979.

3 Smashing time

I RETURNED to work for Dula once the 1978 season had finished. Paul Duncombe didn't mind me attending to my own bike after work – despite the fact that it was fitted into the frame of his rival in the frame-making business, the East London-based Hagon! Paul always stayed late and at the end of the normal working day, I'd join him after 6pm to work on my own stuff. It was an ideal situation for me, because I had a great workshop in which I could do all the trick bits and stuff I wanted to do to my bikes – skills I had learned from Paul and his partner, Trevor, who was also a tremendous engineer.

Relatively speaking, I am quite mechanical, although I wouldn't say that I was mechanically minded – it was a case of applying a reasonable amount of commonsense combined with what I'd learned from a good teacher in Paul. There were very few jobs that I did well when I first started working for him but he taught me how to weld and use a lathe. It enabled me to do most jobs in the workshop and while I'm not especially proficient at any of them, I could get by and make bits and pieces.

After working through that winter, Pete Webb was then able to help with the purchase of another engine and a chassis for the following year. I sold the chassis that we had and invested in two new Hagon frames, which were of a slightly different style. What I'd basically tried to do was start the 1979 season with two complete grasstrack bikes.

But my plans suffered a setback when I crashed and wrote off my sponsored Ford car on a trip to Wales. The accident happened at Builth Wells, where I was also to suffer another bad injury on the Royal Welsh Showground track. Bruce Carter was in front of me in the 500 final and I managed to get my foot stuck in his back sprocket while trying to bully my way past him. It was very sideways and slippery at Builth Wells, my foot went into his back sprocket and round his wheel. It broke his shock absorber and bent the bike's swinging arm but, to be honest, I was more concerned for myself.

As I lay on the ground in agony, I thought I was dying, fearing that my foot had been ripped off. It was quite muddy and there was blood oozing through the mud – and it was coming out of my boot.

When I got to hospital, they cleaned everything up and stitched my foot back together. I had broken the three toes where the sprocket had gone straight through my boot, it looked as if a shark had bitten my foot! I was lucky not to lose those three toes.

I was out for a few weeks with that injury although, what with that and the fact that I'd smashed up my sponsor's car, it could have been worse. At least I was still in one piece and the people at the Norman Reeves dealership were very understanding.

My move into speedway began in the winter of 1978-79, when I managed to get myself a speedway bike and attended a number of training schools, at Reading and Weymouth, using a second-hand engine and a very old speedway chassis I acquired from Larry Ross. I also purchased a diamond and a back end, plus some bits and pieces for £40. I fitted an old Weslake engine into the speedway bike and went off to be trained by John Davis and Jan Andersson, the biggest stars at Reading, as well as grasstrack veteran Lew Coffin at Weymouth.

This was just to keep my hand in so that when the grasstrack season started I'd be really fit. The sole purpose was to keep active and be more fluent on the bike – I had no thoughts of

The earliest action shots of Simon practicing speedway at Weymouth.

becoming a speedway rider at that stage, especially after an early pile up at Weymouth.

I started going to occasional speedway training schools again. Lew Coffin, who ran a school at Weymouth, knew me from the grasstrack scene. At the end of the session Lew organised a few races but the track hadn't been watered, so when I overtook two guys, there was no dirt to hold me up and I just went straight through the fence.

I had cut the handlebars off too short and I had a Jawa twist grip with a steel barrel on it. It was hanging off the end of the handlebars and when the bike hit the fence I ended up with my groin virtually impaled on the end of the handlebars. I hadn't blocked out the end of the bars, which buried itself into my thigh about an inch from my wedding tackle! It acted like an ice-cream scoop, slicing across my leg and taking out a great chunk of flesh.

I was rolled up in agony before being carried back to the pits. Then in the changing room, I curled up like a ball again. Eventually I took off my leathers and saw a big hole, exposing all the fat tissue. I was nearly sick on the spot and thought I was going to faint. Thankfully Dickie was with me again and took me off to hospital, where they cleaned me up, inserted 16 stitches in my groin and sent me home.

I think my first-ever public speedway ride was at Oxford in 1978. I don't recall how it went but I still have the programme from the night of Thursday, October 12 – when the Cheetahs faced Mildenhall in the National League – which shows me scheduled in a 'Challengers Romp' second half race against fellow juniors Barry Allaway, Paul Mitchell and John Pragnell. Ironic that I should go back to a much changed Oxford six years later as one of their most expensive British League signings. Having said that I made my public debut at Oxford, I have another programme from Reading, for their home meeting against King's Lynn on September 11, 1978, that shows me entered into the 'Junior Jaunt' along with Andrew Nichols, Barry Allaway and Phil Vance.

In fact, I was bullied into signing a contract at Reading. I didn't have any money, nor a proper bike and I had no intention of becoming a speedway rider.

To make matters worse, my car sponsorship with Norman Reeves ceased when Bobby Schwartz signed for Reading in 1980 and they were persuaded to back the new American signing. The Speedway Controller at Smallmead, Brian Constable, got onto Norman Reeves, pointing out how Reading Speedway was able to give the Ford distributor a lot more coverage than I could as an individual, plus the benefits of corporate hospitality evenings and staff jollies.

It was a bit of a blow that, in a sense, triggered in me a resentment of speedway at that time.

I told Reading that I couldn't ride, that I had one grasstrack bike while my speedway engine was effectively the engine for my second grasstrack machine. All I had was a speedway chassis. I had the bike as part of my Windsor Comp sponsorship but hadn't been making any money – just getting by, paying engine bills and putting tyres on my bike. I didn't even have transport to get me to and from meetings.

Reading then decided to help me with an old Audi that their Polish rider, Henryk Gluklich, had driven previously. They lent it to me for my first grasstrack booking of the season – in Germany. Grubby Sharpe, who was a very well known character throughout the sport, came with me as mechanic and co-driver. We had reached Hasloch, where it was freezing cold and there was snow everywhere. It was mid-March and the heater didn't work! For me it was a great adventure, as I hadn't driven this far before, having previously only gone abroad as a passenger with other riders, Barry Meeks and Tom Leadbitter.

I noticed a massive poster promoting the event. Everybody who was anybody was listed – including Simon Wigg! I thought, 'Christ! – I'm here with all these boys.' It was only two years earlier that I'd been drooling over them at Hereford as a star-struck kid.

Then we looked at the track – well, you couldn't see the end of the bloody thing! I had never seen a grasstrack in England bigger than about 600 yards, but this monster was 1,000 metres long. We decided to grab a couple of hours' sleep and then go out on the Saturday evening to have a few drinks and meet people. Anyway, by the time we woke up it was 8am the next morning. We had slept from 6pm and missed everything, including Egon Müller's cabaret show, which we'd heard about and were very disappointed to miss.

I spent the next day at the meeting getting blown out of sight. I'd not seen anything like it in my life, having never been faster than 60mph on a motorbike before, but by the end of the straights at Hasloch we were doing 110mph. It was very deep and very bumpy – and scared the pants off me. Meanwhile, Müller, Georg Hack, and Christoph Betzl were floating around there as if it were a Sunday afternoon stroll.

I remember the last race, where I cheated at the start. I went 10 yards back, dropped the clutch and must have been doing 20mph when the tapes went up. But to underline how uncompetitive I was that day, I was still back to last by the time I changed gear. The guys were going so fast, I couldn't believe it. By the end of the meeting, I felt destroyed, especially after the way the afternoon ended on a sour note.

My appearance fee was £200, which was just enough to cover the trip and despite the fact that I had a contract to confirm the deal, the promoter, Fritz Kissell, decided to cut my money by 50 quid because I'd ridden so badly.

The place was packed, so the promoter must have made good money, and although I had ridden my balls off, my Hagon-Weslake was nowhere near fast enough and the frame was wrong. Like a naive beginner, I had tried to race top blokes like Egon Müller – with his super-fast Otto Lantenhammer engines – on a standard speedway motor. Everybody in the pits had an OL except me. I didn't know what to expect and wasn't really ready for it.

The promoter and I shouted and screamed at each other. I called him every name under the sun but as we were leaving, Grubby shouted: 'B******!'– the only English word the German understood. That was it . . . he began chasing us down the pits at about 90mph, so Grubby and I just jumped into the car with the £150, realising that we were lucky enough to get away from the place with that much in my pocket!

Kristian Praestbro was also travelling back to England with his protégé, a young fellow Dane called Erik Gundersen. Kristian had finished seventh but he was not a longtrack star and was really a sandtrack specialist. This was Erik's first trip out of Denmark and he would have been about 18 at the time. We stopped at the services and all ate a meal together, laughing and joking.

Now Grubby happened to be a tremendous Belle Vue fan. Even though he lived down in Salisbury, he would go everywhere to watch his beloved Aces. Kristian had ridden for Belle Vue before moving to Cradley Heath, so Grubby was full of smart-a*** remarks telling Kristian how well Belle Vue were going, especially since he'd left!

Leading grasstrack rookie Bruce Penhall in the big Western Winner at Exeter, 1979.

A hilarious personality, Grubby could tell you that your mother was a cow yet you wouldn't be offended. I don't know how he got away with it.

When we got home from that first German trip I had to completely re-think my whole strategy. I had quite a few meetings booked in France, we still had the Audi and were also still trying to fit in second half speedway rides at Reading. I was really struggling to combine both grasstrack and speedway, and at that stage I wasn't doing either particularly well. I'd also naively assumed that following my success of recent seasons, I could go to Germany and beat everybody. Instead, it was me who had been blown into oblivion.

I did go to Bergerac, France the next week and had a reasonably successful meeting against the likes of Sture Lindblom, who was a tremendous competitor, a wily Swede who had everything going for him. Great style, lots of class and with good bikes, he was very safe on a bike. He might be outpaced by the Germans but he could beat everybody else most of the time. Sture rode in the majority of meetings that I was booked for and I felt encouraged when I ran quite a few second places behind him.

As I had quite a few weekend bookings, I eventually decided to pool my earnings and go to Don Godden for one of his 'Gold Top' engines – a specially tuned job on the Weslake. It would cost £300, which was just about all I had. My speedway engine had blown up, so I was down to one engine anyway – and that was already in the bike.

I'd run out of money and didn't have enough financial resources to ride speedway as well as grasstrack, so I decided I had to finish with Reading. There were other guys doing both sports, like Phil Collins and Sean Willmott, who were at my level and of the same generation, but they had the advantage of greater financial backing and access to more machinery. I found it all a bit difficult at that stage, but persevered.

I tried to a find a faster engine and Don built one for me which I rode in a meeting at Celle, Germany a few weeks later. Everybody was there, including Ivan Mauger and Peter Collins, and I managed to just scrape into the final, the last eight, which I was more than happy with considering the fact that I was among a world-class field.

On the last lap of the semi-final I managed to get my foot stuck under the footrest and broke my big toe again. Sture Lindblom pipped me but I was given the 'Unluckiest Rider' award by the promoter. The next day I was at Gutesloher for another grasstrack meeting, so I wrapped my foot up and headed off. At this stage my girlfriend, Jackie, who was a secretary at Windsor Comp, was driving me around to meetings in a Volkswagen van that she used to tow her horsebox!

I was in the B group, while the A group included big names such as Briggo, Ivan, Egon and PC. I was second in my first outing before hitting the front in my next race, so I was suddenly leading a German grasstrack – and with a bad foot, too. Three laps went by and I was really enjoying it when, coming towards the finishing line with 50 yards to go, a conrod snapped and came out of the front of the crankcase. We were knackered. I hadn't got another bike and still had another three races left.

For a bit of British companionship, I had parked next to Peter Collins and his mechanic in the pits, and PC lent me a bike for the remainder of the meeting. It was a fantastic gesture and one that I never forgot. I had no options – it was either ride PC's spare bike or go home. He didn't need to be helping a young kid out, so it was very good of him to come to my aid in that way.

With girlfriend Jackie and the Cortina Estate supplied by Norman Reeves, long before the luxury motorhome had been invented.

The problem for me was that I had one blown-up engine with a rod sticking out of it, plus a box of bits that I carried around with me for spares. The next meeting was at Libourne, in the south of France, and we were travelling there straight from Germany, with Jackie driving and us both having to sleep in the freezing cold car overnight. We didn't have enough money for hotels and I had to save more cash to put together the damaged engine in the south of France.

Down in Libourne, we looked up Bernard Tison, who was a top French grasstracker in his time. I had two boxes of exploded engines with me and there I was, asking him to put one together for me. I didn't know how to do it and I'm not sure he did either. He managed to get it all together somehow, though, before handing me the bill.

It wasn't exactly money well spent either. For I reached the Le Baule grasstrack venue, went three-quarters of a lap in practice and blew it up again! So I found myself hunting around the pits, trying to offer all the juniors some money to borrow a bike for the rest of the meeting. I managed to borrow a longtrack Jawa with a twin cam engine and no suspension on it. I actually finished third on it, behind Sture Lindblom and the Dutchman, Ab de Groot.

The bike I used that day came courtesy of Serge Duchamp, who had a very good Weslake with a crappy, old Jawa as a spare. I borrowed his Jawa but all my thoughts soon turned to the need to get home and try to put everything back together again.

"For a bit of British companionship, I'd parked next to Peter Collins and his mechanic in the pits, and PC lent me a bike for the remainder of the meeting. It was a fantastic gesture and one that I never forgot"

Back home at a few meetings in England, I found that I wasn't quite as competitive as I should have been. I wasn't winning races and found life very frustrating. The harder I tried to win, the worse I seemed to go. Halfway through the season I received a booking for a meeting at Hechthausen in northern Germany. Alois Wiesbock was a World Champion and the Swede, Conny Samuelsson, had been runner-up in the World Ice Championships in 1977. They were among some very good riders there but I ended up winning the meeting, passing Wiesbock on the last lap of the final.

Dickie Staff, my old grasstrack contempory and a very good friend, used to accompany me to meetings at this stage – and boy, did we celebrate! I thought it was the greatest thing ever to be standing up there on the rostrum, with German star Alois Wiesbock on one side of me and Conny Samuelsson on the other. I was 18, still raw, and they were world stars. This notable victory was a major stepping-stone for me and got me noticed around the northern Germany tracks.

I had a few more successes in France and then finished second to Trevor Banks in the British Championships at Braintree, Essex. By the end of the season I had gone on a bit of a run again, winning a few big meetings, including the Portsmouth Airport event. I also hoped to win the first-ever Ace of Aces but fell off in a semi-final while leading, leaving Mike Garrad to snatch glory.

The 1979 season had seen a lot of ups and downs. What with vehicles blowing up and exhausts falling off, and cars breaking down in the middle of nowhere and in freezing cold conditions, I'd seen plenty of strife in some pretty weird places. And these mishaps were by no means rare!

It was all character-building. There is no use in life being full of ups, because then it doesn't prepare you for coping with the downs. I regard all these experiences of life as just as important as any training schools. All those trips . . . breaking down in the middle of nowhere with no money in my pocket, wondering how I was going to get to the next meeting. It's all those setbacks and heartaches which make the good times all worthwhile. You dig deep for motivation at times in your career when you really need it. It's a formative period — and not only in your career, but in terms of maturing as a person, too.

4 Letter to Otto

IN the close season of 1979-80, I knew I had to have a rethink machinery wise. I had a blown up Weslake, which was probably worth nothing, in bits, while my other one was fairly worn out by this stage. So I decided to write to Otto Lantenhammer, the legendary engine-tuning wizard, whom I read about in *Motorcycling Weekly*.

I had read all these stories at the time about engine tune-ups costing £2,000, which was an awful lot of money then. I didn't know if any other English blokes were doing this sort of thing but I just thought I would contact Otto and ask him how much he could do me an engine for? Within a week I received a letter back saying: "We are pleased to prepare a full engine for £450."

A new engine cost £700, as I recall, and I thought: 'Well, I've got two heaps of dung here. If I get rid of this rubbish and buy a new one, it will cost me £700. I'll only get £400-to-£500 for these things, so I'm probably going to get a completely re-built Lantenhammer engine, which will be better than anything brand new.' I thought I just had to go for it.

So I shot down to Otto's place with Dickie Staff and a car borrowed from Norman Reeves. Thanks to Jeff Bing who arranged the deal for me, I was effectively 'selling' cars for them by driving around in new models which weren't quite to showroom standard.

Dickie and I jumped into a Ford Capri and drove all the way to Munich . . . to visit the famous Otto Lantenhammer.

Otto and his wife, Ingrid, were very pleasant. We left the engines with him and returned to England to sort out a trip to Australia – well, I was 19 and wanted to race a bit more.

Bill MacDonald, who had been Australian Champion on a number of occasions on the dirt track scene, was a very good friend of my brother's and the Baybutt family. I wrote a letter to Bill, asking if he would be able to put me up for a little while until I sorted myself out.

I didn't have enough money to buy a complete ticket but I read that British Caledonian were promoting cheap standby tickets to Hong Kong for £140. I reached there and stayed for a couple of days, on my own, trying to find a cheap ticket to Brisbane and back, as you couldn't get into Australia on a one-way ticket. So I had to buy a Hong Kong-Brisbane return, which I found for about £240 in the end. Trouble was, I was in Hong Kong for three days, on my own, staying at the YMCA. It was quite a scary feeling really – for even though I'd driven around Germany, I'd always had someone with me. This was different.

When I arrived in Brisbane, Bill was there to greet me with his wife and two daughters. The family took me in like a son, they couldn't do enough for me and in future years I would always stay with this fabulous couple when in that part of Australia.

Bill had a motorcycle shop, a pick-up truck and a lot of contacts. When I told him that I was very keen to ride short circuit, he fixed me up with a loan of a bike from a mate, plus many other items that I needed. The MacDonalds kept their word and treated me unbelievably well, with Bill lending me his pick-up truck or a bike to go anywhere that I needed to.

Bill was a friend of Julian's from when my brother had toured Australia to race short circuit in the early 70s. Short circuit is the Australian equivalent of grasstrack racing, except the Aussies have right and left-hand bends and their tracks are normally 1,500 metres in length.

Bill's wife, Margaret, bought me a speedway bike from Brisk Sales in Brisbane, whom John Titman used to work for. Part of the agreement was that they lent me one of the short circuit bikes, a Hagon-Weslake.

For the speedway bike, we did a deal with promoter Bill Goode to ride at the Brisbane Exhibition Grounds. I made a lot of friends on my first visit, including Rob Ashton who was then riding at Exeter. Stan Bear, Steve Regeling, John Titman, Mike Farrell and Alan Rivett were also

Above: Grasstracking on Boxing Day, 1982. Below: Ripping up the grass at the Wimborne Whoppa, 1982.

among the Brisbane crew at the time – a bunch of complete and utter lunatics but great fun to be with! This, plus the fact that I didn't like England in January or February, marked the start of my regular trips to Australia.

5 Weymouth Wildcat

I REGULARLY used to spectate at Reading Speedway. With the Racers running their home meetings on a Monday, I was normally returning from the continent that night, so it suited me to pop in on my way from Heathrow airport and watch the likes of Bobby Schwartz, John Davis and Jan Andersson leading their British League challenge. I also used to see those guys at grasstracks on occasional weekends – and would take great pleasure in beating them.

Mervyn Stewkesbury, a businessman who had just taken over at Weymouth, happened to be standing next to me at the Reading pits entrance one night. We got chatting and before long he invited me down to Weymouth, where the prospect of riding him for him in the National League appealed to me.

Allied Presentations had sold the promoting rights at Weymouth Speedway to Mervyn, a millionaire property developer, who had acquired me as one of his new assets. He had never previously met me and his attitude was simply a vase of, 'As we've got you on contract, I suppose you might as well come down and ride!'

I explained that I was struggling to get my finances together to do full justice to what I had already taken on in grasstrack circles and didn't have a bike for speedway, too. I'd spent money on an engine from Lantenhammer and the grasstrack scene was about to happen for me, with quite a few bookings already lined up in Germany that season. So I told Mervyn that while I would love to race speedway for the 'Wildcats', I'd only do so provided it could be fitted in around my grasstrack commitments. That had to come first and foremost.

There were lots of Sunday tracks in the National League – or second division – but Mervyn didn't mind, because it was a case of either Weymouth having me whenever I was available, or not at all. We had a good understanding and got on tremendously well from the start.

Which is more than I can say for my early season form, because I started the 1980 campaign

Leading the way in his first season of speedway . . . Wiggy ahead of Berwick's Steve McDermott, May 1980.

dreadfully. For my first meeting, against Oxford, I had a Phil Pratt-tuned Jawa, an old bike that used to belong to team-mate Malcolm Corradine, which I couldn't ride at all well. My first pointless meeting was followed by my scoring three points in the next match, my NL debut against Stoke.

Other regulars in the expensively assembled Wildcats' team in my first season included Martin Yeates, Brian Woodward, Bob Coles, Chris Pusey, Mark DeKok and Terry Tulloch. Phil Lock was team manager.

In my second season on the shale, Neil Street took over as team manager and new riders for 1981 included Malcolm Shakespeare, who had made such an impression on me in my days as a schoolboy spectator at Ipswich, plus Steve Schofield, Les Rumsey and Steve Crockett.

I managed to boost my average by almost four points a match, to just over 10 points a match, as Weymouth soared to second place in the league table – eight points behind champions Middlesbrough.

We enjoyed a very good sponsorship deal from the VW dealership in Dorchester, who bought everybody in the team a new Weslake. The deal was that our team manager and ace engine tuner, Neil Street, would look after all the engines for the year and that we wouldn't have to pay for them. I took delivery of my new Wessie in time for Oxford's visit to Weymouth. I was number seven and scored 14 points, beating Dave Perks – the National League number one – three times! The crowd went berserk.

My speedway career took off from that point and although there were lots of ups, there were very few downs. However, I do remember going to Exeter and walking the track with Chris Pusey, which was the worst thing that I could have done. Chris, who was nearing the end of his successful career, convinced me that it was the most suicidal place on the planet – and, not surprisingly, I scored only three points from five rides. When I visited the County Ground again at near the end of the following season, I made a point of walking the track with Neil Street before the meeting – and this time I scored 14.

The way Neil approached a meeting was different and I found him fabulous to talk to. If ever I had a doubt or a problem in my mind, I would talk to him. He is not only enthusiastic but very understanding too. He could understand what we riders were going through. If you had a psychological problem or something you were trying to come to terms with, he'd talk you through it. He is a brilliant bloke – simple as that – and no wonder Jason Crump, Neil's grandson, has come on as quickly as he has. He wouldn't tell Jason how to ride the bike but it's very encouraging for a young rider to have someone of Neil's experience and know-how behind him and offering background support.

Team-riding Wildcats' pair Simon and John McNeill combine for a 5-1 against Rye House's Kelvin Mullarkey.

6 Making a stand

ON our arrival in Munich, Otto Lantenhammer was waiting for us with two engines. He explained how this was wrong and that was wrong, that he'd had to throw away certain items, and the whole bill had come to a lot more than £450 per engine. However, he said he'd stand by the amount he'd agreed he would do it for.

I was by now anxious to go try out the engines he'd prepared, so we went to a grasstrack circuit very near to Otto's place, where we bolted the engine into the frame and started it up. The sheer speed produced by this four-valve pushrod engine came as a shock to me – it was just unbelievable compared to what I'd been using at the time. I let the clutch out and the bike just wanted to go to the moon – it was the most amazing sensation that I could ever imagine, like the thrill you experience when, having only ridden a 350, you try a 500 for the first time. I'd been riding 500s on international grasstracks for a year or so and now I thought, 'this is it . . . no-one is going to get near me now.'

The day Wiggy 'arrived' in Germany – beating Peter Collins and Egon Müller at Vechta, 1980.

In the UK, I started thrashing everyone out of sight, winning other meetings in France and several low-key events in Germany. Then came the European semi-final, at Damme in Germany, which I won from reigning Euro champion Gerald Short to earn a lot of respect among many influential promoters.

After seeing me win at Damme, the promoter at Vechta rang me about their big June holiday meeting, wanting me as a replacement for Tormod Langli who had to withdraw after breaking his arm in a hang-gliding accident. The international field included Ivan Mauger, Ole Olsen, Anders Michanek, Peter Collins, Scott Autrey, Gordon Kennett, Chris Morton, Egon Müller and Sture Lindblom. Everybody who was anybody was there but I went through the programme and beat them all, winning from PC and Müller in front of a packed crowd.

By now I had acquired a full-time mechanic – Adam, who was my girlfriend's brother. He was 18-years-old and although I was only able to pay him a weekly basic of £20, I'd also give him 10 per cent of my winnings. At that particular meeting I won £400, which was a lot of money to me at the time and enough to pay for another tune-up. By this stage I also had enough to buy Julian's other engine from him, which meant I had two Lantenhammer-tuned motors. If anything happened to one, I had the other to fall back on.

I also changed frame manufacturer, to the Hagon sandracer that Egon and most of the other top guys were using. Joseph Jay, an Englishman who was a main parts and engine distributor for longtrack and speedway in Germany, had advised me that I'd been using the wrong frames. He was very correct, so he got hold of a sandracer frame for me and I was very successful using that as we approached the European final at Bad Waldsee, Germany.

I honestly thought that I was going to win it – I was on a roll, having thrashed everybody out of sight two weeks before. I thought, 'this is it . . . I'm going to be European Champion.' And it was looking good when I achieved fastest time in practice on the Saturday, having just been down to Lantenhammer, who'd worked on both of my engines for the final.

In my first race, Franz Kolbeck, a wily old German rider, made the start on me. We were going into the third corner at the end of the back straight when he started turning very early. I thought, 'this is great, I've got him.' So I just kept going straight longer before driving underneath him. Then he heard me coming and tried to block me, and I hit him in the back so hard you wouldn't believe it. The pair of us collided and crashed spectacularly and although concussed, I vaguely remember trying to get up and mumbling: 'European Championship! European Championship!' to the doctors who were trying to hold me down.

I collapsed back down on the track and, like Franz, didn't wake up until the following morning. My girlfriend and her mother had made the trip to Germany, along with Pete Webb from Windsor Comp and Tom Pink of Norman Reeves Motors. They travelled in hope and expectation of seeing me become European Champion but it was all over for me on the third corner of the first lap. Local rider Willi Stauch won it from Gerald Short.

My girlfriend found accommodation with a local family so that she could be at my bedside while the rest returned to England. I was still in hospital the following Thursday when I received a message from the promoters at Cloppenburg. After my Vechta triumph, I had bookings coming in thick and fast, with all the northern German tracks wanting me to ride for them.

Cloppenburg was one of the fastest and most famous grasstrack events in the world, all the top boys were there and I was desperate to join them. I'd informed the promoters at Cloppenburg that I couldn't attend because I was in hospital and, having been unconscious for a long period, the doctors were unwilling to release me for another five days. The club sent a message back saying that if I didn't ride in the meeting, then I would never ride there again!

So my girlfriend and I waited until 11pm on my fourth day in care before sneaking out of the hospital, albeit still feeling severely under the weather. I could hardly stand up – and I was certainly in no fit state to drive. My head was spinning and, looking back, discharging myself was one of the most stupid things I ever did. Under the circumstances, I was driven by fear, thinking that I simply had to get to Cloppenburg or else miss out on so many more future opportunities there.

My girlfriend drove us up to north Germany with me laid out in the back of the van trying to sleep. When we got there, I set up to fulfil the booking even though I couldn't even see where the bloody track went! It was the fastest track in the world, where riders averaged speeds of 85mph. I was in a right mess, failing to score a point, which did my reputation a lot of damage in the eyes of a lot of promoters, who came to the conclusion that I was just a flash in the pan.

Next I was caught up in trouble over the British Grasstrack Championships, which had been staged over three rounds. The Evesham club staged the opening round at Shipston-on-Stour on the side of a hill. It was 500 yards around, had a highly unusual steep gradient of about one-in-six, with bends at both top and bottom, and was the bumpiest course I'd ever ridden.

Opinion among the riders as to whether we were should ride was split. But to my mind, it was totally unsuitable and a disgrace to the sport, so we really shouldn't have ridden. I organised a petition and although many riders agreed that the track was dangerous, when it came to the crunch, a lot of riders decided to give it a go – except me and Gerald Short, who were headlined 'The Evesham Two' in *Motor Cycle News* the following week. We wanted the meeting abandoned but officials insisted it went ahead. After we both missed our scheduled second rides, Gerald and I returned to take our third outings, but it wasn't good enough for a British Championship.

And I paid the price by not being crowned British Champion and finishing fifth in the overall points scorers – behind Trevor Banks, who retained the title, Chris Baybutt, Jeremy Doncaster and Alan Gardiner. Having won the second and third rounds, at Portsmouth and Exeter respectively, all I needed to have done at Evesham to clinch the title was finish at least fourth.

"There I was, a young rider willing to state my case and stand up for what was right. People think that I've got like it with age and status. No! I stood by my principles way back then and thus started a history of brushes with officialdom"

But I feel very strongly about the credibility of the sport. I don't think the big meetings should be run like Mickey Mouse affairs. Having experienced the Continental scene, and seen what was achieved in the mid-70s at Hereford, to see a British Championship on a moto-cross track . . . well, the Auto Cycle Union (ACU) shouldn't have allowed it. You have got to have quality control and ensure good standards are adhered to.

So there I was, a young rider willing to state my case and stand up for what was right. People think that I've got like it with age and status. No! I stood by my principles way back then and thus started a history of brushes with officialdom.

To help compensate for the furore over the 1980 British Grasstrack Championships, I had the satisfaction of winning a lot of open meetings around Europe later on in the season. In doing so I managed to get my foot back in the door with the big boys in Germany again. After Cloppenburg, I had endured a lapse in form for about a month afterwards, then I gradually got back into again. I finished the season quite strongly and won several of the big end-of-season grasstrack events in England, including the Wimborne Whoppa, Bewdley Bonanza and the Holbeach and Shropshire championships.

On the rostrum in Holland with Gerald Short (left) and wily Swede Sture Lindblom.

7 A wasted year

LOOKING back on my three speedway seasons at Weymouth, between 1980 and 1982, I enjoyed some great highlights. I had some big scores here, there and everywhere and also a few disasters along the way.

Like the zero I scored on my first visit to Exeter and a couple of ones elsewhere. Once, I arrived at Glasgow too late for the match because I'd been stuck in a traffic jam and didn't even get a ride that night.

My speedway experiences in 1980 helped to make me a much better grasstrack rider. The opportunity to make a lot more starts every week, and the closeness of the first corner, it added a new all round edge to my racing. I sharpened up my act by riding speedway and, every Sunday, it paid off for me on the grass.

Before I took up speedway I'd watched blokes like Phil and Les Collins on the grasstrack and I couldn't quite live with them. It was around 1979 when I recognised that they were a little bit better than me, so I identified the key to progress – riding speedway in the week would raise my all round game.

Speedway was useful, rather than a priority, yet things just happened for me. I wasn't perhaps giving it the full attention I should have done but I was still making progress. Before long, I went out and beat established speedway stars without really thinking about it.

The following year – 1981 – I got fairly serious about everything. I had undertaken a trip to Australia that winter but struggled a little bit at Brisbane because I was down on power.

When I returned in 1981-82, though, at least I was fit and raring to go. I'd worked hard on the bikes before going to Australia so that most of my equipment was set up and ready for when I returned home. I had one speedway bike rebuilt – including a re-paint of the frame, bits and pieces polished and a new bearing fitted – but it was still an old speedway bike. Gerald Jackson was doing a fair bit on my engines at that stage, from his place in Twickenham. Nothing too special but between what Gerald and Neil Street did, I had reasonable motors. While Otto Lantenhammer worked on my grasstrack engines, I couldn't afford to have him work on all my motors. Besides, another plus with Gerald was that he'd also help me with grasstrack engines if I was stuck.

When the speedway season was in full swing, I went on a roll, banging in good scores and finishing second to Newcastle's Joe Owen in the National League averages. As the new Weymouth number one, ahead of Martin Yeates, I made it to the National League Riders' Championship at wet and windy Wimbledon, where I finished second to Canterbury's Mike Ferreira, who scored a maximum. I dropped my only two points to Ferreira and Edinburgh's Neil Collins in my first ride.

Less than 24 hours after the biggest speedway meeting I'd ever ridden in at Wimbledon, I managed to win my first British Grasstrack Championship at Uckington, Shropshire, completing a maximum nine wins to finish 14 points clear of Trevor Banks.

Life at Weymouth was always great fun, it was the key to our success. Mervyn Stewkesbury came into speedway promoting with no preconceived ideas. If he'd presented what he did at Weymouth down at Poole at the time, you wouldn't have known where to put all the people. At Weymouth you had a cold, old, windy stadium that had nothing but the most basic of facilities and yet Mervyn did a great job with what were very limited resources.

Wherever we went it was a great giggle. Although Phil Lock, my first team manager, was very serious, no-one else was. Alan Hodder, the club's press officer who went on to become manager of the NL's head office, was good fun while Mervyn was continually coming out with practical jokes, like stink bombs in the bar. On one occasion he brought down Phil Crump for a series of races against Les Rumsey, Martin Yeates and myself. He placed some colour bombs up Phil's exhaust pipe while he was waiting to be pushed off, and soon there was red smoke everywhere. It was hysterical.

In 1982, Martin Yeates enjoyed a lot of success and it was announced in the press that they were going to have a couple of Penthouse Pets come and present him with a prize. So they had this Rolls Royce, with blacked out windows, drive onto the track and circle for a lap or two. Then Phil Lock and Mervyn, dressed as bunny girls, leapt out of the back of the Roller and jumped on top of Martin! They were pulling stunts like that every week.

That is what speedway misses. Although the sport is really very important, everybody seems to have forgotten about the fun aspect. These days, it's all about the points you score and the emphasis on the team winning. Yes, that's important, it's got to happen, but first and foremost, speedway must be an entertainment.

I had a great time with my Weymouth team-mates plus a super bunch of juniors they had at Radipole Lane back then. I brought Stan Bear over from Australia, while Steve Schofield came on the scene in the second half. By 1981, I was dragging people along with me to Weymouth, telling them what great fun it was there.

Stan was a great character, well liked by the fans. It wasn't just the points he scored on track, he was also a good value person to have on the team. Unfortunately, people just tend to look at the points a rider scores and not the other things that he can bring to the table. Stan, Martin and myself used to team up to go on the northern tours – and we had an absolute scream.

Having said how much I enjoyed my three years at Weymouth, I made a big mistake in not going up into British League – or first division – a year earlier than I did. I hadn't put a foot wrong in 1981. My only disappointment that year was missing out on my first World Longtrack Final, thanks to two blown engines in the semi-final at Pfarrkirchen, Germany.

It occurred to me that I'd made a mistake in spending a third season at National League level after I scored 20 points out of 21 at Crayford one Tuesday evening, followed by 21 points at Middlesbrough just two days later – all on the same back tyre. In fact, I'd ridden six successive meetings on the same rear tyre!

At the end of the '81 season I wanted to keep active and went back to Australia. Weslake contacted me about being a factory rider for them, so I did a deal with them to ride their engines on the Continent. I was a full-time professional at this point, having enjoyed a fantastic year abroad with a lot of big wins, including many in all parts of Germany. Although I had missed out on a first World Longtrack Final appearance, I'd finished third in my quarter-final at Harsewinkel, an event with its share of drama.

I now had a Ford Transit of my own, which Dickie Staff and I took to the event with two pushrod engines from Otto Lantenhammer, while Windsor Comp had helped me with a single-cam engine. I'd spent a lot of money with Lantenhammer to acquire the latest state-of-the-art longtrack engines, so I had two bikes and a spare engine – the oldest pushrod engine being the spare.

On the first lap of practice at Harsewinkel the best pushrod engine blew up, so then I came out on the new single cam and that also blew to pieces. After just two laps of free practice on

Left: The highlight of Simon's National League career – runner-up to Mike Ferreira in the 1981 NLRC, with Bruce Cribb third. Right: With team-mate Jan Verner on a guest appearance for Cradley Heath, 1982.

the Saturday, I was down to my last engine. Walter Grubmüller, an Austrian rider who rode speedway briefly at Exeter, had also blown up two engines in practice, as had Ivan Mauger. So Walter came to me and said that with six blown engines between the three of us, the plan was for him to drive down to Munich after practice in my van (I can't remember the details but something had happened to his). Walter would phone Lantenhammer on the way, to let him know he was coming and what was needed from the ace German tuner.

As well as the time it would take Otto to rebuild six engines, you are talking about a minimum 12 hours' drive there and back.

Well, Walter was back in the pits within three-quarters-of-an-hour . . . having now blown up my van! It was only able to do 40mph, so Walter had coaxed it back to the track. The World Longtrack quarter-final was looming the next day, with only my third engine available. Anyway, I survived the meeting and finished third behind Mauger and Anders Michanek. Then there was a special race to climax the meeting for a trophy, which I won ahead of Ivan.

While the meeting itself had a happy ending, we endured a dreadful drive home. By the time we got back to the UK and through London, we were down to a maximum speed of 25mph, just to keep going. We actually managed to drive all the way home . . . but it took us a-day-and-a-half. The engine had blown up but we managed to get it fixed for the next week – and went back to Germany again.

Dramas like this happened all the time but they were all good fun and games. We managed to get everything built up for the World longtrack semi-final later in the year but, on a very hot day, I blew two more engines. I was very despondent because I was sure that I was going to make it to the final.

"After giving Ole's offer a lot of thought, I had to apologise to the Danish superstar, who I'm sure couldn't understand my thinking at the time. In hindsight, I think joining Coventry then would have been a good move for me"

In the early winter of 1981-82, Ole Olsen came to see me, asking if I'd sign for his Coventry team. He phoned first and then came around to my home – I was still living with my parents in the old people's home near High Wycombe. They had an apartment there and Dad had an old garage that he worked from, which had a paintshop out the back where I'd prepare my bikes.

When Ole came to see me we spent the whole morning together talking. He wanted me to ride for Coventry the next year, 1982, but I thought, 'hang on, I'm not supposed to be a speedway rider, I'm a grasstrack rider. Coventry is a Saturday night track.' Ironically, I did eventually sign for them more than a decade later.

I chewed over what Ole had said and there was no denying that it was a tremendous compliment having a legend like Olsen come and speak to me, about riding for a great club like Coventry. I talked it over with my brother and we took into account that although I'd nearly cracked the Continental grasstrack scene and was being well rewarded for results, I hadn't yet been to all the big German tracks. At that stage, I was still writing to organising clubs trying to get starts, for it was still very hard getting invitations to compete in those top events.

Convinced that I was on the verge of cracking it on the longtrack, I didn't want to give it all up and go and ride for a Saturday night speedway club. I had my first experience of a clash of grasstrack and speedway interests when I was fined £500 by the Speedway Control Board for riding in Barry Briggs' Isle of Man meeting when they claimed I should have been riding in Young England v National Select matches at Exeter and Middlesbrough. Even though I had informed the speedway authorities of my prior commitment to Briggo's IOM grass meeting, they ignored me and still named me for those two speedway Tests.

After giving Ole's offer a lot of thought, I had to apologise to the Danish superstar, who I'm sure couldn't understand my thinking at the time.

In hindsight, I think joining Coventry then would have been a good move for me, although I did at least gain some some invaluable senior league experience in 1982, as a guest for the Bees' Midlands rivals, Cradley Heath.

Heathens' promoter Pete Adams took me on a brief loan spell, although I continued to 'double up' with Weymouth in the lower league, and he threw me in at the deep end a bit by booking me into the Black Country track's annual Golden Hammer meeting, which was one of the plum individual events in the domestic calendar. I did OK to score 10 points in top company and then had another enjoyable night among the big names when I finished third, behind Bobby Schwartz and Phil Crump, in the prestige Blue Riband at Poole, where a big following from Weymouth came to cheer me on.

History in the making . . . the first National League rider to reach the British Final, at Coventry, 1982.

To be honest, though, 1982 was a bit of a wasted year for me, speedway-wise, because I didn't do anything more with Weymouth than I'd done the year before. All I did was go through the motions.

The only thing that Neil Street and I would discuss was to see if it was possible to go around every track a second faster than I'd done the race before. I was effectively racing against myself everywhere I went because I was able to beat all the opposition comfortably most of the time. A lot of the challenge went out of it as I toured the National League for a third season, although I did enjoy winning the Best Pairs title with Martin Yeates at Swindon, where we were undefeated all night and beat Long Eaton's Dave Perks and Alan Molyneux in the final.

There were a couple of individual highlights, too, in that I made history by becoming the first NL rider to qualify for the British Final, one of the classic meetings of the season that formed a vital stage of the World Championship. And on the grass, I managed victory in both rounds to win the first-ever British Masters Grasstrack Championship.

However, as far as speedway was concerned, I should have made the jump into the British League a year earlier than I did.

Challenging on the outside of Mildenhall's Richard Knight.

Hans Zierk proved a major turning point.

8 Help from Hans

EARLY in 1982 I'd been having a lot of trouble with Weslakes on the Continent. I'd a couple of engines from the Weslake factory but they weren't very fast or competitive. Although Weslake boss Mike Daniels and the lads at the Rye, Sussex factory were tremendously supportive and tried very hard, they didn't seem capable of finding the same sort of power that Lantenhammer produced for Egon Müller and the rest of the top boys. So, more often than not, I'd take the factory Weslakes with me, only to end up riding OL engines.

A major turning point for me, mechanically, came at an early season meeting at Celle, in northern Germany, where I'd done reasonably well the year before. This time, though, I blew up both factory engines in practice and they were slow anyway. Hans Zierk, another well respected German tuner, was standing in the corner of the pits with his wife. Hans used to go to many of the meetings and I remembered that the year before I'd seen Trevor Banks ride his bikes. Banksy used to have a Roth – an enormous twin-cam machine with a big carburettor on it. It was like a rocketship – so fast, you could barely confine it to the stadium! It was at that meeting that Trevor crashed on his Roth.

The previous winter, Hans had done a deal with British engine manufacturer, Don Godden, to become the main Godden importer in Germany, having previously helped Don to set up his business at East Malling, Kent. They were friends from way back, when Don himself had been a star on the grasstracks and longtracks of Europe.

Hans said to me: "Do you want to ride my bike?" I told him that, for now, I would simply love to borrow one of his engines for the day. So we stuck a Zierk-Godden in my Dula frame – I was riding Dulas by this stage and working for part of the close season with Paul Duncombe again. Paul had allowed me to incorporate some of my own ideas in a good longtrack bike for the Continent. I wanted to continue to use Dula frames but by fitting the GR engine provided by Hans Zierk, I was taking another step up from what Lantenhammer had been doing. Not so much in terms of power, but in the sense of top end speed.

Although I finished second at Celle to Egon Müller, behind me were quality blokes like Georg Hack, Karl Maier, Ivan Mauger, Peter Collins and Sture Lindblom. The Lantenhammer engines were still good but this was the start of my long and successful association with Hans Zierk. It started accidentally and we soon fostered a brilliant working relationship that has lasted to this day – and I've never ridden anything else since.

Based at Hanover, Hans is a Ford dealer who has done tremendously well, having built his business from scratch. My relationship with him is very similar to the one I enjoyed in Australia with Bill MacDonald. Since my brother Julian was such a great help in starting me off and giving me help to get going, Hans has been my main guiding light, a man who has been able to piece the whole Continental scene together for me and point me in a few right directions.

Hans is more than a technical expert. Having qualified for European and German finals as a rider himself, he's been through it all. He'd also been to every longtrack in his country, so he knows what's required everywhere. There is so much more to longtracking than just power – good technique and riding style is also important. My riding style wasn't really right for longtrack – until Hans helped improve my starting technique, plus the advice he gave me on shock absorbers, gear boxes and clutches, the setting up of frames and other things.

Hans is also a very supportive bloke. I can't think of any meeting when I've done badly and Hans has come across and given me a hard time. It's never happened. Never. If I've performed badly and apologised to him, then just like your Dad he would say: 'Don't worry, you did your best.' Or: 'You'll be OK next week, we *all* have bad days.'

Sure, there were days when I've said that the engine is this or the engine is that but he knows me well enough to know that I'm not just making excuses. There have been times when I've won a race and come back in and told him that the engine needs changing or there is something wrong with it. There have been other occasions when I've been beaten out of sight and come in and said: 'This engine is unbelievable – the fastest thing I've ever sat on.'

In contrast, I struggled to get my opinions across to Don Godden when we were trying to modify the Godden engine a little bit. Don didn't seem able to accept input, he'd take what was said personally and that affected his business.

How does this all compare with Neil Street, who invented the Jawa-Street Conversion engine? Well, he is an absolutely gifted guy, who can put anything together that he wants to. But I felt that with Neil, he was always figuring out ways of saving money rather than making the engines go faster. He deliberately worked to a small budget. Speedway and longtrack tuners obviously have a different approach to each other. If you have Lantenhammer making engines for Egon Müller, with Egon earning vast amounts of money, he doesn't mind if he is spending two grand on an engine. He is obviously going to have a different product to someone who is trying to put an engine together for £150.

But spending vast amounts of money to find extra horsepower, which for speedway is not often really necessary anyway, probably isn't Neil's style. He does a great job for what is needed. To put a speedway engine together that is going to do 25 meetings, you probably couldn't find a better bloke to do it than Neil. But in terms of finding extra horsepower or doing a real super trick horsepower job – he is not your man. He is very inexpensive because he builds an engine and no parts have gone into it.

On the other hand, Lantenhammer is the luxury, high-earning end of the market and he charges accordingly. He does the job accordingly – and so does Hans Zierk.

However, Neil is a very clever guy and he does know how to make them go if he really wants to. He has very much got the sport and its future existence at heart. He is always on the riders' side, whether they're seniors or juniors, and is permanently trying to keep the price down as much as possible. He can prepare good motors for junior riders, although, as shown in the mid-70s with his four-valve development, he can also build engines to go faster than the rest.

Looking back at 1982, the link with Hans Zierk was great for me and we had a lot of success together. His GR engines were very fast at the end of the straight. They used to really rev but that was OK if you were riding them flat-out. Although I like something which has a lot of strength – so that from low revs, the throttle can be opened and shut, and you can still change direction and ride accordingly, I don't like riding flat-out. The Zierk engines suited me.

Once I started to use Zierk's engines, I also helped to develop them. Hans had a liking for light flywheels and great big inlet ports, which meant the engine has plenty of revs and a lot of power at high revs, but not much strength from bottom. It makes good, consistent starts very difficult. So we changed that. Karl Maier was using Hans' engines at the same time as me, in 1982, Hans having had had a lot of success the previous year with Georg Gilgenreiner and Christoph Betzl in the World Final at Gornja Radgona, in the then Yugoslavia. Georg finished second to Michael Lee and Christoph could have won it but ran last in the final when he needed fourth place to finish as World Champion.

A very funny guy, Hans really had his heart and soul in the sport. When I started working with him, we immediately got on like a house on fire. I think he liked the fact that I was willing to try anything that he would throw at me, while I felt honoured that someone with his mechanical expertise was willing to use me as a guinea pig.

It's not been all win, win, win, though. We've had some dreadful meetings when we have tried things which didn't work but I can accept that. Although we have developed a perfect situation in recent years, one only has to go back to 1992 when I finished last in the World Longtrack Final at Pfarrkirchen without scoring a point. Hans and I have had a few of those too!

9 Cradley calling

IN the winter of 1982-83 I returned to Australia and mainly rode speedway. This close season was a key period in sorting out my immediate future on the shale as I knew that after three seasons with Weymouth, I had to move up to the British League.

I'd had a lot of trouble agreeing a deal with Mervyn Stewkesbury at the beginning of the previous season and initially withdrew my services. We did eventually reach agreement, which included the proviso that I would be put on the transfer list at the end of the season. To be fair to him, though, once we'd sorted out my basic deal, we didn't have a cross word all season. After shaking hands with him, I just got on with it. Mervyn was fine and I can't fault the guy.

Whatever my regrets about spending a year too long in the National League, Weymouth remained fun for me and from that point of view it was a shame to leave the place.

Early in 1983, Pete Adams phoned and came to see me. We went out for dinner where he told me that he was able to give me access to Jürgen Goldstein, who had been Bruce Penhall's Continental mechanic before the double World Champion retired after retaining the speedway world title in 1982.

The main area of concern about riding for a Saturday night speedway club was fitting it in around my Sunday Continental grasstrack and longtrack commitments. It was the reason, remember, why I turned down a move to Coventry a year earlier, so finding a good bloke to look after me was imperative. As it was, Jürgen lived only an hour from Hans Zierk, and Jürgen had been with Bruce for three or four years so he knew the score. He'd travelled with the Californian superstar all over Europe, not just to Germany, and his knowledge and experience was invaluable. I went to see Jürgen and found him to be a fabulous bloke.

My previous mechanic, Adam, had been outstanding but, tragically, he was killed in a car crash at the end of 1980, aged only 20. In 1981 Dickie Staff used to accompany me quite often and by 1982, along came Greg Williamson, who had worked for Kai Niemi the year before. Greg was a Kiwi from Auckland, who stayed with me until 1985 and based himself in Milton Keynes.

Team-riding at Dudley Wood with Heathens' Alan Grahame (right), one of the finest exponents of the art, 1983.

So, it was decision time. I decided to move up and join a good British League club, one that could have added the 1982 BL championship to the Knockout Cup they'd already won that season but for Penhall's shock retirement immediately after he'd retained the world title in Los Angeles. Pete Adams was such a good bloke to talk to and his team plans looked impressive.

To go from Neil Street to Pete Adams was a perfect move. Again, I was riding for someone who thought about what he was doing. He wasn't just demanding points on a regular basis, but he was putting a lot of thought into how to obtain them.

I quickly agreed personal terms with Pete to ride for the Heathens, who paid a reported £18,000 for me, and It was neither a brilliant deal nor a bad one. I had considered other clubs – there was talk of Bristol making a return, which would have appealed to me – but Pete was very professional and I liked what I heard from him. Significantly, he had fixed me up with Jürgen Goldstein, who would work for me in Germany.

I'd been to the majority of German tracks at least once, so I knew what to expect in terms of travel requirements and other planning. Arriving later at a German track after an early Sunday morning flight from England enabled me to give up those long and tiring journeys by road, so I bought a van for Jürgen to drive the bikes around in Germany and we'd meet up at the track on raceday.

I then spent all my money purchasing a house from Kai Niemi in Newport Pagnell, with a little workshop in the garage and very handily situated very close to the M1.

Once I signed for Cradley, I also had support from Don Godden for some parts for bikes – two frame kits and the loan of an engine. I bought quite a lot of product from him as well. I believed it was time to develop my speedway career as I saw that my longtrack racing would progress naturally. I thought to myself that if I was going to develop as a rider, I would have to put in a fair bit of effort. By then, it looked as if that extra effort was going to be worthwhile, with crowds still healthy and the general speedway scene at that time looking pretty good.

I started the 1983 season as Cradley Heath's number seven in a star-studded team headed by Erik Gundersen and also including Lance King, Phil Collins, Alan Grahame, Jan O. Pedersen and my fellow reserve, Andy Reid. After a month Andy was replaced by Peter Ravn, who was soon joined at reserve by Jan O. as I was promoted to ride at number one in partnership with American star Lance. Erik rode at number three, with Phil and Big Al at four and five. This was widely regarded as the strongest British League team of all-time.

The points development was dramatic. Within a couple of weeks we went from our starting maximum of 45 points to a combined 63-point aggregate in the averages, we were virtually unbeatable and it was fabulous to be part of that scene.

I also made my debut for the senior England team managed by Wally Mawdsley, although it was a disappointment not to be picked for the World Team Cup Final at Vojens. Having done quite well in the 3-2 Test series win against America, scoring double figures in two of the three matches for which I was selected and nine points in the third, as well as playing a key role in our qualification from the UK round at Reading, I thought I'd done enough to just squeeze a place in the WTC side for Denmark.

The big problem for me was that most of the fixtures were scheduled for Sundays – when I was being asked to ride for a lot less money to represent England than many others got for turning out for their clubs in the British League. However, being my first season at Cradley, and bearing in mind that Pete Adams had managed to drive such a hard bargain with me, I was actually earning more riding for England than I was for Cradley!

Although I was happy to sign for Cradley, I was being paid nothing like as much as for England compared to what I could have earned for riding at a Continental longtrack on a Sunday.

The British Speedway Promoters' Association (BSPA) had a habit of scheduling Test matches for a Sunday, which I thought was against the very ethos of speedway itself. Running your most important fixtures in the afternoon seemed ridiculous, when Test matches and events of similar prestige deserved prime Saturday night billing.

At the time fixture lists were congested but I still thought the major events should have been staged on Saturdays kept clear of league racing. The only way speedway will survive is if the big-time events are promoted correctly and allows the grass-roots level to grow on the back of it. On Channel 4 at the time, there was American football with a techni-colour pitch,

Wiggy racing for Cradley at King's Lynn, 1983 . . . in the afternoon.

cheerleaders dancing up and down and 100,000 people watching it live. You see that on TV and then two weeks later you're flicking through your local newspaper and it says American Football is being staged in Milton Keynes. Well, I saw what entertainment the Americans served up on TV the other week and it looked bloody good, so I might just pop down and watch my local club. That's how every successful sport is marketed.

In speedway's case, if the promoters are trying to show something to the general public with the aim of attracting new supporters to tracks, then their top meetings have to be staged at night, under floodlights. They shouldn't stage them in the afternoon for many reasons . . . dirty stadiums . . . empty seats . . . rusty, old tractors . . . and the greyhound tracks with dirty covers. So many factors which, if you are running at night, the viewing public – and television cameras – just wouldn't notice. What you see at night is the illuminated race strip, the colours, the characters and the racing itself looks twice as fast and dramatic, too.

At that stage of my career, being a newcomer to the England team, I tried to talk what I

New boy Wigg fires England

By DAVE LANNING

● ENGLAND debut boy Simon Wigg had the super confident Americans tearing their hair out with a composed first appearance on the Test

Simon on his senior England debut, jetting clear of partner Peter Collins and USA's Bobby Schwartz at Swindon on Sunday, April 24, 1983.
England won the Test series, 3-2.

Looking totally relaxed on parade as team manager Wally Mawdsley has a word prior to the England v USA third Test at Poole in 1983. John Davis, who coached Wiggy in his early speedway days, looks on.

On his first Test appearance against Denmark, Simon tries the outside line against mighty Danes Hans Nielsen and Erik Gundersen in wet conditions during the opening Test of this 1983 series.

Wiggy soaks up advice from Peter Collins and Kenny Carter before winning a vital race for England in the 1983 World Team Cup qualifier at Reading. He was disappointed not to be chosen for the final.

AXED WIGG SPARES ENGLAND BLUSHES

By PHILIP RISING

SIMON WIGG saved England from a speedway World Team Cup humiliation at Reading yesterday and then complained that he had been unfairly axed from his second ride.

Wigg the wonder

Simon powers his Godden GR500 through the turn at Cradley Heath.

thought was commonsense but without making big waves. But every Sunday meeting is a nail in the coffin as far as I am concerned. If you are small-minded and think only about today, and how many people you can get in the stadium on any given date, then run big meetings on a Sunday afternoon, because it's a more convenient time for speedway fans.

But as far as pushing your product is concerned, which speedway hadn't done for 10 years or so, it is dreadful – all the promoters are doing is showing the worst their sport has to offer.

On a hot summer's afternoon, the track has to be heavily over-watered just to start the meeting. Nine times out of 10 it is a dust bowl within eight races, and then there is very little or no overtaking.

For a rider, it's very unfair when the track changes so quickly during such important meetings – a conclusion I quickly came to when I first rode for England. They started slotting in Test matches on a Sunday afternoon just to take a few quid off the speedway fans, rather than put on a real show that could draw new fans from beyond the sport's existing fraternity.

There are factors relevant to sponsors that shouldn't be overlooked either. Ideally, you want to give them a product where they want to come back next year and spend some more money with you. It's all very well having a Sunday afternoon event at Swindon, which is easy to get to. However, I would have thought that a sponsor might sacrifice a day out for a few of its employees in return for coverage in the national newspapers. Any sports journalist will tell you how difficult – no, nigh on impossible – it is to get speedway coverage in the national papers on a Monday morning.

There is so much else going on in the sporting world during summer Sundays – Wimbledon (tennis), the golf majors, cricket Tests, motor racing grands prix and, every four years, the football World Cup and European Championships. So doesn't it make sense that if speedway Test matches, the British Final or any other prestige meetings were staged on, say, a Wednesday evening, there is a much greater chance of coverage right across the media spectrum. And by scheduling their big meetings for midweek, the BSPA would be able to give their sponsors some extra mileage and, in turn, help the sport achieve a higher profile.

But if you are trying only to attract speedway fans along, then your market is restricted. That has been the basic problem with speedway for so long, with the majority of promotions aiming solely at the people who are coming already. Very few promoters aim to reach beyond the converted, to the general public, who don't know what the hell speedway is all about.

At club level, I had no complaints, though. There was a tremendous balance because we had some very serious characters in there. Erik was a great personality and a lot of fun, but he was still a very serious speedway rider. So, too, were his fellow Danes, Peter Ravn and Jan O. Pedersen. However, having fun-loving guys like Phil Collins in the midst of all that stopped anybody getting too carried away with their own self-importance. Phil kept the whole balance going with a fun element.

Even when the pressure was on, someone like Phil would be there with the right joke at the right time. If any team is going to be successful, it has to have the right balance among its riders. Lance was good, Phil was brilliant, Jan O. was lively, while Alan would ride through a brick wall for anybody. I got on well with all the riders and Pete was a tremendous manager in the way he brought it all together.

There was no way you were going to make a mistake as far as team-riding went. Phil and Alan were just tremendous as a pairing, never getting in each other's way even though they had quite different riding styles.

But everything we had going so well at Cradley lasted only a year, because jealous rival promoters ganged up to ensure that Cradley Heath's all-conquering British League and KO Cup-winning team of 1983 was broken up. Year after year the BSPA invent ridiculous points limits and pull every winning team apart. This is because the whole basis of speedway, since that stage in 1983, has been to drag the top team down to the bottom team's level. Which is why it has been in the state that it has been. It can't survive like that – everybody needs to aspire to a higher level.

"England lost a big opportunity with Pete Adams but, having said that, if you stuck him in tomorrow he could still turn it around very quickly"

Cradley was a very good team away from home (winning 12 and losing just two league matches out of 14). We were great value for money and an attraction wherever we went. We used to bring in big crowds and I never thought it was a problem with speedway. We had inherited the colourful image that Americans Bruce Penhall and Bobby Schwartz had left behind at Cradley as well. It was bloody fabulous, simple as that. For the others to want to pull Cradley apart, just because they wanted to beat them, is pathetic.

As for Pete Adams, he is probably the best team manager that I have ridden for. His understanding of speedway and the riders – and their feelings – goes far deeper than most guys I have ridden for. Pete would have made an excellent England team manager, there is no

Simon enjoyed the craic with Erik Gundersen and the rest of the Cradley Heath team.

With the 1983 BL title and KO Cup already in the bag, Heathens' riders and management were at Belle Vue to see Erik Gundersen win the BLRC. Back row, l to r: Pete Adams, Simon Cross, Wiggy, Alan Grahame, Derek Pugh. Front: Peter Ravn, Jan O. Pedersen, Erik, Phil Collins.

doubt about that. Why didn't he take charge of the national team? Politics within the BSPA, I should imagine. The BSPA control the purse-strings of the England team and I don't think that they particularly want someone who isn't one of them.

Pete was always on the riders' side and would guarantee to get 100 per cent effort all the time from everyone who pulls on an England racejacket. England lost a big opportunity with Pete Adams but, if you gave him the job tomorrow, he could still turn it around very quickly.

At the end of the 1983 season, Cradley Heath celebrated winning the British League championship with what many people considered to be the best-ever senior team. We dropped just four league points all season and completed the double by beating old rivals Coventry in the Knockout Cup final. Erik Gundersen – who also won the very prestigious British League Riders' Championship – was our No.1 with an average of more than 10 points a match, but the key to our success lay in our awesome all round strength. Five of us averaged around the eight points mark, while Jan O. Pedersen was pushing seven and young Simon Cross came in occasionally and averaged six.

We were too good to be true as far as the BSPA was concerned, and, thanks to their controversial combined maximum points limit – which was set at 48 that winter – the team had to be broken up. Jan O. went to Sheffield, while Peter Ravn joined Wolverhampton, where Pete Adams became new, sole promoter.

I would've liked to have stayed with Pete Adams more than anything, even at Wolves, which is not one of my favourite tracks. It wasn't to be, though, as Heathens' boss, Derek Pugh, would have been foolish to have let any of his Cradley riders join their most fierce rivals.

Oxford, who were about to return to the top flight after eight years' of racing at NL level, were being developed by ambitious new owners, Northern Sports Ltd. They had exciting, big plans and had to be taken seriously.

10 Top honours at Oxford

NORTHERN Sports took Oxford Cheetahs up into the British League in 1984 and it became clear very quickly that they wanted to assemble a championship-winning team. In the space of just weeks, they bought Danish star Hans Nielsen for £30,000, emerging England international Marvyn Cox from Rye House, another Dane, Jens Rasmussen, also signed for £12,000 after Hackney withdrew from the BL and dropped into the National League, while Mel Taylor arrived from King's Lynn.

Soon after hitting the headlines with the capture of Nielsen from Birmingham, they splashed out another £25,000 to sign myself. We had a good basis from which to start in 1984 – and by then I certainly wasn't sad about leaving Cradley.

New-look Oxford now looked a very exciting challenge, more exciting than even another year at Cradley would have been, especially with Pete Adams having moved on to Wolves. I definitely didn't see joining them as taking a backward step.

As for Hans Nielsen, he has been a tremendous advert for the sport, someone who has done it all and a person I admire immensely. Hans is a model professional every youngster should aspire to, similar to Ivan Mauger in a lot of ways. Hans' riding style is also so different to anybody else's.

On the track he was brilliant to ride with – I've lost count of the amount of five-ones we had together, especially at the end of matches when we were paired in a last-heat decider. We had a few balls-ups but very few. I got on tremendously with him – and always did.

Oxford's Big Three in 1984 – Wiggy, Marvyn Cox and Hans Nielsen led the way in Cheetahs' new era.

I never had any hang-ups about riding in the same team as Hans and, when we were paired together, I didn't care what start position either one of us had. I'm sure that he wasn't too worried about what I wanted either, so we were always able to discuss things and decide between us. It was a good relationship.

Hans is so different in his approach compared to most British riders, which sometimes caused a communication problem between him and some of the young lads. Which is where I came in sometimes, because they could relate a little bit more to me than Hans. I think that between the two of us, we had as near perfect a solution as you could get.

The big problem at Oxford was that there were too many people running it. Instead of having one single promoter to deal with, there were several representatives and the sport never had any clear direction there. The marketing of Oxford Stadium seemed non-existent, which I found very frustrating at times.

"I never had any hang-ups about riding in the same team as Hans and, when we were paired together, I didn't care what start position either one of us had"

I'd carry on all the time, asking questions like: 'Why don't we do this to get the public in? Why don't we try that? Why not more advertising? Why not more marketing?' But you never knew who to turn to. If I took my complaints or ideas to Bernard Crapper, he would tell me to talk to John Payne. Go to John, and he might refer you to John Tremblin. Talk to 'Trembles' and he would tell you it was Peter York's job. Then Peter would say that John Blake had the final say. And, finally, John Blake would say that he had nothing to do with the speedway and was just the general manager!

So you'd go around in circles trying to find someone who could make a decision. It was absolute madness. That is the one single problem that Oxford always had – the lack of a single strong leader at the top of its speedway management team. That's what it needed from the word go, because everything else about the place was perfect.

With a superb stadium with great facilities, including a new home straight stand that housed new bars and restaurant and even squash courts, Northern Sports were a very supportive group to start with, while the foundations were being laid for success on the track.

However, Oxford Cheetahs lacked an entrepreneurial get-up-and-go personality. You have got to have some imagination and try and see the sport through the eyes of the general public,

Great riders, great entertainers . . . Hans Nielsen and Simon gave Oxford a massive lift.

Wiggy covers the outside of the track as he and Mel Taylor team-ride to a 5-1 against Poole pair Sam Ermolenko and Finn Thomsen at smooth and enjoyable Sandy Lane, 1984.

rather than the average speedway fan. It needs someone to get out there and sell the product, to put bums on seats.

On track, we were incredibly successful very quickly. Hans, Marvyn and myself were all improving at the same time and we had a really solid feel about us. It was a very enjoyable team to be part of, we had a lot of fun.

The 1984 season also marked my first appearance in a World Final, held that year at the Ullevi Stadium, Gothenburg. I had a big crash at Newcastle on the Monday before the final, when Diamonds' Phil White fell in front of me, and although I didn't actually break anything, I landed very heavily on my chest and suffered bad bruising to my thigh. I could hardly walk up until the Thursday and was really struggling.

The crash happened at the end of the back straight, where I went straight on and somehow became wrapped around the front end of the bike.

Being in a World Final was a great experience and, having qualified in second place from the Inter-Continental Final in Denmark, behind Shawn Moran, I travelled to Sweden in good spirits.

As the only English rider in the final (Alan Grahame went there as reserve), I scored nine points on the big night but a carburettor stopped twice, which cost me two points. The throttle jammed open in my second ride, causing me to shut off half-way down the straight to make sure I stopped in time. The pin fell out of the body of a new carb, the slide turned around and the throttle wouldn't shut off.

In another race the carb flooded, which was also very frustrating. The engine coughed and spluttered and, again, I was overtaken. I was having a lot of trouble with Amal carburettors at the time and switched to Dellorto shortly afterwards.

Although those problems lost me two points, I don't think they cost me many places in the final reckoning. Perhaps I'd have finished fifth rather than sixth.

Billy Sanders had been among the pre-meeting favourites and we all thought the Aussie was going to win it, because he had not been beaten at Gothenburg for yonks. He had a fantastic run leading up to the final but then failed to make an impact when it really mattered. Everybody was surprised, none more so than Billy himself.

The top three of Erik Gundersen, my Oxford team-mate Hans Nielsen and Lance King were all well-known to me and I wasn't far behind them on the night. I reminded myself that just two years earlier I'd been racing in the National League, so qualifying for my first speedway World Final and winning a couple of races was a fabulous feeling . . . and I wanted more of it.

No Englishman did more to try and stop the dominant Danes from winning the World Team Cup Final at Leszno in 1984 than Simon, who top-scored in Poland with nine points.

Above: Wiggy shows his back wheel to Shawn Moran, who was America's leading scorer on the day.

Left: With Phil and Peter Collins on the pre-meeting parade.

Below: At least Simon was the only rider to beat Hans Nielsen.

Carl Glover's England slipped to a 4-1 Test series defeat by the USA in 1984 but, once again, Wiggy was always in the thick of the action, trying to lift the Three Lions.

Above: Simon scoots away from team-mate Chris Morton while Americans Sam Ermolenko and Shawn Moran put him under pressure on the inside at Sheffield in the second Test.

Below: It's Wiggy's turn to try the inside at Cradley Heath.

Simon at practice before his first speedway World Final at Gothenburg, Sweden, 1984.

Above: Lone Englishman Simon begins his first World Final with a win in heat three from old mates, Kelly Moran, Kai Niemi and Karl Maier.

Above: Simon believed that Billy Sanders – seen above dicing with Wiggy for second place in heat nine – would triumph in Sweden.

Right: No sign of World Final nerves as a relaxed Simon gives a TV interview to former World Champion Bruce Penhall.

11 Top of the world

THE World Longtrack Championship was always right up there as my main driving ambition and in 1985 I fulfilled a lifetime's dream at Korskro in Denmark. I'd built a new bike with Dula frames, which made it tremendous to ride on small corners and tight turns. I'd also learned a lot about frame development – changing engine plates and moving the engine around, plus different steer links and wheel bases – to find out what suited me best.

I'd always ridden what everybody else was sat on but that year I really experimented a lot.

Back in 1983, I'd ridden the Godden frame for a while but I'd really struggled on small tracks. I'd wanted to discuss a lot of the recommendations with Don but he didn't agree with me, so his frames remained unchanged. I moved off the Godden frames – back to Dulas – in 1984, which allowed us to work on the development of a different frame for '85.

The result was that I won the World Longtrack Championship at my third attempt.

My first attempt to reach the final, in 1981, had seen me run into mechanical difficulties in the semi-final in Germany. Then, in 1982, I reached my first final in which I rode the Zierk-Godden in frames that Dula had made for me at their workshops in Watford. That year I won the quarter-final and finished fourth in the semi-final at Vilshofen, Germany, which left me quite hopeful leading up to the final at Korskro, near Esbjerg.

Karl Maier, Georg Gilgenreiner and myself went testing at Scheessel the week before the '82 World Final and our tuner, Hans Zierk, was quite happy with all three of us. I also thought I had a very good bike under me, although I was still fairly inexperienced at longtrack, despite having ridden the big circuits of Europe for only a couple of years, whereas Karl and Georg had been brought up on them. If I'd been in Hans' position, I would have made sure that those two had the best equipment for that particular final.

As it worked out, Karl won his first World Final on a Godden, which also marked a first-ever World Championship victory for Hans and his engines in Denmark that year. I finished 13th with five points and while I didn't have a particularly good meeting, I learned a lot from it.

In 1983 I'd been on the Godden frame, with engines again provided by Hans, and finished joint seventh at Marianske Lazne in the Czech Republic. Although I was relatively happy with the improvement, I still felt that I should have finished higher than a few who scored more than I did on the day.

For me, although 1984 was the first year in which I reached the speedway World Final, it was a stupid year. I was behind Jeremy Doncaster in a race at Vilshofen, which is quite a difficult longtrack in southern Germany, and I tried to pass him at a point where I shouldn't have done. It's an 800-metre sand track, where the first corner is very square – like a very big version of Exeter's speedway track – and it's very banked too. You tend to run right up to the top of the fence, in the middle of the corner, and then down again. Then there's a very long straight and a very tight, deep corner at the end of it. There are no spectators there – just gravestones, because there's a cemetery behind this corner, where the headstones can be seen beyond the fence!

There have been a lot of big crashes there and mine was just another one of them. I nearly T-boned Jeremy going into the third corner, went over the handlebars and broke my collarbone. So I was out of the World Longtrack Championship for another season.

In 1985 I sailed through to the final quite nicely, having put a lot of effort into qualifying. At the final itself, I had a very good practice at Esbjerg on the Saturday and felt confident that I could finish in the top three, if not win it.

One unexpected boost came from Georg Hack, someone whom I'd admired for such a long time, who just came up to me on the Saturday night and said: "Simon, tomorrow I think you will be World Champion." It was one of the last things I heard before setting off to get my head

The fulfilment of a boyhood dream...World Longtrack Champion at Korskro, Denmark, 1985.

Happy landing – returning in style to Oxford with the World Longtrack title. Soon the BL championship would also be won.

Winning the BL Best Pairs at Wolves with Hans Nielsen, ahead of Cradley's pairing of Erik Gundersen/Phil Collins and Reading duo of Mitch Shirra/John Davis.

down for the night. As soon as he said that I thought to myself: 'Well, if Georg Hack thinks I can win, then I am probably going to be World Champion!' I was fired by his confidence in me.

In the first race I got to the first corner at the same time as Egon Müller and tried to pass him on the outside. It had poured with rain all night and the place was virtually underwater, so I remember getting the biggest face-full in the middle of the first corner and coming out about fifth. There was mud flying everywhere and although I dodged a bit of mud and flying dirt here and there, I could hardly see a thing as I lost all my tear-offs in the first corner. Unable to see where I was going, I nearly ran into Vaclav Verner going down the back straight, before managing to squeeze past him and reach third place eventually. Egon won the heat but I was happy to get three points in the end.

I think Shawn Moran beat me in the next race before I won my last heat to leave myself on 12 points. Egon had dropped only one at that stage and was on 14 points. Shawn Moran and I each won our respective semi-finals, which meant we were both on 17 points after the three heats and the semi-finals. I set a new track record in the semi-final after Hans Zierk came over and advised me to change the gearing, which I did.

For the final I had an unfancied gate position, on the outside, so I was very nervous about that. Having had the outside start in the first race, and been filled in by Müller, I was very worried that if I didn't make a good, clean start off the outside, I'd been in big trouble because the track was very wet and it was also windy.

I recall that the other four guys in the final – Bobby Schwartz, Peter Collins, Jiri Stancl and Egon – were all on 16 points. It was that tight. Everything hinged on the last race – whoever won it would be crowned World Champion.

They came around with the helmet colours and I drew gate six, so I was wetting myself! I thought I could do without that. Then I said to myself, 'it doesn't matter anyway, because I'm going to make the start of my lifetime.'

The one good thing about being on the outside, if there is a bit of tape-pushing or whatever going on, you don't usually get involved in it. On either gate one or six you can be in your own little world. Ivan Mauger always looked at the tapes – he never looked right or left – so he was therefore unaware of what was going on around him. There is a lot to be said for that.

So we'd come to the crunch. I just sat alone in my corner of the pits for 10 minutes, thinking about nothing else but letting my clutch out, getting my balance right and just making the best start ever. I achieved my aim of being in my own world when the green light came on. I just concentrated and concentrated, then BANG! – I made one of those dream starts. The front wheel didn't even touch the ground until I changed first gear. I dumped the clutch and got the

Wiggy has American Shawn Moran in his sights at the World Longtrack Final, 1985.

balance just right. I couldn't have made a better start if I'd practiced it a thousand times and that was the one time I needed to make one.

I got to the first corner and I could just see Schwartz's wheel. Then I got my foot across that . . . and saw daylight! I then prayed that the bike would last four laps – in these situations the last lap is murder. All you can think about is the piston going up and down, and the valves, and you are hoping that nothing is going to fly apart or stop or that the chain won't fall off. I can't even describe what it is like to go from that feeling of immense tension to crossing the line and knowing you are the World Champion. It's the best, the greatest feeling of all time. Something I had dreamt about since I was a kid had finally happened. I felt as if my insides were going to burst, as if my whole chest was going to explode. It's was a fabulous feeling, absolutely incredible. Once you've experienced that, you just want to experience it again and again.

The first reaction you take in are the flags being waved over the fence. The first people you see are your fellow competitors, who tend to catch you up as you are riding back around to the pits. They are all patting you on the back. Of course, everybody wants to win but at the end of the day we all know that whoever has won, whoever has been the man on the day, has deserved it most. I would be the first to pat anybody else on the back if they'd won.

It suddenly occurred to me that all-time greats like Egon Müller and Peter Collins were there congratulating me and that I could now share the status of a world title with them. I was somewhere that I'd never imagined I'd be at this stage of my life, alongside those guys whom I'd goggled at as a kid. I was a long way from Hereford Racecourse at that point. This was the stuff of which fairytales are made.

"It suddenly occurred to me that all-time greats like Egon Müller and Peter Collins were congratulating me...somewhere that I'd never imagined I'd be at this stage of my life, alongside those guys whom I'd goggled at as a kid. I was a long way from Hereford Racecourse at that point. This was the stuff of which fairytales are made"

As for the financial implications of becoming World Longtrack Champion, I had been carving a solid reputation on the Continent, bit by bit, trying to impress most of the promoters who run the big meetings. They knew that if I was coming, I would be there with well turned-out machinery. I was clean and tidy plus I wasn't going to cause any trouble. I was always going to try my best at all times. Obviously, there were going to be days when things would go wrong, but the vast majority of the time I'd go and give Egon and those boys a very good run for their money. That's what the promoters really wanted. They didn't want a race between the

Simon was proud to skipper England to a 3-0 series victory over USA in 1986. Riders pictured with team managers Colin Pratt and Eric Boocock after the Test at Ipswich are (back row l to r): Andrew Silver, Carl Blackbird, Neil Evitts, Richard Knight. Front: Chris Morton, Wiggy, Marvyn Cox, Jeremy Doncaster. The picture is completed by the 'Sunbrite Girls', including Simon's former girlfriend, Chiquita (far left).

top Germans – they wanted some more blokes like Peter Collins and myself to come and race their top guys.

Before Korskro '85, I'd probably been in more demand than most riders who hadn't won a World Championship. Then, after winning my first world title, I had all the bookings I could want. Even those clubs I'd written to in previous years, pleading unsuccessfully to ride in their meetings, suddenly invited me to their tracks.

The German longtrack scene was a real closed shop, very hard to break into, but winning the

Oxford and Cradley Heath contested many important and classic matches in the mid-80s. Here's Wiggy and Cheetahs' team-mate Andy Grahame about to notch up a 5-1 over Heathens' pair Phil Collins and Jan O Pedersen at a packed Dudley Wood, 1986.

World Championship opened every door for me on the Continent. The best thing was to receive an invitation to ride at Hasloch – the track where, years earlier, I'd been forced to make a rapid exit after a row with promoter Frits Kissell. I have to say that I took great pleasure in telling the Hasloch promotion that I wasn't coming! They came back to me but I quoted them a price so high that there was no way that they could afford it in a million years!

It was, of course, my way of saying that you shouldn't have screwed me for £50 when I was 18 and I really needed the help. I hadn't gone there to ride around last, I'd ridden flat out, but they tried to rip me off.

As it turned out, Fritz and I got on well later and I rode quite a few meetings there before they closed down in the early 90s. I'd rib Fritz, who came to respect me for what I had achieved, by reminding him about when he'd ripped me off for that money – and how the boot was now on the other foot. On the first occasion when I was invited back, however, although I could have done with the money, I took great pleasure in sitting at home that day as World Champion.

Winning the World Longtrack Championship did, however, bring a potential clash with my speedway commitments. The earning potential in speedway was reasonably good and still can be. However, there is no denying that the Continental longtrack and grasstrack scene is well rewarded. Certainly, there are World Champions, like Hans Nielsen and Erik Gundersen, who have looked after their money and become wealthy, which reflects well on the sport.

Even so, despite all the overseas longtrack bookings, I still found the time to take over the England captaincy in my first season back following the end of my year-long international speedway ban. I was always proud to pull on my country's body colour and took great pleasure in leading the Sunbrite Lions, managed by Eric Boocock and Colin Pratt, to a 3-0 whitewash of the USA. Not even some stupid and petty referees, who excluded myself and one or two others on both teams for pulling wheelies as we crossed the finish line, could spoil our celebrations. It also helped to make up for our 4-1 Test series defeat by the dominant Danes earlier in the season.

I finished with an average of more than 10 points a match, Oxford retained the British League title, while Hans Nielsen and myself won the BL Pairs Championship. Speedway was not a distraction, it helped me. I became a better longtrack rider by racing on shale, and my speedway was proving successful anyway.

Riding for Oxford was also a very enjoyable experience for me – not only because we were successful, but also as I had a lot of fun there, among plenty of friends, and it was only up the road from home. Our Friday race-night was also perfect in terms of slotting it in with my weekend longtrack meetings on the Continent, although I was naturally gutted that my defence of the world title ended in the semi-final with mechanical mishaps at Harsewinkel.

But there was trouble brewing in 1987 . . .

12 Capital losses

I'D had no problems whatsoever at Oxford for three years and then one day, Kevin Hedderley, one of the financial management team of owners Northern Sports, confronted me with a proposed pay cut for the 1987 season.

Having been a World Champion, and brought a lot of profile to Oxford and its stadium, which I felt they never exploited at all, I felt quite bitter about being asked to race for less money.

A move to Hackney was mooted after Oxford told me that they couldn't afford to pay me what they had in 1986, so what I did that winter was go out and find a good sponsor. In Australia I met John Old, who was coming to Britain to start the Trueseal business here and had been looking for a way of marketing his product in the UK. When I told him that I was struggling to do a deal at Oxford, he asked me what I could do for him if he put money up on the sponsorship front. I told him that there was a new team entering the British League and that Oxford might be looking at letting me out on loan. The track was in London and they wanted me as their number one.

John stated that if I moved to Hackney he would make up the difference between what they could afford to pay me and my 1986 deal I had at Oxford. It was a good solution for all concerned and I was happy knowing I was going to earn my normal rate, even though it meant a little extra work for me in promoting the Trueseal name and products.

The whole business frustrated me, though, as I didn't think that Oxford were doing enough to put bums on seats. They were relying on the team's success as their only way of attracting crowds but there was so much more that could've been done on the promotion and marketing side. I thought that if more effort went in to increase attendances in the first place, I wouldn't have been asked to take a pay cut.

In the three previous seasons I had agreed a deal with Bernard Crapper and John Payne and had always been able to talk to them. Then Kevin Hedderley came along and he couldn't understand my way of thinking. I couldn't understand his, so there was a big breakdown in communication there really.

I would have much rather continued at Oxford on the same deal in 1987 but it didn't happen.

It is very hard to drop your standards when you have set your budget and you are an organised professional. If your planning is all set to a certain standard and someone asks you to do the same job for less money, it becomes very hard. Whatever business you are in, it's difficult to suddenly find ways of cutting your costs. At the same time as trying to win races and score points for your team, you are also expected to look good and turn out professionally, to have clean and tidy mechanics, to drive reliable, quality vehicles – in fact all the trappings you would imagine that a speedway organiser would want you to have.

That was a very difficult situation for me to accept but, luckily, it was solved through John Old and the Trueseal Group, whom I'd met at the Mister Melbourne event, which they sponsored and I managed to win. Seeing me as an interesting way to help put across their message in Europe, they made up the shortfall on what Hackney could afford and I signed for the east London club, who were returning to the top flight after having spent three previous successful seasons in the National League.

It could have been a good career move but the one issue that always made it very difficult for me to immerse myself into the Hackney scene was the fact that I was only there on loan from Oxford. I was still owned by Oxford and I really hated that. Although a situation like that probably doesn't bother a lot of riders, I like to feel part of the furniture, as if I truly belong somewhere. But if you think that you may only be spending just a year at a club, which is the basis of every loan agreement, it is difficult to become totally involved with that team. This also applied in

Simon trying to get to grips with Hackney in this battle with Reading's John Davis and Tony Olsson.

1990 when I went to Bradford. In both situations, I wanted to be bought from Oxford.

The other problem to me was that the Hackney track changed. It had been a fabulous track but they decided to bring the fence in – as I recall, for safety reasons to keep the Control Board happy. The trouble was that bringing the fence in drastically reduced the racing line and restricted a rider's ability to get alongside other riders entering the corners. This made it particularly frustrating if you were at the back, so it was very hard to ride the track fast unless you were in front. It was very difficult to get past anybody on the reshaped track.

The Hackney track was also very slick, much slicker than I had imagined it would be on a regular basis. When they did try and put any dirt down, it always became very patchy. I found that very hard to understand having been at Oxford, where Barry and John had spoilt the home riders rotten. Oxford was the best track in the country at the time, prepared by the two very best track guys, using the most expensive material that they could get their hands on. That's how it should be. When I ride in a motorcycle meeting, I'm expected to turn out with the best bikes and the best equipment possible, so by the same token, I expect track preparation to be done the same way.

The paying public are the ones who pay the biggest price if the product is not right. They always vote with their feet. If you are trying to get bums on seats, one would automatically think that the most important issue, first and foremost, would be good track preparation.

But after what I'd been used to at Oxford, I found it difficult adapting to the Hackney circuit. Also, the alterations they'd made that winter, by reducing the width and bringing the fence in two metres all the way around, only added to my dissatisfaction. I'm not trying to make excuses for any performances but it was very difficult to become excited about going there towards the end of the season.

It was also a pity that their season back in the British League was to prove a one-off, with the promotion unable to sustain the financial realities of life in the top flight. The potential of racing in London was enormous and I know that everyone involved in the management – John Louis, Dave Pavitt and Mike Western – all tried very hard to make it work. I must also accept that there may have been a number of circumstances, of which I am unaware, that made it difficult for them to do what they set out to in the British League.

The Kestrels team was certainly full of exciting potential. Mark Loram was a young reserve at the age of 16 and nothing made me happier than leading such a youthful Hackney team to Oxford towards the end of the season – and winning!

There was a view put forward from some quarters that Hackney returned to the National League in 1988 because I was an expense they simply couldn't afford. I know what I rode for and

When Wiggy won the Golden Helmet at Sheffield in 1987, they had no actual helmet to present to him. Instead, quick thinking *Speedway Mail* photographer Ken Carpenter lent Simon his hat – complete with impromptu sticker – for the presentation by Sheffield boss Maurice Ducker.

I know, too, that my main sponsor, Trueseal, paid a lot of it. It's a load of old rubbish for anyone to say that I was too expensive for Hackney, for Trueseal were subsidising my deal quite considerably. In fact, I probably rode for 20 per cent less at Waterden Road that season than I've ever done elsewhere.

It was true that Hackney's crowds weren't particularly healthy, although I didn't see how attendances there could be sufficient when the racing wasn't as good as it needed to be to maintain the public's interest.

It's difficult to point the finger. It just didn't quite work well enough for John, Dave and Mike to want to go again in the British League in 1988. Instead, they dropped a division and won the National League that season – and no wonder. Riders like Loram and Andy Galvin, who had ridden very well when I had been there in the senior league, were absolutely flying at NL level.

There were times when I didn't do particularly well in league matches and other occasions when things went very well. The boys could pick up what was going on from me and improve their own form and preparation.

Overall, Hackney was successful for me, because I finished the '87 season with an average in excess of nine points, although the last month of the campaign saw me suffer a lot of engine troubles.

Being closer to Don Godden during my season at Hackney meant I saw him most weeks, but I still had problems trying to get my point of view over to him. I never experienced this frustration at Oxford because I never saw him. For years I hadn't spoken to Don a great deal, yet I had been on the GR500 engines since 1982.

At the end of my only year at Hackney, I felt that I was learning a lot very quickly. I felt that I had a lot to offer the Godden set-up by way of development, which, unfortunately, didn't seem to please Don. He seemed to think that I was interfering and sticking my nose into his product, which was a shame.

The product was very good and Don had some very good people working for him, who were really enthusiastic. The GR500 engines needed a few minor changes – nothing amazing or enormous, just some different thinking to produce that little bit extra.

"It's a load of old rubbish for anyone to say that I was too expensive for Hackney, for Trueseal were subsidising my deal quite considerably"

Don has traditionally been a longtrack man, first and foremost. It's a difficult matter trying to explain wheelspin and the need to have a lot of low down power in order to find grip, especially on slick, slippery tracks like Hackney. Longtrack riders have never experienced that for themselves. You can explain it to a speedway man because every speedway rider knows what I am talking about, whereas for the longtrack boys it is a completely different ball game – they cannot have too much power. If ever I said to Don that maybe we should try this or change that or do something else, I always had it thrown back at me that I was trying to make excuses for a bad performance. I found that quite frustrating all the time.

At the end of the season we struggled with an engine going back and forwards all the time, so the last month with Hackney was not particularly good. Generally, the rest of the season was quite healthy really, including grabbing third place in the British Final at Coventry.

Simon gets the better of the Moran brothers – Shawn (left) and Kelly – on their home track during the final England v USA Test at Sheffield, August 1987. Below: The victorious Sunbrite Lions at Owlerton.

Unfortunately I got knocked out of the Commonwealth Final stage at Belle Vue, where Jeremy Doncaster and myself had a run-off for the final qualifying place. On the last corner of the run-off, I was a few yards behind Jeremy and the only thing I could do was aim the bike at him and try to get in his way, in the hope that the referee would exclude him for falling off. Jeremy and I had been knocking each other off for years, so one more wasn't going to make any difference!

I'm sure Jeremy would have done exactly the same if he had been in my shoes. We laughed about it afterwards. Anyway, it was me who was excluded from the run-off, so I was out of the speedway World Championship for another year, but I consoled myself with the fact that the World Longtrack Final was coming soon, at Muhldorf in southern Germany.

Looking for a way past Denmark's Tommy Knudsen, 1987.

I hadn't qualified for the final in 1986 due to two punctures in my semi-final. Everywhere I went that season as World Champion on the Continent, the longtrack scene was fairly healthy and I earned a few bob as well.

Leading up to the 1987 World Final I had a very good year on both grasstrack and longtrack in Germany, having become the sole Zierk-Godden rider since Karl Maier's move to Lantenhammer and GM engines.

I felt I had a good chance in the final, especially with Hans Zierk right behind me. He knew that I'd won before and he was quite happy to put a lot of effort in for the final. As it turned out, it was the most frustrating World Final I'd experienced.

A year earlier, Christoph Betzl's younger brother, Sepp, had come over to England for a holiday. I'd known Christoph for a fair time, having raced against him when I first visited Germany, but Sepp was only 16-years-old and had just started to ride. I remember one particular occasion when he came over with another German, Klaus Lausch, and stayed at my place for a week. I got home one night to find a message by the back door: 'Thanks for letting me stay . . . I've decided to hitchhike back to Germany. Thanks for a great holiday. Sepp.'

I couldn't believe it and was concerned for his whereabouts, so I rang his brother and told him how worried I was that Sepp had disappeared. Christoph then announced: 'It's OK, he's here.' Sepp had managed to get from Buckinghamshire to their place, outside Munich, in the space of 24 hours – without any money in his pocket! Obviously he had thought nothing of making such a trip.

At this time Sepp was learning to ride and performing quite well. Then Muhldorf had an open meeting in 1986, which I rode in. The track was very wet and heavy at first, having rained all morning, and Sepp was competing in the junior races, which were held first. He'd gone out in one race but I hadn't been watching because I was busy working on my bikes. I was then informed that he had suffered a really bad crash. Apparently, he got filled in at the middle of a corner and ran straight into the fence at full bore. He was taken off and we didn't know any more until the meeting had finished.

I just wasn't expecting it when officials at the club, whom I knew very well, came over and explained that young Sepp had died. It was dreadful, especially as I knew the family so well and had stayed with them. Sepp had only just turned 17 – it was devastating. He was young, keen as mustard, funny and a really nice, young man. There wasn't an ounce of badness in him, he'd had a proper Christian upbringing.

I had travelled extensively elsewhere in the following 1987 season, so I hadn't visited Christoph's family. Then, a couple of days before the World Longtrack Final, I decided to go and see Christoph for the first time since his young brother had died.

It was my big mistake. Everyone at the house burst into tears. I was taken to the cemetery where Sepp was buried – his poor mother was dreadfully upset and remained so throughout the day. I obviously felt for the family and could only imagine how painfully they felt their loss, but for me it was far from ideal preparation for the World Longtrack Final.

When I came to the final, although I tried to think straight, I became paranoid, emotional and kept filling up. All I could do was think about Sepp and what had happened to him. It was dreadful trying to overcome these feelings as start time got nearer. I hadn't been back to the circuit since the day Sepp had been killed – and my next meeting there was a World Final. Having gone to see Sepp's family on the Thursday, by Friday I couldn't get the emotional scenes out of my mind and it was driving me crazy.

I had the bikes set up as good as possible and was just about ready and beginning to shut images of Sepp out of my mind when we came to the start line for heat one. All of a sudden flags were being waved and they sent us back to the pits. The delay had been caused by lots of spectators who had entered an exclusion zone on the back straight, so we then had to wait 45 minutes while the organisers tried to get these people out of the way. After the prolonged delay they came rushing into the pits announcing that the riders were on two minutes. A mental picture of Sepp kept reappearing, I was struggling badly.

At the start line, when the tapes went up, I was stuck there like a lemon. I was ready to make a good, clean pull to the first corner despite being late with the clutch. I was on an inside gate, which helped, but we must have gone only five yards off the start when Lubomir Jedek, a Czech rider, ran straight into me, nearly knocking me off.

In longtrack, even if you make a bad start, you can normally regain your balance and shoot past a few going into the first corner. At Muhldorf, you have to get your grip just right because there's such a distance to the first turn.

We'd put together a new bike the week before with some new engine plates and moved the engine back three-quarters of an inch. You couldn't miss the start. Even if you let the clutch out late, you were going to get to the corner in front. It was a fabulous facility.

Not this time, though. I hadn't had a chance of pulling to the corner because Jedek had run straight into me. I was all arms and legs as I nearly fell off. This was the first year that the FIM introduced eight riders per race – and I was back in eighth place for two-and-a-half laps. I managed to get past one bloke and then one more on the last lap. After finishing sixth in heat one, I then won my next heats as well as my semi-final. I needed to win the final, with a two points advantage on meeting leader Karl Maier, to force a run-off with him for the title. So if I won it with Maier third, we would meet in a run-off. If I won and he finished worse than third, I'd be World Champion again.

I made the start in the final . . . gone! Then, looking over my shoulder, I saw Shawn Moran in second for three laps, with Maier following him. It meant I was still on course for the title.

As I came over the start line to begin my last lap, Union Jacks were waving everywhere. Fans were waving and I was feeling so good again after that first race fiasco. But hang on . . . as we were coming down the back straight for the last time, Maier must have got past Moran – by this time, I wasn't looking behind me, only where I was going. As I came into the last corner, all of a sudden this sea of German flags went up in the air. I didn't even have to look over my shoulder to know what had happened.

I went over the finishing line nearly choking. I felt awful, especially knowing that if the first race had gone well I would not only have won it, but cleaned up. That incident at the start with Jedek in heat one had proved a disaster for me.

What's really weird is that, at Muhldorf in 1993, Karl Maier was two points in front of me going into the last race. On that occasion, I needed to win the final with him third or worse for me to be champion. Same points difference, same blokes, same track . . . and he ran last! Which proves that what goes around, comes around.

I mentioned my sadness for Sepp and the rest of the Betzl family but that day at Muhldorf in 1987 also reminds me of another personal tragedy. I had some good people around me at that World Longtrack Final, including my former mechanic, Jürgen Goldstein, who had worked with me from 1983 to 1985. From that point on, I brought my bikes back to England and worked on them there. However, Jürgen was back among the Wiggy pits crew to help us out that day in Germany.

Sadly, Jürgen was tragically killed in the early 90s, aged just 38, when he fell over coming out of his pub, knocked himself out and froze to death where he lay. They found him early the next morning. Jürgen was the real life and soul of the party and it was a very tragic way for him to die.

With mechanic Jürgen Goldstein, who died tragically.

Simon leads Shawn Moran and Simon Cross in the 1987 World Longtrack Final, but Karl Maier's second place in the last race at Muhldorf was enough to give him the title.

Looking back on 1987, my main achievements were finishing second in the World Longtrack Championship and winning the British Masters grasstrack. The ACU proclaimed that you had to finish in the top 20 in the Masters to obtain an international licence, which amounted to blackmail. They should make the British Championship an event in which we are all proud to take part and all equally desperate to win. If the ACU took the positive approach to the event, then the public would get excited about it and want to come and watch it, while sponsors would be keener to back it.

You can't point a gun at someone and say: 'Smile!' It is not how the world goes round and the ACU had the whole motivation thing upside down.

"It's up to the promoters to decide who their drawcards are. After all, we are talking here about world-class riders being refused licences, not complete idiots who have never ridden a motorcycle before"

It's very frustrating to see the ACU's failing to make the changes needed to benefit grasstrack racing. That's why guys like Jeremy Doncaster, Kelvin Tatum and Simon Cross were all refused international licences for various reasons. Andy Smith is another example. Most of them have been faced with speedway commitments on the same day as a British Masters round, and yet the ACU still wouldn't grant them a licence. Well, to me, that's bloody pathetic.

The people who promote meetings are the selectors, the ones who decide who they want to appear at their tracks. If a promoter thinks that you are a good enough rider and he wants you to ride for him, who are the ACU to tell anyone that he is not good enough? It's up to the promoters to decide who their drawcards are. After all, we are talking here about world-class riders being refused licences, not complete idiots who have never ridden a motorcycle before.

What makes it more frustrating is that I've been lucky enough to be in a privileged position because the longtrack scene has been very good in terms of results. The ACU has moved the goalposts for me, and they have done it on numerous occasions, but that doesn't do the sport any good. If a rule is a rule, then a rule is a rule. You can't suddenly say . . . 'well, Simon Wigg is not a bad bloke so we'll give him a 10-year licence.'

A week after I said that it might be best if I took out a German racing licence, the ACU gave me a 10-year British licence. It's nonsense.

Wiggy challenges Hans Nielsen (above) on the inside as the Dane combines with Erik Gundersen for maximum points in the first six-rider World Pairs Final, at Pocking, Germany, 1986. Simon and Jeremy Doncaster (left) struggled in the slick conditions on a sun-baked afternoon in Germany . . .
But there was a much improved showing by the English pair in 1987, when Simon and Kelvin Tatum (below) finished runners-up to the Gundersen/Nielsen pairing, with Americans Sam Ermolenko and Kelly Moran third at Pardubice, Czech Republic.

13 Oxford (track) blues

BY the start of the 1988 speedway season I was back at Oxford – but the once ideal and superbly prepared speedway track at Sandy Lane had, by then, become a disaster and enjoyable home meetings were few and far between.

It appears the people who were employed to cover the greyhound track were not doing their job as well as they should have done.

The greyhound fraternity had a lot of trouble with granite on the greyhound track cutting the dogs' feet, so the use of granite on the speedway track was banned from Oxford.

Our two track curators, John and Barry, being the kind of conscientious guys that they were, knew that they couldn't do the kind of job that they wanted to do without the materials necessary. So they left – and I don't blame them.

It would be like asking Hans Nielsen or myself to do the same job as we have always done, for half the money, or with half a motorbike. On certain issues, you have got to stand by your principles. Either you do the job properly or you don't do it at all. John and Barry were very honest people and they just refused to do half a job.

With Hackney reverting to the National League for 1988, I returned to Oxford, where we managed to do a deal for the new season after I'd been forced to take a cut. We argued fairly loudly about it, and Kevin Hedderley would say that it was only a 10 per cent reduction on my previous deal with them. What people like Kevin tend to very conveniently forget is that, being a speedway rider, you probably spend up to 60 per cent of your income setting yourself up to perform. Even with good sponsorship, you are ploughing huge amounts of money into your set-up in order to do the job properly.

What looks like a 10 per cent gross pay cut might actually amount to a 40 per cent reduction in your net profit, so it's vast in real terms. Accountants would easily appreciate what I'm saying but they conveniently forget when they are trying to do a deal with you. In these situations where both parties are struggling to reach agreement, employers tend to try and leak the details of the employee's proposed pay deal to the media in such a way as to make it look as if you are the villain of the piece, the mercenary, which is again fairly convenient for them.

Anyway, I went back to Oxford for 1988 and soon discovered that the track was a disgrace. The situation was made worse, though, by the new fixed gate position rule.

When the Oxford track was patchy, I always started meetings on the outside grid. By starting off gates four and three in my first two rides, it meant that one of the visiting heat leaders would be to the inside of me. I could usually just about gate on them but not always. Gate four was a b****** of a start to go from early in the meeting at Oxford, although it was not bad later on if there was a bit of dirt out wide.

Early on it was difficult to get across a good trapper on the inside of you. Ninety-nine times out of 100, with a big rut in the middle of the first corner, someone would hit that and T-bone me. I just got sick of it – you can only take so many knocks. From way back when I first broke my leg as a 17-year-old, I had by now broken collarbones, numerous ribs, fingers, etc, and here I was still being banged about.

Luckily, I struck a fabulous vein of form thanks to a new GM from Trevor Hedge, having finished with Godden at this stage. In the winter Don and I had a big fall-out. We were writing each other nasty letters, which, in hindsight, was fairly childish but eventually I moved to GMs.

It took me a little while to sort them out but I eventually managed to get myself a flying machine from Hedgie. It was a standard engine – nothing expensive about it – but an absolutely fabulous piece of equipment that Trevor had put together. I had a brilliant run on it and didn't seem to put a foot wrong.

The first night that I used it, I scored 15 at Cradley and passed both Jan O. Pedersen and Simon Cross twice. Next week I went to Coventry and got 15 again. Realising how good it was, I put it aside and didn't ride it again until the British Final, which I won.

Then I put it away for the Commonwealth Final at King's Lynn, which I should have won easily. I had 12 points after four races and I thought I'd put a new tyre on for my last ride, although I might well have put too much air in the back tyre because I executed a 360 degrees turn just after the track had been watered! In finishing the meeting on 12 points, I let Kelvin Tatum in for the title, with myself second.

Continuing to save this engine for the big occasion, I finished third in the Overseas Final qualifier, despite suffering a nasty injury at King's Lynn in a Test match against Denmark. I was coming into the pits corner chasing Tommy Knudsen when, yet again, I managed to spin almost completely full circle. I tried to save the fall with my left leg and, as I did so, my foot stuck in the ground. The rest of my body and my bike was moving one way while the lower part of my left leg was going in the other direction.

I tore the inside ligaments in my left knee really badly. It happened a week after the Commonwealth Final and, again, I went out just after they watered the track. I was in a lot of pain with it and borrowed an old carbon fibre knee brace from Lance King. Without it I couldn't have ridden. Anyway, the next meeting back was that Overseas Final at Coventry, where I had a run-off with Kelvin Tatum and Simon Cross while wearing Lance's knee brace. I finished third but at least I'd still qualified.

Then, at the Inter-Continental Final in Vetlanda, Sweden, I only just made the cut. I was again carrying an injury after someone had run into me at Oxford, which was no surprise given the consistently rough condition of my home track. I made it to the World Final in Vojens the hard way.

My favourite engine didn't appear to have enough steam in Sweden, although it seemed to suit the English tracks very well. Anywhere small and slippery and it was out of this world but on a big one, it just didn't seem to have enough power at the start.

At the speedway World Final in Denmark, my nine points ensured that once again I finished as the top Englishman in sixth place. By this stage I was riding GMs with Dula frames on the speedway, and Dula frames with Hans Zierk's Godden engines on longtrack. Although I had severed my relationship with Don Godden, I was still riding GR engines on longtracks because they came direct from Hans in Hanover, and my relationship with Zierk was very strong.

The World Longtrack Final of 1988 was at Scheessel, by which time I employed a Danish mechanic, Jesper Klausen, who was a very good guy, very funny and as honest as the day is long. I've been very lucky in having some great characters in my back-up team.

But on this occasion we had a big misunderstanding. What happened was that I told Jesper which first gear I wanted in the gearbox of the longtrack bike, and assumed that he'd set it up just as I had asked him to. We had a little problem in that his English was not quite as spot on as it needed to be and sometimes he would miss the point of what had been said.

Well, I ended up having a dreadful World Final. On the Saturday in free practice, I qualified for the track record over a 'flying lap', and to break a track record before a World Final was very encouraging. For the actual final on the Sunday, however, I was last at the first corner in every race. I didn't make the final and finished eighth.

I was scratching my head all the way home, trying to work out what had gone wrong. I had also tried another bike with a three-speed gearbox, which George Bewdley had made, but that wasn't really the answer we were looking for.

As it turned out, the next grasstrack after Scheessel was the Ace of Aces, near Andover. The start line is very slippery there, where you tend to pull a very high first gear off the start. So when I went to change the gearbox ratios for the Ace of Aces, I removed the end cover from the gearbox, only to find they were already there! So it must have been a breakdown in communication between Jesper and myself, or we had got the numbers wrong.

It turned out that I'd actually used the first gear ratio favoured on a little 500-metre slippery grasstrack for a deep and heavy 1000-metre longtrack World Final!

"Track preparation should have been of paramount importance but I began to feel very frustrated at Oxford. It became disgraceful as meetings were held up and the place began to get a bad reputation"

Overall, though, 1988 was not a bad year, the personal highlight being my victory in the tough British Final at Coventry.

Oxford had a relatively good season, climbing seven places in the BL table, with Martin Dugard having successfully moved up from Eastbourne and Marvyn Cox continuing to make progress.

But behind the scenes at Cowley the atmosphere was very tense and I'd remained unhappy with the state of the track. It is crucial that a small track like Oxford is prepared well. The big tracks, where you are racing around with both wheels in line, like the old Belle Vue and Sheffield, if they are a bit patchy or a bit bumpy, you don't tend to notice them too much, as the bike tends to fire you around the corners.

However, at small tracks where you are very sideways on, if the surface is patchy or full of holes, it can be dangerous when everyone is riding very hard and there is very little space between all four riders going into the first corner.

Track preparation should have been of paramount importance but I began to feel very frustrated at Oxford. It became disgraceful as meetings were held up and the place began to get a bad reputation.

Every time that I opened my mouth, I was accused of being a 'moaner', while any efforts we made in order to try and help were resented by the management. I ended up saying the most because I tended to be the general spokesman for most of the boys, who otherwise had a lot to say among themselves in the pits. Hans Nielsen, the captain, never said that much in public about what he thought but I felt strongly that someone had to stand up and say something.

I did agree, though, with Hans' considered analysis in his autobiography, *Main Dane*, that Oxford's basic problem all along was that there was no one single person there with direct responsibility for running the show. It was a case of too many chiefs . . .

14 Mauger influence

IN 1989 I enjoyed my best-ever season at both tracksports, finishing second in the speedway World Championship to Hans Nielsen and winning the World Longtrack Championship for a second time.

At the end of 1988 I'd split with my former fianceé, Chiquita, having been together for six years since we first met in her native Brisbane. Perhaps I'd been in a negative environment? Anyway, I found a new lease of life on my own and it tended to change my whole outlook. All of a sudden it was one big, exciting world again where I was able to do what I wanted.

At the beginning of the season I said to Mick Day, who had worked as mechanic for Hans Nielsen for a couple of years, having originally come to the UK from Australia to help me: 'I'm not too worried about how much money we make this year. Life's been kind to me, I'm still in one piece and enjoying a reasonably successful career. I'm not desperate any more but I want to be successful on the speedway tracks and everywhere else. We are going to plough all of my money and all of our efforts into the bikes and I'm not going to skimp on a flipping penny. Every effort is going to be made to win everything.'

My new sense of purpose paid its first dividends of the season when I retained the British Championship at Coventry – and on the same GM engine I'd used to win the tricky World Championship qualifier the previous season. In those days, the British Final was a very hard meeting to win once, never mind twice in successive seasons. Every race seems like a war, and it's as easy to come fourth as it is to finish first, at any time in the meeting.

The summer of '89 continued to sizzle along as I won the Commonwealth Final at Belle Vue

Simon has a last minute word with Ivan Mauger before a vital race in the 1990 World Longtrack Final at Herxheim, while brother Julian (left) and mechanic Mick Day stand by.

Hans Nielsen uses every inch of the Munich track to surge under Simon and win the decisive heat 19.

and, back at Coventry, was third in the Overseas Final, followed by a creditable fourth place in the Inter-Continental Final.

But for the World Final at Munich's Olympic Stadium, the track was in poor condition. I'd been there for the warm-up meeting early in the year and, though bumpy and deep, I thought it was fabulous. It was bloody hard to ride but I thought: 'This is made for me . . . big, nasty, bumpy track in Bavaria. The fans knew me better than half of the Germans in the event.'

I should have won that World Final warm-up meeting, having beaten Hans Nielsen and Erik Gundersen, but made a mess of one race and finished second overall to Erik.

However, for the final itself, they tyre-packed the hell out of the track, which was more like a motorway. The place was very flat, square and slick as hell. About the only exciting incident was in heat 20, when Roman Matousek found that you could ride around the wooden kickboards and go like crazy. That was the highlight of the evening.

Still, you have got to go there and do the business, make the starts, handle the pressure and all the rest of it. I was a little bit frustrated but happy to finish second to Hans, who was then at his brilliant best.

Before my last race I needed to beat Hans, with him having to finish in third place in order for there to be a deciding run-off between us. My plan was to trap on Hans and run him across the grass. It was going according to plan when I made the start on him, just reaching the first corner with half an elbow across his front.

The problem with this one good engine I had was that it wasn't so strong off the start, so I pulled the clutch in and out about three times, just to keep the thing going. It was on the back wheel and though it was probably as good a start as I could possibly make, when I got to the first corner I had no revs at all, which meant I couldn't turn the bike.

So, instead of being able to turn across in front of Hans and fill up the track, and do what I liked with him, when I got to the corner I couldn't hold my line. I didn't have enough wheelspin or enough revs in order to turn the bike. With the bike going straight on when I reached the corner, Hans drove straight past me as if I'd opened the door for him.

I was kicking myself but there wasn't much that I could do to stop him. Still, it was good to be second and to experience what proved the highlight of my World Championship challenge in speedway.

The legendary Ivan Mauger, a record six times speedway World Champion, helped me at both the speedway and longtrack world finals of 1989. The deal with Ivan was that if I was successful, I paid him. So while it was an expensive association, it was nevertheless very worthwhile at that stage of my career.

Ivan was very helpful and I continued to use his services years later. We have a different arrangement, where I ride in the longtrack meetings he organises Down Under in return for him coming to help me in the World Longtrack Final each year, an arrangement we are both happy with.

Ivan is someone to turn to in high pressure situations when you need important advice or dialogue. Only people who have experienced that can give you answers to those questions at crucial times. They know what they are talking about from their own experience. Winning World Finals is what it is all about and I admire Ivan for what he's done. He has achieved everything in speedway and longtrack without possessing quite as much natural talent as other riders of his era, but through sheer hard work and dedication. I admire that side of Ivan immensely and have a lot of time for him.

He can be a bit mercenary at times but most people who achieve any significant success are – they don't give it all away.

The 1989 campaign was another successful one for Oxford, who regained the British League championship after denying Coventry a hat-trick of titles, although I suffered a number of injuries from being run into on my home track. I managed to limp through the season and rode in the British Final after suffering three broken ribs five days before the meeting.

Brian Griffin came on board as a sponsor at this time. Brian is a very successful photographer and artist who is involved in TV commercials through his own company called Produktion. A very creative type, Brian followed Cradley Heath originally and has a real love for the sport. He lives in East London, where he does most of his filming and creative work. A very inspirational guy, he supported me with a motorhome, so I no longer had to get changed in the dressing room with the other boys. My bikes went on ahead, which meant I could arrive later at meetings. My motorhome had a changing room, showers, TV, music centre and a bar!

Brian had a very different approach when talking to or approaching people. With my background, I got on well with him and liked him immensely.

At the end of the season, England finally regained the World Team Cup, although our victory at Bradford was completely overshadowed by the crash that finished Erik Gundersen's career.

Simon and Ivan relax and plan strategy between races at the World Longtrack Final, 1990.

Great stadium, shame about the track. Simon found Munich's Olympic Stadium surface disappointing.

Wiggy withstands a fearless inside charge by Czech Roman Matousek in heat six of the World Final.

Heat 16 and Simon makes it to the first turn ahead of Andy Smith, Olli Tyrvainen and Tony Olsson.

Looking at the picture above, you would find it hard to believe that Hans Nielsen had just won his third World Championship, while runners-up Simon and Jeremy Doncaster look totally content at the press conference following the 1989 World Final in Munich.
Below: Hans soon raised a smile, though, when Wiggy got the beers in!

The 1990 season was to prove my last at Oxford. I had persevered but things hadn't changed for the good and getting knocked off my bike as a result of bad track preparation was the straw that broke the camel's back.

I blame Oxford's poor track preparation, and the compromises they made to save money on it, for a lot of my injuries.

Eight days before the Overseas Final, Australian Stephen Davies ran into me in the middle of the first corner in a match against King's Lynn. He hit a hole and took off, leaving me with a broken collarbone.

You read all sorts of wonderful stories about riders continuing with broken collarbones but I know that when you break a collarbone in half, you aren't going to be riding again within a week. There are fractures and there are fractures but break a bone clean in half and you're not going to be doing anything for a month. I've tried to do it before and reckon that I can stand more pain than most people.

I did have a private health insurance scheme and, as I shall explain later, it ended up costing the insurance company a lot of money that year. I went to the local John Radcliffe Hospital after the meeting at Oxford. This was an NHS hospital under pressure and I'd been there for three hours and had still not been seen by any medical staff. It was 12.30am and I was getting really tired, so I didn't hang around any longer – I drove myself home! My car had been brought to the hospital, so after midnight I thought, 'sod this!' and decided to go home. The car was an automatic, which made it just about manageable.

As anyone who may have broken a collarbone knows, trying to sleep is murder. In the morning I rang Gordon Hadfield, the ACU medical adviser, whom I had known for a few years. I explained what I'd done and he said to come down quickly. He examined me at his practice in Woking and after promptly announcing that he was going to operate that day, I went straight into hospital and he put a plate in, which is unusual.

"I blame Oxford's poor track preparation, and the compromises they made to save money on it, for a lot of my injuries"

The following afternoon, I went to the the Berks Bonanza grasstrack, where Julian was riding. Although still feeling very groggy, I knew I had the rest of the week to recuperate and the only real 'work' I did was to speak to Ivan Mauger a couple of times on the phone. We drew up a plan based on which races we thought I could afford to drop points in, because I didn't want to be busting a gut or shoving anybody around and thus risking further damage to my collarbone.

But by the time I'd done two races, I hardly knew that I'd hurt myself. The rules don't allow riders to take any painkillers these days, which is bloody ridiculous, so I just got on with it.

In my first race Ronnie Correy gave me a big smack in the side on the third turn and although I didn't think it was very fair, I got on with it. The rest of the meeting went to plan and I actually grabbed a couple of points that I wasn't expecting to.

In my last race I was expecting the three points that I needed to come my way, which would have left me on 10. I'd led up to the last lap and then blew up my best engine. Of all the GMs I had, seven at one stage, I didn't have anything as good as this one. I could rely on it on slick and slippery afternoon tracks and it was great for dragging me around corners.

It meant I had to go out for a run-off on the GM I favoured for big tracks, and it was tremendously overpowered for the conditions that existed after 20 heats at Coventry in the afternoon. The track was like concrete at this stage, I ran a bad third and failed to qualify. I should have sailed through on 10 points.

Had it not been for that crash at Oxford, I reckon I could have achieved a rostrum place because I was very positive about going there and doing well. Instead, I was out of the speedway World Championships for at least another year, leaving me once again to concentrate on the grasstrack and longtrack scene.

My build up to the 1990 World Longtrack Final at Herxheim included victory, with a maximum, in the British Grasstrack Championship a week or two before the big one in Germany. When it came to Herxheim, it was clear who I had to beat to retain the world title. Karl Maier was still with Lantenhammer engines and the GM scene, he had been World Champion two years

Simon (4) roars to the front on his way to glory in the World Longtrack Final at Herxheim, 1990.

previously and had finished third when I won in Czecho the previous year.

There were eight riders in a race at this time and, perhaps not surprisingly, there were a couple of wild clashes in the first corner as eight abreast is a bit too many at some longtrack circuits, but not all of them. Everybody is going for the same bit of dirt and, on the smaller circuits, eight very determined and forceful riders don't fit into one square metre very well!

Eventually the meeting settled down and Karl was four or five points clear of a couple of us but he'd had the favourable outside starts early on. At Herxheim on that particular day, the outside gates were especially good. Karl had gate positions seven, eight and six in his first three races, while I had one, two and four, so I was quite happy although I had dropped four points in some relatively hard races. I was heartened, though, that my next two were outside starts while Karl had to move to the less desirable inside grids.

In his next race, he actually edged in front and then blew his bike up in what was, I think, the last race before the semi-finals. This threw it all wide open, because Karl was suddenly back on the same amount of points as myself, with Hans-Otto Pingel, Marcel Gerhard and Klaus Lausch all in contention. I then managed to win my semi-final, from the outside, in order to maintain the status quo, as did Karl.

So everything came down to the last race of the day and I drew gate eight, right on the outside. I was changing first gears between races like they were going out of fashion. The starts were that different, depending on your draw, that you needed a different first gear for gates one to five as opposed to gates six to eight. My gearbox was in bits while I waited to see what draw I had before deciding which first gear to install.

Karl made an absolutely dreadful start from gate two, while I made one of the best that I'd ever made, managing to get to the first corner in front. But Maier wasn't the only concern to me – there was also the challenge of Pingel. By wriggling past riders who had broken down in front of him, he was only two points behind me going into the final race, and he was next to me on the start line.

Pingel was an older German rider, on a Zierk-Godden, the same as myself, so I knew he had a quick bike. I also knew that he was going to aim it straight at me and try to run me off the track. I parked so that I had the full width of the start area between him and myself, so that even if he aimed towards me, I'd probably be able to get out of his way.

As it was, he came right across and I just managed to get half a bike in front of him before he came into gate eight. If you watch the video, you wonder what is going on, because I've gone in a straight line to get out of everybody's way, while Hans-Otto has done a big right and left.

The FIM introduced eight-man races for the 1990 World Longtrack Final at Herxheim, Germany.
Even so, Wiggy (4) – on the inside – knew the best line to take when up against main rival Karl Maier (11).

LUK
LUK
LUK Kupplungen
Sparkasse
Sparkasse

Anyway, as I said, I made the start in the final and won it to retain the World Championship.

Mick Day, my mechanic, was as ecstatic as me, particularly as we'd suffered a big drama in practice after a chain came off during the first practice start. I think the back wheel must have been loose, because the back of the bike was destroyed when the rear chain came off. The back wheel wiggled around, causing the chain to go through the shock absorbers and the mudguard. All the swinging arm was twisted and the shocks badly damaged.

This was one of the first finals where I'd actually brought along a third bike, just to sit in the pits and be there for us to pinch bits from if needed. Thank God that we did. After one practice there was nothing left of my first bike, as it lay on the floor in a heap of nuts and bolts, so we did actually take parts from the second spare. Having a third bike with me at meetings – effectively a complete spares kit – became routine after the experience of Herxheim.

It was at the end of 1990, in the the Golden Gala at Lonigo, just two weeks after the World Longtrack Final, that I broke my neck.

I was on a high and everything had been going well. I'd won the meeting in Italy before and had always done well there in the past. It was one of my favourite tracks and I love Italy and everything about it. I was looking forward to it and trying a new clutch for Paulo Bellini.

The track on the day was particularly grippy, which made a slipping clutch very important. In hindsight, it was foolish trying out items like this in a meeting without any practice. However, you have to eventually be in a meeting to find out if they were working or not.

"They had never seen anybody who had done the damage I had to my neck who wasn't in a wheelchair. Plus, after the crash, I had ridden two further races, gone to a disco and flown in an aeroplane! I should have been a paraplegic or even a quadraplegic. My head had gone that far forward that I had squashed the front of the third and fourth vertebrae, breaking the front off them which had split like an apple being squashed"

We managed to burn two clutches out in the first two races in which I scored three points – nothing impressive. Then the mechanic put new clutch plates in for my third ride. They didn't seem to have any idea how to set the clutch in the first place. They didn't seem to have a starting point. I said: 'Do you know how to set these plates? How many turns in do you set them? Where is the starting point?' They replied: 'We don't know. We put them in and if it's too sharp we will come and undo it.'

I thought: 'This is a bit haphazard.' It was a massive mistake to allow someone else to do something like this for me but I thought that they knew what they were doing. If they are clutch manufacturers, they must have some plan and some starting point of what works and what doesn't. But they didn't.

So I came out onto the track and tried to slip the clutch out gently, and do a practice start. The clutch gripped so hard that the bike just took off in the air on its own. The bike had reared so quickly that I actually landed behind my starting position. The thing jumped up so quickly that I went backwards rather than forwards. It was ridiculous.

I ended up landing on the back of my head, with my body rolled over backwards, sort of squashing myself. The chin of my crash helmet was buried in my chest.

I knew that I had done something serious because the pain was intense. After catching my breath for several minutes, I walked back to the pits. A little bit later I went back out for another couple of races on a bike borrowed from Per Jonsson, and finished with around nine points.

Afterwards I was given a surgical collar to wear by a doctor who said: 'Put it on as a safety measure, you may have damaged something.'

It was hurting like crazy but I thought that I had just torn the muscles badly. We actually went to a nightclub that evening with all the boys, to let our hair down towards the end of the season. I thought: 'Bloody hell! I can't go out with this collar on. I won't have a good night out and it looks stupid.'

So I took off the collar and spent most of the night at a disco!

I put the collar back on when I went to bed. When I boarded the plane the next morning, the sight of my collar amused just about everybody and I endured quite a lot of mickey-taking.

To be honest, I felt a bit of a prat.

When I arrived back home I went to see a physiotherapist, who gave me ultra-sound treatment, which sorted out the damaged muscles almost immediately. The process is fabulous for muscles. Strangely, though, my neck was starting to hurt in a different way. I began to feel that there was something more to worry about now than the neck muscles had settled down. I said to the physio: 'Bloody hell! My neck's killing me. It's right in the middle, it's not the muscles at the back. I feel as if there is something else going on.'

He advised me to get some X-rays, so I went to Chiltern private hospital at Great Missenden and requested some. The nurse was in the scanning cubicle sorting out the pictures and I was standing nice and straight when she came darting back out shouting: 'Don't move! Don't move! I'll be back in a minute.' I thought to myself: 'Bit bloody desperate that!' Then a doctor rushes in and says: 'Don't move, we'll get a collar straightaway. Just don't do anything stupid, we have a serious problem here.'

They had never seen anybody who had done as much damage as I had to my neck who wasn't in a wheelchair – especially as, after the crash, I'd ridden two further races, gone to a disco and flown in an aeroplane!

I should have been a paraplegic, or even a quadraplegic. My head had gone so far forward that I'd squashed the front of the third and fourth vertebrae, breaking the front off them, causing them to split like a squashed apple.

Because everything – my head, shoulders and back– had been in an exactly straight line at the time of the practice start, they presumed that was the only reason why my spinal chord hadn't been damaged. If I had landed on my side, it would have been very different.

As it was, they had to take loads more X-rays with me bending my head. The trouble was that I couldn't achieve a gradual bend because there was nothing to support the front.

They told me that they were going to have to wait for a month to see how the bones would mend and then try and sort out what they were going to do about them – if I wanted to ride again. They put me in a fairly big cast, which I stayed in for a month. When I went back for further X-rays, I then had to bend forward and the neck was still only bending in the very middle instead of the whole distance. The bones were just doing nothing, they hadn't fixed and they weren't going to.

So the only option was a bone graft. They took some bone from the base of my pelvis and grafted that between the third and fourth vertebrae, and wired them together.

The insurance company were not very impressed with me. Collarbone plates and a broken neck all in one year. They actually tried to get out of paying for it – they claimed that they didn't know that I was a motorcycle racer. I pointed out that on the letterheads I sent them it stated: 'Simon Wigg, International Motorcycle Racer' and now they were telling me that they didn't know that I did this. They said: 'You are not covered'. And I replied: 'You have to be joking!'

They coughed up in the end but we were fighting about it for a while and it came to £12,000 for the neck operation. I was in bed until just before Christmas and after the New Year I got one of those cheap charter flights to Australia - £500 from Luton, as I recall. I spent a couple of months in Australia recuperating while sitting in the sun.

At the end of the 1990 season I reviewed everything and knew that the time had come when I should change speedway clubs again.

My concerns about the Oxford track just wouldn't go away – we never knew how it was going to be prepared from one week to the next. At the end of the day, although we were all riding for a living and we were all professionals, you have still got to be enjoy the racing aspect. If you are not enjoying it, then it's time to get out.

I was not enjoying my trips to Oxford as much as I had when the track had possessed a lot of granite. A couple of times when they had been desperate, if the track was very heavily watered or had taken a lot of rain, they had a severe problem. To get a meeting on they would put down a load of granite and it would produce a great racing surface. It was so frustrating to know that all it took to achieve a fabulous race track was just a few stones thrown down on it.

But the promotion normally refused to use the granite substance because they didn't want to upset the greyhound people who were, obviously, important, and I could understand that.

The fact was, if the greyhound track had been covered correctly by diligent workers, this

Heading clear at Oxford against Bradford – the club Simon would join next.

problem would never have raised its head.

I'd just about had enough by then – I was no longer enjoying my Friday nights at Oxford. For example, I didn't even know what gearing to put on the bike before leaving home. I'd normally put a 57 or 58 sprocket on my back wheel and load the bike in the van. But in my latter days at Oxford, such were the extremes in track preparation, I never knew whether to put on a 61 or a 58 sprocket.

Hans got on with it and didn't say too much about the unpredictability of our home track. He earned his money and went home again. But I was very unhappy and always made my thoughts known. It probably didn't make me very popular with the management but there are no prizes for keeping your gob shut.

Being laid up with a broken neck gave me a lot of time to think. Although the Lonigo incident had nothing to do with Oxford, I had suffered enough whacks at Sandy Lane to know that I needed to be riding at a track where I'd be really happy, and where I could get out of the way a bit. I needed somewhere with a bit more space, more room to manoeuvre in the first corner.

It was time for me to move on. I didn't want to talk about leaving, as I thought I'd let nature take its course. I didn't really want to ask for a transfer from Oxford, preferring to wait and see if anybody else wanted me to ride for them. I wasn't thinking about anywhere in particular, I just knew that I didn't want to be at Oxford any longer.

In the end I got a call from the Bradford promoters, Bobby and Allan Ham. It was a big decision to make because of the distance to and from West Yorkshire and the Dukes being a Saturday night track. It also meant going back to what I hadn't done for a while – employing a mechanic to support me.

15 Going Dutch

WHILE I settled in quickly following my winter transfer to the Bradford Dukes and liked the big Odsal track, the early 90s were not good as far as the speedway World Championship was concerned.

In 1991, my first year riding the Czech-made Jawa engine, I went out fairly early in the qualifier at Ipswich, while the following season I was eliminated in the Overseas Final at Coventry. The track was over-watered and I wasn't making very good starts, it was as simple as that. I got a bit of a heave-ho from Andy Smith in the first race and my luck ran out that day.

In 1993, when I'd moved on from Bradford to Coventry Bees, I went out at the semi-final stage at my former home track, Cradley Heath.

By 1994 I didn't compete in the British League and rode instead on a Dutch licence, but encountered problems in the semi-final at Prague.

However, there were plenty of positive highlights, especially in major Continental meetings and on the longtrack scene.

In 1994, just before the World Longtrack Final, I won the Czech Golden Helmet at Pardubice, ahead of Tony Rickardsson and Chris Louis. I seized my best engine in the qualifying rounds on the Saturday, then blew up another in the first round. They have seeded riders who come in at the quarter-final stage, which is a brilliant system and is, I believe, how the Speedway Grand Prix should be run now.

The Czech Golden Helmet has a separate qualifying system where a lot of lesser riders start their qualifying the day before. Then the seeded guys join the competition at the quarter-final stage. It's a bit like Wimbledon tennis, where everyone gets a chance but the top blokes are protected from early elimination. You have groups of six riders who race three times from different gate positions, with your two best races counting and the top three going through to the next round.

If you're going to have a Grand Prix series, there has to be GP qualifying. It follows the principle that you are trying to find the best guy, on average. So one engine failure or a crash doesn't necessarily spell the end of the night for a rider, while everybody is allowed to compete for the right to make it to the latter stages. This way, just because you might have a one-off lucky day or a half-bad day, it doesn't mean you are necessarily in or out.

If you are trying to find an aggregate champion, which is what a Grand Prix is about, you have to have an aggregate system – not a one day knockout formula – to decide things.

I'd been in the long-established Czech Golden Helmet three or four times and made the final twice. The winner receives a brand new bike and a gold helmet – and the helmet is worth a bloody fortune, a beautiful object that the champion gets to keep. They make a new one every year, paid for by the host Pardubice club.

The other riders in the 1994 final I won were: Hans Nielsen, Tony Rickardsson, Chris Louis and Bo Bhrel. Tony was second, a week after he'd won his first speedway world title in Denmark and I was pleased to beat both Tony and Hans three time each that day.

The victory at Pardubice, one of the biggest speedway tracks in the world, was a real boost to me preceding the World Longtrack Final at Marianske Lazne, where I'd won the final in 1989. Like Germany, the Czech Republic became almost my second home.

Although I had generally been successful in open meetings, it had been a very hard season in which we had undertaken a lot of travelling. I wasn't quite set up to do the schedule that I was trying to fulfil, so my choice of vehicle was crucial. I had a super van but I was still doing things the way we'd always done them, which is why I opted eventually for a motorhome. Tony

Czech Golden Helmet winner Simon beat Tony Rickardsson, who had just won his first world title, and Chris Louis at Pardubice, 1994.

Rickardsson had showed us all the previous year what a good facility it was. For me it was invaluable, providing complete control in a self-contained environment, which was absolute luxury.

I have never ridden in a final where I've been so relaxed and confident as I was going to Marianske Lazne that year. I had a pair of leathers especially made skin tight by Barbara Miles of BMJ and then airbrushed in Munich by a guy called 'Fuzzy'. So I felt I had a big advantage there not only with weight, but also with streamlining. I had a very smooth suit made of leather compared with other smooth suits like Kevlar, with no writing on it at all, which made it quite slippery through the air.

Also, there were the aerodynamic extras I had developed on the bike over the previous year. We had a very good team there with the mechanics and everybody else, which made me feel very relaxed and at ease.

When I practiced on the engine which Hans Zierk had prepared for me on the Saturday, both bikes felt fantastic and one in particular felt absolutely fabulous. I think I only did four laps at the most on the Saturday because I felt so good about what I was sat on. And we didn't need to go over matters a thousand times because I'd done the work all year long. I knew that I was ready, the bike was in great shape and so was I.

I'd been training and running a lot during a week's holiday on my own, which was my usual routine before a World Longtrack Final. This time, I went to the south of France to go skiing in the mountains. I always felt I needed a little time by myself to get my thoughts together and by the time the World Final came around, I felt like King Kong.

The '94 final was the first that I'd ever won with a maximum. It went so well – I still can't bloody believe it! It felt like I just had to let the clutch out, do four laps and then come back in.

With five World Longtrack titles and many other big meeting wins under my belt, I felt very experienced. Getting to the final is most rider's biggest headache. Once you have actually got there, you are in, and you feel different. I have always felt very positive before major finals. If you are in a qualifying round, you can be as determined as you like but if luck is against you, you'll go out. So I find it very hard, mentally, to prepare for a qualifying round. I never feel comfortable because I have nothing to gain and everything to lose.

But once I go into a final, I know that I can lift myself to a higher level and beat anyone.

I felt elated on the rostrum after my fifth world title success, as jubilant as I'd felt after my first title win in Denmark nine years earlier. The only sad aspect for me was that they didn't play the National Anthem afterwards, despite being told by Jos Vaessen, the President of the FIM, that *God Save The Queen* would be played.

It was very annoying. The licence issue is nothing to do with whether I'm English or not. Who I happen to buy my licence off is my decision. I'll explain what led to me taking out a Dutch national licence . . .

The point is, motorcycle racing is not merely my hobby, it's my *job*, so I have to make a living doing it. There is no golden handshake if I fall upside down in a heap, I have to make hay while the sun shines.

I spent a lot of years trying to build up a reputation on the Continent. I'm fairly happy with most promoters and they'd have me back again the next year. You build up a reputation and you can't afford to ruin it.

I have missed a lot of meetings in the past because of Sunday speedway, which always annoys me from the point of view that I want to earn a living on a Sunday, plus, as I said earlier, there's the added factor of the damage Sunday speedway does to the sport.

I'd missed so many meetings on the Continent because of British speedway commitments but the straw that broke the camel's back came in 1993, when I was booked to ride in a $10,000 meeting at Wiener Neustadt, Austria.

One week before that meeting the BSPA informed Joe Screen, Andy Smith, Hans Nielsen and myself that we were going to have to ride at Belle Vue in a re-arranged Belle Vue v Coventry league fixture on a Sunday afternoon. They gave us just seven days' notice to pull out of the meeting in Austria. The original fixture had been postponed because the Belle Vue promoter hadn't prepared his track well enough. We couldn't ride it, even though it was a nice, sunny evening, so we had to go home instead.

So the BSPA withdrew Joe, Andy and myself from the meeting in Austria, while the Danish Motor Union stood by Hans, which was good of them. They refused to withdraw his start permit, so Hans actually went to Wiener Neustadt . . . and won it!

The big problem I had was that from that moment on was that no promoter on the Continent knew if I was going to turn up or not. Every promoter knew they could spend lots of money having posters printed, advertising my name in the newspapers and magazines, on the radio, etc, but the BSPA wouldn't do the right thing and think about the Continental promoters. No wonder they had few friends at FIM level, where there was an understandable reluctance to allocate Britain the really top meetings.

At the end of the season another problem I had was adapting from the newly introduced lay-down engines onto the upright motors I was still riding in the British League. At the end of the year, I thought the only way for me to go is to ride lay-down bikes all the time, wherever I race. So I decided that from the next year it was going to be lay-downs only for me . . . and then the BSPA announced they were not going to allow lay-downs in British racing in 1994. That was OK for riders who only competed in domestic British meetings but lay-downs were allowed by the FIM in international meetings that year, which created problems.

This, plus the Wiener Neustadt fiasco, made riding in England unrealistic. Also, by pulling out of the British League, it gave me the chance, for the first time, of going everywhere I possibly could as a reigning World Champion.

There were obviously good reasons why I chose to ride on a Dutch licence. The trouble is that we have two different sports – grasstrack and speedway – so I had to deal with two controlling bodies in the ACU and the BSPA. Not only did I have that problem with the BSPA, but the British grasstrack scene is very difficult because they also have control over where you ride. They try to make you ride in the British Masters Grasstrack Championship. Unfortunately for me, the dates for that clash with two very big meetings on the Continent.

I decided I was going to do all the meetings available thanks to the KMNV (Dutch national federation), who were a pretty typically tolerant national body from Holland, which is a relatively broad-minded country. They haven't got a lot of riders there, so they are not very active. The most important issue for me was that they had a good attitude about the European scene and for guys like me who have a problem, they are very open and helpful. They know their job is simply to provide a service to the sport and riders like myself, who just need permission to ride.

To be honest, I don't mind where or who I buy my racing licence from. I need a racing licence in order to compete in FIM events, so I have to purchase it from somebody. Who I actually purchase it

Simon's aerodynamically developed longtrack bike.

from is slightly irrelevant. But the ACU felt that they had been kicked in the teeth.

There had been an issue about my use of caffeine found in the dope test at the World Longtrack Final in 1993, when a lot of the staff at the ACU were very helpful towards me, having really fought my cause. However, the way I saw it, once you buy a licence from them you are actually only buying their services for that particular year.

I didn't feel that I was kicking anybody in the teeth. My main allegiance is to my family and making a living as a motorcycle racer, not to the ACU or any other racing organisation body.

When it came to the new season I didn't want to do the British Grasstrack Championship again. The Ace of Aces is a meeting all riders wanted to do – indeed, the promoter struggles to offer enough places to all the riders who want to do it. If the ACU were to have spent a little more time and energy running the British Masters, they could have creates the same type of prestigious event as the Ace of Aces, which everybody is desperate to be a part of.

But instead, the way it was formed, most of the riders spent time actually trying to get out of riding in the British Championship meetings! That can't be good for the sport, it can't be good for the spectators and I'm one of the riders who would rather not be doing it. It's fantastic to win a British Championship – I've been lucky enough to win it a few times – but winning it again wasn't going to make an awful lot of difference to me.

"I didn't feel that I was kicking anybody in the teeth. My main allegiance is to my family and making a living as a motorcycle racer, not to the ACU or any other racing organisation body"

As a professional, the main question is one of finance. British Championships are poorly rewarded are they are staged over two days as well, which clashes with most of the big fixtures on the Continent. So, once again, as a professional, you are a little bit stuck. You have a dilemma and the trouble is, if you'd rather ride abroad, the ACU has to give you permission to go there. And they are not going to give you permission to go anywhere on the same days as their British Championship.

This is why obtaining a Dutch licence solved a whole lot of problems for me and freed up the diary. The crux of the matter is that no-one has any real control over where I ride. Before, if I had wanted to ride in a Continental speedway meeting on a Sunday, on the same day as an event in Britain, the BSPA would, I presume, try to object.

But when I'm racing on a Dutch licence, they have no control over when or where I ride. Being a professional, I need to be free to be able to ride where I want.

After what happened with that clash of dates between the rescheduled league match at Belle Vue and that lucrative meeting in Austria, that was it for me – the end of telling me where and when to go.

I know that under European law, the ACU has not got a leg to stand on if challenged, and neither has anybody else. I know that anytime I want to go anywhere I could go to court, get an injunction against the ACU and they would have to release me. But if I want to put myself in that position every time I want to go and ride a motorbike, it's stupid.

Now the guys who run the ACU and the grasstrack committee are not professional racers and never have been. It is a very worrying matter for me, as a professional, to have someone controlling my livelihood. So the only way for me to have a reasonably secure future, to maximise income, is to have the freedom which a Dutch licence provides. The KMNV don't object to anything I do and while they would like me to do a few meetings in Holland if I can, they appreciate that I'm a professional racer and must make my own decisions.

Now I'm having a lot more fun racing bikes. My first year on a Dutch licence was the best I'd had for a long time in many ways. I haven't counted exactly how many meetings I did but it was in the region of 65 – a lot less than what I have done in the past but at least every time I went to a meeting I was riding on well-prepared tracks, and at places I usually enjoy going to. Sadly, this wasn't always the case in England.

16 Grand Prix challenge

MY involvement in the Series 500 in Australia goes back to the fact that from my early days spent out there I've always had good results. Maybe that's because the big Australian tracks have to be ridden like European longtracks in a lot of ways.

A lot of my friends and colleagues share my view that Australia has a real German feel about it, it's a lot more relaxed and enjoyable. I don't feel a stressful, negative pressure, which I sometimes feel, and maybe put on myself, when I'm in England. In Australia, you are able to let your hair down, express yourself, have some fun and the environment seems to be a lot less stressful.

When David Tapp was trying to get his tour together, I actually got in touch with him to see what he was up to and we reached an agreement fairly quickly. I wanted to be part of it because I like going to Australia and it was an active racing diary. I felt that if anyone was going to try and do something new and different, a bit like the Speedway Grand Prix, then I wanted to be a part of it.

I also felt that if we got enough television coverage, then it would enable us to attract good sponsorship. Unfortunately, David wasn't able to get quite the TV deals he wanted and I think he discovered that turning his career as a commentator into one as a promoter wasn't as easy as he'd hoped. He discovered petty jealousies and people, some of whom he thought were his friends, didn't want to help him as much as he'd expected them to, especially in the media world.

In the first year he didn't make any real money, it was a learning curve but the important issue was that he wanted to do it again. I think the second year will be a roaring success. The sponsors were very happy with it. Being a television man himself, David knows he has to put a lot of effort into the TV side of the project.

Series 500 were the sponsors, and they want to come back for more, so he must have done something right. To get sponsors is hard enough. Hanging on to them is even bloody harder. I can tell you that for nothing. They were happy with what he did and the way that he did it, too.

We had a lot of fun with Ivan Ballantine and his family who run Series 500. Not only were they the major series sponsors, but they made it a lot of fun for us riders. The tour was iffy sometimes, and there were a few clashes here and there, but it was generally a load of fun. I'd want to go back and do it again.

I was disappointed at not managing to win the series. If, at the start of the series, someone had said to me that I would have finished the series in the first three places, I probably would have been relatively happy. By when the series actually finished, I was left kicking myself. Just a couple of points here and a couple of points there would have been enough to win the whole thing.

A Series 500 win over Sam Ermolenko and Tony Rickardsson.

There were 13 rounds and tracks were very varied. We had a few big ones and a few small ones. What really knackered it for me was something as stupid as a pressure gauge. I bought a new pressure gauge three-quarters of the way through the tour in Melbourne. With everything being chucked around in the truck, the pressure gauge began to malfunction without me knowing it. I did two meetings with what I found was completely the wrong pressure in the back tyres.

I was using Barum tyres for the majority of the meetings over there. I find the Barums tend to work better with relatively little air, so I'd normally run about seven-and-a-half pounds in them. Although my pressure gauge was indicating seven pounds, I later discovered that I had nearly 12 pounds in the tyre! And I did two meetings before I found out the problem. I was all over the place and had so much trouble riding around, you'd have thought I was a beginner at Gosford.

I had a particularly good meeting the first time we visited Gosford, finishing fifth. But when we returned there just a couple of weeks later, I couldn't even ride around the place. Yet I'd had a cracking meeting two nights before in Newcastle and I can only presume that the pressure gauge had suddenly given up the ghost.

In Melbourne, the next meeting after Newcastle, I'd been very poor. We were just checking the tyre pressures before the last meeting in Brisbane when I said to Brett, my mechanic: 'How much have you got on the back tyre?' He replied: 'Seven pounds' and I felt it with my hands. I said to Brett: 'It's nothing like seven. It's bloody hard as nails.'

I borrowed a pressure gauge from Mark Thorpe and it registered 11.5 pounds. I then borrowed another from Greg Hancock and it registered the same. So we promptly let the tyre down and thought perhaps that had been the trouble at the last meeting. On a nicely prepared track, a few pounds here and there doesn't make any difference. But when the track is bad and difficult to ride, that is when you have to get everything right.

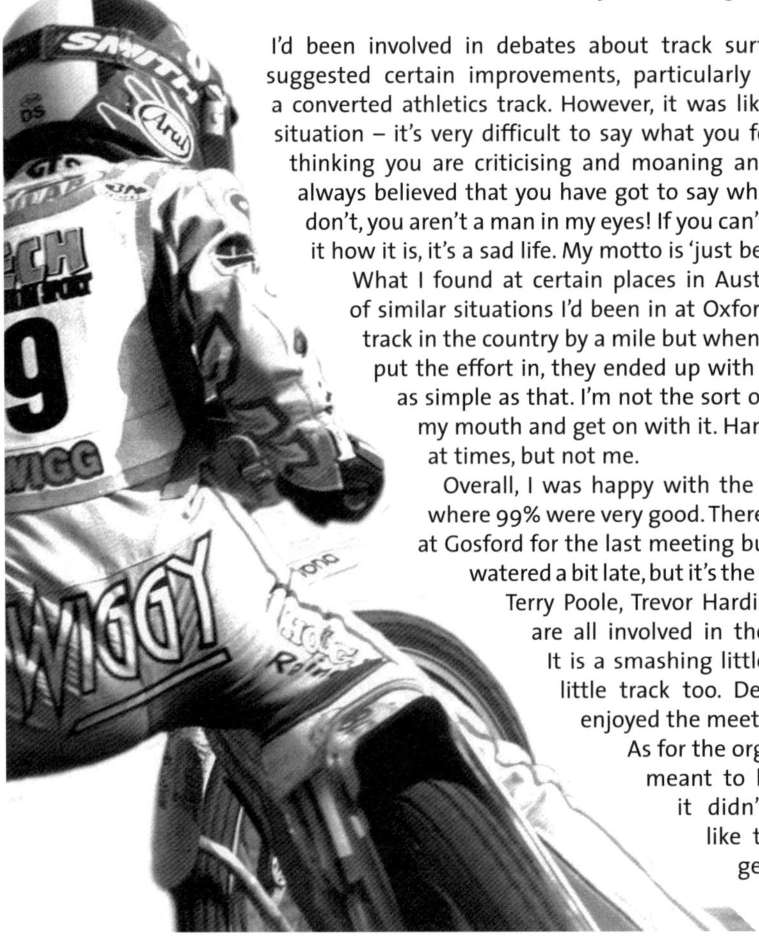

I'd been involved in debates about track surfaces where I had suggested certain improvements, particularly at Melbourne, on a converted athletics track. However, it was like the Don Godden situation – it's very difficult to say what you feel without people thinking you are criticising and moaning and groaning. I have always believed that you have got to say what you think. If you don't, you aren't a man in my eyes! If you can't be honest and tell it how it is, it's a sad life. My motto is 'just be yourself.'

What I found at certain places in Australia reminded me of similar situations I'd been in at Oxford. We had the best track in the country by a mile but when the guys no longer put the effort in, they ended up with a crap surface. It is as simple as that. I'm not the sort of bloke to just shut my mouth and get on with it. Hans Nielsen might be at times, but not me.

Overall, I was happy with the tracks in Australia, where 99% were very good. There was a difficult one at Gosford for the last meeting but one, when it was watered a bit late, but it's the same for everybody. Terry Poole, Trevor Harding and David Tapp are all involved in the promotion there. It is a smashing little place and a good little track too. Despite everything, I enjoyed the meetings we had there.

As for the organisation, we were meant to have one base but it didn't quite work out like that. We ended up getting a bit scattered at times and the accommodation was sometimes difficult. David may have been caught out by the vastness of the project, including the budget for such an event. It was a hell of a project. He learned and knew what to do the next time.

The concept did wonders for the image of a Grand Prix system – it's a great formula. The guys who are most consistent over the whole course of the series reap the benefits, which has to be better than someone winning on a one-off basis. The issue with the GP is that *everyone* has to have a chance – and it's the same with Tappy's system.

Everybody is trying to cling on to this old 20-heat formula but that might not be important now. If you are going to change the system to the Grand Prix, it might not be a bad idea to change the formula and go to a pyramid-style of qualifying, like they have for the Golden Helmet at Pardubice. Here, 30 or 40 guys start the meeting. You are still going to get a big final at the end. You are still going to get a winner. The bottom 16 who get knocked out receive a very limited amount of money to cover the basic costs of travelling there and back, but that's it.

It means the guys who actually produce the goods get paid, which is what the whole concept is about at the end of the day. At least it gives everybody the chance to win the event. The good result from a speedway point of view is that you don't need a £10,000 motorbike to win these competitions. Some young whizzkid can turn up with a bike like Sam Ermolenko's and win the meeting. That has always been speedway's greatest selling point – the fact that some tearaway can turn up and start blowing everybody away. But if he has to prove himself for a couple of years before he is in, he will never get in.

As for promoting events in Australia, a few more riders from different nationalities need to be involved. At the end of the day you still need bums on seats at these events. Australia being such a multi-ethnic country, it would be foolish to confine it to Aussies, Poms and Yanks. You also want Poles and Italians. If you had an Aborigini riding, you would be laughing, wouldn't you? If you even had a Greek speedway rider it would be brilliant. Or Japanese . . . you would pack them in. Hungarian and Czech riders are available – those boys bloody fly, they are certainly no slouches and they would add to the event. I think you need the nationality theme. They have had Russians on tour and people like to see a Russian, no matter *what* he is doing. There still remains a touch of mystery about somebody from the old iron curtain countries.

Coming back to the actual Series 500 tour, we didn't have five minutes to stop and have a holiday and I think I paid the price in the following European season. I was feeling a little worn-out, to tell the truth.

What was interesting is that Charlie and Abigail went to Oz with me. I think that if it hadn't been such a long tour, I might have gone on my own. It was nearly three months, a long time to be away from family. Abi was growing and changing every day and so it was not a good idea for me to miss that. They both had a great time, I think, even though it was very hard for all of us. They didn't get spoilt with where they went or what we did. They were really just tagging along and having to take the rough with the smooth, which is not always easy.

Everybody thinks it is great to go to Australia but when you are stuck in a car for days on end, the novelty soon wears off. You soon wish you were sunbathing on some beach somewhere, doing as little as possible, rather than roaring around the globe.

My summary of Series 500 is that it was a good start by David Tapp and it showed the Grand Prix is such a fine idea. I admire anybody who just gets off their backside and has a go at it. They have to be commended. Tappy really took the bull by the horns. There were a lot of doubters who said that he was stupid and he was this and that, but he had a go at it and has done a bloody good job really, all things considered.

I remember saying to David at the beginning: 'The only issue that matters to me, David, isn't money – it is whether you want to run again the next year. If you want to do it again, then it has been a success.'

There were times when I thought he wasn't going to do it again - lots of hassles and so many problems that he had to deal with. Guys like me gave him problems at times – I call a kettle black. I don't always make myself popular by doing it but you are not here to be everybody's best mate. You are here to get on with the job.

David did huge amounts for speedway in Australia. He approached the project very professionally and made the whole nation a lot more aware of speedway, which is important. The crowds were generally very healthy, although attendances at some places were very ordinary. When we went to the last meeting at Gosford, it was poorly attended, as was Canberra. But Mildura had the best crowd they have ever had. Bunbury was excellent – we had 7,000 there. Perth was excellent. Brisbane was good on both nights, with about 12,000 there on the second occasion.

More important than anything, he raised the profile of speedway and created awareness again. It's a difficult matter trying to turn a ship around while it is in mid-stream. Speedway, in general, is going in a certain direction and it's guys like Tappy who are trying to turn it around, pushing to get the sport some credibility.

There were a lot of people against the Speedway Grand Prix when it was introduced to replace the traditional, one-off World Final in 1995. I'm all for it, I think it's a brilliant concept. The whole idea is what speedway needs, especially now I have been involved a little bit. Having seen what TV3 have done with slow motions, it's absolutely out of this world. The television that came out of the first meetings has given speedway such a shot in the arm. I saw it live when it came in to the studio on the night, then helped the guys to edit it because they weren't really speedway people. Then I went back in the studio on the Tuesday evening to talk through the event.

Problem is, every time you open your mouth, people claim that I'm only saying something because I am this, that or the other. Obviously I'm looking at the whole scene from my point of view, as much as looking at the sport from the general public's perspective. I like to think that what I'm saying is not just being said because it happens to suit Simon Wigg, but because it is what is genuinely needed for the good of speedway. I open my mouth when I think there's something that needs to be said.

"I like to think that what I'm saying is not just being said because it happens to suit Simon Wigg, but because it is what is genuinely needed for the good of speedway. I open my mouth when I think there's something that needs to be said"

It's like the Sunday speedway issue. I talked to Colin Pratt about Sunday speedway and the first thing he comes out with is: 'You only want to go to the Continent on a Sunday afternoon.'

Of course I would. But at the end of the day, I would much rather be riding in England on a regular basis, if only the sport here was in a healthier state.

I can see what damage Sunday speedway has done to the sport, though. It's like going to a rock concert and handing out earplugs to everybody before the gig, or going to the movies and making everyone wear dark glasses.

I've always maintained that afternoon speedway devalues the product – it takes away the excitement. That's why I feel very strongly that the biggest meetings should always be run at night and, ideally, in midweek.

With respect to the Grand Prix, what needs to be improved is the fact there are so many riders who can contribute to world speedway in a Grand Prix, who aren't in it at the moment. That is the big gripe, the main problem, but how do they break into it? Getting into the elite group is nearly impossible.

What the FIM has been trying to do is cling on to all the traditional, old World Championship qualifying rounds, so that promoters across Europe have their so-called prestige meetings with all the top riders on standard money. From Europe's viewpoint, I'm talking about the British, Commonwealth, Overseas, Inter-Continental and Continental Final with its quarter-finals and semi-finals.

As well as having a Grand Prix, they want to have their cake and eat it.

The problem for us now is that the likelihood of not getting through is so great that you would have to be fairly foolish to even start the qualifying rounds. It's a very long road to get there, because at the Inter-Continental stage only four guys go through to the Grand Prix Challenge. Now, I've been to a lot of meetings where riders have been fourth on 12 points or

Simon takes off in Australia, January 1991.

fifth on 11 points and you can go out. You could win the British semi-final, British Final, Overseas Final and get all the way to the Inter-Continental Final, have three wins and a second then an engine failure, even a bout of 'flu, and you are eliminated.

Can you imagine Boris Becker having 'flu on one day and them chucking him out of the ATP tour? Or Bernhard Langer suffering a cold one day, or hitting a round 12 over par, and being throw off the golf tour?

That's the problem they have with speedway. Since the Grand Prix was introduced, organisers Benfield Sports International (BSI) haven't just created a different way of finding the champion, they have changed the whole principles of the sport and the way it is run. They have changed it from a knockout or sudden death qualifiers into something in which you have to pace yourself and your results over the course of a season, to decide if you are champion.

Under the same system, your results over the course of a season should decide if you are in or not. So if you are going to have six qualifying rounds to get into it, the organisers have got to say that if you score more than, say, 74 points, then you are through to the elite group of riders. At the moment, you only have to be average to stay in the GP, so you could be in forever!

I would like to see every round run like Wimbledon tennis, where a young British guy still knows he can enter and if he plays well enough he can be on Centre Court to meet Andre Agassi and win Wimbledon. That's the fairytale dream the public want to see.

17 Man of the world

WHEN I was at school, around 12 years of age, I always had pictures which I had taken from magazines of Teterow. It was such a famous event in the grasstrack world that I had pictures of Don Godden and Chris Baybutt riding around Teterow and ever since then, I always wanted to go there.

It was a fantastic event and just the way grasstracks should be – fast jumps and right-hand bends.

Funnily enough, some of the meetings which I rode in when I started, especially in the Midlands around the Bewdley area, always seemed to have a jump or two. Really that was part of the excitement of grasstrack for me, much better than having a circular track, like a glorified speedway.

So, when I was awarded an international licence at 18, I wrote to the club at Teterow, in east Germany a lot. Of course, we couldn't go because of the place was located in an area ruled by the most Communist regime in Europe after Russia. They didn't want westerners going there, especially as we might win and beat their local favourites! That certainly wouldn't have been good for propaganda. (I heard that they eventually stopped western riders appearing there after some of the boys climbed on top of the town hall one year and stole the East German flag. From that day onwards, western riders were banned – not sure how true that is but that is what I heard anyway.)

Westerners had been and done very well at Teterow. Don Godden had won it and I think that Kelvin Tatum's dad, Martin, also won there one year. Of course, Hans Zierk, the guy who tunes my engines, was sort of king of the place, winning there every year from the time he was 17-years old until he fled from the East in the 60s.

For Hans was originally an East German, from near Rostock. As a young rider, Hans had been the hero there and he and I would often talk about it, saying that when there was a chance for us to go there, we'd both love to make the trip.

Eventually, after Communist rule ended in 1989, they invited a couple of Swiss riders and some Dutch moto-crossers to Teterow. Then, in 1990, they had a full-blown international. Hans organised a practice for me very early in the season and I went over to Teterow and rode a dozen laps on a bike belonging to Thomas Diehr, the new local hero. It was the most heart-stopping, awe-inspiring moment that you can imagine when you look at this mountain and know you are going to ride a longtrack bike around there. You can't even begin to describe what the place looks like. You can see all the pictures in the world but when you look at the place and you are actually there, you can't believe you are going to ride a longtrack bike there.

It's very big, the mountain is so high, the track is long and some of the bends are very tight . . . it's madness!

You start riding around very slowly to first, getting to know where the rights and lefts, the jumps and the bumps are. Once I got the swing of the place, it was the most fabulous sensation ever. Even when there are 50,000 people watching, you think you are the only one there. You can concentrate your thoughts on where you are going and what you are doing but you have to concentrate on every bit of the track.

It's nearly two kilometres long, so it's twice the size of a longtrack, but it's built on two sides of a mountain in the form of a figure eight that doesn't meet. The elevation from the start line to the middle of the straight, where you have the first right-hand bend, is 50 metres. That's within 400 metres of the start. Then on the back straight, you've got the side of the mountain where there is one big jump – the *hechtsprung*. At the bottom of the *hechtsprung* is a drop and then this hugely steep climb. And when at the top of that, you are probably doing 90mph at

Simon tackles the spectacularly unique Teterow grasstrack,with its high speed jumps, twists and turns.

the point where you leave the ground for the big jump.

In 1994, for the first time, they had a prize on offer to the rider who could make the biggest jump but we didn't actually get to do anything much because it was pouring down with rain all day. I managed to leap 40 feet in the difficult conditions.

At Teterow you really need to be winning races as slowly as possible. There are 14 riders in a race, with about 100 competing at the start of the meeting. It's a tremendous event – there's nothing like it in the world.

I've won the Golden Helmet at Teterow three times, and been second in that event once, in addition to winning the handicap final three times. In 1993, I won a brand new Ducati motorbike. The positive publicity from doing well at Teterow has also been quite a launchpad for my career in that part of Germany, where there are a lot of sandtracks and speedway tracks.

Indeed, that's how I came to sign for the Berlin speedway team in 1995.

I don't mind the travelling at all. Everybody has to get out of bed, get in their car and go to work. I'm quite busy in that part of Germany. I found supporters get right into it too and I receive a lot of support when riding there.

My profile is as high as it can be for the sport that I'm involved in. We would like to get more exposure for our activities but the image has to move with the times a little bit. This is difficult because the sport is not run by one association. Each club does its own thing and most of the federations and associations don't actually make the sport happen – they allow it to happen. So the clubs and the organisers have their own ideas and the whole sport lacks any general direction.

That's really a big problem with speedway and grasstrack worldwide. The two sports need clearer direction. The problem in Germany is that for every good organiser, there is a bad one. The big, traditional clubs like Herxheim and Cloppenburg are very well organised, whereas some clubs don't even get involved in the marketing of their own meeting – they contract it out to a marketing company, such as one in Offenburg, in the Black Forest. But they do very well, attracting around 15,000 people there every year. Look around the grandstands and it is not a bunch of speedway fans sitting there, but members of the general public going for an afternoon's entertainment.

As for the sport in the eyes of the general public, I think it could do with a bit more of a governing body. Organisations like the ACU and the DNK (Germany) . . . all they do is allow the clubs to run. They don't get involved specifically or influence the way it is run, so they are almost riding on the back of the sport. I don't think that they do enough for grasstrack and could do a lot more than they do.

German speedway is run on a four-team formula. There are five meetings a year, which include four qualifying rounds each at the four tracks in the group. Then the top two teams go through to the German final. There are only two groups representing North and South, so there are only eight teams contesting the Super League.

Gerd Sievers, whose team I ride for in Berlin, is making a fabulous go of promotion and attracts the attention of the newspapers. He does a first class job of pushing the sport. However, for one Gerd Sievers there are another two who don't bother with any marketing.

One idea Gerd suggested to the other clubs was to change their name from that of their local village to the nearest population centre, in a way that the media and the public can identify with. But the other teams threw up their arms in disgust – Olching, for example, should be called Munich, while Diedenbergen ought to ride under the name of Frankfurt. But while you have got these little villages outside major cities who want to cling on to their heritage, it's an uphill battle for those who want to move things forward.

I also think the four-team formula is a mess. I sent a plan to Gunther Sorber at the FIM in the late 80s. My suggested meeting formula still involves four teams but instead of riding as individuals, they ride as pairs – over 28 heats, if I remember rightly. The format is that each of the four teams in the tournament has two riders who ride as pairs, with each pair against every other pair in the meeting once. It's a perfect format for a four-team tournament – and it would be a perfect tournament for the World Team Cup. Instead of having individual racing, the format would embrace team racing with everybody racing each other in pairs, which is the whole essence of team speedway.

On the subject of teams, I honestly believe that we should have the same bikes and the same costumes, so that the general public can very simply identify each team. I hate yellow as a colour but the Berlin 'Grizzlys' team runs in yellow, so we all ride yellow bikes. At a rain-affected match, we wore our yellow over-suits. At least the public in attendance, as well as those watching on TV, knew us as the 'Yellow Boys'.

The problem is that speedway is designed and run for the speedway fan, it's not simplified to appeal to the general public. We have numbers on our bikes now, which is starting to make matters simpler, but so much more needs to be done to make speedway a public-friendly sport.

Every decision – whether it relates to tape exclusions, track preparation, interval attractions, the centre green, the promotion, the presentation, helmet colours, rules and regulations – has to be designed with the general public in mind, otherwise they won't know what the hell is going on.

If a lot more thought went into changing speedway for the benefit of the man or woman on the street, without its insular rules and self-serving regulations, the sport could be enormous almost overnight.

But, instead, we make so many confusing changes every year, especially in Britain. One minute we stage matches over 13 heats, then 18 heats, then 15. If the BSPA honestly believe that is going to make an iota of difference to the general public coming into a speedway stadium, they have got their heads up their a***! All these rule changes mean nothing.

Every rule should be simplified and re-written with the general public in mind. If the speedway authorities did that, they will have cracked it.

There is no real need to advertise meetings in the trade speedway magazines, which is preaching to the converted. Even for those tracks who can't afford to spend huge amounts of money on advertising, a good publicist can dream up stories and marketing ideas that the general public should become interested in. Then television would want to come along with their cameras, and national newspapers would send along reporters. That's how every other sport operates. It's down to good PR.

"Once speedway finally realises that it is really another commodity, another form of entertainment, it will take off"

Speedway doesn't seemed to have grasped this at all. The problem is that the sport doesn't have clear and strong direction from the top. They haven't got a captain steering the ship who understands that speedway is just like another branch of McDonald's, or cinema and you have to get in there and fight with all the other leisure pursuits. Once speedway finally realises that it is really another commodity, another form of entertainment, it will take off.

But while the promoters still only think of it as a sport and it remains small-minded and does not look at the big picture, failing to realise that it is an entertainment fighting for crowds and attendances, while they still operate in their own little cocoon . . . it will never become a big sport again, let alone one to be taken seriously.

Let me cite the example of Marmande in France, which is very well organised grasstrack and where the show is aimed at the general public. It's one of those sort of events you'd be happy to take anybody along to, because you'd be showing them the best points. I often take a video tape of this event to potential sponsors, because it is something to showcase and be proud of.

Marmande, which is almost really a speedway circuit in terms of the size and everything else, is very well presented. If you look around the grandstands at Marmande, I'd say that the majority of the crowd is around 60 per cent youngsters who are just out for a good night's fun. It's a one-night event – and it's the night before Bastille Day, so the following day is a national public holiday and it works out very well. It is really aimed at the general public, not simply speedway fans.

They run a similar event 25 miles down the road, at La Reole, with very much the same riders and they are lucky if they get 25 per cent of the crowd that Marmande attracts. The issue with La Reole is that unless you are a speedway fan, you wouldn't actually go and watch it. They try very hard, and I'm not criticising them because they are still a very good club, but it isn't run along the same lines as Marmande.

At Marmande, it's like going to a party with a few motorbikes thrown in for good measure. The music is very important, it really makes the atmosphere so special. You can hardly hear the bikes for the music thanks to the fact that they have two very large speakers on the centre green the size of a bus! Personally, I think that is what is needed – an evening's fun with people enjoying themselves and a commentator to add more flavour to the proceedings.

They will employ someone to call the races and give the results, but the commentator will be somebody who is nothing to do with speedway. He will be there just to keep the crowd entertained between races, perhaps by telling stupid jokes and chatting generally.

While still on a party theme, Berghaupton is more of a motorcycle meeting, a very traditional

German grasstrack in the Black Forest. With its delightful picture-book scenery, they hold a big party the night before the meeting in the town hall with up to 3,000 people present. It is a super track, in a gorgeous setting with a lake in the background and trees surrounding it. It's some set-up, with loads of beer stands around the track. They don't tend to go in for the loud music but it is still a very entertaining day, with good commentators who keep the show flowing. It is held once a year, in September, and the riders love it.

A similar event is at the very picturesque Altrip, which is a 400m sandtrack event held a few weeks earlier. All these events attract the best riders in the world. Anybody who has been World Champion and remains active will always be there.

They have two or three other events for the club members in the year and then they run the big one to get the funds in to finance the whole operation. They are very well supported and the crowds think it is great.

Having criticised the BSPA, I must say that it's very much harder for the British promoters, who are running week in and week out for 25-30 weeks of the year, to provide such an interesting and entertaining formula when they are presenting basically the same product every week. It's most definitely a lot easier for the big clubs in Germany, where they have only one big show and only a handful of other meetings to put on each year – but that doesn't mean the Brits can't do a lot better at promoting their sport.

In this country the annual Ace of Aces is a highlight of the grasstrack calendar, although its success does seem to depend much upon the weather, and the organisers have been unlucky in that respect over the years. If the weather is good, the meeting is on a par with most of the top events abroad. They really do try hard and it's a pity that there are not more meetings like the Ace of Aces for the public in England to enjoy.

The Tonbridge club try very hard with their big one a week later, although they are competing with the Ace of Aces in a sense. The Ace of Aces is like Disneyland in grasstrack terms – and you don't go to Disneyland once a week, do you? If they could run the Tonbridge event two or three months earlier, then perhaps it would have greater spectator appeal.

Looking at other events and promotions which I have been in around the globe, I have enthused already about the Czech Golden Helmet. This is a big, traditional race event that everybody likes, it's so well run and such a classic. The prizes are so good and the line-up so competitive, that the public seem to come from across Europe to enjoy Pardubice. Crowds are probably not as good as they once were but they still have up to 25,000 in attendance.

Turning to my Australian experience, I have a lot of time for John McNeil – a former team-mate of mine at Weymouth in 1982 – and the way he runs his meetings. He definitely aims to draw in the general public by staging the spectacular one-off events and he was fortunate that he could run one once a year at the Melbourne Showground.

John's event is more of an evening's entertainment, where there are always lots of other attractions going on. The big problem is attracting people through the door. Most of us traditional speedway folk find all of these intervals a bit of a pain in the backside, because you would much rather see more racing. The problem is that you have got to get the general public through the turnstiles first, and then hopefully turn them into speedway fans once they're lured inside. So the challenge is to induce them to come along. But as I've already said, I think that you need all the other attractions to provide enough of an exciting product to bring the people along in the first place.

That seems to be John's main aim – he has clowns, a good band and it's a very good presentation, a really big show. As the norm, he attracts up to 15,000 spectators to the Melbourne Showground, which, when you think of it, gives us all a lot of hope because the city of Melbourne hasn't any speedway fans as such to draw from. So if John pull in 15,000 people to watch speedway in Melbourne, it really tells me that all you have to do is decide the direction in which you need to go.

I am not saying that John McNeil has all the answers. One factor he should deal with is to take more people on board to help him. John tends to try to do everything himself but he could do with more help at the event. John has a lot of people around him who would like to help, if only he'd allow them to assist him. That is probably John's only weakness – a bit like a speedway rider not having a mechanic.

The first one he ran was in 1985, as part of one of Ivan Mauger's world series tours. It was excellent and he had top blokes like Hans Nielsen, Peter Collins, Kelvin Tatum and Phil Crump on the bill. He has tended to go for a cheaper meeting in recent years, with a few more local riders and whichever international happens to be in the country at the time. Sometimes I feel the racing could be slightly better at Melbourne, and they could do with a few more riders in the meeting. He tends to go for a 12-rider format but I think that could also be improved upon.

To promote his meeting, John concentrates on television advertising, spending the equivalent of £20,000 to reach a broad audience. As they say, you only get out what you put in. If people don't know, people don't go. Even though there are a lot of other activities in such a cosmopolitan city, everybody knows when the speedway at Melbourne Showground is running. John has a good name for his main event – 'Mister Melbourne', which is ideal for him. A catchy sort of name which the public can easily remember.

I have always done very well at Melbourne, it's a big track that suits me and my style down to the ground, and I've actually won the Mister Melbourne title five times.

Unfortunately, John had a lot of trouble with the council in 1994 and the meeting didn't take place, which led me to believe that he could probably do with a few more friends in high places.

Other good points in Australia arose from Trevor Harding of the Kwik Snax organisation putting a lot of money into speedway. Certainly, without Trevor and his investment in the sport, a lot of it would be in the doldrums. Having said that, I think that sometimes Trevor puts his enthusiasm for the sport before the basic finances. A certain amount of money needs to be coming in to enable the promoter to carry on next week. Unfortunately, Trevor got very excited about a Swedish Test team a few years before, plus the Russians, and ran a couple of very high profile events. However, they didn't make enough money to pay for themselves.

Trevor really had to take a back seat with the organisation of speedway for a few years to put the finances back in place. He certainly puts his love of speedway before financial considerations. You have got to commend the guy on that front.

With Dave Tapp's 500 series, Trevor got right behind that and he is a larger than life character – one of those guys you either love or hate. He got right behind it in a massive way and, to be honest, if he hadn't been there I don't think it would have happened.

I've also ridden in most of Ivan Mauger's meetings, injury or business commitments permitting. Ivan has been over in Europe since 1989 helping me in speedway and longtrack World Finals and we've had a pretty good strike rate since then.

One of his regular meetings is staged in Hamilton, New Zealand, while he also runs some big meetings in Australia. I've done most of the Aussie ones and although he doesn't always run his meetings at the same venue, he became a regular at Canberra.

Ivan's meetings tend to be motorcycle events. The first time Ivan runs a meeting anywhere, I think he's laughing because the novelty aspect of seeing the nine times World Champion makes it attractive for everyone to want to go and have a look. But then to entice them back again is another matter. If they're not out and out speedway fans, I don't think they will return.

There's a very fine balance between promoting a motorcycle-only event, that only motor bike fans are interested in, and a family show which is devoid of a certain amount of two-wheeled racing and has broader appeal.

I've won Ivan's Australian Grand Prix Longtrack three times and the superb New Zealand Grand Prix, at Hamilton, once. I think it's a lot simpler to run something big in New Zealand compared to Oz, because they are not as spoilt for choice. In a country town like Hamilton, they still have enough people to fill up the stadium but there are not a lot of counter attractions there. I could compare it to somewhere like King's Lynn. It's not exactly a big metropolis but there are enough people living in the town to put sufficient bums on seats to make it work.

Ivan has been good with his selection of venues. If you go to Auckland you are fighting against rock concerts and cinemas and other leisure outlets. Ivan's deal in Canberra, where he has run the Australian promotion, is difficult and I don't think that he has made any huge amounts of money promoting there.

Most of these tracks are trotting tracks. There are many across Australia, which means plenty of potential venues for longtrack racing. It's the same in Germany – they are trotting tracks, perfect for the horses and the bikes. They co-exist well and it all seems to work. The clubs get on well and that is pretty difficult in these days of the green environment.

We need guys like Ivan to put all their years of experience back into the sport, because he has a hell of a lot to offer. Obviously, though, if he is not making any money doing it, he will not want to keep promoting long after his retirement as a rider.

Ivan has been a great help to me in many aspects over a period of time and I have a lot of admiration for the guy. He has done it all. What I admire most about him is that he did everything without an abundance of talent. He certainly wasn't a natural like Peter Collins or Kelly Moran, who could just turn themselves inside out on a bike. He certainly had to work on his technique, focus hard on his starting and just about everything else that he did around the racing scene. His success resulted from hard work and dedication. That's probably why I admire him more than anybody else, because of the work he puts into it.

Enjoying himself on Ivan Mauger's World Series tours. Above: A winning night ahead of Larry Ross and Neil Evitts, 1986. Below: Lining up with the tourists in front of a huge Melbourne Showground crowd.

I think it will be a long time before we see a rider who works as hard to become a true World Champion as Ivan Mauger did.

I work hard at it and so do Hans Nielsen and Sam Ermolenko. When the American star turns up at a meeting with as much equipment as he does, you realise that he is not spending a lot of time doing anything else, that's for sure.

Ivan was the hardest-working rider in his day and he reaped the rewards because of it. A lot of us looked up to guys like Ivan and Ole Olsen and, later on, Bruce Penhall.

As a promoter, Ivan is a bit like John McNeill in that he likes to do most tasks himself. At Canberra, I hardly saw anyone else helping him. He is a real loner when it comes to that side of affairs. Whether it's a good or bad, I don't know. If I was Ivan, I would probably want a few more people helping me.

I must mention my American perspective. One thing I would like to do just once is to contest the mile race in the States on a Harley Davidson. My only experience of speedway in America was the 1988 World Team Cup Final in Long Beach, where, unfortunately, I never got over jet lag. I felt absolutely dreadful the whole time that we were there. The funny thing is, the minute I got off the plane back home, I felt fantastic again. I don't know why that was.

We didn't really have much time to settle in California, I never slept the whole time on the plane and didn't really adjust to the time difference. I really felt very much at sea the whole time that we were there. No, I haven't done much in America.

I fancy the mile racing, though, because it's a bit like longtrack, although it takes place all across the country. It's a very similar set-up to Teterow, with jumps and left and right-handers, producing all sorts of fun and games.

"Why not invent a new product, possibly called Super Flat Track, with riders from both grasstrack and longtrack contesting a new World Championship?"

They should do more with longtrack – by increasing the engine capacity up from 500cc to, say, 650cc, and try and get manufacturers involved. Maybe they should change the bikes a little bit, to try and persuade the Japanese to invest.

Longtrack is out on a limb as a specialist activity, whereas flat-track in the USA has the backing of companies such as Harley Davidson. In Europe, besides Germany, the only other longtracks are to be found in the Czech Republic and Scandinavia. The longtrack scene is healthy but there are not enough tracks outside Germany.

There are a lot of grasstracks around, and there has been a lot of talk about bringing the two sports of grasstrack and longtrack together, which is not a bad idea. Why not invent a new product, possibly called Super Flat Track, with riders from both motorcycle spheres contesting a new World Championship? I don't know if a Grand Prix system would work, though.

The FIM were trying to form a working party to discuss possible ideas. With the Speedway Grand Prix you have got Ole Olsen driving the bus, which really makes all the difference. Ole is professional and full-time, he is on the case and it's his livelihood at stake, so he is obviously going to give the SGP everything possible to make it successful.

But if it is left to the FIM, unfortunately, the way circumstances are, most of the guys have other interests in the week and have limited time to spend on such ambitious projects.

Grasstrack would work quite well if it was driven by an overall race director, in the same way Olsen runs the speedway GP for Benfield Sports International. It needs someone to grab the bull by the horns, do television deals and get the project off the ground. I wouldn't mind helping the sport when I have finished, because I do enjoy that side of it.

Meanwhile, maybe Egon Müller, who is without doubt a fabulous ambassador, could be used in the same way SGP employs Olsen. In his prime in the early 80s, he really used to get the crowds going, having spent a lot of time and effort projecting himself publicly. Everybody in Germany knew Egon's name. Even today in longtrack circles, they know Egon Müller and what he represents.

I'm not sure if this sort of leadership role would be his cup of tea. What I do know is that you need a captain steering the ship and then the rest can follow. You can't have committees running affairs – it never works.

I've not ridden that much in Scandinavia, although I competed in the Swedish League at Kumla for a year, when we won the league for the first time in the club's history, and Vetlanda for two years. The problem there was that after my first season at Vetlanda, they introduced a pay scale. These are echoes of the problems I encountered at Oxford, where the promoters were effectively asking someone to take on the same job for less money. I found it difficult to get fired up at all and a real challenge to warrant spending vast amounts of money on my machinery when there wasn't the return.

I did sign for Vetlanda again, but under the old terms. As the third foreigner behind Leigh Adams and Brian Karger, my schedule did not involve many meetings. At Kumla I rode alongside the likes of Henka Gustafsson, Lars Gunnestad and Stefan Danno, who were all relatively new on the scene back then.

I helped to bring Roland Danno to Hackney in 1987, having been friendly with him for a long time. He asked me if he could come to race in the British League and, later, it was him who paved the way for me to ride in the Swedish League.

We had some good lads at Kumla and ended up winning the league, it was bloody great. The travel wasn't bad – I flew out of Heathrow for every meeting and had my own bike waiting for me in Sweden.

I had a similar arrangement when I rode in the Polish League for Tarnow, in 1992. That was also very enjoyable. The club mechanic, Henryk, always prepared my bike well and he also used to look after my engines in Poland.

18 Simon Says

I DON'T know what my future plans are, because I'm so happy riding motorbikes that the question of retirement hasn't even been considered. Obviously I can't ride forever and grasstrack is the main area where I'd like to think I can play some future part in its development.

With respect to my possible involvement in speedway promotion, there are so many people with a foot in the door already that I don't see it as a realistic option for me. I wouldn't say it makes life difficult but it would not be as easy for me to have an influence in the speedway world as it would in grasstrack circles. At the moment grasstrack doesn't really have anybody of significance who has any answers at the top level within ACU headquarters. So if an opportunity came on the ACU front, I'd consider it – but I'm definitely not a committee person. I don't think you should be holding a vote every time a decision needs to be made.

I probably know grasstrack, and the way it works, better than I do the speedway world.

I would like to earn a living by continuing to be involved in motorcycle racing, although at quite what level, I don't know. I really don't want to worry too much about it, because I have probably worried too much about my future in the past.

It's OK planning for tomorrow all the time but if tomorrow isn't going to come – or something happens . . . or, God forbid, you have an accident, all your plans are a waste of time. People have got to live for today, take it a little bit as it comes.

However, I don't see myself walking off at the end of my career and thinking: 'That's it, a phase of my life has ended and I don't want to be connected with it any more.' Far from it. I still want to be involved in some form or another.

I would really like to see grasstrack racing move forward in a big way. The grasstrack scene from the mid-70s, when I was a youngster, has gone backwards quite considerably. The year that I started riding there were seven or eight top international grasstrack meetings in the calendar. It has proved very difficult for the promoters to survive, never mind progress, although I don't think enough is done in that respect to keep them going. There were quite a few meetings in the 70s where you could go and watch the top riders in action. I've got some ideas and I wouldn't mind doing something with them . . .

Essentially, I have been a grasstracker more than a speedway rider for most of my career. I've been a grasstrack rider *trying* to be a speedway rider. One of the insights I learned fairly quickly was that it is better to stick to what you know best, whatever line of business you go into.

And the grasstrack scene is what I know best.

"It's OK planning for tomorrow all the time but if tomorrow isn't going to come – or something happens . . . or, God forbid, you have an accident, all your plans are a waste of time. People have got to live for today"

I'm asked about the potential for longtrack in Britain, and I consider grasstrack and longtrack to be the same entity. Sure, if it is done right, it can happen but there aren't the stadiums here in Britain to accommodate longtrack meetings. If there was a World Longtrack Championship qualifier held here, it would draw a good crowd. If it was promoted correctly, aimed at the general public and not only the out and out speedway fan, a longtrack event here could prove successful.

But to go to the expense of building stadiums to run motorcycle events these days is not a commonsense proposition at all. Unfortunately, unless suitable existing venues can be adapted, longtrack racing in Britain is really not viable.

Deep in thought, Simon at home in 1999, contemplating the future...

As for the future direction of British speedway, an Elite League is essential. One big league, which fans tend to clamour for, was a mistake. It's like trying to sell McDonald's hamburgers to customers at The Ritz, or offering a £30 sirloin steak to customers of Burger King. People know what they've got, they know what the market is.

Also, we need stepping stones for British youngsters. Unfortunately, promoters tend to think it's important how many races they have on a night, or how the regulations are structured, or whether the team aggregate points limit is set correctly. Those are all negative aspects of speedway.

The complicated stuff is destroying things. But the genuine businessmen involved in speedway know that all those things are relatively unimportant.

An important consideration is second halves. What is the logic in not having them? I don't understand. Promoters should send their customers home at the end of the night on a high. They say that the final heat of the main match has this effect, but it doesn't.

Heat 15 is not necessarily an entertaining finale – it's a winner-loser situation. So depending upon whether his or her team has won or lost the match, supporters leave the stadium either happy or down in the dumps.

But anybody in business will tell you that the aim must be to send your customers away happy as often as possible. By reintroducing a second half to follow the main event, at least it's a logical way of defusing the frustrations experienced by supporters of the night's losing team. Victory by their star rider over the home favourites could at least be seen as some consolation for losing the match itself. On occasions when the match itself is a bore, the rider-of-the-night finale can often turn out to be the most exciting part of the night's entertainment.

It would also provide a chance for the kids to ride against the good blokes. The old second halves were a perfect system, an ideal chance for youngsters to measure their progress.

When I started in speedway, second halves were a great way of gauging how well I was doing. There is a vast void between the Third Division (or Conference League) and the senior league and riders who can take on everybody and compete at the age of 16 are very few and far between, so they need to be offered stepping stones to the top.

From a rider's point of view, the second half programme was also a chance to try out a spare bike, or to experiment with equipment, without letting down your team or supporters.

If every member of the BSPA were making a million quid a week running speedway, I would listen to them. But they are not. Most are busting their a* to survive – and then tell each other how to run their show. I find that incredible.***

Charlie's story

By the woman who knew Simon best

By Charlie Wigg-Booden

I FIRST met Simon when I was working for a travel agent in Buckingham. He came in with a group of other guys and made an enquiry about a booking to Hong Kong. I put some work into their request for details but the booking never materialised and I came to the conclusion that it was a set-up.

Then I was out in Milton Keynes one night with a friend and we bumped into him. Simon apologised that he hadn't got back to me and asked if he could buy me a drink. So we went out for a drink and then he asked for my number. He did pursue me for a while before I agreed to go to dinner with him, which was followed by an invitation to a party at his home.

When I arrived there, I thought: 'Oh my God, what am I in for?' You can imagine my reaction driving through those big iron gates and seeing this wonderful house. It was really large but what I began to like about him was that he had this very nice property but was still such a normal guy, someone you would be happy to live with in any kind of place. His home was not something that he bragged about.

Simon never told me that he was a speedway rider and, initially, I couldn't work out what he did for a living. I presumed that he was some sort of businessman who went in and out of the country a lot, because he was frequently off to Germany and Prague. Simon announced that he was in England for one week but then off to Australia for three months! I was only 20-years-old when I met him, and had grown to really like him, but I couldn't understand why I couldn't see him more often.

Once I knew he was a speedway rider I didn't go and watch him race for quite a while. I'm not the sort of person who likes the limelight so when I knew that Simon was in the public eye, I didn't know if this really was for me.

Growing up, I was always very family-orientated. Also, I like to know what I am getting myself into. I don't like being somewhere where people are looking at me, so I was a bit nervous about being around him at speedway. In addition, Simon was 12 years older than me, which meant a lot of his friends were older, too.

I felt happier about what he did after accompanying him to a presentation by the Mayor of Bradford following yet another Knockout Cup success by the Dukes. I was introduced to Gary Havelock's fiancée, Jane, who said: 'I haven't seen you around.' I replied that I didn't really like the speedway scene. However, I soon began to take to her and feel that I'd be more comfortable going to watch in future. Jane was the first speedway girlfriend that I'd spoken to and knew that I could spend time with her because she was down-to-earth.

I didn't start going to speedway regularly until Simon joined Coventry in 1994. There I became friendly with Michelle Jorgensen and Michelle Smith, the wives of John Jorgensen and Andy Smith, which made me feel even more comfortable.

Simon and I were married on November 9, 1996, although I'd started travelling abroad with him to meetings after Abi was born.

If you watch any dangerous sport in which someone whom you know and love is competing, the fear factor is at the back of your mind all the time. I always felt confident of Simon and didn't see him involved in many crashes until his last year of racing – and later we realised that he'd become ill during the 1998 season with King's Lynn.

The other challenge with having an emotional attachment to a motorcyclist is their long-term love of the sport, which is normally greater than the love they have for their wife or partner. I was no exception but in this respect I had a lot of support from my Mum, Louise, and Dad. When they were first married, Dad went to play football in South Africa, so Mum knew what it was like to have been in a relationship with a professional sportsman. She had been in the background while Dad had to focus on his career. She really helped me so I could accept where I stood in the scheme of things with Simon and his racing career. Mum got across to me the point that if you get involved in this type of lifestyle, you have to be prepared to be a follower. In many senses, though, I was pleased to be in the background. As I've said, I didn't like the media spotlight or being surrounded in the van by fans. However, I did get used to it as I grew older.

When I first went to speedway it did feel intimidating. Simon received a lot of female attention and there were stories going around. Maybe, being a bit more mature for my age, I was always confident that there was nothing for me to worry about. To be honest, one of my best friends, Carolyn Ravn, is one of Simon's ex-girlfriends. I have a good rapport with her and she stays with us – and vice-versa – when I am in Australia, so it's not something that worried me. Obviously my relationship with Simon was true.

I am often asked what it was like being married to a man who was constantly on the go and always full of ideas. Well, my eventual advice to Simon was to take a pad and pen to bed with him, because the ideas that were whizzing through his head meant that he wasn't getting a proper sleep. He would go to bed late and awake very early. There was just too much going on in his mind and I have to tell you, Simon wasn't that good at prioritising.

Yes, I'd support him 100 per cent and he would talk his schemes through with me. He would talk about the speedway clothing and the helmets and all other aspects of his sports. I tried to push him to write everything down. He definitely had a fertile mind, it was always buzzing.

It could, of course, be frustrating at times when I wanted to talk about the kids and how they were getting on. I tried to get across to him that there were other interests in life beside his racing. However, I'm a pretty laid-back person and accepted that his racing was what was current and believed that the period *after* his retirement would be our time together.

"He would talk about the speedway clothing and the helmets and all other aspects of his sports. I tried to push him to write everything down. He definitely had a fertile mind, it was always buzzing"

Many people speculate what Simon would be doing with himself these days, if he had lived. Well, even though we went to live in Australia, it's my belief that given the way Sky TV has developed its coverage of speedway, he would have played a key part in that in some way. Simon was involved with presenter Keith Huewen from the beginning and was one of the first of his regular studio guests. I imagine that Simon would have spent the majority of his time during the UK season with television commitments, because he loved the camera and the attention. He loved getting his point of view across. Also, it has to be accepted that a lot of Simon's original concepts are now part of speedway in the new television age.

Simon would also have been interested in a promotional role around the grasstrack scene in Britain. The farewell speedway meeting we ran at Oxford in March 1999, after he first fell ill, was right up his street. He loved every single minute of it.

Simon was also very interested in doing something to help the youngsters coming through the speedway ranks. He had a lot to give to other people and developing British talent would have been a mission close to his heart.

Anyway, back to his career in which King's Lynn was the final phase. I remember ringing the promoter, Buster Chapman, to tell him that the contract he'd prepared for the 1999 season would remain unsigned, it wasn't going to happen.

Simon had never really argued with Julian and always listened to what his brother had to say. Julian had been a very good influence all his life and, of course, Simon respected him enormously.

But one night, there was an incident when we were coming home from a party, when Simon really turned on Julian quite nastily and he was upset by it. In hindsight, we can understand now why these things happened but at the time I thought that Simon wanted to take a different path to that which he had followed with Julian. He was certainly ready to disagree with his brother.

The Wiggs' former period country home, The Old Stables at Sandhill, Middle Claydon, Bucks. When Simon was unable to drive, the family had to sell it and move into town.

There were also occasions in our own relationship when, inexplicably, things became quite strained. It was like one minute Simon was with it but the next minute, he wasn't. He seemed quite blank on occasions.

I think his problems started in 1998. He wasn't well at the beginning of that season, showing what were flu-like symptoms. Simon went to the doctor, who carried out blood tests but didn't find anything wrong. It was presumed to be viral 'flu, so he was rather slow to start the '97 season.

Then he had a big crash in Holland from which he suffered a quite severe concussion. This was followed by another pile-up at Exeter after which he missed several meetings. Finally, he had a major crash with Gary Havelock and Piotr Protasiewicz at King's Lynn, at the end of the '98 season, when he hit the wooden fence head-first, and couldn't remember it happening.

Simon had now suffered three bad concussions in a year.

Looking back to the bad incident at King's Lynn, he remembered going into the corner but nothing else from that point. At the time everyone thought that was a bit strange, then time passes and no-one thought any more about it. Even after a couple of days with concussion, he didn't feel well overall. He felt faint and his colouring was poor, and you could tell that he wasn't right in himself.

Then the season finished and he was getting his bikes together to go to Australia in the winter of 1998-99. They were due to be collected the day after Simon was to suffer a massive fit. He actually collapsed on our second wedding anniversary – November 9, 1998.

I'd been talking to him in his workshop and then went back indoors to put some washing away. On the way upstairs I heard this noise and thought: 'My God, it sounds like someone 's having a heart attack!'

Simon had come out to see the young lad who was cutting the grass in the courtyard. I remember looking out of the window and seeing Simon clutching his chest. I dropped the basket of washing and ran back down the stairs. By the time I reached him, Simon had fallen onto the gravel and was fitting quite aggressively. I'd never seen anyone fit before – only in episodes of *Casualty*.

Memories of watching that popular TV programme actually helped me to know what I needed to do. I put him in the recovery position and sent the young lad around to a neighbour whom I knew was a first-aider. I also knew that he happened to be at home because of his shift patterns. By the time he rushed around, Simon had began to come out of his fit.

I phoned the ambulance service and gave them directions, because our house wasn't the easiest to find. We managed to get Simon sitting up in the passenger seat of our car, parked nearby, and I treated a nasty cut on his head, which he'd sustained when he collapsed onto the gravel. As Simon came around, he thought that he was at a speedway meeting and had crashed. He couldn't work out why he wasn't in his leathers and kept asking about his bike. Simon was very agitated.

The ambulance arrived and I explained what had happened. On the journey to hospital, Simon's eyes started to roll and he began to fit again. When we arrived at Milton Keynes Hospital, they couldn't get him out of his fit so they put him on a life-support machine.

I still couldn't work out what might be wrong with him. Had he had a heart attack? Was it the meningitis that was going around at the time? Everything goes through your head. Not knowing anything about epileptics or fits – no-one could confirm anything at that time – I was very worried about what the outcome was going to be. I could hear the doctors and medical staff saying: 'Come on, Simon. Come on, Simon' as they tried to get him out of his fit, to which he was not responding.

Then they came and fetched me to see if he would recognise my voice. There was still no response, so that was when they decided to put him on a life-support machine.

A lot of tests indicated that he had suffered an epileptic fit. Julian had arrived by now and they had to inform us that Simon would have to lose both his racing and driving licence for a year. We were actually more concerned how Simon was going to take that news than the fact that he had suffered an epileptic fit. For racing was his whole life and there was now the prospect of him not riding and being stuck around the house. It wasn't as if we were based in a town or a city – we lived in the heart of the Buckinghamshire countryside. I was worried about that side of it as much as what had happened to him.

We asked the doctors not to tell him that bad news about the fit when he did eventually come around, until one of us was there to give Simon support. But I was so amazed how well he took the news. The fact that he treated the whole episode as if he had a broken leg that would mend, is in a way a good outlook to have – but it's not practical or realistic.

We had many arguments over this, as I felt that something still wasn't right. I just sensed that he hadn't suffered a typical epileptic fit. Most people fit and carry on normally with their work but Simon couldn't. As he had never witnessed a fit, and knew nothing about epilepsy, he thought: 'Oh well, it's happened. Let's carry on.' So there was a downside to this somewhat blasé attitude. I wanted the problem to be investigated but his spirit was a double-edged sword. It's good to be upbeat but you have to be realistic, too.

We went to see a specialist in Milton Keynes a couple of times and I had rows with him because of what he was saying. He stated that he saw 10 people a week and it was a one-off occurrence for them – he didn't put Simon on any medication. I took the line that people don't just fit without a reason. I requested various scans and this particular doctor told me that he didn't know what my problem was. He said people have fits – so deal with it. He told me to go away, get some leaflets and read up on it. It was so frustrating and remains so in hindsight.

I tried so hard to get across to the specialist that Simon wasn't an ordinary person off the street. He was a speedway rider and had experienced three really bad concussions within a year, with the crashes unexplained. Logically, there had to be an underlying problem and eventually the doctors agreed to a scan.

Meanwhile, we decided that we would go to Australia simply for a holiday, because Simon couldn't now take part in David Tapp's speedway series. While in Australia, we received the result of the scan which revealed that there was a slight abnormality to the left side of his brain. However, the doctor stated that we shouldn't worry, as many people have this!

I told Simon that if it were me, I'd seek a second opinion.

While in Australia we started looking at properties. Simon said that if he couldn't race, then he wanted to be away from England. He loved Australia, it was a second home to him, and he'd decided that Australia was where he wanted to be.

Again, this was the Simon that even I didn't really like at times. There was no consideration for what myself and the children might want. Abi was four when Simon fell ill, while Ricki had just had his first birthday. Like I said earlier, I am close to my family, we're very close and do a lot of things together. Simon was making these decisions alone and saying this is what we are going to do.

Although, in a sense, moving to Australia excited me, I still had concerns that we needed to investigate his problems further. Maybe it's the kind of person I am – I need to know the ins and outs of everything before I make a decision, whereas Simon viewed the problems with his head like he would a broken arm or a broken collarbone. In his eyes, everything would be alright again in a few weeks.

Julian had his concerns and I had mine. I spoke to Julian about it but we couldn't get any sense from Simon. As far as he was concerned, he was OK and he re-emphasised: 'I'm going to Australia. I'm starting a new life. This is fine.'

It was a difficult period for me. I felt that I was pulling one way and obviously Simon was pulling the other, towards this new life – a future in which, according to him, no problems existed. He was in denial.

While in Australia, there were a couple of episodes where I thought that there was something wrong with him. He was a bit vacant and not sure of what was happening on occasions, but nothing to suggest that he was going to have a fit.

We had been staying with Allan Rivett, the former Exeter rider, and were meant to be flying home at the end of our holiday. We checked into Brisbane airport but the plane was delayed, so the staff there said it was best if we went away and had a meal before returning. We all got back into Allan's car and he said: 'You might as well go back to my place, as I'm only 10 minutes away. I'll bring you back later.'

On the return journey to the airport, Simon suffered a massive epileptic fit. We were going across a single road bridge at the time when Simon, who was sat in the front passenger seat, tried to grab the steering wheel. It was just so frightening and Abi was hysterical. There was also one of Allan's boys in the back with me. I was trying to hold onto Simon from the back and pull him to the correct side of the car.

Allan drove very fast to reach the hospital while I was saying to him that I didn't know if Simon was going to come out of this fit. It was very, very frightening because he had ended up on a life-support machine the first time, and I just didn't know what was going to happen. These were my worst fears unfolding, as I'd always sensed the problem was something deeper. Then I started questioning myself – why didn't I do this or why didn't I do that?

Simon had begun to come out of his fit as we pulled into an ambulance bay. Allan sprinted inside to alert the medics, who came out and got Simon onto a stretcher. Simon came around quite well at the hospital, where the doctors were fantastic. They couldn't understand why Simon wasn't on medication to control the situation. I obviously gave them his medical history. I'd also kept a private diary in which I'd noted the strange happenings, the various episodes that he'd had. I had read up on the condition in a lot of booklets and leaflets.

The doctors prescribed medication for Simon and we stayed in Australia for an extra two weeks, although of course, all our bags were checked onto a flight that we didn't make. I rang Julian in floods of tears to tell him what had happened to Simon, before starting to worry about us getting back home safely. Doctors gave me some injections to administer if Simon suffered another fit on our home-bound flight due to pressure changes in the cabin. So now I faced a flight with a four-year–old, a one-year-old and Simon, who was basically out of it.

We made it, though, and my Dad met us at the airport to ensure we all us returned home safely. We revisited the same doctor who had seen us before and this time I insisted that something had to be done.

Simon was put on a brand new, more sensitive, MRI machine in Milton Keynes. This doctor called us in and said that he was referring Simon to a Mr. Adams in Oxford. I remember the matter-of-fact way he just told us that a tumour on the brain had been confirmed.

Now I could have told him that there was some sort of pressure there. This should have been dealt with earlier – from Simon's first fit the previous November, it was to be the following May before Simon went into the Cromwell Hospital in London to have his first operation.

I went down with him on the day and they removed a tumour the size of a plum. But Simon came out of the operation so well and there was an amusing incident to follow. Joe Screen and Steve Johnston came to visit him and had shaved off all their hair, thinking that, following an operation to his brain, Simon would also be bald.

But as they walked in ready to show off their new look, they were greeted by Simon with every hair on his head still in place! The surgeons had simply lifted his hair before entering his skull through the left side. With only a tiny scar, you wouldn't even know that Simon had undergone an operation.

Simon nearly rolled out of his bed with laughter. Joe and Steve thought that by having their heads shaved they would make him feel better – and, in a sense, they did! Difficult though the situation was, there were still so many laughs in the hospital.

As I said, Simon came around after the op' very well and he was only in the Cromwell for four days. The surgeon had sat me down – I'd stayed with him at the hospital the whole time – and told me that the tumour was benign and had probably been there for some time. The knocks to his head from speedway had certainly done Simon no favours but I felt a great sense of relief as we went away to Greece for a week's break.

"I started coming to the conclusion that the crashes he had in recent seasons weren't due to racing incidents, but may have been caused by him suffering mini-fits on the track"

When we returned from holiday, Simon started his course of radiotherapy, for which he had to go to Northampton on a daily basis. When that was completed, we had a farewell party in readiness for leaving the UK and moving to Australia. In the meantime, we bought a place near my Mum and Dad, in Milton Keynes.

Unfortunately, at the party, I slipped and broke my wrist and was put in plaster. Despite this setback to our plans, Simon still left for Australia on his own, leaving me unable to drive and having to feed the kids with great difficulty. Julian was not very impressed and tried to talk to Simon, to ask him to delay the trip for a few weeks. But Simon was adamant and it was almost as though he thought that once he reached Australia, he would be embarking upon his new lifestyle.

Simon had a real passion for Australia, he loved the weather and enjoyed having a tan. I suppose at this time it was the 'feel good factor' after all he had been through. I recognise that now. That was how Simon viewed his illness. He believed that when he got over there, he was going to feel so much better. This was his new start in life, as he could no longer ride a bike – although, convinced that he was OK, he still had plans for a comeback!

I stayed in the UK until I had my plaster off and while Simon had found us somewhere to rent. He left in the October and I arrived the following month. I liked Australia but, again, there was the challenge of being thousands of miles away from my family. Throughout Simon's illness my Mum had been a rock for me, she had given me such great support and, being a nurse, was so understanding. Towards the end I couldn't have done without her really. She was there for me all the time.

When I joined Simon in Australia, he looked well – or at least so I thought initially. In time, though, I began to have my doubts again. I'm not saying that I'm a negative person but I was very concerned. Two small children, moving far away, and not convinced that Simon was 100 per cent . . . deep down, I knew that the old Simon would never have left me on my own in Milton Keynes with a broken wrist. I just knew that wasn't the real him.

This is when I began putting two and two together. My memory went back to his arguments with Julian before the whole situation developed.

I also started coming to the conclusion that the crashes he had in recent seasons weren't due to racing incidents, but may have been caused by him suffering mini-fits on the track.

My Mum was very concerned about my going to Australia, partly because of an issue of medication. When someone is on medication the doctors have to try and get the balance correct. So why would he want to go and fly to Australia while this was still being sorted, with the risk of a fit while he was alone? What Simon did by going to Aussie ahead of us was irrational.

Yet when I got to Australia and viewed houses, which were very suitable for the children, and could see that his mind was working sharply, I began to feel more at ease. However, I did suggest that we should live in rented accommodation for a year – just to make sure that everything was alright before we definitely committed ourselves to Australia.

Two days before Christmas, Simon went for a check-up in Brisbane by a specialist to whom we had been sent by Mr. Adams. Simon felt that he'd been given information that everything was fine, even though we were still awaiting the latest test results. Simon went out for a while and came back with a kitten he'd bought for Abi. I said to him: 'This is a rented house, we can't keep animals here.' Simon replied: 'Yes, but we're moving next week – I've bought a house!' He had actually been out and bought a property that we had looked at several times. It was a gorgeous house, at Paradise Point on the beautiful Queensland Gold Coast, but he had gone ahead and made the decision on his own.

Looking back, I think that Simon was just being so positive about everything. It was almost like while I was urging us to be a little wary, he was saying there was absolutely no need to be cautious. I suppose having been ill and gone through the operation, he believed what he wanted to believe. In a sense, Simon was coping but not in a realistic way. Having said that, he did take the information that he couldn't ride remarkably well for someone who we thought would break down once given the devastating news. That wasn't the case at all. He was so positive and planned his comeback with a fitness campaign.

We moved into this new house on the Gold Coast the week after Christmas. It was a gorgeous house on the waterfront, everything that he wanted. You could drive down under the house, where there was enough car parking space for eight cars. It was in there that Simon planned to set up his new workshops. Once we moved in we rarely saw Simon upstairs in the house, as he was absorbed downstairs setting things up.

I started to think that maybe we were getting back on the right track. He seemed so focused on what he wanted to do in the house and began talking about running speedway training schools out there.

Simon, who had always been very fit in the past, got himself back in good shape again by cycling and swimming a lot. But while I began to think that we were doing alright, deep down I was scared. I was in a different country, a long way from my family and with no friends of my own. If something did happen to him again, who would I call for support? It was a big worry that remained at the back of my mind.

In the February of 2000 I had decided to come back and see my Mum on her 50th birthday.

The lovely house at Paradise Point, on the Queensland Gold Coast, that Simon bought and where he planned to spend the future with his family.

I wanted my parents to see the kids, too. The American rider, Ronnie Correy, had actually been staying at the house with us for a while, so I felt quite comfortable knowing that somebody was around Simon. Ivan Mauger, who lived fairly close by, was also keeping an eye on him, so I flew back with the children for a family reunion.

My Mum came to the house a couple of days later and said: 'I don't know if I should be telling you this but Simon is actually flying in and he's taking you to Paris for your birthday. Julian has dealt with all the arrangements.'

Mum prompted me that when I got to Milton Keynes Station believing that I was going away for the weekend with a friend, it was actually Simon who was going to be there to meet me. Which was all very romantic! Obviously I went to the station and pretended that I didn't know anything about his surprise. We went off to Paris for a romantic weekend and had a lovely picture taken together while dining out on the Seine, while he still looked well.

In Paris, Simon was completely with it and there seemed to be no problems. Then things changed again for the worse. Within a few days I happened to ask him if he wanted a bacon-and-egg sandwich and he looked at me as if I was an alien. I also began to notice that his speech was slightly strange. Then I heard him on the telephone calling Paradise Point, where we lived in Australia, 'Daradise Doint'.

I contacted Mr. Adams and told him that the December check-up had revealed some signs of growth but that we had been told it would be many years before this would require a further operation. Now, I believed, the tumour had grown much quicker than anticipated.

Mr. Adams told me to bring Simon in the next day and they would run an MRI scan. So my Mum and I took him over to Oxford and, once they saw the result, they booked him in for an operation the next day. They explained that with this operation, the left side of the body could become weak.

I spoke to Simon the next morning and he was chirpy as they prepared him for the op'. I travelled down to London to be there when he came around. I was still upstairs at three in the afternoon, so I rang my Mum. I told her that there must be something wrong, because after his last operation, I'd been taken down to see him in recovery a lot earlier. No-one had been to see me and I had been left waiting alone in this room for many hours. Nothing seemed real. The registrar eventually fetched me and said that Mr. Adams needed to speak to me while Simon was still in recovery.

He took me in an office and stated: 'I think you need to remember your husband as he was and not what he is going to become.' So I replied: 'What are you saying.'

The way Mr. Adams explained it to me was like a pot of white paint, and if someone dropped a blob of red paint into it – the spray effect was like little veins. Although they had removed the majority of the tumour – the size of a small melon, the veins had gone into parts of the brain that they couldn't reach to take out.

They informed me that he would have six months to live – if he were lucky.

With a young family around Simon, they wanted to give him chemotherapy, to keep him going for as long as possible. I didn't agree with this course of action, as I felt this wasn't what Simon would have wanted. I knew him too well. He would not want to stay around unless he was 100 per cent. But the medical people said: 'No, with a young wife and young family, we want to do this for him.'

They said that they would not tell him that he had only six months to live.

Again, I didn't agree, as there were things we would want to say to each other as a family. If Simon didn't know the full facts, we wouldn't be able to express ourselves because he would be asking why I was saying certain things.

Anyway, Simon came round after his second operation and, to everyone's astonishment, said that he was hungry. The staff in the intensive care unit had never heard anything like it before!

Meanwhile, I had to face up to some serious issues and, unable to contact Julian, I rang his wife, Lynne, instead. I spoke to Julian in the evening and asked if he was coming to the hospital. I explained that I couldn't do this on my own. So Julian came down and saw Simon. It was very hard for Julian to stay strong once he was told of the finality of the situation. Eventually Julian took me home that night, dropping me off at my parents' home. I went back in the next day but Simon had taken a turn for the worse. He was very swollen and didn't look like the Simon we all knew at all. He couldn't speak and he was in a lot of pain. He was not moving very well either.

One for the ladies, Simon was once credited with having the sexiest arms in speedway.

Early days in speedway at Weymouth, 1982.

A happy Heathen, 1983.

Riding for title-winning Cradley Heath in his first full British League season, 1983.

Oxford's finest, the 1986 British League champions and joint KO Cup winners. Left to right: Jon Surman, Wiggy, Per Sorensen, Hans Nielsen, Bernard Crapper (team manager), Nigel De'Ath, Marvyn Cox, Andy Grahame. Below left: BL Pairs champion with Hans Nielsen, 1985. Below right: Fast-moving Cheetah.

Captain of Hackney's HL1 Kestrels in 1987. Left to right: John Louis (team manager), Mark Loram, Alan Mogridge, Wiggy, Malcolm Simmons, Randy Green, Allan Johansen, Andy Galvin.

Above: Bradford pair Simon and Gary Havelock combine against King's Lynn at Odsal, 1991.
Centre: After the Dukes clinched the KO Cup in 1991.
Below: Challenging on the inside of Belle Vue's Shawn Moran, 1992.

Top left: Coventry, 1993. Top right: Berlin, 1995. Centre: Leading for Exeter, 1997.
Bottom: Winning for King's Lynn ahead of Ryan Sullivan and Lee Richardson, 1998.

Simon takes top spot on the rostrum at Coventry – ahead of Kelvin Tatum (2nd) and Chris Morton – after winning the British Championship for the first time, 1988. Inset: He retained the title a year later.

Top left: Early days on the grass, at the Aces of Aces, 1980.

Top right: Golden days as winner of the Golden Helmet at Teterow, 1990.

Left: Wiggy loved the unique twists and turns of the Teterow grasstrack in Germany. He1s pictured racing there in 1993.

Below: As spectacular as ever.

The closest Simon came to winning the speedway World Championship, when he finished runner-up to Hans Nielsen in the 1989 World Final at Munich, with Jeremy Doncaster third.

Always proud to pull on the England racejacket, here's Wiggy leading a World Team Cup qualifier at King's Lynn in 1984 from the USA's Bobby Schwartz and New Zealand's David Bargh.

Above: Captain of the England Sunbrite Lions, 1987. Left to right: Simon Cross, Kelvin Tatum, Wiggy, Martin Dugard, Paul Thorpe, Marvyn Cox, Colin Pratt (team manager). Front: Andy Grahame, Chris Morton.

Left: Wiggy leading Lions partner Chris Morton and USA's Lance King during the 1984 Test at Sheffield.

Below: Powering clear of Denmark's Jan O Pedersen at King's Lynn, 1987.

At the end of the speedway season, Simon would organise his popular fancy dress party which, apart from providing plenty of fun and frolics, also benefited the Speedway Riders' Benevolent Fund.
Left: Wiggy dressed as Bart Simpson in 1991.
Above: As the *A Team's* 'Mr T' with Egon Müller, 1990.
Below: Wizard of balance, showing off his top-of-the-range longtrack bike and luxury motorhome.

Simon's five World Longtrack Championship wins.
Top left: Korskro, 1985.
Top right: Marianske Lazne, 1989.
Centre: Herxheim, 1990.
Above left: Muhldorf, 1993.
Right: Marianske Lazne, 1994.

Finding extra pace in a specially made lightweight suit for the 1993 World Longtrack Final at Muhldorf.

Man and machine in perfect harmony, Wiggy going flat out at the 1995 World Longtrack Final.

Above: Simon with the riders who contested his Big Day Out farewell to British speedway meeting at Oxford, March 1999.

Above: With the finalists, Jason Crump, Greg Hancock, Armando Castagna and Billy Hamill, plus model Teresa May, who joins Wiggy (below) on a lap of honour.

Below: Simon thanks the competitors and the huge crowd that turned out to pay an emotional tribute to him.

The Wigg family – Simon, Charlie, Abigail and Ricki, December 1998.

Below left: Simon before the 1997 Speedway Grand Prix in Prague.

Below right: One of the last portraits of Simon, February 1999.

Charlie and Simon on their last trip together – ready for a meal on the River Seine while visiting Paris in February 2000.

Family and friends at the uplifting reception held at the National Hockey Stadium, Milton Keynes that followed the funeral and thanksgiving service on November 27, 2000. In keeping with Simon's wishes, the occasion was very much a celebration of his life and he would surely have approved of the men wearing shirts in his trademark green!
Left to right – standing: Alan (Charlie's cousin), Kip Hewitt, Dickie Staff, Julian Wigg, Karl Maier. Seated: Hilary Staff, Louise Milne (Charlie's mum), Sharon (Willen Hospice), Andy Milne (Charlie's dad), Brett Walton, Mary (Christopher Wigg's partner), Christopher Wigg, Charlie Wigg-Booden (with Alexz Wigg on her lap!), Steve Brandon, Elaine (Charlie's aunt) and her partner, Brian.

This went on for 28 days. We actually got to the stage when we thought that he wasn't going to come out of the hospital. My Dad, who actually knew Simon's other brother, Christopher, having worked together years ago, rang him and told him to come over. That night they had decided to double Simon's steroids so when we took Christopher in for what he presumed was a death-bed visit, Simon was in the bathroom shaving and singing! All this thanks to having his steroids intake doubled.

The hospital soon informed me that I could take Simon home, which I was petrified about. Word had got about and it only takes one person to say: 'Sorry to hear, mate.' I was very concerned about him hearing the worst.

I sorted out a property to rent that was bigger than our house, because I knew that we wouldn't be going back to Australia, whether he wanted to or not. We needed support and I would turn to my parents and Julian for that. Obviously, Simon couldn't understand why we were renting a house.

There were a couple of instances where people rang up, and though they never actually said anything, Simon would come off the phone and say that the caller had made some strange comments. He was picking up vibes that there was something wrong but couldn't fathom what the problem was. He was also very frustrated that he didn't feel as good as he did after his first operation.

"That day was the first time that I broke down and cried in front of Simon. He then told me: 'Look, I'm 40-years-old. I have a beautiful wife, two fantastic children and I have done more than most people ever do in their lifetime. It's my time to go. I'm OK with it, so be strong.' That heartfelt statement was to see me through"

Then, one day, I came in to find Simon crying. I asked him what was wrong and I presumed that someone had said something about his terminal condition. He replied: 'I know I've got to fetch Ricki from school but I don't now where it is.'

Ricki was at nursery across the road from the house – and it was so close that you could see it from the window. But Simon couldn't remember and his frustration, compounded by him sensing that there was something seriously wrong with him, had boiled over into tears.

I said to my Mum: 'Look, I've got to tell him. I can't live like this.' For instance, we couldn't have any nurses coming in because otherwise, Simon would wonder why they were there. It was such a strain and it's a horrible secret to keep.

My Mum said that we should go and speak to Mr. Adams about it. He said: 'Fine, I'll see him. If he asks me the question, then I'll tell him. If he doesn't, then I am not prepared to tell him.'

So my Mum and I took Simon back to Oxford. I went in with him and Simon was asking sensible questions such as: 'How many of these operations do you do? What per centage of patients survive?' Mr. Adams did tell him – quite bluntly – that Simon should make sure that he had everything in order. We then came out and obviously my Mum was sitting outside not knowing how we would be when we came out. I decided to go back in and say to Mr. Adams that I *had* to tell Simon the truth. I explained: 'There are things I want to say. Also, we've got a house in Australia and I've got to have paperwork in place for the sake of the children, as I don't know where I'm going to be.'

Mum and I sat down with Simon and told him the truth. We led up to it by discussing how he felt about the fact that he wasn't getting any better and couldn't understand why. Simon turned to us and exclaimed: 'Oh well, s*** happens!' And that was that.

We went out for a walk later that night with my Dad. Simon said: 'Andy, you know I'm going to die?' My Dad – well what do you say? – came out with: 'Yes mate, I heard that.' That was it, that's how easily Simon accepted it. Strangely, he never once mentioned the kids or how they were going to cope, or commented on the fact that he wasn't going to see them grow up. I found it quite heartbreaking when I thought about these factors myself.

Obviously Simon and I talked a lot while sorting out the paperwork. He did have chemotherapy but began to deteriorate too quickly, losing his speech and coordination. I spoke to Mr. Adams about the fact that the chemotherapy wasn't working and that I would like it to stop, because I didn't think it was doing Simon any favours. It was in tablet form, so it wasn't as if he was

undergoing the laser treatment. Mr. Adams was very fair and said: 'OK, we'll stop.'
They did another MRI scan, which confirmed the tumour was growing rapidly.
That day was the first time that I broke down and cried in front of Simon. He then told me: 'Look, I'm 40-years-old. I have a beautiful wife, two fantastic children and I have done more than most people ever do in their lifetime. It's my time to go. I'm OK with it, so be strong.' That heartfelt statement from him was to see me through.

After that we did a lot. We went to a pub that provided Christmas dinners out of season. The whole family went along and we all put on our hats and did the usual things. Our last Christmas together – although somewhat in advance.
At this point Simon's speech was getting very limited. I remember that he fell over a wall and Jeremy Doncaster had a hell of a job helping us to get him back upright, because Simon had put on so much weight. Simon was lying in the bushes laughing his head off with three of us panicking while trying to pull him up. Simon thought it was hilarious!
He was very, very positive with the twinkle still in his eyes and that cheekiness about him. He was so heavy, partly because of the effect of the steroids and partly because of his new passion for chocolate. He wouldn't let you in to visit him unless you brought him cakes or chocolate! Someone visited once and gave me a box of Ferrero Roche, with Simon receiving four chocolate eclairs. He got the hump because the chocolates were not for him!
Word got around that all visitors to Simon had to bring him chocolate treats. He had spent more than 20 years religiously watching his weight and eating sensibly, but now he'd gone to the opposite extreme.
We had an early 40th birthday party for him at our new rented house in Milton Keynes in May 2000 and it was fantastic. Some 40 people attended, including Barry and Tony Briggs, and Simon was the life and soul of the party.
The sad side to the good side was that he could get aggressive occasionally. He was in the shower one day when Ricki tried to get in with him. Simon got worked up because he didn't know who it was around him. It was distressing for the children to hear him like that, too.
He also suffered quite a few fits and the medics told me that if he had a major one, it would kill him. Every time the ambulance came, the paramedics would ask me why I still had Simon at home? They told me to get him into a hospice as they felt the situation wasn't good for me.
Eventually my Mum and I were having to bath him and he had to live downstairs. I got to the stage where I was physically drained, I wasn't sleeping and I wasn't really eating. I remember hearing a noise one night and I had reached the point that I was so scared of finding him dead or fitting that I rang my Mum in a state at 2am. She came round, took a look at him and he was fine. She then said to me: 'You've got to start to have the McMillan nurses coming in to help.'
Next day my doctor arrived with some nurses from The Willen Hospice. He explained that normally they didn't take long-term patients at Willen but they had a meeting about it and because of the difficult situation with the children and myself, they were prepared to take Simon as a long-term patient. I had him at home for as long as I could and I was very reluctant to let him go but, on the other hand, it was the best decision that I had made. The time that I then spent with Simon was quality time, when I was his wife again and not his carer.
However, he liked the fact that I could shave him rather than have the nurses do it for him – he wasn't very approving of their handiwork! I did spend all day at Willen and I helped them to bath and feed him.
I don't think that I would have admitted to myself at the time that I needed help. Unfortunately, I endured some pretty nasty comments from some people when I agreed to him going into The Willen Hospice. What those people didn't seem to realise is that Simon had been ill since 1997. That is a long time to have been an active and constant support.
Also, our eldest child, Abi, wasn't coping too well with the strain either, although Ricki was obviously very young and didn't remember a lot of it.
Simon was actually at Willen Hospice three months to the day he died. It was good of them to have taken him under the circumstances. They were very flexible about visitors, even allowing both Barry Briggs and Terry Russell to take him out. Terry was actually with us in Australia when we had news that the tumour had started to grow back again.
Terry arranged for Simon and I, plus my parents, to visit Coventry Speedway for the 2000

World Team Cup Final. By now Simon was disfigured and a lot of people found difficulty in approaching us. Terry was involved in the meeting in his role as Chairman of the BSPA. He and his brother started to carry Simon up to the seats but halfway through Simon started pointing that he wanted to go to the toilet. I was thinking: 'How do I manage this? I can't move him.' I had to run and find Terry's other brother, Ronnie, who came and helped them carry Simon to the loo. The Russell brothers were absolutely fabulous to us that day.

One day, Terry came to the hospice in his new Mercedes with all the extras, and Simon thought that this was the business! Simon had a lot to do with Terry over the years, especially when discussing the concept of the team suits that are now commonplace in the Elite League.

Back at The Willen, Simon had developed the habit of saying: 'F***ing Hell!' and 'Jesus Christ!' whenever the vicar came to visit. Simon is fondly remembered for the fact that if anybody came down the corridor he would presume that they were coming to see him and shout out to them, loudly and clearly: 'F****** Hell! F****** Hell!'

He was also fond of going down to the smoking room, which I couldn't stand. So he had to wait until my Mum came in at 2pm and as soon as he saw her he would try to jump out of his chair. He couldn't move but he could shuffle. She would say: 'Come on then' and push him down there in his wheelchair, so that he could have a cigarette.

When someone came to visit him and he found it intrusive – some fans did turn up unannounced – he would look at me, wink and pretend that he'd gone to sleep. This gave me the opportunity to apologise for him feeling so tired and ask them to leave. So in many respects he did know what he was doing and he could be so funny with it.

Simon actually had more visitors, two weeks before he died, after Oxford's local radio station, Fox FM, mistakenly announced his death on air one morning. Their blunder caused quite a knock-on effect, because somebody posted the misinformation on the internet and news spread world-wide. Sympathy cards and flowers even began to arrive!

More immediately, I took a call from Julian who was absolutely distraught because he thought that I hadn't rung to tell him of Simon's apparent passing. Of course, I didn't have a clue what he was talking about. Then I started to panic, thinking that the hospice hadn't been able to get hold of me and that perhaps he had really died.

I think that the whole confused situation shocked a lot of people who had wanted to see him but were scared to. Then they realised that they might not have the chance to see him again, so Simon had a different set of visitors from the sport within the next week.

Lots of people, however, still wanted to remember him as he was and did not visit. I understand it now but I found it hurtful at the time.

Just before Simon passed away it was almost as if he was determined to hang on for certain special occasions. Ricki's third birthday was at the end of October, soon after Simon's 40th. This time the party went on to 2am – in the hospice! Karl Maier, Simon's great friend and rival from the German longtrack scene, flew over for that one. We had our wedding anniversary at the beginning of November.

He had made it through a busy period for the family. Then I went in one night and Simon was suffering from what they call 'terminal agitation'. He really didn't know what he wanted – whether to lie down or sit up, or to be dressed or undressed. I begged them to do something, as it was distressing for everyone to see the state Simon was in. When you know what is going to happen, then you want it to be as quickly and painless as possible.

I put him to bed that night and for the first time since our trip to France the previous May, he uttered the words: 'I love you.'

They sedated him and I rang all the people who were closest to him. Julian, of course, plus Dickie Staff, Olli Tyrvainen, Paul and Simon Cross, Steve Brandon, Brett Walton and my parents. They came to say their goodbyes.

Two days later, on Wednesday, November 15 and exactly one month after his 40th birthday, Simon passed away with Brett, my Mum and myself beside him.

Not long after that conversation about how much he had done in his life, he told me:

'Do you know what? I want the biggest and best funeral ever!' He had a list of requests including a bike to be present and a selection of the music that he wanted played. Simon emphasised that he wanted the whole affair to be big and loud. That's what we tried to do and a lot of what happened that day was down to Simon's input.

We had a band and Rosco (Swindon promoter Alun Rossiter) even brought his disco! The reception was held at the National Hockey Stadium in Milton Keynes, simply because they had the largest function room available locally.

The whole day was surreal and I expected Simon to walk in at any minute with a big grin on his face. It was almost as if it was *his* party.

I remember that before we left for the funeral, I was so nervous because I knew that some people would criticise the kind of music that had been chosen. I actually said to my Mum that I didn't want to go and I really don't know how I got through it. I made a speech thanking everyone for attending but can't actually remember giving it.

It was, though, a hell of a send-off and one of which Simon would have been proud.

A Service of Thanksgiving
for the life of

SIMON ANTONY WIGG

15/10/1960 - 15/11/2000

Church of Christ the Cornerstone
Central Milton Keynes

Monday 27th November 2000 at 2.00 PM

Simon taught me that life moves on. Today I'm married to Pat with Abigail and Ricki having a new sister, Libby, born in March 2005. Pat played in my Dad's football team in Milton Keynes for a few years and they were close. Pat's father, David, was chairman of the football club that employed my Dad, so we had known of each other for quite a few years.

Simon was in the hospice at the same time as Pat's father, who, coincidentally, was in the next room. Pat and I were visiting the hospice at the same time but only spoke about three or four times during that period.

The week that Simon passed away, I also lost a male friend in a car crash and Pat's father died. So from having never previously

Simon / Daddy

If tears could build a stairway
And heartaches make a lane
We would walk straight up to heaven
And bring you home again.

We all love you and miss you now and forever.

Charlie, Abigail and Ricki

Charlie, Abi and Ricki with Libby – the latest addition to the family in 2005.

been to a funeral in my life, sadly I attended three in one week.

It was six months later that Pat and I met again at a football presentation – I was there with Mum and Dad while Pat was on his own having finished a long-term relationship. We sat at the same table but never spoke to each other all evening! We bumped into each other a few months later. We spent a lot of time talking about Simon, Pat's father and how cruel life can be. I hadn't really spoken to anybody like this and realised that we had a lot in common.

We decided that we would like to see each other but I wasn't interested in taking it any further unless it was long-term. I had two children to think of and I didn't want anyone coming into their lives, only to drift away again. It wasn't something that I wanted for myself either.

Pat helped me through a lot of difficult times. There were a lot of tears and tissues, but eventually we were married a year to the day that we first sat down and talked heart-to-heart. The children took to Pat so well and they now had a male in their life again. I felt that was especially important for Ricki. Sadly, he didn't have the play-fighting and fun he has with Pat with Simon, because Ricki was still very young when Simon's illness struck. So Ricki thought this was fantastic.

Now Ricki talks about his 'Daddy Simon', who is in Heaven, and his 'Daddy Pat', who is with us today.

Julian and his family are very supportive of me and the children. Simon's brother and I have shared tears in private since Simon has gone, and Pat is so understanding about this.

Libby is the positive sign of my new life and I know that Simon would truly want me to be happy.

The Willen Hospice, where Simon's family were very grateful for all the loving care he received throughout his final weeks and days.

Tributes

How others remember Simon Wigg

Simon's good friend, former Radio One DJ Adrian Juste, at the opening of the Crazy Coyote restaurant that Wiggy and Kai Niemi owned in Milton Keynes.

FAMILY

Abigail Wigg on 'Daddy Simon'

I HAD my eleventh birthday on June 14, 2005 but I can remember when I was a five-years-old in Australia. Every morning Daddy would get up, then wake me up and we used to go for bike rides for a couple of hours. On weekdays, we didn't walk to nursery but took a bike ride instead. Sometimes we were late and we didn't stop. Daddy had bundles of energy and he would never stop anyway, so I used to get worn out! Once I knew my way to nursery, we would have races. I had my own little bike and enjoyed these rides – pedalling along really fast was great fun. I also noticed that I was getting browner and I like having a tan.

I remember getting a Barbie doll from Daddy Simon and a cat called 'Tiger', which I really liked. He was grey with little white stripes all over his face. 'Tiger' kept on jumping up and walking on his back legs. That was funny.

We also had a fishpond where we'd sit down and watch the fish go round. It was lovely, a triangular shape, surrounded by big flowers. I also remember looking out of a window at the blue jelly fish which had been washed up on the shore. There were also crabs with big heads and we used to go along and pick them up by their heads and put them in a bucket.

I used to love to go to speedway meetings. I got to ride around on the big truck at the end of meetings at King's Lynn and stood on the rostrum in Germany. I was at King's Lynn standing on a platform near the pits, watching Daddy race into the corner, when shale flew off his back wheel and split my lip. It was a big cut and I've still got a scar there now. Daddy came off the track and I was in the ambulance! On the victory parade I used to sit on his lap when I was quite young but as I got older I sat beside him.

Simon having fun with baby Abi.

I used to make friends at the speedway. I had this one friend who was a boy and he brought his little model motorbikes when I went to King's Lynn. We used our fingers to make the shapes of tracks.

When I travelled around Australia to watch the racing, I'm told that I used to make the fans look round at me because I knew that Daddy Simon rode in green – but so did Shane Parker and I was calling out: 'Daddy! Daddy!' to him as well. So everybody was confused but the other riders thought it was very funny.

Shane Parker became one of my favourite riders. I remember that we visited him and Angie and their little girl. I also knew Jason Crump and Greg Hancock and liked them very much.

I still go to speedway at Oxford with Pete and Penny Seaton, who are kind enough to let me take my friend, Sarah. My favourite rider now is Nicki Pedersen. We have fun bets on the speedway on television and I always choose Nicki or Crumpie to win. Nicki is very entertaining and when I went to watch him at Oxford one night, he got off his bike after one race and had a fight, which we rushed to watch.

I've got a collage in my room of Daddy Simon and loads of pictures of him holding me as a baby with me wearing my 'Number One Dad' hat.

He wasn't like the other dads who just sit around and watch football on television. He wasn't the sort who, if you said that you wanted to go out to play, would tell you 'perhaps later.' If you wanted to play tennis or go in the paddling pool, he would come out and join in. We also had lots of play-fights, rolling around on the ground. He used to let Ricki and I ride him like a horse despite our weight. He was great fun.

I have a baby sister now. She is cute and she laughs a lot. I was looking forward to having a sister. One day I will be able to help her with her hair when she is getting ready for nursery in the morning. I look forward to teaching her dance routines and letting her borrow my clothes. When Ricki was told that he was having a sister he shouted: 'Oh no. Not a girl!'

Libby and I already have a good relationship. When she wakes up after a sleep, I get her bouncer and her teddy – I've just bought her a new one – then I put her in her bouncer and we watch TV together.

Alexz Wigg on 'Uncle Simon'

UNCLE Simon and I didn't really have any good chats because I was only riding trials for enjoyment when I was a child. I had my eleventh birthday only four days before he died. I did travel with him towards the end of his racing career, though.

I remember going to Skegness with him in the big motorhome for a grasstrack meeting. He was leading in the final and dropped it on the last corner. He wasn't too happy, I recall. On the way home he was still chatty and bubbly with me but he wasn't impressed with himself.

I went to an Ace of Aces meeting with him as well. I remember that he made a fantastic start – it was textbook, it couldn't have been better and he led from start to finish. I was lying on the top of the van watching the racing and him in particular. When he won this feeling of emotion came over me. I started shouting: 'Yes! Yes!' and my arms were shaking. To watch someone that you were close to win an event – it was awesome. I was about eight at the time, so I remember the downs and the ups with Uncle Simon. The down was obviously Skegness and the up was him winning the prestige Ace of Aces.

I was aware that he was a very good all round motorcyclist. My Dad, Julian, explained that his younger brother was a World Champion who won many titles. I've got loads of videos of him racing when he was younger, including footage of him riding speedway at Oxford and Cradley Heath in the 80s and from when he won his first World Longtack title, in Denmark – it's nice to watch old films of him in action. Now that I'm into competition myself as a trials rider, I really do appreciate what went into his reaching the very top. Of course, it would be great if he was still here, to offer me extra advice and input.

I have always been interested in the sports that my father and uncle took part in. Actually, I originally wanted to do moto-cross too when I was quite young but Dad thought better of it. He knew all about injuries as, between him and Uncle Simon, I don't think there was a bone that hadn't been broken. Dad preferred that I took up something more steady. When I started to take an interest in trials and wanted to ride more frequently, that's when it picked up and we've carried on with that. I now enjoy it so much.

Trials is a very skilful motorcycle discipline and I think that if you can ride a trials bike well, then you can ride anything well. Trials riding teaches you balance and throttle control – like when to bring in the power and when not to. You really have to feel for the grip – you can't just rely on the power to get you up a bigger step. You have to put all your body into it and consider so many things at once. After a while it becomes second nature,

Preparation is also important and I've picked up on my uncle's example in this respect. He understood how a bike worked and I have to do that too.

From Uncle Simon's example, I know that it is not going to be an easy ride to the top. I have been lucky enough to observe a World Championship in my sport and you can only dream of doing it. Uncle Simon once had that dream and progressed to achieve it. Progression is coming with me but that makes you realise how much more there is to do. I'm the European Champion for the under-16 category and I won that title when I was 14 – it's a stepping-stone really. Luckily, I hate losing at anything, be it tiddlywinks or school sports.

Even with the support that I've received it, it has taken me time to get to the stage I'm at now. I have to concentrate on being a trials rider even though I have been tempted to have a go at speedway. I know people want me to convert because of what Uncle Simon did and was. However, I don't know how long it would take me to get good at speedway. Also, I am not going to be the next Simon Wigg and he would be a hell of an example to equal, especially having won five World Longtrack Championships. If he had lived there would be no one better for me to turn to for advice. I'm only sad that we didn't get to know each other well. He had been there and done it and I'm so sorry that I can't access his knowledge.

My aspiration is to become the World Champion in my chosen sport. It would be a remarkable family double. It's a brilliant challenge for me to match him but in another motorcycle discipline. So similar but so different. You need a factory to take you on for ultimate success in my sport, whereas Uncle Simon had to do it as an individual.

My conclusion of Uncle Simon, who I didn't get to see as much as I would have liked because of his schedule and then his illness, is that there were two sides to him. He could be the funny and relaxed person but, come race day, he could turn it on and be a true professional. When he was riding he seemed able to cut it all off and be very switched on. And at the end of a race meeting he could return to normal.

Alexz is now a European champion trials rider.

SPEEDWAY WORLD CHAMPIONS

Barry Briggs MBE

SIMON was an arch-rival of my son, Tony, on the grasstrack scene in the late 70s, so I couldn't help but notice him. At that time he had no inclination to take up speedway, this would only happen a few years later.

Simon basically went to Weymouth to help improve his grasstrack, although he was good at speedway from the off. In both sports, he had good equipment and presented himself well.

Essentially Simon was a motorcyclist and didn't treat racing as just a living – he loved the whole scene. However, it's my opinion that his grasstrack background actually hindered him reaching the top in speedway. You need more precision as a speedway rider than you do as a grasstrack rider – the grasstrack style is untidier.

The mutual love of motorcycling created a natural bond between the Wiggs and the Briggs. We always got on well and I took trips with Simon abroad. World Championships were always the most interesting for me, because I understood what was required – and not just on the bike. Simon had a good support team and was one of the first riders to get his act together in that way.

He also understood how important the mental attitude was towards winning, yet he could be philosophical in defeat. I've been with him at a World Longtrack Final when he hasn't won it and Simon coped very well.

His relationship with Julian was an important part of this and in terms of his whole career. There are brothers and there are brothers, but Julian and Simon had a close relationship. Simon had someone he could discuss things with that he might not raise with others, while Julian knew the racing scene from his own racing days and is a very straightforward character. You only have to look at Alexz Wigg to see what an excellent input Julian provides as a senior member of the family, not only as a knowledgeable adviser. Alexz will make something of himself in the world of motorcycle trials. The lad is not only very talented but has an excellent attitude. So you observe Alexz and appreciate the benefit Simon enjoyed from having Julian as his closest adviser.

Simon was a real star and you saw that in Germany in particular. Wiggy knew how to make an entrance – last out of the pits gates usually – and the fans there loved him. He looked the part too and he had such a warm rapport with everyone. Simon was blessed with a great grin, so even if was p***** off occasionally, he still looked happy and welcoming. That's a great plus in life, being able to give other people a 'feel good' factor.

Briggo, Ivan Mauger and Simon before the 1984 World Final in Gothenburg, Sweden.

Simon also lived life to the full – and beyond. In my career, if I had a booking in Munich, for instance, I would turn up, perform, collect my money and go home. Simon was much broader than that. He'd phone up Tony and tell him that the snow looked good and invite Tony out on the ski-slopes with him. Wiggy was always active. He died young but lived twice the life of most.

His medical condition does make me think and I relate it to the fact that there are good mechanics and bad mechanics. The difference is, a bad mechanic tends to miss things that he should spot. And the medical profession is no different. It's understandable that we all have high expectations of doctors and I've been close to a harrowing death with my late wife June in recent years. I'm curious why Simon's real problem wasn't diagnosed earlier. Sometimes I find doctors can be insensitive to situations.

Which brings me to the difficult memories of Simon's last days. We loved Wiggy as a family and went to see him on a regular basis. I'm of a different generation to Simon but Tony and him had so much in common – even down to both breaking their necks in their racing careers!

I want to retain my better memories of Simon. For example, to see him race on the longtracks was very special.

As an ambassador for his sport, Simon was the English Bruce Penhall.

As a rider, Simon had pride in performance. He gave promoters and fans good value. He always set out to try.

As a person, Wiggy had that rare ability to return to the pits and switch from being competitive to friendly.

Wiggy was a great rider – but a great guy, too.

Peter Collins MBE

I HAD broken into the German scene at a time when it was very competitive. Simon was coming along as a younger rider and spending a great deal of money on tuning. In a sense he was trying to buy success and I became concerned for him given the amount he was investing. However, in the long term, it proved worthwhile, as his many titles show.

His work rate and dedication were exceptional, especially the fitness regime. He was definitely more Briggo than PC in that respect! I relied on regular racing and rest before meetings to keep myself sharp. Simon was the very opposite but it worked for him. He was also consistent with a good diet and knew his weight at all times. Me – I kept away from the scales!

Having first got to know Simon from his early days in Germany, we were later matched up for a room-share on one of Ivan Mauger's Australian tours. Simon would be up at 6am, pull on his shorts and set off for a 10-mile run. I'd still be in bed at 9am. He would always be saying to me: 'What are we doing today?' Simon couldn't sit still. He wanted to be active. In fact, he was hyperactive and that carried into his racing to good effect. He would be off karting or water ski-ing or powerboat racing. I would sometimes tag along but Simon was the instigator and organiser.

From the time Simon opened his eyes in the morning to the time that he fell asleep at night, he was always on the go. He packed twice as much into one day than most others manage in two. Even though it is no comfort to his family that he died at 40, Simon lived a very full life in his short years.

He was so professional too. With Germany as a second home, Simon took the trouble to learn German and spoke the language fluently a lot quicker than I'd managed. Most riders didn't even make the effort.

PC and Wiggy watching from the pits.

When Ivan was trying to expand the Australian and New Zealand longtrack scene he imported Simon. Wiggy was technically way ahead of the other riders with road racing seats, spoilers, fairings, etc, and he was way ahead on the track, too. Unbeatable.

Simon's ambitions were rooted in his being able to travel around with Julian on the grasstrack scene as a kid. It was an insight into a magnificent era for grasstrack and longtrack rather than speedway. There was a reverse symmetry with our respective careers. I was a speedway rider first and foremost and turned my hand to the continental grasstrack and long-track scene. I won the speedway World Championship (1976) but my peak in longtrack racing was as World number two. Simon became World Longtrack Champion five times and his speedway peak was as World number two.

Although I've highlighted Simon's focus and dedication, and would describe him as a man on a mission, he was not at all boring. He was great company and full of fun. He had a particular thing about funny jokes, which cracked him up! Among my favourite tales is the time I reversed the trend with Simon, who was a serial prankster. We were both booked at the Western Winner grasstrack in the early 80s. I was riding at Belle Vue on the Saturday night, so it was the early hours of Sunday morning when my mechanic, Rob, and I arrived at the circuit. Simon was fast asleep in a single camping tent that he had brought along.

Rob and myself engaged in a very loud conversation next to Simon's tent, on the premise that we were going to hitch his tent to our vehicle and drive off. Suddenly there was this scratching and rustling from inside the tent. Then Wiggy emerged in just his underpants, shouting and waving, and proceeding to chase us across the field. He had been convinced that he was in imminent peril!

Jason Crump

IT was during Simon's earliest speedway days, at Weymouth in the early 80s, that I first related to him. My grandfather, Neil Street, was the Wildcats' team manager at the time and to me – a kid of seven or eight years of age – Wiggy stood out in his bright green leathers. I know my grandad rated Simon very highly, he was a regular topic of conversation in the Crump family.

I got to know Simon personally and we were very good friends once he became a very frequent visitor to Australia. I always admired him for the way he presented himself, his immaculate machinery and his colourful appearance. He made time to talk to everybody – even me, despite the fact that I used to pester him in the pits!

Whether he was enjoying water skiing on a lake in the Australia sunshine or freezing at Oxford Speedway on a cold night in October, Simon always looked pretty happy with that trademark smile of his.

He was deadly serious when it came to winning the World Longtrack Championship, though, and I never did manage to get to grips with that form of motorcycle sport. I was thrown in at the deep end really, competing initially with greats like Simon, Egon Müller, Karl Maier and Gerd Riss. I was out of my depth against them and I think they found it quite amusing when I messed up.

I did get my own back on Simon one day, however, when we raced against each other in a grasstrack at Nandlestadt, Germany. This time, as on a number of other occasions, Simon, Donkey, Simon's mechanic Brett, my father and myself travelled together to the Bavarian meeting in Wiggy's motor home.

While Donkey and I had just the one bike and one spare back wheel each, Wiggy took with him three bikes, 25 spare wheels and around 50 sets of shocks! Anyway, I'd finished second, third and then last in a couple of races before winning my last two and the semi-final. I had got my act together and was confident going into the final.

Just before the final, Simon came up to me and asked what gearing I had on. It was ironic, because I'd remember, a couple of years earlier, being at the same longtrack meeting as Simon and asking him what gear I should use. He'd tell me, but in a jokey sort of way, and it turned out to be a couple of teeth out from the gear he really had on, which made the bike that little bit harder for me to ride.

So when the chance came for me to dupe him in the same way, I took it. I told him I was pulling some crazy gear compared to what I really had for that particular final race – it was probably as much as five teeth out! The result was that Simon's bike was damn near unrideable.

Wiggy looking unimpressed with Jason's slogan.

We were about half way home when we stopped off for a couple of beers. It was then that I confessed to Simon what I'd done in giving him the wrong gearing information and he saw the funny side of it. He realised that I rarely got the chance to put one over on him and didn't blame me for taking the opportunity.

Aside from what he achieved in Europe, Simon also did a lot for David Tapp's series in Australia and I don't think people fully appreciate how much Simon did for the sport in Oz. It's hard to say that he made the biggest impact of any English speedway rider in my country, because Nigel Boocock also did an awful lot back home over a very long period, but Wiggy is right up there as one of Australia's finest imports. He certainly made the biggest impact of his era. He was like an American-Englishman, someone who oozed charisma.

I saw a lot of Simon socially and he was always great company, fun to be with. When I moved into Troy Butler's house near Northampton in 1996, Simon and Charlie were very helpful to me, a great support.

That same year they threw a surprise 21st birthday party for me at their place. Typically, Wiggy had arranged for the unexpected visit of the biggest Fat-o-gram I've ever seen! There were regular parties over at Simon's house – we shared great times together.

There are still days now when I get out of bed and think of Wiggy. The undying image I have of him is standing on parade at the World Longtrack Final. He was one of the best all round motorcyclists we've had and the riders who can successfully combine speedway and longtrack today are very few and far between.

I had trouble coping with Simon's deteriorating illness. Although I went to the house to see him with Steve Brandon, I couldn't face going to the hospice. He wasn't the same guy I knew and I didn't want to remember him that way.

But Wiggy will always be in my thoughts. On the wall of my garage hangs the plaque I received for appearing in the Simon Wigg Memorial Yeovil Traders grasstrack meeting in 2001. I look at it every day and think of him.

Erik Gundersen

I FIRST met Simon at a grasstrack meeting in Germany, when I accompanied the late Kristian Praestbro. We all headed back to England together and, being a similar age, Simon and I hit it off immediately.

I saw him around the Continental grasstracks after that but then Peter Adams pulled off a masterstroke and convinced Simon to move up to the British League with my team, Cradley Heath, in 1983. By now Simon was a top rider in the National League at Weymouth and it was a good career move for him. He was an immediate success and blended well into what proved a very strong team. We were all young guys at Cradley at the time and we had great fun together. The spirit in the dressing room was very good.

I had a particular game going on with Simon during that season – we used to spy on each other's bikes and then see who could come up with the latest gimmick for their equipment. It was quite competitive but it was a laugh at the same time. Simon was always full of ideas but didn't mind copying some of mine either!

As he became more immersed in the German racing scene, so he began to absorb ideas on presentation and PR. He was particularly observant of how Egon Müller would work to enhance his profile outside of the sport and attract TV coverage. Simon also looked at how the American riders presented themselves. For an English rider he became exceptional and began to appeal

Fuels
GTS
GM

There was usually fun in the pits when Simon and Erik Gundersen got together.

to both the public and the media.

Simon made his World Final debut at Gothenburg in 1984 and as a contender for the world crown myself, I knew that he had the ability to be a danger. Not only was he capable of beating me in a race, but I saw that he had the potential and the ambition to actually win the meeting. In the final analysis, I took my first world title and Simon finished a very creditable sixth.

I give him full praise for becoming 'top dog' on the longtrack scene when the competition was so rich. Karl Maier, Egon Müller and Alois Wiesbock were very tough to beat but he did it. He adapted very well from his grasstrack background and his aggressive style, together with a natural talent, meant that Simon Wigg was the man to beat.

It should be remembered that he won a hell of lot of meetings against top class fields. He also had a first class support team with Julian Wigg and the late Jürgen Goldstein, backed by an excellent working relationship with Hans Zierk, who provided his engines.

As a personality, he took Germany by storm. He was a true English gentleman, popular with fans, sponsors and tuners alike. Although you could tell when not to approach him, he would normally speak to anybody. He could communicate in a friendly manner with kids and use the correct way to talk to the top brass of the FIM, usually in the same breath. Simon was always respectful and became an ambassador for his country as well as his chosen sports. He could socialise but his behaviour was always appropriate. I never saw him drunk.

His life was 'full gas' on and off the track. Simon did have a lot of pressure to cope with and he would work it through himself. There was a lot of expectation surrounding him and a heavy workload on his shoulders.

We saw a lot of each other in England over the years. Simon would come and visit me in Tamworth or I would go down to the Old Stables at Middle Claydon. We would spend hours talking about equipment and also how to take speedway forward.

Our friendship didn't prevent us from racing very hard against each other on the track. Cradley versus Oxford matches were always highly competitive anyway. Although he was a tough competitor, Simon always left you room. He was very fast and a real handful. We had many races in our career but we could finish every race on a handshake. We often went to meetings abroad together, flying from either Heathrow or the East Midlands Airport. We were rivals in the pits but travelling companions, too.

In that context, one of my favourite tales of this period concerns Simon's diplomatic skills and my rivalry with Hans Nielsen. After one match involving Cradley and Oxford, Hans, Simon and myself were booked to ride in an Easter meeting in Germany, with Simon having made all the arrangements.

At that time Hans and I were daggers drawn – there was absolutely no conversation between us. On the flight out, Simon obviously sat in the middle of us and spoke to each of us in turn. In Germany the meeting was washed out and so we searched out our hotel. There was one single room and one twin room reserved for us and Simon had decided to put Hans and myself in together – even though there were obvious alternative options! So Hans and I were forced to communicate as we unpacked.

Then Simon took us out for a meal and suddenly the ice between my fellow Dane and me began to thaw. By the end of a great evening Simon had got us back on good terms with each other. Simon had obviously been on a mission and he had succeeded.

I think that Simon Wigg's profile emerged at just the right time for speedway. With Bruce Penhall retiring and Kenny Carter taking his own life, there were a lot of negatives around in the early 80s but Simon's presence lifted the scene again.

His fancy dress parties were a factor in this and I went to all of them when I was fit. There would be up to 500 people present and they raised a lot of money for the Speedway Riders' Benevolent Fund. This was partly due to Simon's good heart and also the fact that he wanted to keep busy – he *never* wasted time.

Although he went to Australia in the winter to unwind, he still kept fit by racing and working out. He did work on his strength for the grasstracks in Germany, for they could be rough and bumpy. I've seen him turn through corners on those types of tracks in Germany as smoothly as if he were riding at Cradley. Simon put a lot of effort into various aspects of his preparation. It was a sign of his mental strength that he could keep driving himself year after year.

The top German guys were in training, too. They sought a perfect combination of weight for bike and rider, so Simon also became very accurate in his weight management. In fact he became accurate with everything – even down to the amount of Loctite applied to a screw on a mudguard.

He was 110 per cent about everything and was always searching for new ways to improve. I was amazed by his great energy – not only in coping with his constant trips back and forwards in Europe, but getting involved in other projects. His opening of the Crazy Coyote restaurant in Northampton would be a prime example – how did he manage to find time to do it, especially as he was never half-hearted about anything that he took on? It's no wonder that most of what Simon tackled proved successful.

I won the World Longtrack Championship twice but only rode about five longtrack meetings in the preceding part of the season. Simon rode every Sunday – and bear in mind that speedway and longtrack racing can conflict with each other if you're not careful. Simon's ability to adapt was *the* difference and why he was that much more successful than myself.

After my serious accident at Bradford in 1989, Simon was a great support to my wife Helle. When I was well enough to receive visitors, Simon's time with me would lift my spirits.

I kept in touch with him once we settled back in Denmark and after his first operation I met up with him at a Grand Prix in Vojens. I last saw him at a Grand Prix at Linkopping, when Olli Tyrvainen brought him over to Sweden. It was very upsetting to see the deterioration in his condition. But his spirit shone through the misery and the pain that he must have been suffering. That night he made the effort to get around to everyone. It was as if it was his farewell tour.

Simon was a great team-mate and I so enjoyed being on track with him when we were paired together at Cradley, for you knew exactly where he was. He was a fair rival, too.

Above all, Simon Wigg was a positive human being whom I made friends with when I was 18 and who still remains strong in my memory today.

Celebrating Bradford's 1991 KO Cup victory with Gary Havelock.

Gary Havelock

SIMON Wigg was the complete package. The way he conducted himself . . . so neat and professional, everything co-ordinated and meticulous. He had such a positive image and was always fun to be around!

If I had a choice of either living Simon's life or living until 80 as a boring b****** . . . well, there's no contest.

I was quite young when I broke into the England squad following my move up from Middlesbrough to Bradford, so guys like Simon and Jeremy Doncaster were quite a few years older than me. In those days we rode a lot more as a team abroad in Test matches, World Team Cup qualifiers and pairs events, whereas today we tend to ride abroad much more as an individual. So I spent a lot of time away with the squad, even going to America for the World Team Cup in 1988.

Simon was normally a great ambassador and got on with everybody. He did have his moments, however. On one World Team Cup trip to Prague, I remember coming out of the lift door at our hotel and seeing some bloke with his knee on Simon's throat while punching him at the same time. I dragged the guy off and pushed Simon into the lift. It appeared Simon had been trying to sort out a confrontation and it all ended up in a massive brawl. I rescued him, when he was supposed to be keeping an eye on me!

The only other time I witnessed anything like it with Simon was in Australia once. I was on a Lions tour and Simon was on holiday and not part of our itinerary. We went sailing one night, with the Brits on one boat and a group of Aussies – and Simon – on another. As we reached land

The England Test team to face USA at Sheffield, 1984. Back row, l to r: Dave Jessup, Alan Grahame, Carl Glover (team manager), Neil Collins, Chris Morton. Front: Les Collins, Wiggy, Michael Lee, Peter Collins.

again, we became aware of an argument involving Simon and someone who I will just describe as a lippy Australian rider who now competes in the Premier League.

Once we'd landed, they ended up rolling around on the jetty in quite a punch-up. Everyone – and I mean everyone – was rooting for Simon! It was rare, though, for Wiggy to be involved in anything like that.

I was lucky enough to have been in dressing rooms with him for both England and Bradford. He always had a new joke to tell, which made everyone laugh. He also geed everyone up before a match. He was a great team man and a great team rider.

He was helpful, especially to younger riders, while I also appreciated his time and advice. When I became World Champion in 1992, the attitude of some riders towards me changed in a negative way, but not Simon. He was pleased for me and never changed.

In the course of a career it is inevitable that there will be some team-mates you get on and others you don't. There can be friction but this never happened with Simon.

I also enjoyed his company in a different way. In the early 90s, when I was at the top, the sport was going through a fallow period in terms of profile and attendances. Simon would always want to chat about how the sport could be improved. He had real vision and I enjoyed listening to him.

My greatest bond with him? Simon was proud to be British and he was, indeed, a great Briton.

Michael Lee

I WENT to a few grasstracks with Wiggy when I was banned from speedway. Then, later, I was helping Steve Johnston with his engines at the time and Wiggy also looked out for Johnno. Simon got Johnno into the 1996 European Grasstrack Championships and we teamed up, although I didn't know Wiggy that well at the time.

He had the big Wulfsport transporter and the guy was a total professional and kind of opened my eyes in a way. He was the first to have the big motorhome and Tony Rickardsson has taken Simon's ideas to the next stage.

Man . . . Wiggy was a character! He wasn't the best speedway rider in the world – and Wiggy would tell you that himself if he was here – but he was a great grasstracker.

I was always organised when I was racing and it surprised me when I first saw Wiggy's set-up just how totally organised he was, too. I went down to Wiggy's place and I hadn't seen anything like it since our own set-up. He had all his bikes lined up and he said he remembered seeing the same scene pictured in my old workshops, so we had a giggle about that.

In a way, Wiggy was probably too big for British speedway. He was a bit like myself in that he wanted speedway to progress and although he would make his own progression without help from others, he badly wanted to drag the sport forwards with him. He was able to do that in Germany, which is why the country was so important to him. They permitted him to become a star in their country and he really was a superstar in Germany. Whereas here in England, the authorities didn't want big stars or personalities – it was almost as if the stars were suppressed out of it. A lot of the big names had already drifted out of speedway before Simon really came on the scene. Bruce Penhall had retired, I'd been punished and Kenny Carter had done his thing. A number of the biggest names had gone. Suddenly, speedway was an unheard of sport – not on TV, not written about in the press and crowds everywhere were dwindling.

Wiggy came along and tried to bring it back and he did his best. It was hard for him to do because he wasn't a natural speedway rider, but he worked hard at it and became successful.

But at longtrack and grasstrack, the geezer was on fire.

In Germany, when Wiggy arrived, the crowd went mental. Everyone waited for him to appear at the track. I didn't realise just quite how big Wiggy was in Germany until I saw the crowd surrounding his van at a meeting out there one day. He was completely mobbed and I always jokingly called him 'Herr Wigg' after that!

I was the first Englishman to win the World Longtrack Final – at Gornja Radgona in the old Yugoslavia in 1981, when it just all happened for me on the day. That achievement, which was a shock at the time, means more to me today than it did back then, so I can imagine what five world titles meant to Wiggy.

I last saw him when I was helping Johnno and all three of us met up at a grasstrack meeting in France. It was just so sad that he died so young.

Mark Loram

MY first season in speedway was 1987, as a 16-year-old at Hackney. Simon was joining on loan from Oxford as our number one. Now I knew the grasstrack scene and recognised that in a minority sport in the UK, Simon was a big fish in a small pond.

He was a superstar as far as I was concerned and my hero as a kid. So as a youngster trying to make a go of British League racing, I would have looked up to my team's top rider but Simon had a real presence about him, too.

Wiggy with the then 16-year-old Mark Loram (right) and another Hackney team-mate, Randy Green, in 1987.

As I discovered throughout that season, Simon could be quite frank in his opinions and advice if you sought it. He would tell you where you were going wrong and he would tell you where you were going right, but come straight to the point. You knew exactly where you stood with him. So I listened and benefited. That was important to my career.

Not that he couldn't be fun to be with. I used to really laugh at his many jokes as they appealed to my own sense of humour. He would always have a few beers with the boys too and mixed really well.

It was nearly a decade later that we became team-mates again. By this time I had also taken on a heavy schedule of speedway, grasstrack and longtrack commitments, so I competed against Simon regularly at home and abroad and also saw a lot of him socially.

In 1996, my club, Exeter, was looking for a support

rider for me at the top end of the team. Norrie Allen and I spoke to Simon and convinced him that Exeter was a track that would suit him, which was perfectly true and so it proved.

It was a strange adjustment for me to be his number one but we did settle down well as a team-riding duo whenever the chips were down in a match.

As a younger rider, Simon had arranged my first-ever rides in Slovenia. He was always striking deals with promoters in far-flung venues and I didn't mind that Simon was on a super-deal, much more lucrative than mine – the opportunity was always welcome.

Well, Simon was still at it when I was a senior rider – his 1996 trip to Togliatti in Russia, which he organised for the Exeter team, is the stuff of legend and well described by my team-mate, Graeme Gordon, elsewhere in this book.

By this time in his career Simon had achieved what he had prioritised – the World Longtrack Championship – and won it on five occasions. I was first and foremost a speedway rider who took on the other motorcycle disciplines. It has to be accepted that Simon was the best all-rounder of all-time.

I became World Speedway Champion (in 2000) because it was my priority and I was also pretty good at grasstrack and longtrack. Simon came at it from the opposite direction and he was outstanding at all of it. Whatever our personal decisions, it worked for both of us.

One common interest in our blood was the grasstrack scene. In this country we've lost the Ace of Aces and The Yeovil Traders as major meetings in recent years and that downward trend for the sport in the UK is of concern. Simon would have been capable of getting the big meetings going again – and, as ever, wanting us to ride for free! The big event at Marmande in France, with its lively, loud musical background, would have served as his model, I'm sure. Grasstrack racing in this country suffered more than it realises by his passing.

When Simon could no longer ride, I inherited the opportunity to work with Hans Zierk on my Continental diary and really appreciate the technical input of Simon over those previous years. I was able to relate this in person through a chance encounter in Australia in 1999. I was a guest at Ivan Mauger's home when Simon turned up on a visit. He was very upbeat about the state of his illness and though I did have doubts at the back of my mind – he did make me feel positive about the situation.

He was even talking about a comeback when he had his driving licence back. That was my last proper exchange with the Simon I knew. When I last saw him, it was at the British Final at Coventry, where he was in a wheelchair and in a sad state of deterioration.

Simon Wigg was a remarkable person. He could make moves that the rest of us would be reluctant to take. I am not a flamboyant person, so I really admire him for things like having the big motor home before anybody else, and for riding a speedway bike at 137mph along a runway at Bruntingthorpe airfield near Loughborough, for a publicity exercise in the mid-90s.

He was so switched on and not only a great all-round rider, but an all-round personality, too.

Simon goes for the gap between Mark Loram (left) and Piotr Protasiewicz at the Czech GP, 1997.

Ivan Mauger MBE OBE

THE World Longtrack Championship has never recovered from the loss of Wiggy. For 20 years, from 1970 onwards, the world's top dozen or so speedway riders rode in it and during that period there were also loads of world quality longtrack riders such as Egon Müller, Karl Maier, Marcel Gerhard, Alois Wiesbock, Wiggy and others.

Simon's departure from the scene coincided with Egon and Karl retiring and all these guys were personalities in their own right. But certainly, from when Wiggy appeared on the World longtrack scene in the mid-80s, it was him and Egon who were the major stars and both excellent showmen in their own right.

I knew Simon's brother, Julian, quite well from grasstracks in England and Europe and then Wiggy started coming over to the European grasstracks when he was about 17. We struck up a friendship almost immediately and I raced against Simon many times during the last five or six years of my own career, all over Europe, on longtracks and grasstracks.

During that period Simon often travelled to European meetings in my transporter. Most Fridays, my mechanic Norrie Allen would take my transporter from our base in Cheshire to the Continent and if Simon was in the same meeting, they usually teamed up and travelled together – at that time Wiggy was not doing too many speedway meetings in England. That was the beginning of our very close friendship that remained until Simon passed away.

Simon rode in most of my 30-year Jubilee speedway meetings in Europe and did the complete New Zealand and Australian series.

My daughter, Julie, brought my oldest two grandaughters, Josie and Sadie, over to New Zealand for my last few 30-year Jubilee series meetings. Josie and Sadie used to join in the swimming pool antics with all the guys but they really took to Wiggy with his big grin and bubbly personality. For years afterwards, the two of them, who really had no interest in speedway, used to look for his photo in speedway magazines that arrived at my place.

They were also concerned for his welfare. A few years later, after one of his World Longtrack Championship wins, I got a card from Wiggy that had his address printed on the outside, which read 'The Old Stables, Sandhill, Buckinghamshire.' Sadie, who was probably only about eight-years-old at that time, studied the address for quite a while and seemed concerned where Wiggy was living. She said: 'Grandad, now that Wiggy is World Champion, can't he live in the new stables?'

I'm sure that statement, coming from Sadie at such a young age, summed up our family's association and love for Wiggy in a few words.

When we settled on the Gold Coast, I soon began promoting the Australian Longtrack Grand Prix and also a series of International Golden Helmet Speedway Series and Wiggy rode for me in just about everyone of them up until the time that David Tapp introduced his speedway series. Tappy had good connections with television and was able to gain very good sponsorship for his series.

He used to call me quite regularly to seek advice and phone numbers of different rider, etc, and it was during one of the conversations that I told him that he really needed a very good English rider, because of the huge English population in Australia. I suggested Wiggy's name to him, because Simon was a great personality, a great rider and someone who could speak very eloquently on television interviews, on radio and to newspaper reporters.

Anyway, a short time later Wiggy called me from England to tell me that Tappy had called him to offer him a lot more money than I could ever pay him to do my longtracks. It was a measure of Wiggy's loyalty that he was still prepared to do my meetings and turn Tappy down. However, I was very impressed with the series that Tappy was putting together. I thought it would be very good for the Australian speedway scene, so I told Simon to take the money for a few years and, in the meantime, I will bring Egon Müller, Gerd Riss or somebody else over. Tappy's series only went for a few years before Wiggy rode in mine again.

I had known Simon as a rival racer, a travelling companion and as his promoter. I had known him as his manager and motivator. And I had even known him as a neighbour. But, most of all, I had known him as a friend.

There are so many stories, so many memories that I could fill the whole book. But throughout every aspect of knowing him so well, he was always perfect to deal with, and that included the

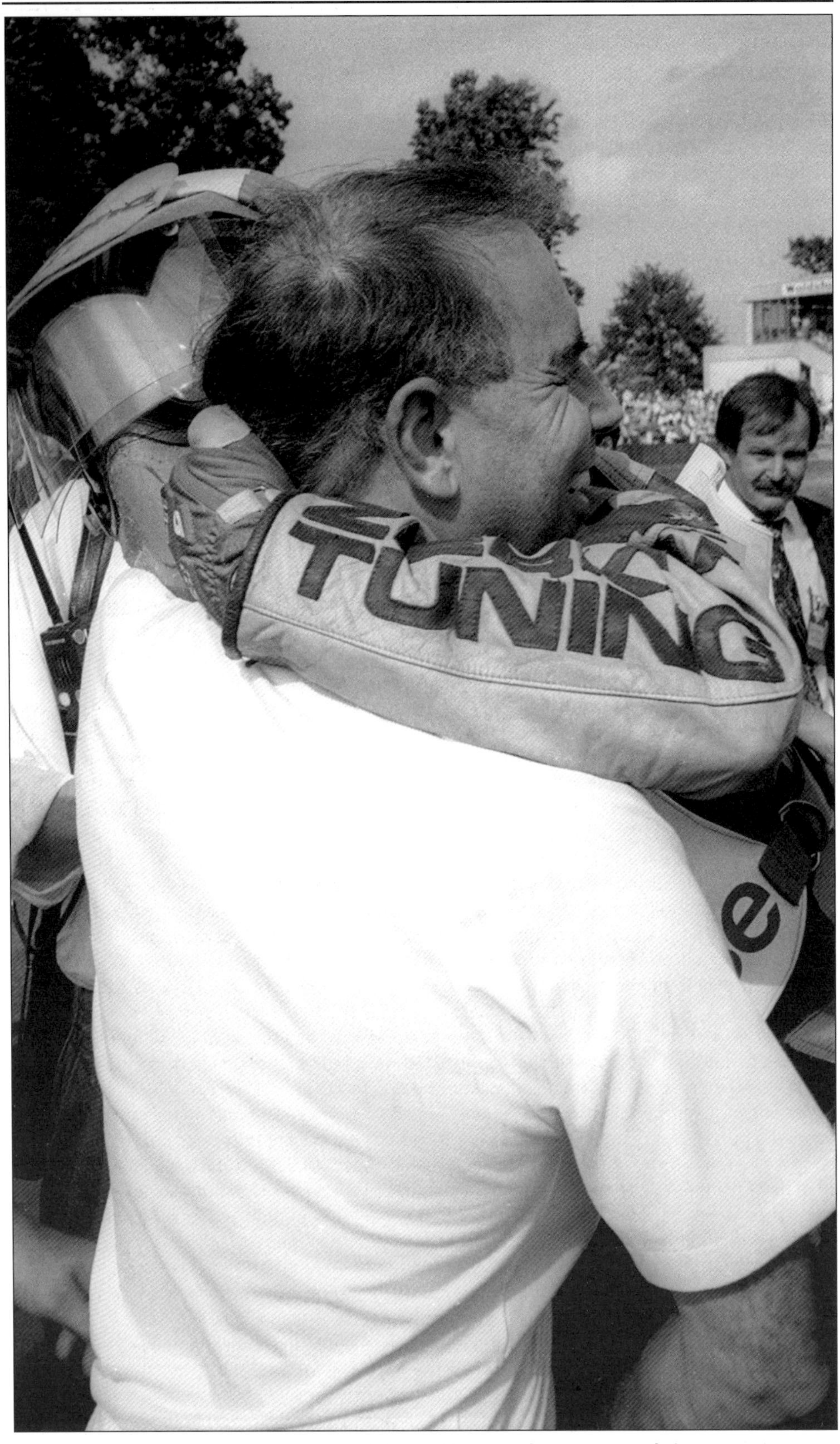

Simon and Ivan embrace after Wiggy retained the World Longtrack crown at Herxheim, 1990.

time I was heavily involved with him, helping him from the late 80s.

My last competitive meeting was in New Zealand in early 1986 and not long after that I began coaching Hans Nielsen on speedway and longtrack. Simon had been having an unusually lean spell and, in 1989, he asked me to help him, too.

In a three-year period he won the World Longtrack Championship twice and was second (to Nielsen) in the speedway World Final at Munich. I was proud of our association and Simon's complete trust in following out our game-plans.

He didn't question things. We agreed that I would always be the last one to speak before he went to the tapes – I'd have five seconds in which I was the last one to talk. He always kept to that and he'd do everything I told him to. It's satisfying when someone trusts you, does exactly what you have asked them to do – and goes on to win a World Championship.

I remember one particular World Longtrack Final when we were together at Pfarrkirchen, Germany in 1992. Having just come over from Australia two or three weeks before, I'd been to some longtracks and everything was going fine when we had a private test session in Muhldorf on the Tuesday. At that time I had a bad dose of the flu and was really struggling to concentrate.

At the Muhldorf test session we both rode each of the three bikes and we agreed not to discuss our personal feelings about each bike, or the change of set-ups, until we had finished at the end of the day. We both kept our own notebooks and used our own mechanics.

I had to make allowances when riding Simon's bikes, because Wiggy always had rear suspension settings much harder than I ever did. And although I was struggling to concentrate, my mechanics always knew my golden rule: whatever I tell them the instant I get off my bike at a test session, is what we write down, and it's what we stick to, because too many guys I know change their mind half-an-hour after a test session and you can't go back and replicate that. Too many of those riders ended up confused before big meetings.

Anyway, at the end of the day Wiggy and I both agreed which bikes were first, second and third choice. The next day, we dropped Wiggy at Munich Airport and off he went up to Sweden to do a league match, while his brother Julian, myself and the others went to Pfarrkirchen, where I stayed in bed recovering all the next day. During that day, Wiggy had called Julian and the others and completely changed everything around, so when I went to the workshop on the Friday morning I thought a bomb had gone off – all three bikes were in a million bits. Nothing was recognisable as a bike. Even the gear boxes had been taken out.

The official practice on Saturday was chaotic and the meeting went even worse. Wiggy missed the two-minute time allowance in his first race while he was changing bikes due to a refuelling rule that had been brought in that year, and then he touched the tapes. Things went from bad to worse and he ended up last.

So after the meeting we sat down, had a big talk about it and I reminded him that Ove Fundin came last in his first speedway World Final and won it the following year. I also reminded him that Egon Müller finished last in his first World Longtrack Final and won it the following year. Precedents had been set and things happened in threes, so we decided there and then that Wiggy could win it the following year, which he did.

There were never any half measures with Simon – if he did something, he'd go the whole way. I will never forget probably the last example of that driven approach he had, when he was living a few miles away from our home on the Gold Coast in Australia. By this time he couldn't drive and I told him I had a push-bike he could borrow and Simon said he would walk over to our place. Time went by and I got worried about him, so I thought I'd better drive around in case anything had happened.

And then this nose and great big grin came through the gate and there was Simon, looking as if he had come straight from the *Tour de France*! He had everything – the cycling shorts, cycling shirt, special shoes, helmet and the sunglasses! He had everything, including the bike.

Halfway between our two houses there is a bicycle shop and on his way over, Wiggy had stopped and bought not only a racing bike, but everything to go with it.

That was so typical of him and it is an abiding memory.

He was – 100 per cent – going to end up living in Australia and I'm glad that he did, albeit for such a brief period. We had so much fun together on jet-skis, racing each other, jumping over waves and generally being speedway riders off duty. We also had great times in New Zealand, where I also had jet-skis, especially during the Jubilee Series.

Quite often Simon's jet-ski used to be kept either on my boat ramp or in my boat shed and he would just come around to my place and off we would go at it, sometimes at six o'clock in the morning, especially in the early days of us living on the Gold Coast. Lots of other guys would come out with us, including Mike Farrell, Troy Butler, Mark Carlson and other local speedway boys, as well as some of the Aussie motocross guys.

There was a bit of competition jumping over the waves and it was also occasionally a bit dangerous. But lots of times, there was just Simon and me together. We'd go off on our jet-skis and then sit on one of the little bays or beaches and just talk about everything possible for the improvement of speedway and longtrack. We'd discuss bikes, equipment and the following season's World Championship rounds and where they would be, etc. We often made decisions at these times that we would carry out to the letter seven or eight months later at some longtrack in Europe. Sometimes we would be so engrossed and sit there for hours because the conversations were timeless. There were 100 different things to talk about and those were precious times and conversations.

Another abiding memory is of the last time I ever saw him, at the hospice in England.

After we had left him for the last time, just as we were about to leave in the car, my wife Raye said: 'I think Simon would like to see you on your own, Ivan, why don't you go back.'

I went in by myself and I gave him a big hug and told him: 'I've always loved you, Wiggy.' As clear as a bell, he said: 'I know that,' and he put both his arms around me in a big cuddle. It was a really private moment and in that instant he wasn't like how we had seen him for the months before – it was like the old Wiggy, when he was racing. It was something I will never, ever forget.

As I said earlier, there are many aspects of my friendship and association with Wiggy that I will never forget but one thing I am very grateful for is that both Charlie and Julian always realised that his heart was set on living in Australia and they both knew and appreciated the fact that Simon and I spent so much time out on the water together. A few months after Wiggy's funeral in England, Charlie and Julian and their families came over to the Gold Coast to have a memorial service at The Firth Memorial Chapel, Tonga Place, Parkwood, Queensland.

It was decided that Simon's ashes would be spread into the water and we had quite a function around at Wiggy's house. I'm not sure now how it came about but I was asked if I would perform this ceremony – and I have to say I was very, very proud that they thought of me – so we went down to the end of the jetty and I sprinkled them into the water. As it happened, the tide was just coming in, which I thought was just great – it signified to me that part of Simon would always remain in the area that he loved.

In the first Australian Longtrack Grand Prix that we did at Bathurst, I had TV cameras there and Wiggy was the star of the show. During afternoon filming, he did a beautiful wheelie all the way along the front straight. The sun was shining on him and, being such a very clear and spectacular clip, we used that action shot of Wiggy in all our television commercials for the longtracks from then on. After he died, I talked to both Charlie and Julian and my family and we all agreed that I should continue using that particular bit of film. So now I include that special sequence of footage in all my longtrack TV commercials. I'm sure it is the way Wiggy would like to be remembered – entertaining the crowd and giving his all!

Receiving last-minute advice from Ivan while mechanic Mick Day checks the bike.

Even when promoting the World Championships in New Zealand, I still manage to get that bit of film in somewhere on the TV commercials and it is a way of saying 'thank you, Wiggy' for your friendship to me personally, my family and for all the efforts you put in to riding in my speedway and longtrack meetings.

Egon Müller

WIGGY was a good friend of mine. When he came to Germany to ride he would stay with me, and I remember him coming to me and saying: 'I want to be World Champion.'

On one occasion he was sitting in my house studying photographs of me in action and asking me what I was doing and why I was doing it. I had won World Championships and he was determined to learn from me.

He went on all night like this. At 5am I said to him: 'Simon, it's five o'clock! I have to take you to the airport!'

He was a great asset to motorbike racing. When he was riding he was always 100 per cent professional in what he did.

From the moment he got up in the morning, all he thought about was how to go faster, how to be better and how to bring the sport to the public. He loved the sport and he wanted to find ways of bringing more people to come and watch it.

I was very pleased that he did because he worked hard for it and he deserved it.

Some people were very jealous of him but I could not understand that – what right did they have?

I rode against him many times and to start with – no problems – it was easy to beat him. But he listened and learned and got better and better so that it became very difficult to beat him and, of course, he went on to achieve his aim of being World Champion.

I said to him that if he concentrated on speedway, he *could* be World Champion, but that if he did too many longtrack meetings, it would adversely affect his speedway.

I think that if he had done more speedway, he would have been World Number One.

But he can be very proud at what he achieved, he was a credit to the sport.

Unfortunately I was not able to come over for the funeral, but I wish that I had.

Last meeting of two tracksport giants – Egon Müller and Simon.

Hans Nielsen

ALTHOUGH Oxford in 1984 was the first time that Simon and I rode together as teammates, with 1983 the first season that we competed against each other in the British League, it was in fact at Weymouth that I first became aware of him.

My team, Birmingham, went down there in an inter-league challenge in 1982 and I soon noticed this pacy, young Englishman.

When Simon signed for Cradley Heath we were both part of the Midlands speedway scene but a year later Northern Sports bought Oxford Stadium and wanted to put their team into the British League. They bought Simon and myself in the transfer market and thanks to the active social scene for supporters at Cowley, we were quickly able to get to know each other a whole lot better. You will have heard this from so many other sources, I am sure, but I was taken by his bubbly and happy personality.

Simon had these qualities and yet was dedicated to his career. Most times his focus was excellent but not always, in my opinion. He sometimes tried too hard and not just on track.

I used to take him to task for experimenting with his machinery during meetings when things were already going well for him on track.

My constant comment was: 'For Christ's sake, Simon, leave it alone!' He would have been better off spending time on analysing how to improve his riding style. I think that Simon would have benefited from having had the same arrangement that Bruce Penhall made with Eddie Bull. Eddie would set everything up and Bruce's role was to sit on the bikes and perform. With Julian Wigg being so knowledgeable and capable, that kind of set-up would have been possible for Simon too but I do accept that Simon had a genuine interest in the mechanical side of motorcycles – so mission impossible!

The early years at Oxford were a great time for everybody involved and we enjoyed tremendous success. Oxford Speedway employed two outstanding track curators, called John and Barry. Then the accountants cut their budget and, to their credit, the track guys refused to do half a job. The knock-on effect was that the Oxford track was by no means as good from that point onwards.

Hans and Wiggy signalling an historic collection of silverware at Oxford in 1985, with Simon adding the World Longtrack title to the British League, KO Cup and Midland Cup trophy haul.

Now it is obvious that Simon and myself were different personalities, so we had different ways of dealing with the situation. My preference was to keep quiet during the match, concentrate on the task in hand, then go and have a quiet – but pointed – word with the promotion afterwards.

Simon's reaction was to make an issue of it immediately.

Simon and Bernard Crapper were both larger-than-life characters and sometimes it all got very loud! It was good that Simon was his own man and wasn't afraid to complain but it affected his psychology. The fact that there was a bump on the first bend or a hole somewhere was at the front of his mind. In my opinion, in a sport where confidence is a key factor in performance, it is better to put potential problems right to the back of your mind. Simon was therefore prone to distraction before and during some meetings and this was likely to impact on his performance.

Simon also had an extra dimension to his brain and he was full of great ideas – plus some that were not so good! Sometimes I have wondered if his active mind, although an admirable quality, added to his distractions.

Friends . . . and sometimes rivals. Although they teamed up many times to steer Oxford Cheetahs to victory, Simon also enjoyed getting the better of Hans Nielsen at international level.

Obviously Simon's great priority was longtrack racing and a record of five World Championship titles is outstanding. Particularly for a British rider in a sport that has no base in the UK. Simon had natural speed and his mechanical preparation was first class. I did ride longtrack, too, and appreciate just how good Simon was at his favoured sport.

However, 1989 proved an outstanding year for Simon on the speedway front too. He finished runner-up to me in the World Final at Munich and this Oxford 1-2 meant a great homecoming for us at Cowley the next Friday. To have made the next step up to the top of the rostrum would have meant a different set of priorities for Simon and, in reality, it wasn't going to happen. Longtrack was his big passion and there was no way he would have put the sport aside, even for one season, to concentrate all his efforts on winning the speedway World Championship.

Away from our racing schedule we did spend some time together. I remember being in Australia on a tour with him and we would take a break and go off on moto-cross bikes for the day. Simon was great fun to be with and was a bundle of energy from daybreak to the time that his head hit the pillow at night. We also went for a ski-ing holiday in Austria, where Simon managed to guide us down the wrong slope and into . . . Switzerland! Despite not having passports on us, Simon managed to blag us back safely to base.

In Simon's later years Susanne and I were kept informed about his illness and monitored the situation with concern. I competed in his farewell meeting at Oxford in 1999 when the presumption was that epilepsy was the cause of his illness. This was bad enough in itself but then came news of the tumour and the operation.

Following Simon's second operation, Susanne and I went to visit him. We found it very hard to come to terms with his speech problems, in particular, as Simon was always so articulate. I knew when we left him that day that it was our final goodbye and I confess that it was very difficult for me.

The human memory, however, is marvellous in that it proves capable of selecting out the painful parts so that you can clearly remember the good bits.

On track, I like to remember his team-riding – not only with myself and our record of 5-1 heat wins, but with any team member. Off track, it was his positive attitude and sense of fun.

I shall always think of Simon as you will no doubt recall him too – young and full of vitality.

With Phil Collins and (left) having fun on mini bikes.

Dear Charlie, Abigail, Ricki, ... Julian and Family.

Feelings into words, ... I've tried for weeks and weeks.
We will all miss Simon, our thoughts are with you all.

Love from Phil, Lisa
Grace Abby & Lilly
(COLLINS.)

Simon

Dear Abigail and Ricki,

I Knew your Daddy along time before you were born. We were the same age and we both raced motorcycles.

We raced all over the world and we often travelled together in vans, taxis, boats or planes.

I liked your Dad, he was funny, he loved to tell Jokes and make people laugh and he always had a smile on his face.

All over the world every where he went he would bring his infectious Smile and good nature.

Your Daddy Loved racing his motorcycles and he was the best in the world, nobody's motorcycle gleamed and sparkled liked your Daddy's motorcycles either.

He was also very strong and handsome and he dressed very smartly too.

Knowing your Daddy the way i do, i bet he was the best Daddy in the world too.

We know he's in heaven now, watching over us all, but he still lives on inside of you two children. He will always be with you.

Love
Phil

Give Mum a big hug.

Copy of a letter sent by Phil Collins, Simon's former team-mate for England and Cradley Heath.

ENGLAND SPEEDWAY TEAM-MATES

Simon Cross

SIMON and I shared a grasstrack racing background – except that he came to it comparatively later than me. I was five-years-old when I first rode but Simon was about 13 when he took it up.

For me it was a case of natural progression but Simon made his name quite quickly. I know that Julian was a big influence on him but you can have all the help and advice in the world but you have to have ability, too – and Simon definitely had it.

We had many common points in our speedway careers too in our early days. I signed for Cradley Heath as a teenager and went on loan to Weymouth in 1983, with Simon transferring in the opposite direction. I then also rode for Oxford in the National League before the new owners took the Cheetahs up into the British League and signed Simon from Cradley – the club I subsequently rejoined in 1984!

With both of us riding in the British League, plus the fact that I was also getting involved in the Continental grasstrack and longtrack scene, we saw a lot of each other as rivals. Off-track, however, we got on well. We had a lot in common and would enjoy a meal or a beer together once a meeting was over. Even though grasstrack and longtrack are sports for individuals, if either of us got into dire straits abroad we would often help each other out. Then we had another happy coincidence of making it to the England speedway scene at around the same time. I also went on tour to Australia with Simon in 1990.

We all have painful memories of the World Team Cup Final at Bradford in 1989. Even though my handlebars ripped through my goggles and inflicted facial injuries that saw me accompany Jimmy Nilsen, Lance King and Erik Gundersen to hospital after that appalling pile-up in heat one, my injuries were not life-threatening, whereas those of my Cradley club-mate Erik were. Simon had to cover for my rides that afternoon and although England won, it was never going to be our happiest memory.

As for out time in Australia – well, Simon was an action man who loved sports. He loved to participate but he wanted to do well so whatever we did, it was competitive!

Simon loved to top up his tan while keeping us all busy.

Being an energetic guy over a wide range of activities, he had also invited myself and my brother, Paul, to accompany him on a snowboarding trip to Austria. He didn't tell us that he was booked into an indoor meeting in Germany on the way home! So while the cost of his trip was already covered, we were chipping in for our travel costs. We also ended up having to pay to watch him ride! The funny thing with Simon was that he would be the first to comment on other people's perceived tightness, but we would just smile to ourselves.

In trying to assess Simon Wigg you have to look at him as a man who was single-minded at his work but different away from it. A flawless professional who could excel for himself and his sports. Someone who was full of ideas, always stayed one step ahead, but who had time for his family, friends and other interests.

His end-of-season fancy dress parties were typical and he would go to town on those. He worked flat out and was always looking for something different for himself. Seeing him dressed up as Bart Simpson and Mr. T remain classic images. After the fancy dress party, it was back to his home at the Old Stables for even more fun and frolics. Simon was spectacular on those occasions and loved being the centre of attention.

We also loved competing against each other. We had each twice won the Trophy Saumond

Simon Cross and Wiggy after defeating the USA in the Test series at Sheffield, 1987.

at Marmande, which meant that whoever won on the third occasion would keep the silver trophy. Unfortunately I broke my back in 1991 and Simon had the ability to go on and win it, which was no easy task. We also chased the British Masters grasstrack title together on many occasions too.

After Cradley lost its base I moved to Coventry – the club that Simon had just left. There, I began to lose interest and wound my career down during the 1997 season. That year I was watching Simon at a meeting in Germany when he came into the pits turn and just fell off for no apparent reason. It was out of character and I thought it was a bit weird at the time. Perhaps, in hindsight, that was a significant incident . . .

Later, I was fully up-to-date with his collapse and the epilepsy situation. I'd been a friend for a long time and Charlie kept me informed as his condition worsened. Having retired from racing, I was involved in car delivery, so after Simon's second operation I was able to work some routes to ensure I got to see him quite often. Each time I could see that he was getting worse and his deterioration was obvious towards the end. I went to say a proper goodbye the day before he died and, sadly, he was vacant by then.

There was a funny side to the visits, too. From a fitness fanatic who lived on salads to someone who scoffed big desserts and closely guarded his sweets!

His funeral was the best that I've ever been to. Every time I hear Blur on the radio, I think of Wiggy and that day. When I look back on it, his end seemed slow at the time but it was all too quick. If you have such belief, then let's hope that Simon has been sent to somewhere better. Charlie assures me that he was not in pain at the end but, in a strange way, I was happy for his sake when he was gone.

It was characteristic of him that he had such a great send-off. I've been thinking that I'd like something similar when the time comes.

I now enjoy a new life in the south of France – a tranquil contrast to my racing life with Simon. As he would no doubt tell me: 'No going back!'

Jeremy Doncaster

SIMON and I knew each other from schoolboy grasstrack days. Once we had entered the adult category, Simon was well away, thanks also to Julian's input. I was still on my learning curve! So Simon was the man to beat for me and us two, along with Martin Hagon, had some great tussles. Although he had the advantage of that insight into the sport that Julian gave him, Simon was above all a superb all-round motorcyclist. That, allied to investment in top-class kit, gave him further confidence.

Eventually we both strayed into speedway. Simon served a proper apprenticeship at Weymouth in the National League, while I jumped into the deep end with Ipswich in the British League. I don't think either of us imagined we would end up together on a World Final rostrum, as we did in Munich in 1989. Although, ever the businessman, Simon did lean across and whisper to me that we could now ask bigger booking fees in Germany for 1990!

Simon's priorities were the world longtrack and European grasstrack scene. He had a plan and he worked at it. Besides his mechanical preparation, his mental approach was spot on, too. He was also a tough lad. I've been with him on the Continent when he had to lie down between races, because he was in so much pain from injuries. I'd question him but he'd just say: 'I've got to do it!' He was very driven.

Of course, when you travelled with him there was inevitably an adventure or two.

I remember one particular racing trip to Germany, when we went in Simon's palatial motorhome with his mechanic, Brett, and ace tuner Peter Johns. The first complication was that Brett, as an Australian, required a visa to sail into Europe. So we hid him on the top bunk. Once over there, Peter realised that his passport was out-of-date. Then Wiggy packed his passport in the wrong travel bag, which was taken off in another direction.

We realised all this just before our arrival at the French port on the return journey. Wiggy said: 'Donkey, you are the only one in the clear, so you'll have to drive through while we hide.'

There was a mad scramble as Peter hid in the toilet while Wiggy slid under the bed. Problem was that I couldn't manage to adjust the seat to reach the clutch pedal, which meant the vehicle then started to 'kangaroo' across the harbour! Inevitably, this attracted attention and I got pulled over. When asked if I was alone, I just managed to croak the word 'yes' but my heartbeat went through the roof as the guy asked to look inside the van! Fortunately, there were bags and equipment all over the place and his efforts to open the toilet door were foiled by Peter holding the handle, which was spring-loaded.

Once I was given clearance, I couldn't get it into gear. The customs bloke must have thought what a terrible driver I was, and how uncomfortable my journey across Europe must have been! I was in a state of shock when the ordeal was over but Wiggy was rolling about wetting himself with laughter.

I also recall that Simon was a great diplomat but he could handle himself, if necessary.

On a trip to a World Team Cup qualifier at Pardubice, we were asked by England managers Colin Pratt and Eric Boocock to chaperone Gary Havelock, who had been in a spot of bother with the authorities for one thing or another. Unfortunately, we were in the hotel bar in Prague when Brian Karger tried to avoid paying his drinks bill.

The situation got heated and there was some pushing and shoving going on. Simon, ever the diplomat, tried to intervene and calm everyone down when, suddenly, someone punched him on the nose.

Next thing I heard was: 'NOBODY touches my nose!!' and all hell broke loose. Simon got involved in a massive brawl and laid a few guys out in the process. From diplomat to prize

'Donkey' and Wiggy trying to put things right in the pits during the World Pairs Final at Pocking, Germany, 1986.

fighter in one easy lesson!

We enjoyed the England scene together. The Danes were dominant at the time and we had to raise our game against them. It was a pity that our World Team Cup victory at Odsal in 1989 was overshadowed by Erik Gundersen's terrible accident, although that was obviously understandable.

Overall, I had a great time in Simon's company – at home, in Europe and Down Under.

When I visited him in Willen Hospice at the end of his days, his memory was failing. He couldn't remember any of his World Longtrack Championship triumphs but if I mentioned a good time we had in Poland or Czecho, that famous smile would cross his face and we'd have a good laugh together.

Simon had bags of personality and I'm pleased to say that it never deserted him, not even in his darkest hour.

I have many happy thoughts and memories and they are the ones that will stay with me.

Wiggy loved bikes, but actually 'making love' to one?

Simon and Jeremy greet supporters after another winning England performance at Bradford.

Chris Morton MBE

A happy England camp. Mort offers Wiggy some victory champagne, while Kelvin Tatum offers his congratulations and Marvyn Cox looks on.

IT was a sign of Simon's rapid adjustment to British League racing that in his first season at Cradley Heath in 1983, he qualified for the British Final for a second time. Simon actually featured in the key race that brought me the British title that year. I had to make the start for once in my life, off gate four. Simon and Kenny Carter had a coming together on the first bend at Coventry and a re-run was ordered. So I had to do it all over again!

By 1984, Simon was a world finalist in Gothenburg – such progress in a short time. He suffered his ban in 1985 while I was out of favour for England selection. When Colin Pratt and Eric Boocock took over in 1986 they restored both of us to the England scene. In fact, we rode as team partners for England on many occasions.

I do remember having problems with my neck at the time and wearing a collar on the flight to America for the World Team Cup Final. I was dozing but became aware of a lot of mirth around me. As I turned my head I became aware of the figure of Simon next to me with a re-fashioned newspaper wrapped around his neck and posing for a photograph. The good thing about Simon was that he could take the mick but you weren't offended. You could see the funny side of it. Quite a visual joke when you think about it and I suppose I was quite flattered to be his latest victim.

Simon was a very balanced character. When it came to racing motorbikes he was serious but away from that he was great company. He couldn't have developed that with time – it was his natural personality. He was full of vitality and must have been since childhood. Simon could certainly help to kill the inevitable tension before a Test match with a laugh or two.

I came to speedway from a grasstrack background. It was a good grounding for many riders of my era. So I appreciate what a good all-round motorcyclist Simon was. I had great respect for his style, for I judge a rider on how much man and machine blend as one. Simon had that factor in his riding. Now despite being small myself, I don't subscribe to the view that being the equivalent of a jockey is the best size for a speedway rider. My view is that guys like Simon, Hans Nielsen and Tony Rickardsson, at five-foot, eight inches-plus, are the ideal height. They are not too tall but have upper body strength. Simon was strong and also worked out to ensure that this remained an important part of his competitive package.

Simon set himself high standards in everything that he did. He was meticulous about equipment. I stayed with him several times to tie in with our international commitments and his workshop was excellent. Simon was a forerunner of the current scene in that respect. However, I must mention that staying with him was great fun and he was so hospitable.

Longtrack racing was obviously his passion with speedway a sport that he turned to successfully. He was concerned about the state of grasstrack racing in this country and I can only imagine that if he had lived he would have set up a permanent track – something like Collier Street in Kent. He certainly wouldn't have put his feet up, he was full of ideas.

However, there is a lot of speculation about what he would be doing now but you must measure a man by what he achieved in his lifetime. In his chosen pursuits his record was more than decent – it was outstanding. He was a champion motorcyclist but also a very creative person – quite arty in fact. Simon was different to the rest of us in so many ways.

In helping to celebrate his remarkable life I can sum it up by saying Simon Wigg was a visionary but always 'full of beans'.

Malcolm Simmons

I STARTED my racing career on the grass but soon concentrated on speedway. I was obviously aware of Julian Wigg on the scene but my first impression of Simon, when I saw him race, was that he was harum-scarum and going too fast for his ability and experience at the time.

By the time I returned to riding on the grass on a regular basis, Simon was then the number one rider in this country at that discipline. How times had changed! When I was at Poole I used to take part in the Wimborne Whoppa and win it. But I had no chance with Simon around.

I had made a conscious decision to put my grasstrack career aside and concentrate on becoming a good speedway rider. It is very difficult to adjust between the two sports, as perhaps Paul Hurry is finding in the modern era. Simon was one of the very few who managed to make that transition smoothly. Simon not only made grasstrack and longtrack his priority, but he made an early decision that he wanted to break into the Continental – and particularly the German scene.

That was not the usual plan among British riders. I would accept a booking in Germany because I could earn a grand on a Sunday – it was purely the financial incentive and that applied to the rest of the top Brits. With Simon, it was more than just the money. This was what he truly wanted to do. Life is about decisions – you make a decision and follow it, but we went down different routes.

I do believe that if Simon had put the longtrack and grasstrack aside for a few years, he would had stood on the top step of the podium in the World Speedway Championship. In the eyes of many that would have counted for more, because speedway is a global sport, whereas longtrack is mainly a European sport. Not that I necessarily go with that view, as I appreciate the motorcycle skills involved in being No.1 in both grasstrack and longtrack racing.

However, it can't be denied that if, for example, Shawn Moran had won the World Speedway Championship, he would have had a lot more recognition than the fact that he did actually win the World Longtrack title. Yes, Simon quite rightly became a legend in Germany but his longtrack achievements didn't seem to earn him the same credit in his own country.

Then again, why should Simon have given that longtrack and grasstrack scene up? He was a great success and made a lot of money from it.

The motorcycle world is one in which you have many good acquaintances but I did find it very easy to get on with the Wiggs, in particular. We shared so many interests, including trials riding. Simon did dabble but Julian, and particularly his son Alexz, are really into it. Julian's lad is outstanding.

My good long-term relationship was one of the reasons that I stood aside to let Simon back into the trail to the speedway World Championship in 1984. I was with Wimbledon and had started the season well. Then I hit an awful patch of form, which you try and ride yourself out of

An unfortunate incident at Wolverhampton that saw Simmo hit the fence during the BL Best Pairs, 1985.

and by the end of the season I'd done so. At the time I just knew that I wasn't going to progress from the British quarter-final at Oxford, whereas Simon had been unlucky to have been eliminated through injury. This was the fundamental issue which led to so much trouble.

Under all circumstances, Simon was a rider going places and he proved himself time and time again in subsequent seasons.

He was also way ahead and so innovative in technological development, too.

Simon Wigg was a fabulous all-round motorcyclist who had such an impact on his sports. I really appreciate just how good a rider he was.

Andy Smith

MY Dad, Frank Smith, was a grasstrack rider and so I originally got to know of Simon through that particular scene. I first saw him compete against my Dad at a venue near Preston, Lancashire, when Simon was only 16. Simon actually won the meeting that day and the key was his equipment. In his first few years on the UK grasstrack scene Simon attracted the sponsorship necessary to become a success and it was obvious that he regarded his racing as a job, not a hobby.

By 18, he was beginning to pick up rides abroad and making the effort to learn German, which underlined his real progress.

Meanwhile, I had taken grasstrack racing up at 14 and started riding British League speedway with Belle Vue two years later. Soon Simon moved up from the National League with Weymouth to the British League with Cradley and so we were now competing against each other in two sports, as I was still active on the grass, too.

I also got into the longtrack scene and became a consistent performer. Simon was one of the outstanding riders to compete against but I did manage to beat him on occasions, as well as finish above him in World Finals. Simon was the standard that you judged yourself against and to finish in front of him was a major personal achievement.

In 1992 I suffered a serious hand injury in Germany when I fell and Simon ran over me. I was out for three months. The next season I won the British Championship – and Simon was immediately on the phone, teasing me that him having run over me still hadn't prevented me from taking the title!

I recall that when I won the Jim Cole grasstrack meeting, Simon wanted to buy the engine I used that day and offered me a new Eddie Bull-tuned engine and cash in exchange. Simon spend money? He must have been keen!

So we had a lot to do with each other and when he joined me as a team-mate at Coventry in 1994, we enjoyed each other's company from the off. The Brandon track was a little too grippy as far as Simon and myself were concerned but we did have a certain Mr.Nielsen in the team at the time! I did admire Simon for the fact that he wasn't afraid to voice his opinion on the subject of track preparation.

Our wives hit it off and Simon used to always make Michelle blush as he was a real charmer with her. He always paid her compliments every time we met up at Coventry and he was always planting a kiss on her!

Simon was always good to have around when you had an injury crisis. He was a very tough guy himself and would convince you that you could go through the pain barrier and get out there and perform. For example, we were both booked at Marmande in France and, with Simon already abroad at the time, he asked me to look after Charlie, and so I flew out with her and Simon collected us at the airport.

During the meeting I came down and Jan O. Pedersen ran into me. I suffered a broken collarbone and with a World Longtrack qualifier looming, it didn't look good for me but Simon convinced me not to pull out, told me to grit my teeth and give it a go. He really got into my mind with his positive words and thoughts. Simon was mentally tough and thanks to his influence, I eventually qualified for the World Final from third place.

The end of the season meant regular invitations for Michelle and myself to stay over at The Old Stables in Middle Claydon, Buckinghamshire, for Simon's traditional fancy dress party. I remember going once as a Sheik with a harem! I remember that year in particular for Simon's Bart Simpson costume. What most people don't know is that Simon made it himself and was

Simon, who won the meeting, and Andy Smith celebrating their qualification from the Grand Prix Challenge at Prague, 1996.

up until the small hours of that morning before putting the finishing touches to his outfit!

I also toured with him in Australia for David Tapp's Series 500 – a chance to combine racing, earn a few bob and take in a trip to a country that I really like. This, though, didn't prevent Simon from shaming us all by going on runs and keeping his fitness topped up while the rest of us were just content to laze around.

During our time together at Coventry I had more time to discuss mechanical matters with Simon and I have two mementoes in my possession of that period. On my workshop wall is a note from Simon telling me how to set up a carburettor he obtained for me. In a cupboard there, I've also got some clutch plates with his name on. I had these done for him but when he saw the bill, he wouldn't accept them. Simon could be a mean so and so at times!

Obviously, I've got great memories of him and our seasons at Coventry were the best.

When I became the first Englishman to win speedway's British Championship on three consecutive occasions, I soon received a fax from Simon congratulating me. He was very good with other riders in that way.

When asked to assess Simon Wigg as a rider, I have only to point to Teterow. What a challenge for a motorcyclist that place is, but he had it sussed.

As a person . . . well, Simon was a great laugh and I did enjoy his many jokes. Yes, he was serious about his profession but he liked a good time, too. That's a great reflection on him.

Leading 'Smudger' on the grass, 1989.

Kelvin Tatum MBE

SIMON and I were rivals but ours was a friendly rivalry. We came to that point from different directions. I started out in speedway and made a reasonable impact. Eventually I developed my other motorcycle disciplines, whereas Simon was originally a successful grasstrack rider who became involved in speedway later.

Simon was well-established as I began to be a competitive force on the longtrack scene. I won my first world title after beating him to the title in 1995, a year after Simon had won his fifth World Championship – he set the benchmark to which I aspired.

The emergence of two top Brits set his active mind thinking, which led to our appearance on Channel 4s *Big Breakfast* for 'Judge the Grudge!' Patrick Swayze was the judge, would you believe, that morning and there were a series of daft but great ideas, like being assessed on how popular the colour of your race suit was! It was a terrific publicity stunt and to Simon's credit that he could pull it off.

I admired his flamboyance and communication skills, he was a real ambassador. He could converse with anybody. Simon also sought to add colour and excitement to events – he certainly could see the bigger picture.

In racing terms, I realised from early days that I had a big catch-up to emulate him. You couldn't help but observe him, and not just mechanically. He was also meticulous with his fitness and diet. One of his biggest influences on me was my having to recognise that I had to work on my strength and stamina. He had both and I didn't.

Eventually we were both working with Hans Zierk and had similar equipment, which meant that I could again learn from observing his mechanical preparation and style. I could appreciate that he recognised me as a rival force and so didn't tell me the things I had to learn for myself.

My favourite memories of Simon are not the usual humorous ones, as I wasn't part of his social circle. Mine concern the unique opportunities he organised and included me in. In Australia, he took me in a party to the Barrier Reef on a catamaran and we went scuba diving. Whilst in Perth, we got to view the Americas Cup from a floating gin palace. Just two examples of memorable days most of us ordinary mortals never normally have the chance to experience.

My bottom line on Simon? He put 48 hours into every day. Wiggy had a real thirst for life.

Some pre-race encouragement for Kelvin Tatum.

SPEEDWAY TEAM-MATES & FRIENDS

Troy Butler

I WAS introduced to Simon by a gentleman called Bob Cowley, during one of Simon's regular visits to the Gold Coast in Australia as a member of the 1984-85 Ivan Mauger Farewell Tour. Simon was running some training schools and, as I'd had schoolboy moto-cross experience up to 125cc and 250cc, Bob encouraged me to have a go.

I was 16 and speedway was pretty big in Australia at that time. I did show some promise in the training sessions and ended up buying a bike, plus leathers and boots, from Simon. That was the springboard for our friendship and he took a real interest in me from that point.

At that time in British speedway, it was possible for Australians with British parentage to come into teams on an assessed two-point average. My mother is from Manchester but emigrated to Australia with her family in the post-war period.

Back home, I'd only competed in 10 meetings at that stage, never managing to beat Simon, of course, but I did beat Vaclav Verner on five occasions at the 400-metres Surfers Paradise track. Those meetings, and others at Sheperton under John McNeil's promotion, involved all the star names on the Mauger tour but Simon was happy with the way I was coping.

So, at 17, I made my way to England and Oxford under Simon's guidance. I wonder how I would have ever coped with such a challenging situation without his help? Simon provided me with food and accommodation, which made it much easier for me to settle in the UK. Being based with him meant access to a well organised workshop and to Simon himself. I was also able to be mounted on decent equipment thanks to Simon's connection with Don Godden.

What would have been the alternative? A garage and a toolbox plus an inferior diet, to be frank. Simon was like a big brother – or even a dad – to me at this stage and he had a huge impact on my personal development too. I learned a lot about one's attitude to life from being in the company of such a positive man.

Simon finds a way to stop Troy falling off!

Even so, I was still under immense pressure at Oxford, struggled badly and had lots of crashes. I was aware that Oxford had some decent young riders on their books, including Ali Stevens, Nigel Sparshott and Jon Surman. I began to get very down and this further affected my confidence.

In fact, I told Simon that I was thinking of packing it all in. He gave me a stiff talking to and asked me to examine all that he'd done for me. He also asked me to look closely at the way I was and how that also affected me. Although I suffered terrible bouts of homesickness, I did stick to my task. I suspect, too, that Simon had persuaded the Oxford Speedway management to persevere with me and he obviously had faith in me.

That winter, I did well in meetings in

Melbourne and Adelaide and went on to surprise everybody by winning the Australian Championship – and Wiggy was soon on the phone to congratulate me. However, my success was a mixed blessing, because I needed more experience and the confidence that comes from winning races.

A loan deal to National League Milton Keynes was discussed – and my move to The Groveway really turned my career. By 1988, I had a 10.40 average and won the National League Riders' Championship. Within a year, I was back at Oxford and lining up alongside Simon at the 1989 World Final in Munich.

When Simon moved on from Oxford, we maintained our friendship, enjoying snowboarding trips to Austria, and obviously we'd meet up, post-Christmas, in Australia. We'd go off to Ayres Rock for a break and he would come and watch me in the Australian Championship.

I remember once when he convinced me to go on a double date with him. Simon always had girlfriends who looked like glamour models, so I was quite encouraged. Now I have a preference for petite ladies. Sure enough, Simon had the super-model for company while I had . . . the double-decker bus! I told him that I'd find my own ladies after that!

As is no doubt mentioned elsewhere, Simon was a party animal. Even after I'd moved on to my own base in Northampton, he would be the first on my invitation list for any parties. When he opened the Crazy Coyote restaurant in the area, Simon would often be on the phone, inviting me down for a coffee or a meal. He was very sociable but never silly – I never saw him drunk.

Looking back, I'm so indebted for what Simon did for a young man like myself, who was much more of a hassle to him than a boon. He taught me so much about life – how to be a success by just getting on with it.

When he knew that he was going to die he 'phoned me up for a final chat and to impart words of encouragement to me. These I will always treasure. His influence remains with me today – not least with a circle of friends that I have in England because of Simon.

I attended the reunion of the 1985-86 team at Oxford recently and a fan kindly presented me with a portrait of Simon that must have cost him more than a few pennies to obtain and mount. He wouldn't let me pay him, because he knew how much Simon meant to me.

It has pride of place in my home back in Australia, so Simon will never be far away.

Armando Castagna

WE first met in December 1984, when I had been invited to take part in an Ivan Mauger speedway tour that was starting in January. I flew with Zoltan Adorjan, the Hungarian Number One, from Heathrow to Perth and we met up over there. To me, Simon was already a superstar having recently finished sixth in the World Final at Gothenburg, which Erik Gundersen won.

In a galaxy of stars on that tour, Simon was definitely a leader. 'Zolly' and I were very much the kids compared to Hans Nielsen, Kelvin Tatum, Peter Collins, Kai Niemi, Karl Maier, Henny Kroeze and Simon. I couldn't speak English at the time but this didn't prevent Simon from talking to me at a million miles an hour! I did pick up: 'Come on, Armando' because, as I said, he was the leader and I was one of the kids. We were all together for two-and-a-half months, and Simon was terrific with us. He was the first man in the troupe that you would go to for help.

This was the start of a global adventure for Simon and myself. Eventually we both ended up riding on a Dutch licence after I had problems with the Italian Federation. I phoned him for advice and he linked me in with the Dutch authorities.

Now Italians make friends easily – it is in our Latin blood – but Simon was more like one of my family in terms of my affection for him. It is the same with Per Jonsson. I needed Simon's strength to help me through the criticism that I took back home – we were both the black sheep, as it were. With Simon also on a Dutch licence, he began to contest the Continental rounds of the speedway World Championship. But whenever we won a round, we always requested that the local track played our home national anthem, and not the Dutch one.

In eastern Europe, Simon was an absolute superstar and to have a top class western rider in action caused a lot of interest. Lots of riders wanted to be like him, both on and off track, he was different and he was successful.

In Germany, too, Simon was a massive draw. He was fast on track with outstanding equipment,

Wiggy leading Armando Castagna during a Hackney v Ipswich clash at Foxhall Heath, 1987.

while away from the circuit he created a fantastic image.

Now both Simon and I were quite big guys for our sport, so diet was very important to us. However, my family and I run spaghetti restaurants so after a big meeting at Lonigo Simon would come and stay a few days – and eat kilos of spaghetti! In Italy, he always seemed to relax. But elsewhere, he always seemed to be going flat out. Here, he loved the sun and when not on the beach in temperatures of 40 degrees, then Simon would sit outside reading a book. Not the usual image of the oh-so-busy Simon Wigg!

One meeting that we rode in comes to mind. It was the 1996 World Championship Semi-Final in Togliatti, Russia. Sergy Darkin had won the round with Simon and myself tied on points for the second and third places. The run-off was the race of our lives. We knocked into each other repeatedly but such was our mutual respect, we could be racing right next to the fence without there being any intent to put the other actually into the fence. Eventually, I crashed of my own accord and Simon took the higher step onto the podium.

We once had a dilemma at one round in Germany. This time, we couldn't help each other, because we both needed to win our final outing, in which we met. So in order to qualify, we had to race for it. I won on that occasion and put him out of the championship but I did have mixed feelings on the day.

Simon actually found the Continental qualifying rounds a lot harder than he expected. I remember him coming up to me in Hungary early on and saying: 'Bloody hell! These guys are all crazy, It's not like the British or Commonwealth rounds.' I reminded him for many years of my reply: 'It's not Christmas time. Go back to England if you can't take it!'

Armando Castagna (left) and Marcel Gerhard on unusual machinery at Wiggy's 1999 Farewell event.

Problem was that all the Russians, Czechs and Poles wanted to beat him because he was so famous. They did give him a hard time out on the track.

I enjoyed my time around him so much that I regret that I didn't take up his invitation to ride in David Tapp's 'Series 500'. Every November at that time he would be on the phone trying to get me to come to Australia. However, I was committed to be in Argentina assisting a promoter with the sport over there.

Some have commented on how expensive Simon was to book for a meeting. You talk to longtrack promoters in Germany and they will confirm that not only did he put bums on seats, but he also helped to get meetings on and convince the other riders to have a go when the weather and track conditions were difficult. Simon gave value for his money and that's why he was in demand.

Simon achieved so much and I have told Gerd Riss: 'Don't you bloody well dare win more than Simon's five world titles!' I hope that Gerd never wins another one, to be frank.

Simon was a guy who sometimes worked with no logic in this sport. Then again, can anyone tell me what is logical about speedway? He was always experimenting. Yes, it did cost him races and meetings along the way but he wanted the best equipment in the best-looking set-up. In so many ways he was years ahead of the rest of us, be it with bikes, kevlars or even the carbon fibre shoe he wore at one longtrack final – instead of a standard steel shoe – to save 300 grams of weight.

I spoke to Simon regularly through the early stages of his illness and after the first operation. In 1999 I took my Harley Davidson to his farewell meeting. I spent five days in the hospice with him before the end. I said goodbye and returned for the remarkable funeral.

At just 40, it was too early for him to leave us. His life had been full and exciting but when I first met him I presumed that he would continue at that pace for another 50 years.

On my internet website – www.armandocastagna.com – I have nominated Simon Wigg as not only the finest ever rider, but the best sportsman I've ever known.

Graeme Gordon

SIMON presented myself and the rest of the Exeter team with a unique opportunity towards the end of the 1996 campaign – his one and only season with the Falcons – and it was an unforgettable experience for all concerned.

He had been riding on a Dutch licence and had therefore competed in the Continental rounds of the speedway World Championship. This took him to Togliatti in Russia, and while he was there, he had been offered a pretty lucrative contract to ride for, and advise, the local club.

To celebrate the promoter's 50th birthday Simon was asked to bring a team over from Britain. Obviously he discussed this with his current team-mates and an ability to ride Exeter's sweeping County Ground would be useful for the big Togliatti track. Simon organised everything for us and we contemplated the trip of a lifetime at no cost and as an earner, too.

My mother, Valerie, volunteered to be a co-driver with Brett Walton and Roger Moore (no, not the Bond actor!). They took the bikes out the previous Saturday in time to make the Wednesday fixture. After our home match at Exeter on the Monday we ended up going back to Alun Rossiter's pub in Swindon and sleeping – or trying to sleep – on his lounge floor. There was Mark Loram, Paul Fry, Michael Coles, Peter Jeffrey and myself.

We met up with Simon the next day at Heathrow and took a scheduled flight to Moscow. Simon was like our dad, telling us to keep together and in line. When we arrived at Moscow he supervised the clearance at customs. We started to log that the soldiers looked serious and we were entering the sort of society that we had observed on television but never experienced. Eventually we met up with our interpreter and boarded this old bus – like one of those old American school buses. We drove around Moscow on what is their equivalent of the M25 but with 12 lanes of traffic bumper to bumper! After three hours of this we reached the next airport and caught an internal flight to Samera. Luckily, we had drunk a lot on our flight from London, which helped us to cope with the state of the plane that we had to board! It looked like a combination of different planes welded together. It had different colour schemes along its inside length and when Michael Coles went to put his belt on – it came out of the floor! Then on landing, all the fluorescent strip lights with their defusers fell off the ceiling!

Once off we were met by officials of the host club and ushered onto a luxurious new coach. We were taken to the Russian equivalent of a five-star hotel – it was pretty basic! We reached the hotel at 1am and after logging the armed guards in reception, we were soon set for bed.

Simon came around at 8am, knocking on our doors and calling us together. He first mentioned that there had been 'trouble in the night' and then proceeded to explain that the promoter had

Simon led a Russian revolution at Exeter, 1996.

been shot dead! I think the mental reaction was pretty much: 'What sort of place have you brought us to, Simon?'

So instead of a birthday bash, the speedway match became a memorial meeting. The irony was that part of the original schedule was to meet up with the promoter at the very restaurant that he been shot outside. We may have been lucky not to be early on this occasion.

When we finally reached the stadium to set up, we were very impressed. The pits were indoor and superb. The facilities for the public were very comfortable. As for the track itself, it was bigger and longer than Exeter but without much banking. Incidentally, we did spot the promoter's Mercedes parked near us – full of bullet holes! It appears that he was from a different state and had become wealthy through owning a factory that produced cardboard boxes. He had decided to run for Governor and it was presumed by us that he had stood on too many toes at that point.

For the match itself, there was a huge attendance. The Russian lads had top class equipment – they were full-time riders subsidised by the Lada factory. The home riders were good and quick on track, beating us handsomely over 16 heats. What I remember most is the parade. It was played to funeral music and with the track staff carrying huge portraits of the deceased promoter. Despite the surreal atmosphere, we were made very welcome and the whole club was obviously run very professionally.

Back at the hotel, Simon strictly forbid us to go out and said that all he ever did was stay safely in the hotel. Having made that announcement, he retired to his bedroom.

However, we got bored and bunked off to what was described as a 'casino'. Mark Loram paid for all of our admission but all it turned out to be was a bar serving beer at the equivalent of five pounds a pint, plus a dance floor. We knew that we had to be up by 6am to start our return journey with a fixture at Peterborough on the Friday night. We were getting ready to roll back to our hotel when were approached by this huge Russian guy who was accompanied by a very short sidekick.

In English he identified us as the visiting speedway riders and insisted that we had a drink with them. We explained that we had to get some sleep but he became very insistent, quite confrontational in fact. Suddenly bottles of vodka were produced and I turned to Mark Loram and told him that I didn't like vodka. So Mark's reply was: 'Better get to like it quickly!' We couldn't help but notice that the sidekick had a gash on his head. When we enquired, the big guy explained that his mate had been in a fight with the local mafia! He then revealed that he was the Chief of Police and then insisted on taking us on a tour of the town in their vehicles. This took in the restaurant that the promoter had been shot at and the local cop shop! The police chief was pretty drunk at the wheel and nearly wiped us, and the convoy, out at one particular bend.

We definitely should have listened to Simon's advice. We were so glad to get back to the hotel – for only a few hours sleep, unfortunately.

We were especially glad to board the plane for Moscow where we confessed how scared we were to each other. By the time that we reached London we were completely knackered – except Simon, of course. At Peterborough it showed in our performances even though we had kept our best equipment at home. However, I thank Simon for his endeavours on our behalf, for it was an unforgettable episode in my life.

As for the man himself, when he joined Exeter I was the baby of the team and in awe of a multi-World Champion. I presumed that he would be very unapproachable but, like Mark, he proved to be funny and pretty relaxed. Simon had a bit of a sticky patch at first as he sorted his kit out for the demands of Exeter. Some fans began to doubt him but once he sorted the problems out he was superb. Simon was a true team member too and he took an interest in the other riders being ready with advice and help.

I rode at Marmande on three occasions in the Under 20s heats. The year that Simon and I were team-mates was also the year that I blew my grasstrack bike up at the event. I was nervous of asking for the loan of a machine but he was so obliging. The commentator was saying: 'Here comes Graeme Gordon on the Wiggy machine!' I finished second overall to Ryan Sullivan. Simon kept an eye on me and no doubt on the welfare of his bike too! I respect what he did for me when he had so much on his mind at the time.

In later years, and during his first period of illness, he came down to see John Gillard for whom I was working at the time. I spent a lot of time that day chatting. Little did I realise that it would be the last time that I would see him. He was full of advice on looking after my kit.

I was lucky enough to have enjoyed a season in his company. You couldn't help but log so much that was presentable about him. I learned a lot from him and it did sink in.

Simon Wigg still remains an influence on me to this day.

Steve Johnston

IN 1985 I had nothing to do with speedway at all. I was a kid of 12, doing junior moto-cross, when Wiggy was part of the English troupe who came to Perth. He was stationed at our house doing his bikes, so that's when I met him for the first time.

I remember going to watch him at places like Claremont. He was a classic, wasn't he? He would do the big wheelies, or win the meetings, or be one of the top guys. He was a likeable guy whom everyone got on with. Even as a youngster, he made a fuss of you and made you think: 'I know Simon Wigg.'

I came to England in 1992 and didn't see much of Wiggy, other than at speedway meetings. I didn't have a lot to do with him and then, in 1994-95, he came out and did some more meetings in Perth. By then I was racing against him. He had been a regular competitor in Australia for 15 years or more. Simon was a big name out there, because he had won a lot of meetings in his time. He was such a marketable guy and was, by now, a multi-World Champion.

He was always top man, working so hard in every meeting that he rode in, no matter what track it was at. Even after he'd won a race, he would still come in and change things to try and go even faster – he just never stopped working.

We became friends. In 1995, I decided that I wanted to do some longtrack racing and Wiggy got me an open meeting booking. He took me and a pile of other guys and we went in a big bus up to Tallin in Estonia.

The next year, a mutual friend, Martin Hignett, rang Wiggy and said that he wanted to buy one of his bikes for me. Martin was a sponsor and a friend of Wiggy's, and he bought me one of the longtrack bikes Simon had taken to the 1995 World Final. That season, wherever we went on weekends to France, Germany, Holland and all over the place, I was lucky enough that Simon took me under his wing. We hit it off good as mates and I don't know if it went back to that time he did his bikes at my parents' house, but he really helped me out.

I was then only a young guy competing against him but I was obviously no threat to his status. It was my first season and I only had the one bike. There were lots of times when I qualified for finals and finished on the podium, with him having won the meeting, but he still tried to help me.

Most weekends I would drive down to his place at Middle Claydon and I'd throw my bike in his vehicle. We'd take off and be all over Europe with Brett, who was helping us at the time.

If Simon went to a meeting and won his first two races, he would chase the track record. He would always chase the pre-meeting *bahn* record, go all out for it. Wiggy would tend to try out both of his bikes and say: 'That one was really nice out of the start but the other one is quicker.' Then he would ask his mechanic to either change the clutch over or switch the engines around. He didn't just want to win meetings, he was driven to do his absolute best. If you've got the meeting won, why would you try something different? But Simon wanted to go better *every* time he raced – he was rarely content.

If he was around now he would still be racing at a competitive level. He had the drive of an 18-year-old. He was so fit, too. Right up until he got ill, you could look at him without a T-shirt on, on a beach for instance, and he looked like a 20-year-old guy who was super-fit. Building up to his World Longtrack championships, Simon could get his weight down to 66 kilos. Yet he

Back at Oxford, 1998, Simon leads for King's Lynn against Cheetahs' Steve Johnston and Lawrence Hare.

was a bigger build than me – a strong, thick-set sort of guy.

Wiggy loved to have a laugh and a joke – and he was a practical joker too. But for months leading up to a World Final, if you went out for a meal, he would have a salad with no dressing on it. He would order chicken and pull the skin off. He was very meticulous with his diet and I honestly believe that he would have gone on to win more World Championships.

In 1996 I won the European Grasstrack Championship. A lot of people helped me but he was a main man for me. Simon was at home in England and I rang him after the meeting and said: 'You are not going to believe it. I've won this!' He was as excited as me. He was going: 'That's great! That's great!' He was over the moon.

I did a lot with him in 1996 and '97 but I stopped doing longtrack in 1998. It was just too expensive for me at the time, so I was better off concentrating on speedway, including racing in Poland and Sweden.

Then we did a lot of Tapp's Series 500 tour, travelling around Australia. A real classic was the time we had just left Rockhampton – you have to think about the fact that there are 25 guys all travelling around together, accompanied by their wives and girlfriends. We had travelled for up to six weeks, living out of hotels, washing when we could and eating dodgy burgers.

Anyway, Wiggy had been travelling to Oz for so long and knew so many people. He happened to have a mate who ran a motorcycle shop near Fraser Island and owned a house on the island itself. So the troupe all went over on a ferry and stayed there for three days. It's one of those situations when I'm out there sitting on the beach and thinking: 'How lucky am I? I'm in my own country, on Fraser Island, where all the movie stars and celebrities are based, and I'm staying in this plush house.' Wiggy had just gone and organised it all with one of his mates. We had an absolute ball for those three days, in a location most Aussies would never visit in their life. This was classic Wiggy, he just had the ability to organise events – and it wasn't unusual for him to do things like that.

When he collapsed for the first time and had his first fit, he was building bikes for a Tapp series. When I phoned him he told me that he had epilepsy – he was so disappointed. He stated he would have 12 months off and then get back to racing. That was his first reaction.

People know him in Australia and still talk of his exploits around various tracks – he definitely left a big mark on a lot of lives. For me he wasn't just a speedway rider and a friend, but a businessman and an all-round person. He taught me a lot about life and not just riding.

I miss not being able to talk to him. I used to ring him up about matters well away from speedway. I would ask:'What do you reckon about this? What do you reckon about that?' Wiggy was always thinking. He was a very clever man.

Simon definitely touched a big part of my life. I was very fortunate to ride with him, against him and have him as a close personal friend.

Simon, Charlie and the kids have come and stayed out with me in Perth on a couple of occasions, which I was happy to be able to do because he had looked after me for so many years. It was great to repay the favour when he came to my home.

I just feel lucky – honoured, really – that I knew Simon as well as I did.

Olli Tyrvainen

IN our long friendship the biggest impression that Simon left on me was when illness struck him. For he never changed and was still full of jokes while remaining positive. I realised what a great person Simon was at that point.

How many people who, when they are eventually told that they have just months to live, wouldn't get down? But he would say everything was fine and, right to the end, he thought that life was good.

My wife, Sabine, and I would bring Simon down to our home in Worthing for weekends. We would visit Eastbourne Speedway and Simon always looked forward to going over to Arlington.

He was always good company, even after the second operation had affected his speech and the left side of his body. We even went to Sweden together during this period and I took him up to Luton Airport very early to check in, away from even the speedway fraternity. I remember we sat and watched the sun rise. 'Isn't life great?' he mouthed. Remarkable.

We had become firm friends when we were part of Ivan Mauger's farewell tour in New Zealand in 1984. I believe that our friendship blossomed because we had interests in, and discussions on, topics far beyond longtrack and speedway. We enjoyed chatting about ski-ing, travel and business matters and Simon really appreciated that. He had a good mind and could have been successful in other directions if had wanted to. He was a man with a plan and stuck to it. He felt that if you didn't know where you were going, then you were stuffed. Even when we were having a good time and going out for a drink or a meal, we we'd debate serious issues.

Simon had a significant influence on my wife. While returning from a racing trip to Germany, I fell asleep in the back of the van. Up front, Sabine was discussing her future with Simon. He asked her what she wanted to be and she answered 'a psychologist'. His next question was a turning point: 'What is stopping you?' Simon encouraged Sabine to resume her studies. As a result, she subsequently registered with the University of Vienna and today she specialises in sports psychology, working with the emerging stars of German four-wheel motor sport, six times speedway World Champion Tony Rickardsson and has just landed a major contract to run stress-release seminars in Malta. It's all thanks to Simon taking a firm line with her that night.

Coming back to the key factor of him entering the hospice – a death sentence in reality, Simon was still positive that he had a good life. He recognised that he had fathered two great children within a loving environment. Most people are aware of Simon Wigg, the multi-World Champion and his public persona. That aspect wasn't as important to me as to many other people around him. It was the private man that I was interested in.

As a friend, you sometimes had to be honest with him. Although a good businessman, he could also be rather innocent on occasions, so you had to intervene to try and protect him.

Also, his pace of life. When, only five hours after we arrived at his home in Australia, I found him wheeling and dealing on the telephone, I had to say: 'For goodness sake – relax!' However, to retain any good friendship you have to keep one eye shut on occasions.

My summary of Simon is that my wife and I still talk about him. Our lives are emptier without him.

Martin Yeates

NL Pairs champions, 1982 – Weymouth's Martin Yeates and Simon Wigg.

I FIRST noticed Simon when I attended a grasstrack training school run by Ian Barclay in February 1977. I went along to flex my muscles in preparation for the new speedway season. Simon was there with Dickie Staff. He was fast, stylish and had well-presented machinery. You could just tell that he was going to be good and had an obvious appetite for racing.

When he took up speedway properly he joined Weymouth, where I was the number one. Simon improved very quickly and I was impressed by the fact that he could score six points in a match – which was good at his stage of progress – but still be frustrated as he knew that he was capable of more. Eventually Simon, and then Steve Schofield, became heat leaders and the great thing for me was that this kept me on my toes. It was nice that we became the best of pals, which doesn't always happen between heat leaders in one team, when the three of you are vying for the number one spot. Our second half finals were very special and great entertainment, as we all wanted to beat each other.

What Simon and I had in common, in particular, was a habit of tinkering with our machines. I'd turn up one week with a device which threaded ropes for caravans and had adapted it for my throttle cable. Simon had to have one, too! Then he would turn up with an air filter extension. It actually became a competition between us to keep finding innovative adaptations for the bike. The seeds of Simon's later technological advances on the world stage were definitely planted on the Dorset coast.

We also competed to see who could run their back tyre the longest. We would acquire tyres from top riders who discarded them after one or two rides, then cut them and reshape them. My record was to go five meetings on the same tyre – but Simon managed to get to a sixth meeting! He was also piling up the points home and away, too.

Simon was a deep thinker and when we travelled together to away matches he was always keen to listen and learn from a more experienced rider like myself. You could see him mulling matters over in his mind and planning ahead.

Talking of travelling with him, I used to go with him on some Continental jaunts, either as his mechanic or to fulfil a late grasstrack booking. It never failed to amaze me that he could zip across Europe to take bookings in southern France or Germany and yet his energy never faded. I would need a day's rest to recover, but Simon didn't.

Before our National League Best Pairs title win at Swindon in 1982, I met up with him at his home and became concerned that travel time was getting tight. I liked to get to a venue very early, walk the track and set up. However, this day Simon was quite happy to spend time on the telephone, receiving and making calls. Then, when it was very late, he had to go and buy some sweets up the high street.

We got there far too late – the other riders were finishing their warm-up as we clambered into the pits with Julian. After a frantic warm-up, it was straight out to the tapes! Strange to report that we achieved a victory with the first maximum in the event's history.

My final thought of my friend is that if I had never been involved in speedway, I would still have loved to have met Simon in any case. He would be great to have around on a golf course or just socialising at a bar. He was just so effervescent.

PROMOTERS & TEAM MANAGERS

Neil Street

I FIRST knew of Simon when he was 17 – he was already a successful grasstracker and I sold him one of my four-valve mark II engines. When he started riding in speedway second halves at Reading, the more confined track was probably too tight for him at that stage of his development.

I was then team manager at Weymouth, so I discussed with the promoter, Mervyn Stewksbury, about inviting Simon down to try out at Radipole Lane. Weymouth Speedway was one big family and Simon settled in well with his easy-going manner. Although grasstrack and longtrack were his real interests, he soon showed enthusiasm for his speedway racing and was fast from the very beginning.

I know he felt that he stayed too long with us in the National League but I disagree. A rider needs to gain more experience before moving up – too many move up too soon. Leigh Adams spent only one season in the National League with Poole before moving up but his prolonged period at reserve in the British League nearly broke his spirit at the time. Simon had enjoyed success at the NLRC and the Best Pairs, and so he had the confidence when he moved up to Cradley in '83.

I had a lot to do with his mechanical preparation during the Weymouth years, including, initially, his grass and longtrack bikes. He was obviously looking for more speed. The great situation from my point of view was that you could have a proper dialogue with Simon about engines, because he was very interested in that side of racing, too.

I worked on a single-cam Weslake for his longtrack racing in Europe and he was over the moon the first time he beat Egon Müller. Eventually he linked up with top tuners, Lantenhammer and Zierk, in Germany, having earned the bookings and the sponsorship to enable him to work with them on special engines.

I was pleased to be involved in his formative years, it was more of a father and son relationship. When he moved upwards and onwards I always followed his career and we kept in touch. Five World Longtrack Championships, World number two in speedway and a host of grass titles display what a great all-round motorcyclist he was. My own background had seen me compete in scrambling and road racing before developing speedway as a profession, so I can appreciate just how talented Simon was to reach the level of achievement in different disciplines like he did.

My outstanding personal memory of him was how good an ambassador he was for himself and his sports. He always had time for people of whatever age or level.

Simon was typical of those who are taken from us at a young age. He burst like a bright light across our lives and we will always remember him as he was.

Simon Wigg will never grow old.

Peter Adams

I WAS Simon's team manager when he moved from Weymouth to Cradley Heath. It's funny how you remember some things vividly. To clinch the deal we met at a pub in Bristol, because I didn't want anybody to know that we were talking to him, and neither did Simon.

I well remember that we met at a pub called 'The Lamb and Flag'. I'm sure that I'd never find it again in a million years but he told me where it was. We met there on a Sunday evening in their restaurant – we were the only two in all night, so our secret was safe! I clearly recall

Peter Adams, Erik Gundersen and Wiggy relax in the sun on a week's break in Lido, Italy. The team-bonding exercise worked a treat, as Cradley Heath went on to win the 1983 championship in style.

that when we left the pub it was absolutely pouring with rain and we had to run to our respective vehicles so that we didn't get drowned.

I had a good discussion with him in Bristol and it proved fairly easy to get Simon to Cradley because I'd enjoyed three very successful years at Coventry. I was 'the kiddy', so to speak, and Cradley Heath had emerged as the glamour club to be at. So the combination of the two made it very easy for us to sign him.

His greatest strength was his all round ability as a motorcyclist. Simon could ride all sorts of disciplines – he was just fantastic on a motorbike. He could have ridden anything on two wheels and been a success.

With Cradley being a Saturday night track, there was going to be the occasional clash with his involvement in the longtrack and grasstrack scene, and we knew that there would be one or two Saturday fixtures that he couldn't do. It didn't bother him, though, as he saw his move to Cradley as the key that would unlock his speedway potential. The Heathens had a very strong team. The points limit in those days was very high – about 52 points as I recall – so you had the scope for them to be very strong compared to today's teams. We were always ducking and diving at Cradley, chopping and changing to ensure that we maintained our position at the forefront of British speedway. We certainly did that in the three years that I was there and, obviously, Simon played his part in our success in 1983.

I had left Cradley – to re-open Wolverhampton – by the time that Simon was transferred to Oxford a year later. I think he was a bit of a lost sheep once I had gone. Things were never quite the same – he often said that to me. There were many instances, after I'd left Cradley, where Simon wanted me to help him with his individual ambitions. But I was so busy at Wolverhampton, and subsequent projects abroad, that I wasn't able to fulfil those requests.

Simon's first actual appearance at Cradley was in the Golden Hammer meeting of 1982, when he was still at Weymouth. We don't have these really big open meetings these days but the Golden Hammer was a prime event. It was the brainchild of Dan McCormick, the previous Cradley promoter, and it drew a lot of publicity, a prominent field and a big crowd. It was held on a Wednesday evening every July.

I wanted to give Simon a taste of what riding for Cradley would be like, so I invited him to race in the 'Hammer' in the season prior to him joining us. He was gobsmacked. It was a completely different experience than riding in the National League. That's how it all sort of started.

Then we had a few injuries towards the end of the 1982 season – those were the days when you could sign riders from the lower league and have an eight, nine and 10 who you could call upon. You could use them at will to cover absences and that was an opportunity for me to get half a claw into Simon – he was one of three riders I chose. The others were Andy Reid and Steve Lawson but every chance we had to use Simon we did. He was clearly the best rider in the National League at that time and we very much wanted him full-time the season after.

He found the transition very easy to make and the key was his ability as a motorcyclist.

As for his bubbly personality, with lads like Phil Collins, Erik Gundersen and Simon in the team, it was a laugh a minute. I've always said that a happy team is a successful team. We tried to have a laugh at Cradley and we did. We had a couple of foreign holidays together, where the whole team went away with their wives and girlfriends. So once you let characters like Simon and Phil loose on the Continent, anything could happen – and frequently did! We had an absolute ball – they were definitely my favourite days in speedway.

The one thing I would say, and I have to say this, is that what held Simon back was that he was a great tinkerer with his machinery. He was never satisfied. At the end of the day, that's the issue which held him back in speedway. He had all the ability and all the flair, everything you need to get to the very top. But he could never recognise when things were going as well as they could.

Simon always tried to make the bike go that much faster, or do this or that. Those moves tended to backfire on him occasionally. Sometimes he would come to Cradley Heath and record the fastest times and score a maximum. Then he would turn up the next week without the same bikes or set-up. It would be something else that he was going to try out, to attempt to go that bit better. Invariably in those circumstances, what he'd changed to went that bit worse, so it was back to the drawing board.

That was his only flaw. If somebody could have ironed out that weakness in him, then I think Simon could have gone right to the very top in speedway, as he did in longtrack.

Bernard Crapper

SIMON played a major role at Oxford from 1984. Few realise, however, that he wasn't in our original reckoning for a team place. Cradley had a side well over the points limit and talks at the BSPA conference at Bournemouth that winter centred originally around the availability of Erik Gundersen. Erik wanted to stay at Cradley but gave Oxford and Wolverhampton as his preferences if he had to move on.

But we didn't think that a Nielsen/Gundersen spearhead would be fair on either rider. Until 4am, we had discussed various transfer permutations with Derek Pugh, the Cradley owner, although we didn't think that Simon would feature in our talks because he had only been at Cradley for one season. But after 4am, it was decided that Wiggy was going to Oxford – and we were very pleased.

We had already unveiled Hans Nielsen at a supporters' social the previous week, so when we came to announce our next major signing, we hid Simon in the house of the stadium manager, Harry George. When we eventually produced him, there was stunned silence that we had pulled off such a coup.

Simon proved an excellent team man, a popular team-mate and I cannot calculate the number of times that he and Hans pulled 5-1 last heat deciders out of the bag.

It's fair to say that we had our disagreements over track preparation and who he thought we should be signing. Sometimes voices were raised. If that happened, Simon would always apologise and, as he was someone I genuinely liked, this helped to calm those situations.

We had to put our foot down with him on the issue of track preparation. We'd tell him that we would find the track the same the next week, and that he should set his bikes up accordingly. You have

Wiggy no doubt offering Bernard Crapper some more advice about track preparation and marketing ideas at Oxford!

to remember, we also had to consider the views of one of the greatest speedway riders of all time, who also rode for us.

I have quite a few funny memories of my time with Simon, as promoter and friend. Like the time he blew his garden fence up at his home in Middle Claydon! We held a celebration party there the season we won everything in sight. Harry George brought some fireworks left over from the final meeting display – some bangers and maroons. We tied them to a fence post and lit them. Nothing happened at first, except a tame 'phew' sound. Suddenly, one set off into the night sky with a series of terrific bangs. As we looked up, there was this almighty explosion. The fence post disintegrated and the fence collapsed. You should have seen Simon's face! It was nothing, however, compared to his look when the police arrived to investigate the neighbours' complaints!

I also recall the time when Simon decided to mark one of his World Championship wins by getting a mate of his to fly him into Cowley by helicopter. We weren't expecting this and when the pilot nearly struck a floodlight while coming into land, we were even more nervous. I was curious how they had managed to gain clearance from the aviation authority, as there was an exclusion zone over Oxford because of various RAF stations nearby and the proximity of the University. Simon and his mate were completely thrown by the question. There was hell to pay for that pilot afterwards!

However, my favourite story about Simon concerns the occasion that we staged a match race between Peter York and Mike Patrick, who was bedecked in his famous check trousers. As they got ready, Mike had to return to the pits to sort out some popping and banging on the machine. Unbeknown to Peter and the public, it was stage managed – Wiggy was hidden away with the same coloured leathers and wearing another pair of Mike's trousers. So everyone assumed that it was Mike re-emerging onto the race track.

Simon played the part very well. He deliberately collided with the fence on the first bend and wobbled along behind Peter. Until the third lap. Then he stood the bike upright and roared under Mr York on the back wheel. Peter, thinking that Mike was out of control and heading for the tote board, was petrified. In fact, Peter was then stuck to the saddle for reasons we won't go into here!

Simon had *everyone* fooled.

Simon Wigg was game for a laugh. We had a great time, overall, and I still miss him.

John Payne

BERNARD Crapper will have covered a lot of key points about our time with Simon at Oxford, including being spread across Derek Pugh's bed at the BSPA conference, which saw us move Wiggy from Cradley Heath to Oxford after one season in the British League. A step up from the National League that he made very well, indeed.

However, I would like to comment on a couple of matters. First, Simon's willingness to respond to phone calls and letters received at Oxford Speedway, on behalf of children who were ill in hospital – some of them terminally. Subject to his racing diary, Simon would drop everything to visit them and with him around, you knew that the kids would thoroughly enjoy his visit. To many he was their speedway hero and he would certainly live up to their expectations. Football is very good at this special area of community relations but speedway is not so developed. Simon was an exception and his genuine efforts are much to his credit.

I do recall that although Simon was a very positive guy, Bernard would successfully try 'reverse psychology' on him. If Oxford was under pressure for a victory, Bernard would exclaim in Wiggy's earshot: 'Bloody hell, it's Wiggy – we haven't got a chance!' So, with his nose put out of joint, Simon would go out and absolutely fly!

Bernard had a lot more to do with that side of the promotion, while I dealt more with the financial side. Simon did not come cheap, as you can imagine. In fact when I wrote out his pay cheque, my hand was shaking! However, he certainly gave value for his money. Not only for his performances on track, but as a very good all-round PR man for the club, and he never failed to attend a supporters' event.

By nature Simon was very sociable and, in subsequent years, he would come and visit me at the Plough Inn, Wheatley, where I am mine host.

He was a vibrant personality and his end-of-season fancy dress parties were legendary. Again, he did it all for charity. Yes, Bernard and I did attend together on one occasion, as Pinky and Perky! That was Simon's nickname for us. Funnily enough, we took the costumes to a match at Ipswich for a bit of a stunt. We were sitting there waiting in the changing rooms when a local junior walked in, dropped his bag and ran off!

People have asked me what sort of promoter Simon would have made. He was very careful with his money, so I believe that he would have been a tough negotiator with rider contracts and hard on his team in terms of expectation of performance. Perhaps that's not quite the answer that most would expect?

On that matter of his tightness, if I was 50p out in my wage calculations, Simon would be on the phone the next day. Then he would spend a couple of quid of his phone bill enthusing over this topic or that! He was the same with fuel – driving miles out of his way to find a cheaper petrol station. When Jeremy Doncaster had a problem once in a major meeting at Bradford because his bike was too light – we jokingly arranged for a call to go out for Simon Wigg's wallet to please be escorted to the pits, as that would solve the problem!

That said – and it's meant in fun – I will always remember Simon Wigg for the great asset he was to Oxford Speedway.

John Louis

I HAD only the one season working closely with Simon when he was at Hackney in 1987. Strange that I have only recently discovered from Jeremy Doncaster that Simon lived in Suffolk and attended Ipswich Speedway from the time we went up into the British League in 1972. He never mentioned it.

Simon came to us as a genuine number one having stepped out of the shadow of Hans Nielsen at Oxford. To be frank, Simon wasn't totally consistent. When he was good he was very good but he did suffer bad patches and at home, too.

I learned of his concerns about us having to take the track in by a few feet but when that happened in my riding career, you didn't tend to notice. Also, I knew Simon's thoughts on being a loan rider as opposed to a full signing. Again, it happens to a lot of riders and it's not unusual. Having said that, Simon was great to have around the place – his energy and enthusiasm was very welcome and his ability to talk to younger riders, fans, the press and sponsors was outstanding. His equipment was immaculate and Simon was always clean and tidy. He was a pleasure to deal with as a promoter.

Yes, we would also have disagreements about track preparation and track conditions but we never fell out. He was always polite in making his point.

Dave Pavitt and myself had a tough decision to make at the end of that season over our future league status. British League was not working for us in the business sense. We opted to go into the National League for 1988 and bring on our younger assets. I have to say that it proved a very good decision and we enjoyed outstanding success, winning the league title and bringing on the likes of Mark Loram, Andy Galvin and my son, Chris. The switch to the NL meant there was no place for Simon but, overall, I enjoyed our season together.

In summary, Simon Wigg was a diamond of a bloke.

Signing for Hackney, 1987, alongside team boss John Louis (right) and HL1 Kestrels' promoter Dave Pavitt.

Allan Ham

WHEN I first signed Simon Wigg at Bradford, I knew what I was getting as a promoter. I had observed him during his speedway career at home and abroad. He was my ideal rider – colourful, flamboyant and stylish both on and off the track. Simon had an abundance of charisma, was fluent and enthusiastic He was a true professional.

Which was why we negotiated to sign him live on Yorkshire TV in a programme fronted by Harry Gratian. The programme opened with a shot of Simon sitting on his bike in the studio, followed by an action preview before Simon moved to the main table with my brother, Bobby. After the big build up, Bobby produced a Bic biro! It became quite a joke at Odsal, with Simon teasing us about why we couldn't afford a Parker pen for the occasion.

Simon had broken his neck at the end of the previous season while riding in Italy and his comeback was in an opening challenge at Berwick's former track at Berrington Lough. Well, you couldn't get a circuit that was more different than the big, fast Odsal bowl and we got hammered. I was using the early season challenges to study pairings and so Simon took his full quota of rides but only scored two points as I recall.

Immediately I had fans on my back complaining that I didn't know what I was doing by signing him. My reply was that you haven't seen anything of the true rider yet.

Simon wore a neck brace at Berwick and continued to do so until one night at Bradford when he was put on two minutes . . . and in the mad scramble, he initially forgot to put it on. He wanted to go and retrieve it with about 15 seconds remaining and I told him to forget about his neck and get out there, pronto. He won that race by 40 metres and came back in and said: 'You're right, Alan!' He never wore it again and I'm sure he'd been overly-concerned about the injury he sustained in Italy at the end of the previous season.

He went on to have an outstanding season, helping us to win the KO Cup, and we even went back to Berwick in the league and beat them.

I sat down with Simon prior to him joining us and spoke to him at length about our joint plans and aspirations. He was full of suggestions to me as a promoter and at the time Bobby and myself were planning some colourful changes around the track – such as a yellow safety fence and post office red kickboard. Simon was so enthusiastic about this, plus aspects of the presentation for the major events that we staged on behalf of the sport at the stadium. He was keen to impart his broader concepts about putting on a show and reaching a new audience. By coincidence, Bradford were involved in the first team suits worn in British Speedway, which my niece, Tracy Ham, produced. Above any other rider, Simon Wigg had terrific vision.

As a promotion, we provided soup and sandwiches for the boys at the end of a meeting. Even though Simon had a hectic schedule, he would find time to sit down in a corner and discuss issues surrounding the sport. He would never clock-watch during a conversation and there was always a conclusion to the exchange. We ended up singing from the same hymn sheet. I have to say we enjoyed a meeting of minds and there was a good rapport between rider and promoter.

Simon also had advice on track preparation, especially at a time when we were becoming more innovative with the introduction of spiking at the starting gate. Simon had some good suggestions on how we could cope with track preparation during long, dry spells. I would strongly emphasise about Simon that he would encourage a promoter and, in a different context, the team manager, too. Lots of riders try to discourage you but he was like a breath of fresh air around the place.

Last-minute encouragement from Bradford boss Allan Ham.

The ladies working for us also commented on how elegant he was. He carried a briefcase into private meetings and dressed well. In fact my wife said Simon would look elegant even if dressed in a bin liner and we were in suits.

Simon was also aware of the problems that his fixture clashes could cause even though we accepted it as part of the package when we sought his services. The Dukes won the Knockout Cup three years in succession and, in fact, we won it four years out of five. Colin Pratt was running Cradley Heath at the time and organised the return leg on a date that coincided with practice for the Ace of Aces grasstrack, which Simon had to attend. We would not be able to book a guest and Colin knew this. So Simon negotiated with Ian Barclay and worked the oracle. He scored double points and enjoyed our victory celebrations before going off to meet his double obligation. When this hadn't been possible in the past, he would discuss the guest options with me and was very concerned that we covered his absences effectively. He even tried to work on fixture changes to fit in with his availability. I appreciated his genuine input and concern.

I believe that Bradford Speedway saw Simon at his peak as a speedway rider. With no disrespect to him or the clubs that followed us in his career, they did not see him at his best.

As a family we went to Oxford in 1999 to support his farewell meeting. It was our tribute for what he had done for Bradford Speedway in his time with us. I so recalled how he always thanked us over various aspects of our work on and off track. How he offered congratulations when our promotion took on the staging of major events. He used to tell me that driving into the Odsal Stadium and looking down into the bowl immediately whetted his appetite for the sporting challenge ahead.

If Simon Wigg was here today he would surely be involved in the TV coverage of the sport and have an ambassadorial role, perhaps more than a promotional job, for the Elite League and the Speedway Grand Prix. His influence is apparent in modern speedway with the team suits, bike fairings and numbers. His contribution will live on.

I am proud to have had such a personal bond with Simon Wigg on so many important matters in our sport.

Keith 'Buster' Chapman

LIKE many other promoters in Simon's career, I knew who and what I was signing when he joined me at King's Lynn in 1997. I mean this as much for his role as an ambassador for the club as for the points he scored on track and the advice he gave our younger riders off track.

In a sense, I gave him a team place when he was effectively out of a job – his previous club, Exeter, had dropped down into the Premier League. Simon had to accept the budget that we worked to at King's Lynn and he rode for a lesser rate than he'd been used to.

Simon enjoyed a very good first season with us, adding about a point-and-a-half to his average. It will come as no surprise for me to tell you that he was great with fans, the media, and sponsors. Where sponsors are concerned, I know how hard it is to find them and how it is even harder to keep them – Wiggy was very switched on in that department. He kept us involved and informed and was a role model for the rest of us.

Simon would have the occasional whinge but never about track conditions. The good thing about him was that you could have a debate with him without falling out over what was said – and I

His final season, at King's Lynn, 1998.

appreciated his general input anyway.

In 1998, Simon suddenly became an unpredictable performer. He seemed to lose concentration in some races and then came an almighty crash with Gary Havelock at Saddlebow Road. He came down very heavily on his head and was well out of it, lying on the track with his eyes up inside his head. Simon just ran into Gary for no apparent reason and he suffered severe concussion for a while after that fall.

I also began to notice that Simon was suffering memory lapses, which was unusual for him. I used to travel with Martin Hagon to meetings abroad and we used to see Simon a lot. Things that had been previously discussed and agreed, plus other facts, seemed to have slipped his memory, although I suppose it's only with the benefit of hindsight that I realise this now.

Matters came to a head between us towards the end of the season, at Oxford, when King's Lynn were in with a chance of winning the match and Simon was well off the pace. Being my usual undiplomatic and vocal self, I asked him how much Oxford had paid him! That provoked Simon and his mechanic to give me the black looks that I deserved for such comments.

When I charged up to him, Simon was hunched over his bike in the pits with his helmet on the crossbar of the frame. He explained that he hadn't felt very well and, in fact, was wracked with pain throughout his body. I feel that my reaction to that is more justified – that he should have advised me of his feelings so that we would have operated rider replacement.

I now realise that all this was the beginning of the end for him.

However, despite my outburst, I did want him back for 1999 but his health situation meant his time with us marked the end of his racing career. I did phone Charlie to ask about Simon but didn't want to pry too much as, no doubt, she had loads of other calls to cope with.

After Simon's second operation, I heard from Nigel Wagstaff that he was bringing Simon up to a King's Lynn match one evening. I was thrilled at the prospect – until I went to the car park and saw him being loaded into his wheelchair. I'm not very good at facing very sad and difficult circumstances – I couldn't even be with my Dad when he was passing away – so, in tears, I turned on my heel and walked away. I like to remember people as they always were, and not in a sad state of deterioration. I wanted to remember Simon as he was – full of vitality.

That's how I remember Simon – not just as a great personality, but as an outstanding sportsman too.

Terry Russell

WHEN I was first became Chairman of the British Speedway Promoters' Association, the first phone call I received was from Wiggy – summoning me to his house so that he could tell me his thoughts and what I needed to do to take the sport forward!

To be fair, he had many very good ideas, spoke a lot of sense and I'm pleased to say that some of what he told me that day – like the riders' colour coded kevlars – are now very much part of Elite League speedway in Britain. He should always take the credit for introducing that.

I first got to know Simon when he rode for Hackney in 1987 – I was sponsoring Andy Galvin at the time – although I'd just started getting involved as promoter at Crayford when Simon rode there for Weymouth, in 1982. Thank God his clutch burnt out in the last race, enabling us to score a match-winning 5-1!

Simon was fantastic, always full of ideas – from the numbering of the bikes, and his wish that all the machines should look the same, and everything else to emphasise speedway's qualities as essentially a team sport.

The one big regret I've got to this day – and I said it at the time – is that he didn't live long enough to see us go to Cardiff, when the Grand Prix series was held there for the first time in 2001. Cardiff would have been right up Simon's street and I just know his big smile would have stretched from one side of the Millennium Stadium to the other. It's the best thing we've ever done as an association and he would have really enjoyed being there with us in Wales. I'd have loved him to have been part of the British GP and I certainly would've wanted him to have seen it with his own eyes – he would have loved the whole show.

Simon had obviously become very frustrated with British speedway when he decided to take out a Dutch licence, although after I became chairman I think we'd overcome a lot of the problems that concerned him. In fact, I helped to get him back on an ACU racing licence. At the end of the day, it's a nonsense – if you're British, you're British; and if you're Dutch, you're Dutch, so I was glad to have Simon back on board and racing on an ACU licence again.

It was a case of him understanding what our problems and politics were as promoters. I understood his frustrations and why he left the ACU at that time – I wouldn't say he was being selfish and I understood exactly where he was coming from on issues like Sunday speedway. Simon felt very strongly that our big shared event meetings shouldn't be held on Sunday afternoons but we have our own problems to deal with and we've been battling hard to try and get our sport in order. To be fair, I still hear Simon's argument about Sunday meetings in Britain from Leigh Adams today!

In an ideal world, Simon wanted to sit down and work out his full racing calendar for the year. The problem today is, we are lumbered with Swedish league matches on a Tuesday and the Polish league on a Sunday. Oh, and by the way, the boys don't really wish to ride in England on Mondays now, because they don't want to have to come all the way back from Poland and then fly out to Sweden for a Tuesday meeting. See, nothing changes much.

It's very, very difficult for British promoters although, in his latter days, Simon began to appreciate our problems with fixtures, and the difficulties caused by rain-offs, a lot more.

I remember when the Elite League Riders' Championship was televised for the first time at Bradford – Simon just went out of his way to have a special bike to put on a really good show and try and win that meeting. He was the ultimate professional.

I invited Simon and his wife, Charlie, along to the World Team Cup Final at Coventry on what was my 50th birthday, in September 2000 – just two months before Simon passed away. We enjoyed it – even though England were robbed again – and although Simon was in a wheelchair and had been on steroids, he knew everything that was going on around him right up 'till the end.

I was very pleased to be invited to Simon's 40th birthday while he was in the hospice, among what were considered to be his closest friends. As a member of speedway's so-called 'hierarchy', I considered it a special honour to be present! Despite his gripes about promoters and the way speedway was run, Simon hadn't fallen out with me, and I was delighted to be there with him that day, just four weeks before he died.

He had a great reaction to me whenever I visited him, even though his vocabulary was quite poor by then. If he'd been able to talk clearly . . . I don't know, he might well have torn me off a strip or two about something or other!

I had loads of time for Simon, I miss him like hell. Fantastic rider, fantastic person.

Chris Van Straaten

I WAS never fortunate to have had Simon riding for a team that I was involved in, so we were always in opposition. I used to look with envy at teams who did have him on track because Simon was so promotional. Everything about him was so professional – the way he looked, the way he conducted himself, the way he dealt with the fans and the media.

I got to know Simon more on two counts. I have been on the BSPA Management Committee for some years and he came to us from time to time with his proposals. We initially thought: 'What is he on about?' But two or three years down the road, you realised that he was just ahead of his time.

This was the mid-90s – Simon banged on about team colours for four or fives years, as I recall. I was vice-chairman the year we gave him the authority to get some sample suits made up and I can always remember when he brought a sample to a promoters' meeting. John Louis was the victim who was chosen to model it. He had to come back into the room in the suit and he looked like a ballet dancer. There was great hilarity!

But the concept was superb, just what we wanted to achieve. Unfortunately, there was the hiccup that it wasn't the right material – it wasn't tough enough. When they walked out for the parade, it probably looked OK but the riders were complaining that they were sliding on the saddle. We have since sorted the problem, having sourced the material in Britain.

What you see with the coloured team kevlars today was Simon's idea.

The work he produced on machines was exceptional, too. One of speedway's pitfalls has been that the bikes hardly looked much different than they had 50 years before. To get the kids more excited, the bikes needed to look a lot more modern. Again, a lot of the fairings that riders have incorporated today were Simon's brainchild. He was spot on – he even had one made up in Pepsi-Cola branding for demonstration purposes.

I loved talking to Simon, because he was so enthusiastic about the sport. Also, he was never frightened to point out what he thought was wrong with it. If he had run-ins with the authorities in this country, it was about longtrack. That probably brought him into confrontation most throughout his time in speedway, which was unfortunate. I used to talk to him about it and said that I couldn't see what the attraction of longtrack was. I told him that I had been to see it and it did nothing for me. Simon replied: 'You wait until you see it under lights, it's a different spectacle.'

This was how the event at Marmande in France had built up, so it got me thinking about the racecourse at Dunstall Park in Wolverhampton, where they had three all-weather circuits. I opened negotiations with the racecourse company, who were OK about us taking longtrack events there under lights.

Simon became heavily involved in that project. He quickly arranged noise tests at the venue and, in fact, Simon and Steve Johnston are the only riders to have ever ridden bikes around the trotting track at Dunstall Park. They did that for me one afternoon – we did all the tests required and, again, Simon was so supportive, saying all the right words to the people from the council who were in attendance. It wasn't through lack of effort on his part that the project failed. It was the conservationists who stopped it in the end, which was a great shame.

Simon had this vision to put on a great event under lights at Wolverhampton, with its big capacity stadium and full restaurant facilities. He was so excited when I first took him along, believing it would be the making of longtrack racing in this country. It has never taken off because we don't have the venues suitable for it.

His enthusiasm for anything which he put his mind to was contagious. If he had lived he certainly would have broken into the realms of Sky TV. You can just picture him now, just sitting in that studio and offering his opinion on everything.

As I mentioned, his grasstrack commitments caused confrontation with speedway promoters. Grasstrack meetings are, of course, traditionally held on Sundays. Even now we get arguments about Sunday fixture clashes and I am quite often called to mediate between the ACU and BSPA with respect to riders, so that problem hasn't gone away. Any friction that was caused by a conflict of dates between grasstrack and speedway wasn't really Simon's fault, though. If the fault was anybody's, it was speedway's.

Simon Wigg was a man of vision with the brainpower and communication skills to match.

John Berry

WE had all heard of Simon Wigg, the grasstrack rider, long before he threw his leg over a speedway bike. It was a brave move to adopt and adapt to another sport, putting his already established reputation on the line.

Although many speedway riders tried their hand, often very successfully, at the Continental longtracks where the loose surfaces blurred the edges between speedway and grasstrack, Simon was definitely a grasstrack boy who had to learn the different art of speedway.

That he so quickly and easily adapted to the new style said volumes about his natural talent, professionalism and intelligence. The ability to hop from one racing style to another on a daily basis, and at the highest level, put him in a class very few others could cope with. Egon Müller, Ivan Mauger, Barry Briggs and, nearer home, his very good friend Jeremy Doncaster were a few who did manage it successfully. Most times, though, I encouraged riders to concentrate on just one of the two codes because they couldn't cope with both.

As England team manager, I never really had a great deal to do with Simon. In my early stints at the job, he had not yet taken up the shale sport, and he then found a log-jam of world class riders already occupying most of the available spaces.

When he did get the opportunities to ride in Test matches, I got the feeling he didn't place these events at the very top of his priorities. Maybe, with so much talent around him, he didn't feel he needed to bring his 'A' game along.

In the time between my involvements with the England team, as Father Time began catching up with the top English boys, Simon took on more responsibility and became an important part of the England set-up. Sadly for me, in 1985, when he was badly needed, Simon was sitting out his suspension. I am sure, without that unfortunate episode, I would have got to know the man much better.

It was a shame his openness, honesty and gregarious nature, which had served him so well in dealing with press, public, and promoters, should have been the very reason for his problems. The sad thing is, he said nothing more then than is now discussed quite commonly with no great shock-horror reactions.

Not that the episode prevented him from being very outspoken about how he felt speedway should be run. Many riders, when they offer their opinions on how to organise things, do not always realise the realities of speedway promoting life, and many of Simon's ideas were not always practical, but the fact that he cared enough to have them showed his love of the sport.

I suspect, had it not been for what happened, we would have seen Wiggy maintain a strong connection with the sport when his riding days were over. I am positive it would only have been to the benefit of speedway. Whoever or whatever you are within the world of speedway, there is no doubting his loss had an impact on all our speedway lives one way or another.

It is always desperately sad when someone is taken before his time. The only consolation with Simon is that he packed more into his short spell on Earth that most do if they live to be a hundred. A great longtrack and speedway rider, a great personality and a great loss for us all.

David Tapp

WHEN asked to write a tribute for this book, I considered it a huge honour. You see, I class myself as one of Simon Wigg's biggest fans. I am not necessarily referring just to his riding ability, which of course has been well documented, but more so his outstanding qualities as a lovely human being.

For me, Simon Wigg was a person of supreme integrity and I would argue he is one of the greatest ambassadors our sport has ever seen. In essence, Wiggy only did very good things for our beloved sport and, in my opinion, speedway owes him a great debt of gratitude.

Back in mid-1994 I was busy planning the inaugural Series 500 International Masters tournament in Australia and, to be honest, I was really targeting three riders that I thought were crucial to the success of the maiden tour Down Under – Sam Ermolenko, Tony Rickardsson and Wiggy. I was successful in securing all three riders and, as history now shows, the inaugural Series 500 proved enormously successful. The tour ran for six consecutive years and the great Simon Wigg was a major reason it achieved such acclaim across the world.

Simon rode in my series in 1995,'96 and '97 and he was contracted to appear again in 1998 – but, as we know, his world was about to be tipped upside down and hence he missed touring for the fourth consecutive year due to ill health. Ironically, at the time he fell ill, his bikes and equipment had just landed in Australia in preparation for another tilt at the Series 500 title.

I will never underestimate Simon's contribution to the success of my series. He had toured Down Under on many occasions before I decided to enter the promotional scene in Australia and he enjoyed massive popularity in a country Simon described as his second home.

People reading this will acknowledge that Simon Wigg was a master in terms of his professionalism and pure entertainment value on the track. The huge tracks in Australia certainly suited his liking to the wide, open spaces and he was almost

Enjoying the Series 500 experience.

unbeatable around venues like Claremont in Perth and Wayville Showground in Adelaide.

His ride to win the A Final at the Brisbane Exhibition Ground, in the Grand Final of the 1996 Series 500, was his greatest ride ever in Australia. It was a performance that typified the genius of the best Englishman ever to race speedway Down Under.

Simon was a must on the rider list when I planned my series each year. A super professional, he was effective on any track, perfect with the media and always great with the event's sponsors. Yes, he was the complete package and the role he played in helping establish the Series 500 in Australia was more valuable than I could ever put into words.

On my tours, Simon was also in many ways the self-appointed event director. He would organise the other lads and make sure he helped any of the young foreign riders that were touring Australia for the very first time. Simon would arrange the riders' social calendar and he seemingly knew everyone in the country – he was always organising nights out or trips to the beach and he handled the role with passion and precision.

Talking of the beach, Simon *always* had a tan and I often wondered how he managed to achieve such a golden complexion while living in a country that was not really renowned for its warm weather and sunshine!

Many times he would volunteer to drive the tour bus and he'd take charge of the sight-seeing, the riders' nutritional requirements and their alcohol consumption. I remember one time after we had raced at Rockhampton Showground, in mid-north Queensland, Wiggy arranged a trip for everyone to visit Fraser Island, one of Australia's most popular holiday locations at the famous Barrier Reef. Yes, our Wiggy loved a party, a beer and the occasional Aussie cigar.

Simon and I became very good friends over the years and during his tours to Australia Wiggy and his family sometimes stayed at my Wattle Grove residence, located 20 kilometres south of Sydney, and as a house guest he was an absolute delight. He was a bloody funny bloke who always lived every day to its fullest – everyone who knew him would say the same thing.

I make no secret of the fact that I used to confide in Simon quite a lot when I was in the process of recruiting riders for my series each year. I had to be careful and make sure I got sensible lads that were in Australia to race hard and ultimately be a good ambassador for their respective country. I wasn't interested in boofheads who only wanted to tear up hotel rooms and waste my time at great expense. For the record, the people I trusted most when it came to rider selection were Wiggy, Sam Ermolenko, Leigh Adams and photographer Mike Patrick.

I always used to make it my business to pick Simon up from the airport when he arrived in Australia and he always had the same greeting for me upon his arrival – 'Hello Tappy, great to see you, mate. Geez, it's great to be back in Australia riding in your series. Do me a favour and put me down for next year already!'

Man with a tan.

I would like to congratulate the author and publishers of this book as the late, great Simon Wigg deserves such a sterling tribute. It seems entirely appropriate that one of the greatest showmen in the history of speedway and longtrack should be honoured in such a way.

Simon Wigg passed away at a very young age and his death rates as a terrible tragedy. He still had so much to offer as a speedway professional and as a human being.

I am proud to call Simon Wigg my friend and I will always remember those famous green and white leathers, in full flight, under the floodlights at venues like the Brisbane Exhibition Ground.

What a superstar he was.

ENGLAND TEAM MANAGERS

Carl Glover

SIMON Wigg was like a breath of fresh air in my year as England manager in 1984, which was only his second season of British League racing. Looking back, I should have pushed Wiggy a bit harder that year, because pressure never got to him.

I once told him that his bikes didn't have enough speed and he went away and did something about it. I could see he was riding his b******s off but he wasn't getting far.

What a fantastic man. Nothing seemed to get him down and he always had that lovely smile.

He could be a bit mischievous mind. Occasionally, I used to drive him to the airport and Simon used to have one of those stupid plastic things, with different messages printed, that he flipped over and held up to the window as soon as you drew up alongside another motorist. Some of the messages were a bit near the mark but it was just Simon having a bit of fun.

Wiggy gave me 100 per cent every time he rode for England. He was an absolute winner.

Eric Boocock

I KNEW of Simon a few years before he came onto the England scene. He was always very competitive on track and also seemed to have a good mechanical knowledge, how to make his bike go faster.

He was forward-thinking with top tuners and good mechanics in his support team. Simon was experimental with details such as different length exhausts, monocoque frames and spoilers. I went to his workshop at Middle Claydon in later years and was struck by the amount of what I would call 'hybrid' stuff that he had there. It was all so well organised.

But while he was advanced in his thinking, it could backfire on him.

I remember in my days as England co-manager, flying to Los Angeles for the 1988 World Team Cup. There were two of his bikes among the air-freight. Simon was sitting near to me on the plane with a camshaft in his pocket – one that was untried. So I discovered that Simon was about to experiment during a World Final!

When we eventually made it to practice, his engines proved too powerful for the Long Beach track. So he turned the ignition back, but too far back. In my opinion, by not testing at Oxford, and deciding to try out in America where it really mattered, he had lost the plot. Simon failed to score and he received harsh words from me afterwards. His tendency to experiment with his machinery could be a major weakness in an otherwise thoughtful and unbelievably quick rider.

In my own early riding days with Middlesbrough and Halifax in the 60s, I had Charlie Monk of Glasgow lodging with me. He was always in the workshop tinkering and was full of ideas. But many times it was one step forward and three steps back. Simon could be the same.

One aspect of my own speedway career that he reminded me of in a very positive way was that he was organised. Part of that was ensuring your leathers, machinery and transport were always clean. It's a good habit to develop. So he reminded me of myself some 20 years previously – not that I had his ability as a rider. I had a good career

Booey and skipper Wiggy in jubilant mood after England had just beaten arch rivals Denmark, 1987.

but Simon was top of the tree. He had it in him to have been World Speedway Champion but grasstrack and longtrack were his priorities. He was fabulous at both and brought a lot of the skills of those sports into his speedway.

Now normally Simon was super with sponsors, keeping them informed and involved. He was among the riders backed by Coal Products Limited and, to be frank, he was their blue-eyed boy. Ron Baker at CPL was hugely supportive of Simon and of British speedway in general. The CPL sponsorship deal, which included backing of the England Sunbrite Lions, was an outstanding one for the sport. But there was a conflict issue when Simon missed England Test fixtures, especially at a time when the Americans and the Danes were both so very competitive.

To be honest, I can understand that it is difficult to ride in England when you can earn up to five times as much the rates for a Test match by riding in Germany on a Sunday afternoon. But I had a role, with Colin Pratt, to run the England scene.

Also, in the days before riders had the attraction of riding in Polish league speedway, Sunday was our best opportunity in Britain to get 16 top riders together at once.

We also felt it was an awkward situation with the standby rider – effectively the England number nine – if he only felt wanted when Simon wasn't likely to be there. In fact, it probably wasn't good for the team as a whole.

When Simon stated that he would only be available for two out of five scheduled Test matches, it was not acceptable to ourselves, and his withdrawal from a Test match at Bradford – in CPL's heartland – made matters worse. Even they were beginning to express concern about who was basically running the team.

We did sit down and discuss matters with Simon in a rational manner. Eventually we went to the BSPA, who had appointed us, and explained that we were stripping Simon of the captaincy and were actually unlikely to select him for the near future. The BSPA were supportive and understanding.

All this was a great pity, as Simon was an outstanding skipper. He was like a third team manager in the pre-meeting talk. Once Colin and myself had finished, Simon would chip in and pick up points that, perhaps, we hadn't made.

Simon was also on the ball during matches. He would be watching the racing as much as possible. I remember his spotting a 'lazy' starting gate in one Test match, and getting us to inform the referee so that it could be rectified.

I did have a bust-up with Simon over another issue – that of travel arrangements for Test matches abroad. To ensure that we could keep such fixtures in the calendar, Colin and myself had to be very cost-conscious, so we worked with travel organiser Gareth Parry on block bookings in particular. Also, we would co-ordinate collection of everybody's equipment.

But Simon was a bugger for making his own arrangements at the last minute, so he could fit other factors into his itinerary – like hiving off to the Jawa factory in Czecho, if we had an international meeting in Poland.

It all blew up in Denmark, when Simon flew in separately to join the rest of us in time for the evening meal at our hotel. He was always very careful with his money and decided, during the meal, to present me with a bill for his taxi ride from the airport. I exploded and there was such a row – again on the topic of him picking and choosing his meetings – that it ended with me telling Simon where to put his receipt before storming from the table.

However, the great thing about Simon was that he never bore a grudge. His manner was fine and friendly the next morning, which helped smooth matters over considerably.

Other than these few skirmishes – and you know that I am Mister Blunt and will tell you about Simon, warts and all – I had the greatest admiration for him. He was so professional, had an easy manner with people and was superb on the sponsorship scene.

Simon was also quite a big lad for a speedway rider but he trained and watched his weight – he had all the right qualities for success.

I last saw him in a hospitality marquee at Coventry. His wife, Charlie, pushed his wheelchair into the area but I was disappointed that he was being ignored by most – a former golden boy of our sport being treated like that. So I went over and leant down in my blazer and trousers to chat to him. Simon recognised me but he had difficulty conversing.

I can tell you, I was right choked up to see him like that, but I'm glad I made the effort.

Colin Pratt

ALTHOUGH Simon had left Cradley Heath and moved to Oxford in the same winter I took over at Dudley Wood in 1984, I'd been aware of his ability as a rider from monitoring Simon Cross, our signing who rode with Wiggy at Weymouth.

Simon Wigg came across as very professional, someone who knew where he wanted to go and who would work hard to get there. He also had a mind of his own and wasn't afraid to express his opinions.

I was impressed by his ability to attract sponsors for all his sports and, importantly, to keep them. Simon really knew how to attract sponsors.

On the speedway scene, he became a very good British League heat leader at Oxford, despite being overshadowed by Hans Nielsen for the number one spot.

When Eric Boocock and myself became the England managers we had the hiccup of his 1985 ban. So in 1986 we made the decision to make him the England captain. Simon had the ability as a rider and we knew that he could handle himself, his fellow riders and the media. More important than his credentials was the fact that Eric and myself wanted to raise his morale after a difficult period. Simon proved an excellent captain in all circumstances, because he could lift a team's spirit and be very helpful to other riders. He was also very professional and set a good example.

However, Simon and I did have a major difference of opinion on one issue – Sunday speedway and where his priorities lay.

I was, understandably, only interested in the British speedway scene and the England team. It all blew up over a Test match at Bradford when Coal Products Ltd were both England team sponsors and one of Simon's individual backers. Simon, plus Jeremy Doncaster and Martin Dugard, would attend functions for CPL and they were very pleased with the riders' efforts.

But Simon opted out of the Odsal Test to ride, I believe, in Teterow. This was not a World Championship qualifier but, in reality, an open meeting. In going to Germany I felt that he had let down both his country and his and our sponsors in one fell swoop. So Eric and I dropped him until further notice, as we felt that Simon had to get his priorities right.

When he argued that speedway should not be staged on a Sunday afternoon anyway, my retort was: 'So what are they doing at 3pm on a Sunday afternoon in Germany, I wonder?' Frankly, you can't pick and choose, whoever you are.

We did eventually recall Simon, in 1989, as reserve for the World Team Cup Final at Bradford. This infamous meeting will always be remembered for the pile-up which ended Erik Gundersen's career and nearly cost him his life. It also took Simon Cross, Lance King and Jimmy Nilsen out of the meeting. So all the reserves had to race from that point. Although England won the title, helped by Simon's contribution, our victory was overshadowed by the concern for Erik. This was an era when Denmark were dominant in all competitions in world speedway and it was very difficult to secure any victory.

Simon came back into the England fold and was no problem from that point onwards – he became an influence on other riders to raise their game.

Apart from that previous England situation, I can't fault Simon. You never saw him down and he was so enthusiastic, well organised and excellent with the media.

Simon Wigg was definitely right for the sport.

Pratty and Wiggy plotting victory over the Danes, 1987.

GRASSTRACK & LONGTRACK

Trevor Banks

GRASSTRACK racing was the basis of my competitive life with motorcycles. I was just emerging when Julian Wigg was a top rider and a rival of my late brother, Graham. I remember going to the Lydden circuit in Kent as a youngster and seeing Julian in action. I logged his kid brother at the time and used to see him around Julian at subsequent meetings.

We first met on track at Morietz in the south of France. Although Simon was only 17, he had received dispensation to ride in the meeting. Frankly, he didn't ride that brilliantly on the day but I was now conscious of this new guy on the scene.

How little did I realise how much Simon would improve!

In 1979 the British Grasstrack Championship was held at Braintree in Essex. We actually met in the first heat. I was on a JAP with a four-valve conversion while Simon was on a Lattenhammer-Weslake. I made the start, just about held him off throughout the race and went on to the take the title.

After the presentations Simon strolled across, sat on my bike, then pronounced: 'How can you ride a load of crap like that!' He then dismounted and walked off. I wasn't very happy with him at that moment, as you can imagine.

In 1980, we enjoyed many close races including those at events like the Ace of Aces and the British Championship, which I retained. Simon had a more serious dialogue with me about my equipment and convinced me to switch from my home-made frames to Dula, with whom he worked. I met Paul Duncombe and went over to Dula from 1981, when Simon and I got to know each other a lot better.

In the winter of 1981 Simon invited me to take part in a short-track series in Australia that he and Julian were going to compete in. Now I have to confess that I was 26 and had never flown in an aeroplane. So my debut flight was from London to Sydney! This was followed by an internal flight to Brisbane, where Simon would meet me. When I arrived in this hot country, there I was in my English clothes of shirt and jeans. Greeting me was a bronzed Simon in T-shirt and Bermuda shorts. Lugging my suitcases, I was taken to a bar called 'Brekkies Creek' in Brisbane, where Simon ordered two massive jugs of beer! The jet-lag plus the alcohol soon got to me and by the time we arrived at the home of Bill and Margaret MacDonald, I was nearly out of it! Did I get any rest? No – Simon whisked me off to watch a speedway meeting. By that time I didn't know if I was coming or going, it was all most bizarre!

Eventually I lodged with Martin Hagon above the Fraser motorcycle shop and we shared the workshop with Julian. It was great as we had racing bikes to prepare and road bikes available to go out on.

It was quite an insight living around Simon – he was very quick at tackling jobs and so energetic. He would be up early in the morning and occupy himself with designing leathers. Then, by the time that most of us were emerging for a normal day, he would prepare the drawings for despatch to Barbara Miles back in England. Simon was so on the ball and he was ready to go before everybody. He operated at a speed in excess of the rest of us mere mortals. Now wonder he was so successful in his endeavours.

That was a great close season and I particularly enjoyed our trip to Fraser Island. It was also a period when Simon again influenced a personal decision, for he convinced me to have a go at speedway. We went to a track called Radcliffe for a Friday night practice session, where I shared a bike with Martin Hagon while Simon had his own solo machine. When it came to the crunch of a proper race, I made the start and kept Simon at bay. Simon was a heat leader at Weymouth and I realised at that moment that I did have the potential to take up speedway. I also found racing around a speedway track easier than I had imagined.

I was based in Folkestone, Kent and so looked for second-half races at Crayford. It was a Tuesday night track, which fitted in nicely with my weekend grasstrack commitments. It was also a very small circuit and I realised that I had to master it if I was going to be any good at the shale sport.

As I progressed, promoter Terry Russell and team manager George Barclay decided to use me initially for away matches at Peterborough, Exeter and Weymouth where they knew I could get around as the tracks were larger. Wiggy had encouraged me to have a go and he instilled confidence in me, something which I needed at the time.

On the short-track tour in Australia, 1986. Left to right: Martin Hagon, Greg Ohl (Maryborough promoter, on bike), Julian Wigg, Trevor Banks and Simon.

Also that season, the move to Dula impacted positively on my grasstrack career and I began to race abroad more regularly. The German scene was harder to break into and I found that their scrutineering was over-strict. I preferred to race in France where the officials were more easy-going. Incidentally, Germany is now my favourite place to race!

I did go back with Simon for a second winter in Brisbane in 1982. Speedway was the main activity for him during that close season. I recall Simon, Martin and myself setting off to race speedway at Taree, near Sydney. We decided to drive through the night as it was cooler and there was less traffic. No spare wheel and, you've guessed it, a puncture! So we left Martin with the trailer and headed for the nearest town to find a tyre depot. Bear in mind that this is the middle of the night. We actually located one and then Simon shinned it up and over an eight-foot fence into the yard! To add to our good luck Simon managed to locate a mini-wheel after much rummaging.

Once he had safely scrambled back over the fence, we found a petrol station with an air-line. We were back with Martin within an hour and off on our journey again. Just one of many scrapes, I can assure you!

Over the years I had a fascination with Teterow and this I shared with Simon. After the fall of communism it was where we planned to race. It is so andrelin-pumping! Left and right-hand bends, jumps, twists, adverse cambers . . . the ultimate challenge for a racing motorcyclist. Simon always had the edge on me when we achieved our dream of competing there, although in 1998 he crashed heavily when he overdid it trying to get past me. I couldn't believe how fast he went alongside me and I just knew that he wouldn't get around the corner.

Our track records are comparable although, at 49, I'm still racing there and will continue to do so for a couple of years yet. The records were set on the weekend of May 30th and 31st 1998 and they still stand at the time of writing. Simon still holds the Teterow one-lap and four-lap records – the former at 121.795 Km/h and the latter at 118.318 Km/h, while I hold the five-lap record at 118.564 Km/h.

During the last chapter of his life Simon never lost his sense of humour or a sense of proportion. He was still joking and sending himself up about purchasing a great property in Australia and living there just eight weeks before returning to Britain for his final operation. There was always that famous smile when you went to visit him. He probably had private moments of depression but he never showed it to his friends. He was always responsive and made the effort when you went to see him.

Now you never ask another rider for their autograph during your racing career together, that's understandable, so I wanted him to sign a photo of us. It was heart-rending to see Simon struggle so hard but his co-ordination had been affected and he couldn't manage to write his name. I don't have his signature, unfortunately, but I do have happy memories of an incredible guy. He was a positive influence on me and I appreciate that.

I also wish to pay tribute to his wife, Charlie, who coped so well and was so loving and attentive to him in his hours of need.

Finally, our sports, grasstrack in particular, lost a great ambassador with Simon's passing.

Lew Coffin

SIMON first came on to my radar screen when he emerged on the schoolboy grasstrack scene. He and Sean Willmott, a protégé of mine, were the top two youngsters around at that time and they had some terrific battles for supremacy. Young Simon was very determined – he didn't like accepting second place.

Simon was a most marvellous kid, very polite and grateful for any help or advice that you gave him. He would also come up to me at meetings and seek information on gearings. From his early teens, improvement was the name of his game.

Once he reached the adult category, Simon was keen to get into the German racing scene, where I'd ridden for several decades and had acquired lots of contacts. However, I told him that I would let him know when I thought he was ready to have a go. Simon would then phone me every week with the same question: 'Am I ready yet?' I told him: 'When you are ready – off you go – and you'll never turn back.'

I believed that his situation would change from seeking bookings to eventually trying to fit them all in, and so it proved.

Simon also came down to my speedway training schools at Weymouth. He hurt himself in an early crash and then said: 'OK, Lew – now I will listen to you!' Once he had made it into the Weymouth team his speedway career went onwards and upwards. He perhaps stayed too long in the National League but he was very happy at Weymouth and regarded it as home.

Longtrack racing was obviously his main pursuit – and what great achievements he made.

Hans Zierk was a big factor and the engines he prepared were very good. Wiggy used to say to Hans: 'Bloody flying machine!' I still go regularly to Germany to assist riders and bump into Hans. We always ask each other if either of us has a 'Bloody flying machine' in the pits, in memory of Simon.

Wiggy became a legend in Germany and, in fact, he still is. One of his, and my, favourite tracks was Osnabruck, where I won the big meeting on 10 occasions before Wiggy took over my mantle. He was real 'box-office' in Germany, pulling massive support wherever he rode. The spectators were a sea of green, wearing the anoraks that had been produced in Wiggy racing colour.

I was talking recently to Karl Maier, who still misses Simon. They were great rivals who met at their peak but they were good friends, too. Karl was commenting on all of Simon's technical innovations and revealed that Simon even used a wind tunnel to help streamline the bike and sort out appropriate mudguard extensions on his machinery. He was also so adventurous – even to the extent of trying for a land speed record on a speedway bike.

The great thing about Simon was that he never changed his attitude. He was never big-headed even though he became a World Champion. He could still have a laugh and joke. He could still make the effort to keep in touch. I enjoyed it when our paths crossed regularly when he rode for Exeter.

The first time he came to the County Ground as a home rider, Simon couldn't turn his motorhome through the small side streets approaching the riders' car park and pits entrance. It was chaotic, so he arrived by more conventional means after that!

To me, Simon Wigg was the master of racing. Win or lose, he was still the same Simon.

Martin Hagon

I ENTERED the adult grasstrack scene in 1978, a year after Simon who was slightly older than me. I recall him riding a 250 Sieger Montessa and combining an erratic style, where he adopted a leg-trail, with genuine speed.

In the first meeting that I ever contested with him, at Lillingstone Lovell, Simon crashed in practice – he did have some heavy falls and injuries early in his grasstrack career and learned his lessons the hard way. In the 1978 season, I remember Simon riding my 350 in the British Final at Evesham, so we were getting on well by that stage.

By 1981, we had competed against each other many times and were friendly and supportive of each other as Brits abroad. That year Simon was involved, with his brother Julian, in setting up an influx of riders to compete in a short-track series based around Brisbane. Simon invited me to take part and organised everything once I had accepted.

This was a great adventure for a young guy and I did enjoy the whole trip. Simon was great to be around, so full of life.

We had a good set-up at the Fraser motorcycle shop, with racing machinery and road bikes laid on for us to go out on. I particularly enjoyed the opportunity of joining Simon in a local woods, where we thrashed around on moto-cross bikes.

As it was for Simon, grasstrack racing was my main love and we were fortunate to be competing in an era when the sport had plenty of fixtures – not only on the Continent but in Britain, too. You could pursue a busy diary then but I feel for the young guys coming into the sport now. In addition to there being far less clubs operating, the cost of parts and travel has escalated so much.

Germany and France were the places to try and get to for Continental experience when Simon and I started riding. In Germany there would be the international class meetings in both the north and south of the country, plus plenty of club meetings for those who couldn't break into the bigger scene initially. Today the Green Party has become a more significant force in German politics, so many of the venues that we rode at don't exist anymore.

Politics impacted in a different way on the motorcycle lives of Simon and myself when Communism collapsed in Eastern Europe by 1990., for we had both discussed our dream to ride at Teterow in eastern Germany – and what an eye-opener of a place that was, a fantastic challenge for any motorcycle racer. Simon and I had coped with right-hand turns on some circuits in our schoolboy days, plus we were also able to bring some moto-cross experience to the party.

After 1991, I reviewed my own motorcycle interests. I'd finished seventh in the 1985 World Longtrack Final at Korskro, which Simon won and I was very pleased for him that day. I used to take his bikes to meetings on occasions and was very impressed by his set-up. Simon had an eye for detail when it came to the presentation of his equipment and himself, he put forward a good image and deserved his rewards from being at the top of his game. Simon certainly knew how to look after his money, incidentally!

Anyway, I switched to sidecars from 1991, drifting away from Simon's circle for quite a while. Then I started to help out Kelvin Tatum when he rode for the London Lions at Hackney in 1996, which brought me back into contact with Simon more regularly around the British speedway scene. I also went with Kelvin to meetings such as Teterow and, of course, would see Simon there. Later, I began to sponsor Jason Crump, when Troy Butler was working for him, and this also kept Simon and I in the same loop. I picked up on the news of his unfortunate collapse in 1998 very quickly.

The following March, I'd gone to watch ice racing at Assen, Holland and was in a bar in Groningen when Simon walked in and we got chatting. He always had an extra dimension to his mind-set and his illness made no difference to his outlook – he didn't dwell on his problems, as a lot of people do and was positive about himself and the eventual outcome. We then got on with talking about a whole range of general topics about life, love and the world in general.

When assessing Simon, I ask people to look deeper than the phrase 'good all round motorcyclist'. You have to appreciate that Simon rode on a variety of contrasting tracks in his career – some were very rough, like the sandtracks in Holland; some were very smooth, like most speedway tracks; some were very large; while others were very small. He rode as brilliantly on deep tracks as he did on slicker surfaces.

Yet Simon Wigg was a consistent winner on them all and that is how he should be judged. The skill to win and the will to win made him the great champion that he was.

Paul Hurry

AS my Dad, Graham, had raced with Julian, I was aware of Simon even though I was only a young child. By the time I came on the racing scene, Simon was already an established top star. What added to his being my hero was that he raced in all the motorcycle events I aspired to compete in.

In 1987, I was the mascot at Hackney the season that Simon rode there in the British League. It was a real thrill that he took an interest in me, as he knew Graham. I remember saving cable-ties of various colours at the time and presenting Simon with a collection of green ones. His big smile and warm thanks stay with me as a happy memory even today.

Later on in my career, we were both sponsored on the grass by John Gillard of Yeovil, so I began to spend a lot more time around Simon. I was due to spend a weekend at John's place at a time when Simon's illness began to affect him. He asked if he could take a lift with me from the British Masters at Abingdon on the Sunday and down via Exeter on the Monday evening. So we had a complete day, plus the Tuesday morning, together. At that juncture, I didn't know what to do with my racing career, what to prioritise and which direction to take, but Simon gave me sound advice. Those words remain an influence on me.

He also gave me a lot of advice on adjusting my style from speedway to grasstrack, and the harder task of switching from grasstrack to speedway. The two sports have drifted apart, technically, so his guidance on how to set up the bikes also remains clear in my mind.

As a rider who now competes in the same motorcycle disciplines as Simon did, I have nothing but admiration for what he achieved. He must have been so organised to take on that schedule and become so successful over a very long period.

Towards the end of his life, I won the Marmande event, which he had been the front-runner in for so many years. I took the trophy down to Eastbourne, where Olli Tyrvainen had organised a trip out for him. Simon knew what it took to win at Marmande and his handshake and smile that day meant a lot to me.

If he had lived, I am sure that he would still be competitive today. His contemporary, Berndt Diener, is still going well at 46 and Simon was obviously a better rider.

In my opinion, his death not only robbed us of a great British motorcyclist, but a man of vision and energy. Simon would have made an outstanding figure at both BSPA and ACU level. If he had been given the top job in either, Simon would have taken speedway and grasstrack in one obvious direction . . .

Karl Maier

SIMON and I were very good friends, having ridden against each other for many years – mainly on longtrack, but also occasionally grasstrack and speedway, although speedway was more like a hobby to me. Just like it was for Simon, longtrack was my main priority.

I first saw him ride in the 1981 Vechta grasstrack meeting and we've had many great battles since that day, at different tracks all over Germany and other places in Europe.

He was a brilliant rider and although we had some very hard battles on the track, we were always fair to each other and remained very good friends.

One of our biggest battles was at Herxheim for the 1990 World Longtrack Final. I led the final until my bike stopped but there was nothing I could do and he was the best rider on the day. He took his chance and it didn't affect our friendship.

The disappointment of losing the title to him at Herxheim was matched when he beat me to first place in the final at Muhldorf three years later.

The best race we ever had against each other was probably the one at Muhldorf in '87, when I won my third World Longtrack Final and Simon was second. It was very hard work for me to beat him and it meant a lot to me.

We also rode against each other on speedway occasionally but speedway didn't mean as

Wiggy and Karl Maier before practice at the 1984 speedway World Final in Gothenburg, Sweden.

much to me – I can't even remember being in the 1984 World Final at Gothenburg!

Simon was a very professional rider – his life was racing. My life was also racing but I have a motocycle shop to run here in my home village, where Simon visited me many times, and I didn't spend as much time thinking about my racing as Simon did. He spent as much time as possible to ensure everything was perfect – sometimes too much time, perhaps, because he could have worried less about his bikes.

We knew each other for nearly 20 years, much of that time sharing the same engine tuner in Hans Zierk. We would talk about mechanical things on the bike and how our engines compared. There was never a problem between me and Simon, although we both thought that maybe Kelvin Tatum had the fastest engine around from 1994 onwards.

Maybe I didn't work as much as Simon did to win world longtrack titles – I could possibly have won the World Championship two more times, with a little more luck – but I have to admit that sometimes luck comes with hard work.

Was Simon a better longrack rider than Egon Müller – yes, 100 per cent. Simon had a perfect style, great determination to win and I'd say that he is the best-ever longtrack racer.

We went out together many times, socially, after racing – if Simon had one German meeting straight after another, he'd sometimes stay at my house near Munich. We regularly went together to the *Oktober Fest*, for a few beers and good fun. I think the last time we went there together was in 1998, when Simon was not the same person as I'd always known him. He looked a little down – he was *kaput!* – and from speaking to his brother, this was the time when his illness started to take effect.

I visited Simon in the hospice on his birthday and when I saw him I couldn't believe how he'd changed. I cried and couldn't speak to him for 20 minutes, because I was so shocked by how he looked at that stage. When we did eventually talk to each other, he seemed very happy – like he was in another world.

Simon was a model rider, fair and correct, he was happy with his sport and after meetings he was a man for all the people. He could speak German and have a little fun with the fans after racing – and many of them came to the races just to see Simon, Egon and myself pushing each other to the limit.

Time goes on but many people still miss Simon. He was the best friend I had in my career.

Steve Schofield

AS a late developer on grasstrack, I was aware of the ability of Julian Wigg as a leading light in the sport at a time when there was a lot of British talent around. I had logged a younger brother who travelled around with him and when that youngster started racing, he flew from the beginning, making an instant impact. Simon had gained an insight into the sport through Julian, who was obviously a big influence on him.

Once I got to know Simon as we competed around the South Midlands, Midlands and South Eastern centres, I thought: 'What a nice lad.' Chatty, friendly and, for a youngster, he was flamboyant. He also had ambition. When he told me: 'One day I will be a World Champion,' I certainly didn't laugh it off.

I was also impressed by how clean and tidy his equipment was, and it made me start to think about my own kit. I soon began to get good gear together. As we became friendlier, so he became a more direct influence on me.

It was Simon who talked me into taking up speedway at Weymouth. He was always banging on about what a great time he was having. Eventually I sorted out a bike and a fast car to set off from work in London to reach Weymouth by the interval. Simon was straight on my case, insisting that I did practice starts and got the feel of the track before my first race. The first time I didn't take any notice – and nearly tipped the bike over on the line. He gave me a right rollocking for ignoring his advice!

Simon was so helpful to me and to Stan Bear, whom he had brought over from Australia. Stan was really struggling at first. As for me, I got fed up with driving down just to ride in the second half, especially when the weather affected getting on track.

So I told Simon that I was packing it in. 'Don't do that,' he said, 'you'll be in the team next week.' I have no proof but I think that he went to the management and made a case for me.

I really enjoyed my time there, all the lads were great company. Meanwhile, Simon was always nagging me to improve my equipment and get fitter. It worked. My attitude improved. I went to the line feeling sharp and confident.

After Simon left Weymouth we still saw each other and he pointed me in the right direction to seek bookings on the Continent. He provided me with all the essential contact details but warned me that it would be a long slog writing to clubs and hoping for replies. When I reached the point of being competitive on the longtrack scene, Simon was very much in my corner.

With Peter Ravn (left) and Steve Schofield, 1984.

One memory stands out – it was a World semi-final at Muhldorf. I had to get sufficient points in my last ride to reach my first World Final but I couldn't get out of the start very well that day. I asked Simon's advice and he told me to do this, that and the other – and it worked. He didn't need to help me, for he had his own pressures at the time, but that's the sort of guy he was – very helpful.

Simon was also a very caring person. When Sussex-based rider Paul Mitchell was seriously injured and ended up in a wheelchair – the same year as Per Jonsson's accident – Simon realised that Paul wasn't receiving as much attention or support. So he organised fund-raising events and kept in touch with Paul to keep his morale up.

We always kept in touch with each other at the beginning of most weeks in the season, comparing notes on the meetings that we'd ridden in. One week I phoned and I could tell something was wrong by Charlie's reaction. Simon had had his first fit.

Sadly, it was the beginning of the end. I'm

pleased that he had some time in his beloved Australia before the final chapter. I have happy memories of our many times together in Oz, surfing and having a busy period together.

I couldn't bring myself to visit him on his last lap. Some could. Some couldn't. I last saw him at Eastbourne in 1999, being kindly looked after in Bob and Margaret Dugard's pit-side caravan. He couldn't speak very well and that really upset me inside. I wanted to remember Simon as he was. I always will.

Dickie Staff

I FIRST met Simon at Gawcott in Buckinghamshire when we raced together in a schoolboy grasstrack event. I was 15, a year older than Simon.

In the first race I made the start but this young star on a 200cc Triumph Tiger Cub came around the outside like a bat out of hell, with the throttle wide open. Suddenly he and his bike were vertical and he fell right in front of me. I had to make a split-second decision to avoid him and run over his bike.

Once I had composed myself back in the pits, Simon approached me with his hand out and thanked me for saving him from potential serious injury. That handshake began a quarter-century of friendship. Rivals on track but mates who stayed in each other's homes. We ended up at that season's presentations with me having pipped him by one point for the centre title.

His progress was upwards and onwards from that point. Despite a broken leg early into the adult category, Simon attracted lots of good publicity and sponsorship, which enabled him to acquire good kit.

Away from the grass, I took an interest when he started to dabble with speedway. We had a grasstrack meeting at Portsmouth Airport one Sunday in October, so Simon came to stay with me in Andover, to take in a Lew Coffin training school at Weymouth on the Saturday. This was the day that he suffered a severe gouge in the groin.

Once I got him back home I called my doctor and Simon ended up in the local medical centre having the wound cleaned out and stitched up. He wasn't that well and for once I convinced him he was in no fit condition to ride the next day.

When Simon first started seeking rides abroad I used to travel with him as his mechanic. I remember going with him to Hechthausen in 1979. When we arrived on the Saturday we searched for a hotel. The only item we could understand on the menu was mushroom omelette. So, to be safe, we ordered it for every meal during our stay! In the meeting he rode a Hagon LTR , which Windsor Comp had provided and which Simon had top tuner Dave Nourish prepare for him, but he was stone last in every race. As we packed away, Simon firmly stated that if he was going to have the career in Germany that he so desperaterly wanted, then he had to get a loan and obtain comparable equipment to German trio Müller, Maier and Duden, who were outstanding that day.

He did. He went to Vechta the next meeting and was top of the pile. To his credit, besides obtaining the loan, he would cut grass and clean windows to fund himself - he was so determined. Not only did his machinery improve, but so did his transport and the vehicle's presentation as time went on.

Although I had a bundle of laughs, including some heart-stopping moments while evading customs, my favourite story about Simon again reflects on his professionalism.

When he won a World Championship title at Herxeim and had parked up by the pits, he took his helmet off to be interviewed by the presenter. The guy asked him in English: 'How do you feel?' There were 15,000 German fans there and so Simon made a three-minute speech in fluent German. He felt that the paying public should be communicated with in their native tongue. After all, as he explained to me, they paid his wages.

They stood to their feet in appreciation at the end of his victory speech. Thoughtfully, Simon had also organised autograph cards to give out to supporters, showing him pictured in action and portrait, and bearing his printed signature – the first in our sport to do so.

Wiggy took every opportunity to exploit PR, encouraging GMTV and Channel 4's *Big Breakfast* to highlight the rivalry between himself and Kelvin Tatum abroad. They were filmed at Hackney, just before the Grand Prix in 1995, wrestling for possession of the World Championship trophy.

Simon with Dickie Staff, one of his dearest friends from their early grasstrack days together and right till the end. They are pictured here on a visit to the Berghaupton track, September 1999.

By this time my days as his mechanic were long passed, having been offered a promotion by my employers, Stannah Stair Lifts, but it was a wrench to leave him.

I became involved in the Ace of Aces grasstrack meeting at Salisbury, where Simon was instrumental in helping Ian Barclay and myself raise the event from national to international status. He had extensive personal contacts and convinced all the great German riders to appear. at our event, at a time when the Ace of Aces was regarded as the unofficial World Grasstrack Championship.

Simon was influential in other directions, too, and convinced us to give emerging talents a chance, including some Russian riders plus the Gollob brothers from Poland, as they began to get noticed.

The acclaimed Ace of Aces was a major grasstrack occasion that remained dear to Simon's heart. Here he is after winning it for the last time, in 1997.

Simon had two particular favourite spots – Berghaupton in the Black Forest, and the Broadwater area of the Gold Coast in Australia, where he had a property. By 1999, he had lost his driving licence because of what was presumed to be epilepsy, so Ian Barclay, photographer Alan Whale and myself drove him down to Berghaupton on a glorious day. We had our photos taken together with a spectacular backdrop – a symmetry of a shot we'd had taken together as young men and one that I will treasure forever.

At the end of Simon's days I went to see him in Willen Hospice every two weeks. Although he had trouble speaking, he was able to utter 'F****** hell' not only regularly, but very loudly and clearly! At first the medical staff found it embarrassing but it soon became part of his persona and added to his popularity around the place.

One of my last memories is helping Simon to 'wheelie' along a corridor in his wheelchair, with him shouting: 'F****** hell', to express the fact that he was still having fun despite his obvious physical deterioration and the pain he was in.

After he passed away, my wife Hilary and I joined Julian and his family, plus Ivan and Raye Mauger, as Charlie and the children spread half of his ashes on the back garden of his Gold Coast property, where he'd been so happy.

My final thought? . . . 25 years of friendship – and never a dull moment!

MORE FRIENDS & SPONSORS

Clint Dunn

I FIRST set eyes on Simon at our local recreation ground, in Haslemere, in 1974. I suddenly spotted another lad on a pushbike travelling a distance of half a mile on his back wheel! I felt that I had to get to know him and we got talking.

We found that we belonged to the same youth club so we became pals and joined a local youth fellowship scheme together. There we would play pool and table tennis.

I had a paper round and Simon was looking for one having just moved from Suffolk, so I recommended him to my newsagent.

Meanwhile, he told me about cycle speedway, which he had competed in successfully back in Suffolk, and how he was into bikes. He needed the extra cash to spend on his interest. I'm talking mainly about pedal cycles here, although he was also just as keen on motorbikes. He told me that his big brother raced in a sport called grasstrack racing, which I'd never heard of.

Simon used to be fascinating to watch as he changed gear ratios on his bike and experimented with different parts.

He soon moved into motorbikes when he acquired a Tiger Cub, riding in four meetings at the end of the 1975 season. That winter he convinced me to take up racing too and so sold me the Tiger Cub for £110. Simon bought a BSA and from that moment we were inseparable.

He would even come around my house at 7.30am on the weekends and wake me up so that we could go cycling. One of my favourite memories with the pushbikes was taking them into the woods to find the steepest hill to slide down – with no brakes. I should add that we had to get into a slide early and we were travelling at some speed. To stop, we would lock up at the bottom of the hill. One day, Simon got into his slide too late, locked up far too hard, high-sided and flew over the top of a holly bush, disappearing with a thud the other side. I kept back in case he was embarrassed by any discomfort. Lo and behold, Simon emerged through the bushes both beaming and exclaiming what a fantastic experience he'd just had! Then he was straight back up the hill and on with the show.

Simon always had this extra dimension in everything that he did. Whether it was preparing the bikes, experimenting or having a go. He thought about bikes 24 hours a day. Simon had total commitment and that is what took him to the heights that he achieved.

After leaving our respective schools at the end of each afternoon, we'd spend as much time as possible before bedtime in his shed working on our motorbikes. Even when we got to 16 and 17 and started going out socially, Simon would invariably arrive late having put the finishing touches to his racing machine.

Simon's dad took my brother, Tony, and myself with Simon to meetings. We had a big, green box trailer behind a Toyota Space Wagon. We mainly raced around the South Midlands centres with occasional trips to Wiltshire and Kent. In 1976, Simon finished second to Sean Willmott in the British Schoolboy Championship after suffering a few mechanical hiccups. I knew then that Simon was going to be very good in the sport. It was now his goal, his chosen profession and, suddenly, Simon announced that he was off to Australia to gain further experience. Now lots of people talk about what they would like to do but Simon just went out and did it. I couldn't believe it when he told me and I questioned him about work and income issues. He was positive and replied: 'This is what I want. If it doesn't work out, I'll still want to ride. The money doesn't matter.'

His mind-set was also interesting in another way. Even though we began to compete at different levels, we met up every Sunday evening to talk over how the day's racing had gone.

Now I was getting in the top six at local level while Simon was in the top three at national level. However, if Simon hadn't won his event, he didn't want to talk about it – only about my performance. Even at 17, he really did have a great desire to win.

Coincidentally, my Dad was a driving instructor and taught Simon, who passed his test first time. Little did my father realise how many miles Simon would go on to clock up in his career.

Simon eventually got me rides abroad and we would travel together. I bought a spare set of his green-and-white leathers from him and at one night meeting in France, Monty Banks – Trevor's dad – came up and complained that this could be very confusing in a race. 'Don't worry,' I replied, 'I'll be the one who is far behind!'

We were about 19 or 20 at the time. Simon so wanted me to be as good as him. He helped and advised me at every opportunity. It was the strength of our friendship. He would tell me to follow his line at practice and he'd slow down for me.

I continued racing until an incident overtook me when I was 24. Luck had deserted me in the opening meetings of the season with mechanical failures and falls while leading the finals. At Abingdon I had gone from a semi-final straight into the final in consecutive races. My arms felt weak and I dropped it on the pits turn. From 70 yards back, Kerry Gray managed to ride down the middle of my back and split both my kidneys. His engine plate actually ripped my leathers clean off.

That was my last race and I decided to follow Simon in a different manner by purchasing a property. I also turned my hand to acting as a mechanic for Simon on some of his grasstrack trips abroad. By this time Simon was an established star, yet he was still down-to-earth, always had time to talk to people and was so full of life.

I remember one trip when I spent five or six days on the road – his schedule was incredible. We based ourselves in Hamburg ready for a grasstrack on the Sunday. Simon had a speedway Test match in Denmark for England on the Friday, then he had to fly back for a British League match at King's Lynn on the Saturday and return to Hamburg for practice and the meeting on the Sunday.

Unfortunately the match at King's Lynn saw only one ride completed before the rain came down. There was a further problem on the Sunday, which I spotted, that nobody at Hamburg had made arrangements to collect him from the airport. A helicopter was scrambled at the last moment to fetch him. After he'd walked from the helicopter to me, I then had to explain that I had noticed a demarcation in the engine plates, which concerned me. Simon immediately shared that concern but with only 15 minutes until the end of compulsory practice, we needed the help of Bob Dolman to change the engine so that Simon was able to get on track for the last five minutes of practice.

The other riders had been there for over a day in some cases, so it must have demoralising for them when Simon went straight out and broke the track record in heat one. Simon went on to win the meeting and also claimed the flying one lap record. I felt shattered even before the meeting had even begun, despite having slept properly. Simon had basically to grab some rest while flying and yet he was unfazed. A quite amazing man.

When we were kids, Ivan Mauger was one of Simon's speedway idols. We used to watch him, including visits to support him at Wembley. In fact Simon once wrote to Jimmy Saville at *Jim'll Fix It*, requesting a meeting with Ivan. He never heard back.

When Simon was on the last lap of his life, I went to Willen Hospice to see him. As I sat there, in walked Ivan Mauger. How I enjoyed the justice of that moment for my good friend.

We were like brothers together. He was Best Man at my wedding and the perfect person for that role. Everything was correct and well presented, as you can imagine.

I miss him and there is not a day goes by that I do not think of him. His impact on my life remains and I am so glad of that.

Pete Webb

I FIRST knew of Simon when he was a 15-year-old member of the Slough moped club. He had a 50cc Gilera and took part in off-road activities. Simon seemed to also enjoy the social side of club life, being a friendly and outgoing lad.

At that time his elder brother, Julian, was a well-established and top class grass-track rider at both national and international level. Windsor Comp Shop was very proud to be associated with Julian. And it was him who gave us the tip that his kid brother was a very good rider and could go a long way.

When Simon went straight into adult racing at 16, we set him up with a complete bike. Simon being Simon, incidentally, he came back to us over the next six months asking for a change of various items such as frame and engine. He was already planting the seeds of a rider who wanted to be involved in development of his machinery.

At the very start of his career I remember accompanying him to a full Easter weekend of racing at Great Missenden. On the Good Friday, Simon was displaying a lot of promise. At this time Chris Baybutt was the British Champion but by the fourth day – the Easter Monday – Simon was beating him. That's when we really knew what potential.

Strangely enough, I also accompanied him to his last ever grass-track meeting, at Don Godden's estate in Kent on a wet bonfire night in 1998. Simon and his mechanic, Brett, came and collected me.

With my business commitments, I didn't have much chance to travel with Simon in the intervening years. I do recall dashing across to Germany with Tom Pink, of another sponsor, Norman Reeves Ford, for his appearance in the European Grass-track Final when he was 18.

Simon could be an impetuous rider in those days. He would often makes moves that others would not dare contemplate, especially blasting around the outside in all the loose stuff. On this occasion he came down in his first race and suffered major concussion, leaving Tom and I to shrug our shoulders and head back home.

One could never doubt his courage and skill, though.

Windsor Comp Shop were involved with several riders from different motorcycle disciplines but from very early on Simon repaid our investment in him with respect to the profile he achieved for the company. It had always been my ambition that our logo would one day be seen in *Motor Cycle News* and, thanks to Simon, there soon appeared a double-page action shot in the *MCN* with our logo prominent on his leathers.

We were delighted that our company was able to provide Simon with a platform for his career, knowing that one day he was going to be a star on a bigger stage than the UK. But while he inevitably attracted the support of manufacturers and Continental sponsors, Simon always appreciated what we had done for him and never lost touch. For instance, he was straight on the phone after winning his first world title in 1985 - a pattern that continued.

I would often pick him up at Heathrow when he had a speedway fixture at Reading and Simon would sometimes stay over.

I'm proud to have followed that career from new kid on the block to five times champion of the world. At the time of speaking, this is my 49th year in the motorcycle business. Nearly half a century, of which the 25 years spent with Simon, from my first sight of him at 15 to his sad death at 40, is by far the most uplifting of my memories. A colourful and positive period with the greatest all-round motorcyclist of his era.

I last saw Simon three weeks before he passed away. He was terribly bloated as a result of the treatment but the eyes, the teeth and his famous grin had not deserted him. I have to confess that when I left him that day the tears were rolling down my cheeks and I had to be comforted by Charlie.

Simon, I shall always remember you as a winner - in every way.

Jeff Bing

I DID once indulge in grasstrack and moto-cross myself as a youngster, so I was aware of Julian Wigg when he began to make a name for himself and first met Simon when he was a 15-year-old schoolboy.

I was based about a mile away from his parents who were wardens at a sheltered home in Hazlemere. Simon appeared one evening and said: 'Hello, I'm Julian's brother and I wonder if I can have a look at your bikes.' He was very personable and outgoing. He was also a clever young man, as he attended the John Hammond School in High Wycombe in the days of selective education in Buckinghamshire.

Simon was taking part in schoolboy grasstrack meetings at weekends. Even then, he had a plan for his future motorcycle career and there was no lack of confidence about pursuing it.

By 1979 I had become General Sales Manager at the High Wycombe branch of Norman Reeves Ford, who had various branches in the region. Through my business and sporting interests I knew Pete Webb, who worked at Sid Morehams, a motorcycle centre, which Pete eventually came to own. It was Pete who set up Windsor Comp Shop. He also knew Simon and his family socially, so began to take an interest in him.

Pete approached my boss, Tom Pink, about helping Simon with transport, although we were involved with football at the time. Tom was interested in motorbikes too and the whole situation began to gel. This was helped by the fact that Simon was a local lad, had talent plus a very positive attitude. Simon was keen to promote us and so when he was old enough we provided him with a Cortina Estate, for which his dad, Tony, provided the signwriting.

Simon made a good start to his racing career and we went to watch him at home and abroad. He was very presentable with clean leathers, a distinctive style and a different personality than most motorcyclists.

Our company became involved with Reading Speedway in 1980 – the year the Racers won the British League championship under Dave Lanning's management. We became involved as a sponsor of Bobby Schwartz. Simon rode in the second half at Reading during that season, incidentally.

Now Americans are superb when a microphone is pointed at them and they also handle the press very well. Bobby was no exception. However, it should be noted that from very early in his career Simon could match the Americans in terms of being both articulate and saleable. We found the comparison interesting.

Eventually Simon took up speedway properly at Weymouth and I was very pleased because I had been a speedway fan since the sport came to the old Tilehurst track in Reading. Simon would come into our showroom in the week and talk about his speedway racing at Weymouth with great enthusiasm.

When he became good enough to ride for England, I saw him beat Bobby Schwartz in some great Test matches against the USA.

We had pride as a company in providing a platform for him in his earlier days before the later successes with Oxford, England and in the various World Championships. Simon was a pleasure to deal with and even as a World Champion, there were still times when he would call in on us or phone.

We kept in touch with Julian throughout the illness and at one time we were optimistic when Simon and his family set off for a new life in Australia. Sadly, it was not to be. Pete Webb was strong enough to visit Simon on his last lap in Willen Hospice. Now I regret that I didn't visit him, too.

I am so proud to have been associated with the remarkable life of Simon Wigg.

Nigel Wagstaff

THE first time I met Simon Wigg was through my interest in grasstrack. One week my family would go to a moto-cross event and another week to road racing. Then I looked in *Motor Cycle News* and saw the Berks Bonanza was on, so we went along. It absolutely poured with rain – and I think Steve Schofield won it – but there was something about this rider in green leathers that stood out.

As a very young speedway fan, I remembered that Nigel Boocock of Coventry wore blue leathers and Mike Broadbanks of Swindon stood out in all-red, while everybody else wore traditional black. This made them look so professional – and so did Simon that day. Everybody else, with respect, were raggy-a**** grasstrack riders but Simon's bike looked perfect.

With Nigel Wagstaff – long-time friend and sponsor – at the opening of Waggy's Houghton Hams factory, where Simon again 'did the business'.

Although a mechanical problem denied Wiggy the title that afternoon, my young son, Paul, immediately took to Simon. From that day on, and over a period of years, we built a friendship that was reinforced when I became one of his sponsors through my company, Houghton Hams.

Simon had an aura about him in the grasstrack world. Not only did he have that ability to embrace strangers, but once you got to know him a little he'd not only make a point of recognising you but also your family, which left a big impression on me. He always had time for everybody, possessing great communication skills.

While we have 24 hours in our day, Simon seemed to have 48 in his! You could phone him at his workshop, but he never told you to go away or say that he didn't have time to chat. Sometimes, of course, he'd explain that he was working flat out, but that he'd ring back later. I fondly remember the hours we spent talking about different issues.

I would go to his house on lots of occasions and it didn't matter if it was at Newport Pagnell or, later, in Middle Claydon, or even in Australia, there was always a rider living at Wiggy's.

Simon had this wonderful ability to mix with everybody and it wasn't just idle chit-chat either. He'd take out his pen and paper and do something to help, whether it was obtaining a car from Germany, getting a rider or finding a sponsor. He seemed to be the one who always led the way.

The top riders all now have motorhomes but I never forget going to the first British Final that he won, in 1988, when Simon turned up at Coventry in a black camper van, a quite luxurious model. The vehicle was owned by Brian Griffin, who eventually became my co-promoter at King's Lynn and was a good friend of Simon's. The other riders usually drove a Citroen with a trailer or a bike-rack on the back but, Simon being Simon, years ahead of his time, he wanted to arrive for the Britirish Final in something a bit special.

He walked into the pits at Coventry that day like he had set his stall out, there was an aura about him, sending out a message that he was better and different to all the rest. Anyway, he won the meeting and then had the audacity – or self-belief – to turn up the next year in the same vehicle and parade the British Championship trophy in the window! Simon could use psychology to his advantage when he wanted to.

He raised his game in a technological sense, too. Take the example of the front wheel spoilers. He'd look and say: 'What do fast riders do on straights? They tuck their knees in and have road-racing seats.' If you'd watched Simon before he used a front wheel spoiler, he had got one arm across and a leg hanging off the back of the machine – he altered the whole concept, which no-one else really followed.

With respect to his special air-brushed leathers, I know that Barbara Miles at BJM was always worried that Simon didn't have enough protection.

A man of great vision, Wiggy and I sat down for hours talking on the phone about how to try and turn the longtrack series into something like the tennis ATP tour, where riders accumulated points and there was a facility for all the best riders in the world to participate.

Simon said that the greatest thing about being a speedway rider was that you would wake up on March 15th and when you got out of bed, you'd have the opportunity to become World Champion that year. But that doesn't apply to the majority of the speedway riders around the world at present, because it's so difficult for the majority to break into the Grand Prix series from one season to the next.

Going back to when the British Final was an important qualifier for the World Championship, I recall Simon riding at Oxford in a semi-final in 1984 despite a broken collarbone. He had to turn up and try to get enough points to make the British Final at Coventry – that's how determined those riders had to be. When Kenny Carter rode in that same meeting at Oxford with a broken leg, he didn't phone up to pull out or ask to be used in the next round as a wild card. Both Kenny and Simon *had* to qualify.

If he'd lived, Simon would be well on the way to reviving grasstrack in the UK by now. He would have probably bought a farm and turned one of the fields into a grasstrack, where he would have staged a massive event with lots of music.

As a potential speedway promoter, I think Simon would have become frustrated with the scene and got bogged down with the politics and the incestuous way it's all done. Simon would go ballistic at some of the things that go on – I know, because it's driving me mad!

Thinking about some of the classic lines Simon gave me about speedway, he'd say that maybe his biggest failing as a speedway rider was that he always thought of the *next* race. What he presented as a failure, I pass onto my Conference League kids at Oxford as such a vital key in the make-up of what they need to become good riders. When you're 15, it's a long season and, hopefully, they can look forward to a lengthy career. What they mustn't do is try and put everything into that one race – because you are not going to win every race, are you? I want my riders to remember Simon Wigg and look at his example of thinking of the next race – he has to be their role model.

Not that he wasn't tough, for Simon's pain threshold was legendary. Sometimes after he'd crash, he would produce one of his classic comments. I'll never forget being at King's Lynn for a World Team Cup qualifier, and I was standing on the second corner with my family. The solid, board fence at Lynn was very hard and Mitch Shirra of New Zealand was involved in a coming together with Simon, who hit the fence with such force that it was a mess. He took a long time to get up and I feared that he'd be more seriously hurt.

When he returned to the pits, they stuck a microphone under his nose and the presenter asked him: 'Simon, you just had quite a bad crash. Where does it hurt?' Quick as a flash he answered: 'In my pocket!'

The great thing about being friendly with Simon was that he'd phone up and invite you to join him and his friends somewhere or other. He'd tell you that it was going to be the greatest thing ever, a real adventure.

Everything you did with Simon was fun, he never stopped laughing or exploring opportunities. If you'd said to Simon at any point, 'Would you swap what you've had for an extended life?', I'm not sure that he would.

Like I said, he seemed to cram 48 hours' activity into each day. I don't know how he did it. He seemed to have another pair of hands – and he could also party better than anybody else, too!

Simon never rode for one of my clubs and, strange to say, I'm not sure that it would have worked anyway. Jason Crump and I were friends before he rode for me at King's Lynn and although we're still mates, it doesn't necessarily mean that you are going to become Morecambe and Wise.

But my friendship with Simon was a constant, he was always only a phone call away. It didn't matter what I wanted him to do, he'd be there, including the opening of my Houghton Hams factory, for goodness sake. I wasn't one of his sponsors at the time – I just phoned him and we had all the press there to see Simon dressed up in a white coat and doing the business for me.

When I ran a 'Save the life of a baby' campaign, Simon helped me with that, too. It didn't matter what you mentioned or asked him to do – Simon was responsive.

When we won the Knockout Cup at King's Lynn in season 2000, he was at the hospice and I took the trophy in to show him. Although he wasn't the best at talking by then, you could see he knew it meant so much to me to win a trophy in my first year as a promoter, so he just sat there in his chair, kicked it and winked at me. It was a lovely moment.

I did struggle, like many others, to visit him in the condition he was in, but Charlie said to me: 'He would want you to visit him. If it was *you* in here, he'd be in to see you'.

The number of chocolates – especially Celebrities – he consumed in the last few weeks ... well, he ate boxes and boxes of them.

Another pleasure he enjoyed was to pull wheelies in his chair, shouting 'Yahoo!' as he flew down the corridor.

But the most poignant moment, for me, came at his funeral when they played Blur's *Song 2*, which includes the 'Yahoo!' chant in it.

As promoters, we should encourage our riders to be like Simon was – to make the time to speak to different interested parties at meetings and, if necessary, to go out into the community to help spread the word. Travis McGowan is like that for me now – no matter what the request. I'm also trying to get this message across to my Conference League boys.

You could say that Simon Wigg was the perfect role model.

Brian Griffin

I FIRST saw speedway as an 11-year-old at a one off meeting at Cradley Heath in 1959. It was part of a Mike Parker promotion called 'A Cavalcade of Speed', in preparation for the introduction of Provincial League racing from 1960.

My parents had been involved in the speedway supporters' club at Cradley in the post-war period and thought that I might enjoy the sport. I was hooked immediately but little did I realise that, 30 years later, I would sponsor one of the greatest riders of all time and become a speedway promoter.

In addition to speedway, I became equally enamoured of grasstrack racing in the UK. By the 80s I took a further interest in longtrack and could afford to fly to Germany and stay in hotels, which was a bit of a difference from finding the petrol money to go to an away match at Coventry! As I began to indulge my interest so I formed the idea of becoming involved with a rider. Through my Cradley connections, the obvious possible candidates were Simon Wigg and Simon Cross. I rated Simon Cross highly as a future speedway World Champion, although a serious back injury eventually curtailed that prospect.

I was watching through the pits fence at a meeting in Germany when Simon Cross started scurrying around looking for a certain tool and eventually went to Simon Wigg to borrow one. It wasn't hard to form the conclusion that Wiggy was very organised and Simon Cross less so.

By sheer coincidence, on the flight home I sat next to Steve Brandon, now the floor manager for Sky TV's coverage of speedway. We got chatting about speedway and I asked him to recommend a suitable rider to sponsor. His answer was Simon Wigg and Steve subsequently set up a meeting between Simon and myself. I had photographed some famous and powerful names in my own career but I was more excited that Wiggy was coming down to visit me at my London studio. I think it all goes back to being a childhood fan of the sport and having viewed speedway riders as heroes. It was a strange reaction all the same.

When I met Simon, I was immediately drawn to his nervous energy. I was entering into a sponsorship arrangement but seeking to have an intellectual influence on a rider whilst seeking inspiration from them in return. To meet someone who would energise me to work better in my own sphere. Surely I couldn't have found a better candidate than Simon Wigg?

There was no difficulty in sealing a deal, because I knew it was a relationship that was going to work. In time we were able to inject contributions into our respective spheres of activity, there was an affinity and a mutual respect. I recognised the focus and discipline required in motorcycle racing, while Simon recognised the same factors were needed in photography and editing.

Simon also realised that in this sponsorship deal, I wasn't trying to sell a product off the back of him. My professional life was irrelevant and none of my contemporaries had a clue about speedway. So in a sense the deal was 'pure'.

The 1989 season was a magic year in which to be linked with Simon. His speedway saw him victorious through the key qualifying rounds and he eventually finished second to a supreme Hans Nielsen in the World Final in Munich. As for following his longtrack exploits, it was an aesthetic experience for me. Simon was truly balletic on his bike – all the way to his world title. The danger factor accentuated the situation and his achievements. For me, it was the equivalent of attending a bullfight.

The British Final at Coventry is a particularly strong memory from that season. We set Simon up in a Winnebago with all his favourite food and drink on board, plus an integrated shower and piped music.

We carried the trophy that he had taken home after the previous season's British Championship at the same Brandon track. He told me firmly that we would be returning with the trophy back on board. So it proved as Simon retained the title in style.

Afterwards, we entertained fellow competitors and Simon's friends such as Kai Niemi and Mitch Shirra. We laid on wine and champagne and it was a superb day from beginning to end, Simon loving every moment of it.

In later years I did travel to watch his major longtrack events. Sometimes he would come up and insist – as he did to so may others in his time – that I went to Germany with him the next day.

He did this to me one night in the bar at Coventry Speedway when he was riding for them in the mid-90s. I had already booked into a hotel near Brandon Stadium and obviously didn't have my passport with me. I ended agreeing to join him on the trip, which meant about an hour-and-a-half of shut-eye at the hotel before heading back to Rotherhithe in London, where I was based. It was then off to Heathrow to meet up with Simon and Mitch Shirra. It was then that I found out it was going to cost me £470 for the flight! Oh well, on to Germany.

When we arrived I was sitting next to Mitch for the journey to the racetrack. I got into a deep discussion with him on how to focus on an activity. I then told him that he had better go out and win after all this – and he did!

Knowing that Simon would listen to advice too, I began to bring my trained powers of observation to watch the mannerisms of his key opponents, to try to interpret their mood and psychology. It was a normal part of my work as a photographer being incorporated in Simon's jigsaw of preparation for races. It also reinforced how rounded our own working relationship was. It was a two-way street based on mutual respect and Simon certainly assisted me to fulfil my potential to a further degree.

At the same time I had to take on board that to fulfil his ambition, Simon had not only to be determined but selfish, too. However, he was generally a very giving and helpful individual, and many people will no doubt testify to that statement.

I found dealing with his eventual illness very difficult and feel that this was a weakness in me. When I saw him at a Grand Prix in Linkopping, Sweden, the sight of his deterioration upset me. I was too sensitive and regret that I didn't see him beyond that point.

I thank Simon so much for providing the intellectual relationship I desired and for being so attentive. It was a beautiful friendship and I shall always appreciate him.

John Gillard

I FIRST saw Simon when he started riding speedway at Weymouth, where he made good progress to become a heat leader and represented the club at the NLRC and the NL Pairs during his three seasons there.

My real interest – unusual for an Englishman – was longtrack racing and I used to travel to meetings in Germany with Lew Coffin from the time that I was 14. I followed Simon's longtrack career and then, in 1995, he came to ride at my local track, Exeter, when they had the one big speedway league.

I took on the organisation of the Westernapolis, as well as the sponsorship, for Colin Hill from 1998 and Simon would help us to get riders for that. I had been providing Simon with a van on behalf of my company, Stoford Commercial Centre, since his Exeter involvement. The deal included me being able to join him on occasional trips to longtrack meetings when my various business commitments allowed. I was also sponsoring Paul Hurry and Simon was very helpful to him through our joint association.

Simon was excellent to deal with from a sponsor's viewpoint. He was always in touch and would bring keepsakes, such as laurels, back from meetings. I wish that I had started to be involved with him years before. I had some good trips abroad with Simon and Brett Walton, his mechanic. For instance, we would park the motorhome outside a certain bar in Herxheim, which had a fantastic collection of memorabilia and photos on the walls. We would have a great social evening and then fall out of the door and clamber straight into the motorhome in time for bed. I remember having a mad dash from King's Lynn to Dover and only just arriving for practice.

With Simon's input and help I promoted the Yeovil Traders grasstrack meeting for several years. While Ian Barclay and the Ace of Aces progressed from a club meeting to international status within a period of time, we gained an international licence immediately.

With my vehicle hire business, I had accounts with over 300 customers in the Yeovil area, so I was quickly able to put together a lot of sponsorship. Through Simon, we were able to negotiate with big names from home and abroad and bring them to the showground near Yeovil, making many thousands of pounds for charity.

I followed Simon's advice on promoting the events like they do in Germany and at Marmande – lots of ancillary entertainments plus good facilities for the public. It was very successful but eventually I got fed up with the ACU telling me that I couldn't do this and I couldn't do that.

In 2001, the season after Simon's sad demise, I re-branded the event as 'The Simon Wigg Memorial'. Charlie came down to present the trophy to its first winner, Kelvin Tatum. We raised thousands of pounds that day for the Willen Hospice, in which Simon had passed away.

Sadly, in 2002, our efforts were wasted, despite their being thousands of potential spectators already outside by 11am. We had to refund advance bookings, of course, and by the time of this event the differences with the ACU were well and truly getting to me and so I pulled the plug.

We had always attracted top names and once Simon's name was associated with us, it created further interest. I believe that was testimony to the high regard in which the fans held him.

When asked to assess Simon Wigg, I think of the fact that in every sport you will find a champion whose personality and contribution outstrip even their talent. Muhammad Ali comes to mind in boxing. Simon was very much in that mode as our sport's ultimate hero and true star. He was unreal.

We will wait a long time to watch another Simon Wigg.

Steve Brandon

IN 1985, my first year in the UK, I was a mechanic for New Zealand racer, Larry Ross, and my fellow Kiwi, Greg Williamson, was spanner-man for Simon Wigg. I met Simon and Greg properly for the first time at a longtrack meeting at Muhldorf that year.

At the time I lived near Heathrow and so my base became a halfway house for riders, which reinforced the contact.

In 1989 and 1990 I was a Sales Manager for Truseal Products, who were one of Simon's major sponsors, and this saw me following his progress up close for his twin attempts at the speedway and longtrack world titles.

I was acting as a liaison between the racing team and the sponsors, making sure that everybody was happy at the event. I was also instrumental in setting up the sponsorship deal for Simon with Brian Griffin, having met Brian on a plane on the way home from the 1988 World Longtrack Final that led to Griffin Racing.

I look back upon my time with a friend whom you could drop into any situation and he would look smart whether dressed formally or casually. As soon as he met Brian, for example, I knew the deal would be done – Simon could present a sponsorship proposal intelligently while at the same time knocking people out with his charisma.

In most cases Simon knew that he was a human billboard, so we worked hard on achieving exposure and giving sponsors something tangible for their money – invitations, newsletters, photographic press coverage.

Courtesy of Brian, Simon was able to travel in style to meetings and the provision of hospitality for sponsors and guests was outstanding. Simon realised that a motorhome could fulfil several functions beyond simply transporting his bikes and support team – he could entertain people in comfort and this was another part of his broader vision as he sought to optimise his income.

Simon could also see the future potential of Sky TV when they started showing highlights of the new Grand Prix format from 1995. Sky would record on a Saturday and then turn a highlights programme around by the Monday evening, with Simon there as a studio guest. Martin Turner was then the producer and Simon introduced me to him, which led to me assisting with the making of the programmes. Thanks to Simon, that involvement with Sky is a constant influence on my life today.

In the years that followed, I represented the GP riders in their liaison with the FIM over meeting issues. Technical changes became contentious and there was a confrontation with Ole Olsen and the FIM over the solid block tyres that they tried to introduce. My advocacy of the riders' case has not prevented a subsequent working relationship with Ole in my current role as floor manager for live world feed coverage of the Grand Prix series as we both want to achieve the best image for the sport.

We all recognise that Wiggy's impact today includes the team-suits but he wanted the branding identity to be much more comprehensive. At Coventry, in the mid-90s, he discussed the possibility of the club colour scheme embracing the bikes as well. He looked at football and saw that everything was colour co-ordinated, from the mascot upwards, and the Silver Machine concept by Nigel Wagstaff at Oxford is the nearest development to that in the Elite League.

Simon saw commercial spin-offs as well as much improved presentation. He envisaged, for instance, potential sales of BMX bikes in the team colours. Given the modern technology in vinyl graphics, there are lots of possibilities for these concepts.

I'd moved into the finance and banking sector from 1993 and this reinforced our dialogue about the sport in this country having a greater business perception. With match income and TV rights, British Speedway has a multi-million pound turnover but one wonders if the BSPA has a five-year business plan to accompany this? Simon would certainly be asking that question – and many more – if he was here today.

Simon also believed that attempts to reach out to youngsters, with riders visiting their local schools, had only been worked on by a handful of clubs, while he felt that the sport had to promote itself to a younger audience to attract new spectators who would bring their kids along to meetings. And once having enticed those new supporters into the stadiums, he wanted it to become easier for them to identify the fact that speedway was primarily a team sport – so two riders wearing red against two riders in blue would ensure that and help bridge the transition from watching speedway on television to seeing it as a live event.

I share Simon's view that unless speedway addresses the situation, it is in danger of relying on a continually aging fan base, whereas Simon had the personality and confidence to open doors and to have found more new opportunities for the sport.

I can also visualise him as our equivalent to Jamie Oliver, in the sense of grabbing the political agenda with respect to national concerns on the state of health and fitness among the country's youth. Wiggy would have led by example, emphasising that motorcycle sports require diet and fitness from their competitors.

Simon could never have taken it easy once he quit racing, he never wasted a day if he could help it. We have lost a crusader as well as an ambassador and it would be nice to think his desire and talent for co-ordination will be remembered within the BSPA and prompt thoughts of a five-year growth plan. Now while we all take on board that speedway promoters have their own winning team at the top of their specific business agenda, Sky TV has provided a new opportunity for the sport in general, plus you must accept the truism that you have to speculate to accumulate. I was privy to Simon's beliefs on these issues, having spent many hours mulling over them together.

Back in 1998, Simon was involved in some very heavy racing accidents. The Simon I knew was safety conscious, he didn't tangle up that often and rarely on corners. At the time the crashes were unexplained and there may have been a 'chicken and egg' situation – was there a health issue that was affecting him on track, or did an accumulation of falls, plus a punishing schedule, take a fatal toll on his health?

Obviously riders have to maximise their income but fatigue does set in when they're racing five or more days a week and taking on return air trips as part of that gruelling diary. This was not unique to Simon, of course, and all top riders who race from one country to another must get run-down as their hectic season unfolds.

I think that there was a certain significance about the timing of Simon's collapse at the end of the 1998 season. He'd wound his season down at the Bonfire Burn-up grasstrack meeting in early November and then worked on packing his bikes away for the David Tapp series. As soon as that process was complete, and the perpetual motion suddenly stopped, it was if his body hit a switch and then . . . wallop!

This was the beginning of the end but such was his fitness and so great was his spirit that he lasted through the rollercoaster of operations, radiotherapy and chemotherapy, emigration and a last lap in a UK hospice for a much longer period than the medics had predicted.

Simon lived life to the full as long as he could – even in a wheelchair he was lively and there was always that famous grin. He attacked the end of his life as he'd approached every day of his life up to that point – full of enthusiasm.

He continues to influence many lives – not least those of many of today's top riders, who learned from Simon's example to explore the margins of preparation and psychology. I also hope there may be an opportunity for his name to live on by association if a national training centre is ever set up for speedway in this country, as Simon had his own plans for rider development in the UK.

The name of Simon Wigg should be honoured and never forgotten.

Paul Cross

I DID race in schoolboy grasstrack but, at 17, began to mechanic for my elder brother, Simon Cross. So I had the enjoyment but no risk! I knew of Simon Wigg around the grasstrack scene and when my brother signed for Cradley Heath, the two Simons were then involved in what amounted to a swap deal between Weymouth and Cradley.

Erik Gundersen and Shawn Moran made a successful fist of their involvement in longtrack racing but Simon Wigg became the superstar. You could always tell where he was in the pits before a meeting, for there would be more than a hundred people surrounding him. Hordes would turn up to study what he was up to off-track.

He did have a series of very good and different set-ups. He was the first to have a proper motor home and at one Ace of Aces event I remember that he set up a sponsors' unit at trackside, which was unheard of at the time. For the bulk of his career Simon Wigg was well ahead of the pack.

He had a lot of input from Steve Brandon with respect to dealing with the media and with sponsors but the great thing with Wiggy was that he had the ability to back up all of these initiatives.

He could get away with ideas that most riders wouldn't dream of attempting. I remember watching a Central ITV news feature following him while taking his motorcycle test. Most people would want to keep that secret, but not Simon Wigg – he could certainly sell himself and his sport on television. Yes, he loved being the centre of attention but it was doing the profile of his sports a power of good. With this approach comes the reason why he made what was a hobby to many into his profession, and later made such a big impact on the longtrack scene.

Obviously my family saw a lot of Simon Wigg as our Simon progressed in his career – my brother moved to the British League with Cradley in 1985 and began to compete on the grasstracks abroad with more regularity. Simon Wigg was willing to help and offer advice – even if it was blunt in its delivery. My brother once asked Wiggy how he could improve his speedway and the reply about his leg-trailing style and the 'hobnail' type boots was scathing! It was observant and to the point.

Wiggy knew what he was about and would give his all to make the best of his opportunity. It wasn't just monetary – important though that was to him – he wanted to leave a legacy.

Ten years ago longtrack racing was very competitive with the likes of Karl Maier at their peak, so it was very difficult for Wiggy to be at the very top of his game at longrack racing and also duplicate that form in speedway. Ask a current top speedway rider about their prospects of going for the World Longtrack Championship, too, and they will look at you with incredulity. Yet Simon Wigg was meeting the demands of that schedule and going for titles in what are basically different sports. He could go from a 1000 metre longtrack on a Sunday and arrive at Wolverhampton Speedway on a Monday night and go unbeaten on a 300 metre circuit. He took it all in his stride and got on with it. One sport can affect the other in an adverse way but he coped with the constant change between these motorcycle disciplines.

Yes, people say that Simon Wigg took a lot out of his sports but, as you have seen, he also put a lot back in. Even his legendary fancy dress parties come into that category . . . all in a good cause and always memorable.

Another legendary factor with Wiggy was how careful he was with his money. I remember going with my brother to Marmande and on the way we saw posters advertising a bullfight at a nearby venue to the track. So we fancied a look at something different. On arriving we logged the Wiggy motor home parked right up against the wall of the arena. Perched on top and seated in chairs were Simon Wigg and Brett Walton – having a free show!

Another time my brother and I agreed to go with Wiggy to Austria on a snowboarding trip. In theory, a cheap trip with us splitting various costs. As Wiggy didn't run the heating at night, we were freezing in the motor home and so decided to book into a hotel after a night or two. Then, on the third day, my brother and I crossed over too close on a slope and he cut a knee with his blade, causing an injury that required 25 stitches and a stay in bed. To top it all, Wiggy suddenly announced that he was booked into an indoor meeting in Germany. Sure enough, there were the bikes in the back, so the mean so and so was getting his travel costs for the snowboarding jaunt covered anyway!

I hasten to add that this didn't affect us remaining good pals for many years. We attended his emigration party after his first illness and the outlook seemed positive. Once his tumour returned and he returned to the UK, then I visited him regularly. Simon was always optimistic but Charlie was very realistic about the situation. By the time that we went to his 40th birthday party in the hospice, he was very ill. But there he was, still grinning from ear to ear as he sat in his wheelchair squirting everybody with a giant water pistol that Trevor Banks had bought for him. As for his jokes, they were so bad that they made you laugh! The mischievous part of his character never deserted Simon.

Charlie eventually called to let us know that the end was near. Once we had said our final goodbyes I remember my brother, Steve Brandon, Brett Walton, Julian Wigg and myself all sitting together in this side room. We had a drink and stayed 'til the evening, talking about the man with a sense of serene acceptance. No-one was in bits and it was nice to be there. Every day that we had seen him was a bonus and when the news came that he had died, I had a sense of relief that he would no longer have to go from one extreme to the other in terms of his health, which I found so cruel.

His funeral was upbeat and different. Any passer-by who strayed in and saw the bike and heard the music would have known that this was someone who was that bit special. Anyone walking into the function that followed would have presumed that it was a 21st birthday party! That is what he would really have wanted.

It is said that in life there are two types of people. Those who follow and those who leave a trail. Simon Wigg is the latter but he sadly died before his time was due.

Christopher Eyes

Chief Executive, The Willen Hospice, Milton Keynes

EVEN though it is almost five years since Simon passed on, staff at The Willen Hospice still remember him with affection. Simon had endearing qualities – his cheeky way and his grin.

Even his choice language didn't cause offence, for it is symptomatic of his condition. Sadly, some patients become aggressive in their terminal phase but Simon wasn't. He was regarded as a 'gentle giant' around the hospice and was even forgiven when he sat on a hand basin to use it as a toilet, causing the whole structure to collapse off the wall!

A factor in his extra weight gain was a passion for chocolates, which our nurses commented on when I discussed this book with them.

We were all struck by how many friends Simon had . . . and how some managed to disappear down the local pub with him all day!

The nursing staff have also mentioned the mystery of how someone who couldn't walk would be found in the bathroom on many mornings. Obviously, he was a man of great spirit who got himself there by sheer willpower.

When Simon sadly departed this life, I attended his funeral. What an amazing and positive occasion it was, like nothing else I have ever witnessed in this context. Simon was a personality when he was with us and stamped that personality all over his great goodbye.

Finally, we all wish to record our best wishes to Charlie and her family as they build their new life.

Tribute to a biking legend

FRIENDS and family of speedway legend Simon Wigg have paid a fitting tribute to him after his death.

His wife, Charlie, had asked for donations to Willen Hospice instead of flowers at the funeral of the five times world champion in November.

Simon died in Willen Hospice aged 40, after a long battle against a brain tumour.

"We are grateful to everyone who gave money to Simon's memorial," said Charlie.

After Simon's death, his widow Charlie and daughter Abi presented the Willen Hospice with a cheque for £5,500 – the amount received in the form of donations to the hospice from Simon's family and friends. In this newspaper cutting, Charlie and Abi are pictured making the presentation to Christopher Eyes, chief executive of Willen Hospice, with staff nurse Julie Hopps and auxillary nurse Angie Thomson also in attendance.

TECHNICAL EXPERTS

Otto Lantenhammer

I STARTED working with Simon in the early 80s, when he first started to make an impact in Germany and he was still riding Weslake machinery.

I worked for Simon for two years and I had no problems with him – we worked good together and he won a lot of races.

Simon was a very hard rider, so determined to win. Sure, I could see that he was going to become a World Champion – he was very aggressive and had good reactions. I wanted to find a boy who could win big races and Simon was the answer.

He often came to our house to stay and was always welcome here.

After two years he moved on from me to Hans Zierk but I wasn't very disappointed, because many riders move tuners in our business. I tuned Egon Müller's engines for 11 years and, later, I did motors for Karl Maier, Billy Sanders . . . there are so many.

The last time I saw Simon, having not seen him for many years, was at the Dingolfing sandtrack. He was riding that day and, I think, he won the meeting.

I always called him 'Wiggy', but I think it was Barry Briggs who first called him by that name.

Mrs Ingrid Lantenhammer:

The very first time Wiggy came to us at our old house, near Munich, he brought his brother with him – I think Simon was the beginner and Julian the star rider then. Simon loved his brother very much and he told us of his ambition to become as big a star as Julian one day.

Simon was very excitable and totally ambitious. He'd say to my husband: 'Otto, please make me the very best engines, so that I can be World Champion.'

We accepted him here as if he was a member of our family – we gave him the guest room to sleep in, although he didn't seem to sleep for long. I would make him and Otto sandwiches and coffee while they were working very late in the workshop and, in the end, I'd go to bed and leave them both to it.

I don't think Simon understood a lot about engines, but he learned a lot from working with Otto.

Simon was a really nice guy and we were shocked when we heard that he had died – we were all shocked here.

Otto Lantenhammer in his racing days.

Don Godden

I WAS at one of the Lydden Internationals in Kent, the last major of the year. I can't remember the date but it was the late 70s. I was talking to Barry Briggs and we decided to walk from the pits to the track to watch practice.

Simon Wigg was going around and Briggo turned to me and said: 'There is a future World Champion'.

Simon was about 17 at the time and Barry had seen him around the racing scene already. Simon certainly had his own style and it was impressive. In subsequent seasons I began to see more of him. Obviously I knew Julian Wigg, who had started in moto-cross but made a successful transition to grasstrack racing, and we were friendly rivals at one time. Simon had talent and benefited from Julian's influence.

Simon raced Weslakes initially and seemed to be spending a fortune on engine preparation – all engines are fragile but his seemed more so than others. I was still riding my own bikes and engines, plus I had a good relationship with Hans Zierk, who was importing my equipment into Germany. I brokered a deal between Hans and Simon for Wiggy to take a Godden and use it regularly on the Continent – I already had commitments to other riders, whereas Hans could give Simon more direct support. They sustained a very good working rapport even after Simon's much later switch to Jawa.

Through this initiative Simon didn't have to worry about the cost of engines, leaving him to focus on his racing. Back-up would also be provided as the season progressed.

However, it wasn't all beer and skittles. A rider should accept the manufacturer's opinion – discipline is required and friction would develop on occasions.

A manufacturer has pride in what he does and the essence of the business is that he must ensure customers believe that they have a competitive product. But whether the engines were Weslake, Jawa, GM or Godden, you have some tuners effectively promoting their own beliefs about how to achieve success. That, though, is not what a manufacturer wants to hear.

We were able to give Simon a useful insight in circumstances surrounding a speedway meeting at King's Lynn, when he received a late call-up for what I believe was The Pride of the East – or maybe another individual meeting at Saddlebow Road. He phoned and told me that he didn't have an engine ready for that night, so I took one up to him at King's Lynn – it was straight out of the box.

Don Godden and Wiggy – both grasstrack greats.

Simon won the meeting – point proved.

For he did like to tinker – and usually at his own expense in terms of performance – and you could say that we had a dialogue or two on this issue!

In all sport you need discipline and in most areas Simon certainly had it. Champions, however, also require inspiration. In my lifetime I've been lucky enough to have been directly involved with several World Champions. I have travelled around the world and seen Simon perform. When he switched on, Simon was tremendous. He could have won even more than the five World longtrack titles that he did, both during his career and if he had lived to contest more World Longtrack Finals.

It is also my belief that Simon had the capability to have been speedway World Champion if he had truly put his mind to it.

Away from the track, Simon was what I describe as a very human person. Career-wise, he did have black years but he stuck to his plan and saw it through. He was strong on self-analysis and the experiences of the highs and lows of life, Simon turned to advantage.

Simon had a vision of his future and its link with the state of grasstrack racing in the UK. We were very much on a wavelength over this. Now that I've had an active involvement with the ACU in recent years, until my resignation, I know they are people led by deadwood. Most are there for their own aggrandisement, they have never ridden and haven't earned the right to occupy the positions that they do.

I know how they view people who become involved to try and improve the lot of the competitors and Simon would have found that his presence would have been resented. I think that he would have had to withdraw his involvement even though, in my opinion, the ACU would not have been as bad as any involvement he might have had with the BSPA or Speedway Control Board!

Simon would have had to assess his position. Like many of us ex-riders, he would have initially let his heart rule his head. I've been there . . . and I'm no longer there.

Towards the end of Simon's life, I met up with him at a grasstrack meeting at his old club centre. He was suffering and, although I did chat to him, I was fighting back the tears. As I said earlier, Simon was fired by an inner inspiration and yet he was so inspirational to others, too.

I'm proud to have been involved in his path to becoming a great World Champion.

Hans Zierk

THE day that Simon won his first World Longtrack Championship, at Korskro in 1985, was also a great occasion for me, too, and I'll never forget it. He wasn't the favourite that time – Egon Müller was expected by many in Germany to win – but Simon made the best start in the final and won it.

I remember thinking before that race that his bike had felt a bit 'tight', and I noticed that the rear chain may come off, so we attended to it just in time.

We had a big party in Denmark afterwards – Simon was a nice boy, always smiling. He spent many weeks at my house and my wife and I treated him like our own son. We do have a son, but Simon was like a second son to me.

I stopped riding in 1977, after I broke my neck in a big crash at Stockholm, and my wife told me that I had to finish for good. I was 43-years-old then, and spent 40 days in hospital here in Hanover, so I had to find something new to do.

I started to tune Godden engines in 1979 – Hans Nielsen was my first customer on the longtrack – but I was helping Karl Maier at the time I met Simon, at a German grasstrack called Celle, in 1982. Both of Wiggy's Weslakes had broken down and I offered to lend him one of my Godden engines, which meant just a 40km drive back to my house to collect it. I'd seen him do very well at Vechta the previous year and I thought then that he had a very good future in longtrack.

There was only about half-an-hour before the start when we fitted the Godden engine into Simon's bike – I was the dealer for that engine at the time, but now I prepare Jawa engines – and it just went from there. Egon Müller was the big hero here in Germany at that time but Wiggy beat him from the start in the final and Egon had no chance. Wiggy and I worked together from that time.

I prepared the Jawa engine that Gerd Riss used to win his fifth World Longtrack title last year, equalling Simon's record. It would be nice if Wiggy could share this record, although he should have won more World Championships himself – I'd say seven, no problem. One time we had a carburettor problem in the Czech Republic, where there wasn't enough time to practice with the lay-down engine.

Simon was at his very best, three years later, when he returned to Marianske Lazne and won his fifth title, in 1994, beating the German riders Andre Pollehn and Riss. As the only works Jawa rider that day, he was so fast and won the meeting with maximum points.

He only lost out on a record sixth win at Scheessel the following year after Kelvin Tatum beat him in a run-off for the title. Kelvin got to the first corner two metres ahead and no matter what Simon tried, either on the inside or the outside, he just couldn't pass Kelvin, who I think was 10 kilos lighter than Wiggy, which made the difference. When he first came in from the

Hans Zierk's smile says that the 1990 World Longtrack title is coming Wiggy's way at Herxheim.

difference. When he first came in from the track, Simon just said: 'S***!' – but he always seemed to cope well with any disappointments. On those occasions, he'd say to me: 'Next time, we come again!' He was always very positive.

I also prepared his speedway engines when he finished second to Hans Nielsen in the '89 World Final at Munich. But Simon was not so good on speedway – it is very hard for the very best longtrack riders to also be at the top in speedway, but Wiggy was better than Nielsen on longtrack.

Our relationship was always good, there was never a problem between us. Simon was a great man and, in Germany, he was more popular than the German riders! He spoke German well, he was intelligent and had gone to a good school.

He brought about five different girlfriends with him to our house over a long period and each time he'd asked my late wife, Johanna: 'What do you think . . . is *she* good for me?'

I saw Simon on his last visit to Germany, at the Berghaupton track in September '99. He was bald following all the chemo he'd had and I noticed how big he looked compared to his normal weight. He told me then that he was feeling OK and that he was looking forward to going to Australia and maybe becoming a promoter there.

The last time I saw Simon alive was when my wife and I visited him at the hospice, it was about two weeks before he died. He spoke slowly and perfectly to us for a long time and he was happy to see us both – he thought a lot of my wife. It was a nice place and because the weather was wonderful, we sat outside where he could have a little smoke.

For me, Simon was the absolute best.

MECHANICS

Greg Williamson

I FIRST crossed paths with Simon in 1981 when I was helping out Kai Niemi and we used to team up with Simon for trips to the grasstrack meetings abroad. There was a good camaraderie between the three of us, which made the journeys a good craic. I started to ride speedway at Milton Keynes and, when not working with Kai, would help Simon out on his trips to France, along with Dickie Staff and Julian Wigg.

This led to my cementing a place in Simon's support team and eventually being based with him. This gave me some stability and I worked for my rent, which was another benefit. It was always a good working arrangement and lots of fun.

Up close, I realised that Simon Wigg was a young man on a mission. He knew what he wanted to do and he was something special long before he became recognised as something special. Simon was larger than life and an inspiration to be with. Yes, there was lots of shouting and screaming in the workshops – but that's part of the deal. It's the bit the fans would never see leading up to a race day.

Simon could make you feel upbeat. It might have started as the worst day of your life but once Simon came along you felt better. That's the effect he had on others. Now a couple of beers and the alcohol can bring the best of your boasts out. When Simon was relaxing and telling you that one day he would be a World Champion, it wasn't just the booze talking. You just knew that he wasn't going to give up on that dream.

When it came to his first love – grasstrack racing – well, as soon as Simon put his leg over the bike, the other riders were aware that they were facing stiff competition. This soon translated into his longtrack racing and he even had this effect on the top German boys. They knew that he was the complete package and this would lead eventually to glory.

A cuppa with Greg Williamson, 1983.

Although I was still riding for Milton Keynes in the National League, by now I was putting more into my work as a mechanic than my career on the shale. I became available to share in Simon's breakthrough years of the early 80s.

The workload was very heavy but the set-up was so professional. The year spent with Cradley Heath in 1983 was particularly memorable for they tracked an unbelievable team who were a happy bunch of lads too. It was this season that Simon realised how good he was on a speedway bike. Previously, Weymouth had been a party for Simon. He did become selfish as success developed but you have to be that to make progress in any sport. Simon was making a positive transition in a sport which was originally simply an addition to his first love of grasstrack racing.

Oxford was a great move for him, too. Simon was part of a strong heat leader trio with Hans Nielsen and Marvyn Cox, which meant they could carry the other team members to a certain extent. Simon also recruited riders and took them under his wing.

Troy Butler – or 'Trojan' as I call him – was a great example. Although he was very raw when Simon brought him over from Australia in '86, there is no doubt that Simon could spot talent. Simon got Oxford to persist with Troy when he was crashing at every corner. Simon taught Troy how to regroup and was always there for him. Simon put his balls on the line with the Oxford promotion but it all came up trumps.

His team-riding at Oxford was also excellent. He could shepherd Jon Surman round as effectively as he could combine with Hans Nielsen for breathtaking 5-1s, with the pair crossing the line on their back wheel.

There are critical observations I would make of Simon. He would get himself all twisted up over issues such as track conditions or mechanical problems. Instead of putting it by and getting on with the next meeting, he and Julian would analyse matters to death. I wasn't in a position to contribute to the dialogue but on journeys back from meetings I'd realise that I was going to get to bed at 2am but have to be up at 5am to cope with the workload created by that analysis being converted into me having to pull the motors out and apart the next day.

Simon did try and get too involved in the technical set-up. He was a hands-on person, admittedly, and couldn't help himself but he could be a nightmare for a mechanic on occasions. It was only when he became ill at the end of his life, and we were talking, that he conceded that he perhaps should have been more relaxed about these matters and left it for others.

Having said that, I give full praise to the build-up for his first World title win. Simon put in so much effort and one aspect was more akin to Formula One. Hans Zierk lived near a one kilometre sand track that was actually a public road. I would drive over to Germany with the bikes and then Simon would fly in solely to practice starts and ride flat out against the stopwatch. It was a form of advanced testing to help him stay one step ahead of the other riders.

Hans must have tipped off the local residents, because Simon was travelling at over 100mph up this sandy road without any vehicles coming in the opposite direction – although I can tell you I was sweating!

Hans also had a big dyno available for bench testing and once these sessions were over, then Simon would be off to the airport. A lot of complex and hard work went into that 1985 longtrack success.

On the day, Julian assumed the role of chief mechanic and I sat happily in the support team. This had been the procedure in the qualifiers and semi-finals, too. When Simon won the World title I was elated. It's such a thrill to be part of the story and Simon deserved all the congratulations that came his way.

These were the golden years of my motorcycle life but there was to be a new direction in 1986 when I met a Pommie lady from Poole. Romance blossomed and after our first child was born in Aylesbury, we decided to set up our family base back home in my native New Zealand.

Simon always showed great loyalty to those involved in his life and we stayed in touch. I was a guest at his wedding in 1996 and ended up on a trip to Russia! I came over to work on his farewell meeting at Oxford in 1999. That was the night he received a roasting from Charlie for expecting me to freeze my nuts off in the motor home in the car park of a local hotel. Simon and his money! Eventually I did end up sharing a room with him in the warm.

When, in 2000, I phoned Charlie and found out how bad the situation was becoming, I told her that I was on the next available plane to England. Not only did I want to see Simon, but I wanted to give Charlie some help. I was amazed that he seemed to have put on about 10 stones in weight. And when I took him around a local supermarket, I soon realised why! We got to the check-out and Simon had managed to lodge about 10 packets of chocolate biscuits in his lap. It was a strange role reversal – suddenly, I was the adult and he was the big kid.

Simon was very child-like after the second operation but this was understandable and he remained good fun. I managed to stay five weeks but had to return to New Zealand before the very end. I didn't come back for the funeral as I felt that we had experienced a long goodbye.

I will always appreciate Simon for taking a young Kiwi of 20 and helping me grow up. Simon was a vital part of my own personal development. Today, in my home in Auckland, I have many mementoes on display with a silver helmet standing out from a collage of many photos.

It's my personal shrine to the late, great Simon Wigg.

Mick Day

I USED to ride speedway on the Gold Coast in Australia and was friendly with Troy Butler – and I first met Simon through Troy when Wiggy was over on one of his winter trips.

One year I hurt my shoulder and so decided to recuperate by coming to England for a look. I phoned Simon before travelling and, through his introduction, I went to work for Hans Nielsen, who had been looking for a mechanic, for the 1987 and 1988 seasons. Hans was so professional and gave me a good foundation.

When I decided to pack up and go back to Oz, Simon phoned me up and asked me to return to England and work for him – the clincher was that he promised me lots of fun! He kept to his promise, because the next three years were the best of my speedway life.

I had to work flat out – never allowed the luxury of a day off – because of Simon's hectic schedule but I did have a paid tour of Europe in the process. The bulk of my time was spent in England during the week and in Germany on the weekend but there were plenty of other places to visit in the season. When Simon was successful, you knew you had to go the extra mile, too, and that you'd made a difference. Once the relief of one success was over, then we'd work even harder – but I loved every day of it.

When I was younger I'd been trail bike riding with Mick Doohan, who later approached me about joining the support team in his global road racing set-up. It was a great opportunity but I had to think about it. Working with Simon, I was the chief mechanic and, in a sense, just one heartbeat away from the rider. With Mick, I would be one cog in a big machine. Also, I found road racing boring compared with speedway and longtrack racing. It was a tough decision but I joined Mick with Simon's blessing and best wishes.

Simon and I had become good friends, I lived with him at the Old Stables in those days before he got married – and he was as great at organising parties as he was at organising his career! He was a real 'action man' when he got his teeth into a project and if he tried enough things – well, per centages said that something *had* to work! I had a straightforward working relationship with him – I wasn't somebody who responded to: 'Do as you are told' and I had my opinions, which Simon respected me for. Successful people don't want to be surrounded by 'yes' men anyway, so we had dialogue and he did listen, which, in turn, I respected him for.

Most working situations that function well follow a basic pattern of organisation. There are things that you do and there are things that you don't, it can be as simple as that really. However, our schedule in 1989 was, to be frank, crazy – I drove about 60,000 kilometres that year on my own.

When Simon signed for Bradford in 1991 I hardly got to see him race at Odsal because I had to drive out ahead of him for meetings abroad. We also had the complication by then that Simon had switched from GM to Jawa on the speedway because the Czech company wanted to retrieve some of the market and needed a high-profile rider to support.

The only problem was that the engines at that time were crap, so consequently we spent a lot of time at the Jawa factory near Prague trying to sort things out.

As a rider, Simon had enormous character. When it came to grasstrack or longtrack, he could be hungry, tired, sick or have half a leg hanging off – and still end up on the rostrum. His speedway results were less predictable, though, and I couldn't work out how he could look so good on some rough grasstrack but sometimes appear more awkward on a smooth speedway circuit. Simon had a great style on the longtracks and really attacked the World Championship, it was his great passion and he also earned a lot more from this than anything else.

As a person, he ran his life very much like his career – in a strong way and flat out. I would also emphasise that he didn't have harsh words for anybody and he certainly didn't do bad things to others.

Despite the fact that my commitments in Australia took me out of the loop for a while, Simon was always loyal to those who had been a part of his life and we kept in touch. After his first operation I spoke to him regularly and Simon was always positive and upbeat. I've never heard him downbeat, not even then.

By now I'd become involved in a company which set up sound systems for music promotions back in Australia. I had just come in from working on a school's bands festival when Troy Butler called me at 11pm to give me the news of Simon's death.

I'd had a few problems in my life at the time, what with a broken relationship and business pressures, and the news of Simon's death was the triple whammy. In fact, I was so upset at Simon's passing, I cried for the first time in my adult life.

Today I'm still part of the Wiggy fraternity, thanks to my friendship with Steve Brandon. Pat and Charlie have also been good friends and I try to visit them whenever I can. With my new involvement in the motor racing scene, I'll be based in England regularly and so those golden years with Wiggy will, happily, never go away.

Brett Walton

I AM from the Gold Coast in Australia and used to occasionally help out Mark Carlson and Troy Butler when they were racing at the Exhibition Grounds in Brisbane. When the overseas riders came on tour they didn't have a mechanic with them, so I'd help out.

My first sight of Simon was actually on television in the 1985-86 close season. There was a promotion featuring Simon in his distinctive green leathers going down a straight on his back wheel. I was impressed and then I had the chance to assist him at Brisbane, where we quickly hit it off.

In time Simon based himself with my family in south-east Queensland, plus we could also help him if he was stuck for a vehicle or needed his leathers and bike kept clean. His full-time mechanic over in Europe was Mick Day and in October 1991, Mick had the opportunity to work with Mick Doohan on the world road-racing scene. This meant him being available at very short notice to fly, for example, to Japan, which wasn't going to fit in with the conventional European scene. It was better for Mick to be an 'in-house' mechanic for the road-racing schedule.

Always game for a laugh, Wiggy and mechanic Brett Walton in 1986, doing what comes naturally!

I'd finished my apprenticeship in green-keeping and was looking after local bowling greens and golf courses. One golf club was high above the airport at Brisbane and I used to watch the planes taking off wondering where they might be travelling. I always hankered to go to England one day.

Well, the opportunity was about to arise quicker than I thought, for Simon asked me to take on the job as his mechanic. I told him that I needed a month to hand in my notice and make preparations for the trip.

So Simon went back to England ahead of me and eventually I arrived to live with him at the Old Stables in Middle Claydon. Thanks to my green-keeping skills, Simon also had the best looking lawn in Buckinghamshire – complete with stripes! Chris McGhee, a New Zealander, was also on board at the time. So Simon made sure he got value out of us and we proved quite handy around the mansion too!

Simon was always very careful with his money but did realise the virtue of injecting investment into his racing career as time went on.

But little did I realise the pressures of the race schedule and by August I was knackered, although thoroughly enjoying myself too. It was especially good to visit countries like Germany and Poland for the first time. I wouldn't have missed the experience for the world.

The pressure wasn't just the pace or the cycle of meetings-preparation-meetings, it was also Simon's own success. He was so good on track that it was essential that we matched that standard off-track. If a world title had been achieved, then Simon had a target on his back as far as the other riders were concerned at every single meeting that he contested.

Leading up to a World Final, Simon was really dedicated but the great thing about him was that he was an extrovert so he could still socialise. Hans Nielsen was the opposite. He was introverted and would prefer to retire to bed early. Tony Rickardsson, for whom I have worked in recent years, was also an extrovert, although the dieticians have got inside his head in recent years. Tony 'beats himself up' over a burger these day. Simon actually had a chart in the workshop with the weight of the other World Champions listed, so that he could remind himself of Hans Zierk's assertion that the finest form of tuning was not to put on weight. In longtrack racing, weight, power and speed are the interlinked aspects of performance.

Simon also knew how important it was to get away completely to be able to think and analyse in complete peace and quiet. Which is why snowboarding and sking were important breaks for him. With all that snow and a lack of noise there, Simon could mull over the answers to questions that had bugged him about certain engines or certain events. The solitude also fostered a creative phase, for it was on a ski lift that he really thought out the action plan for indentical team suits. He was riding for Coventry at the time and saw what a clash there was between his green leathers and their yellow/black colour scheme. All this came after a season of between 120 and 130 meetings with a support team of one – me!

When Simon signed for Exeter in 1996, this proved an exceptionally demanding season. By now he was flying back from Germany or Poland on a Sunday while I would get the motor home back to base by 2pm on the Monday. We would immediately load up the van to head west and my head would not hit the pillow until after 2am on the Tuesday morning. I probably hadn't slept since Saturday night. Then I'd be up to prepare six or seven machines across the week before the sequence started all over again the following Friday.

When the handcuffs were unlocked from the steering wheel at the end of the season, I tended not to get involved in the Australian bookings. Charging off to Perth or Adelaide in such a big country as mine didn't have an appeal after the mileage of a jam-packed European season. I needed to recharge my batteries as well. Not that everything wasn't stimulating. Whether it was Heat One at Oxford Speedway or the final of the World Longtrack Championship, you invest as much time and emotion into that particular race. It didn't matter what race it was with Simon, I felt the same buzz.

You also developed as a person. I learnt to cope with pressure and deal with the fact that not everything was always going to go well. I adjusted to different patterns in the diary and different sets of demands. Working with Simon was based on making sure that we got everything right.

Julian was like a father figure in this respect. Everything from tyre pressures to setting up the engine was analysed. Simon was therefore able to hit the ground running and this organisation was married to his talent.

I became influenced by the fitness regime and the working breaks. Simon traded in his jet-ski with Pete Webb for a KX 500 moto-cross bike. Julian and myself bought one and we would all go and work out on them.

I accompanied Simon on his jogging sessions and then we took our fitness to a new dimension by taking up squash. These were fun sessions, too, with plenty of argy-bargy. We even booked a temporary membership of a club while in Cannes in the South of France.

It was also good to hook up with the dietary preparation. One of the many reasons for Simon importing the motor home from America was not only the left-hand drive but the ability to store and prepare healthy food. Normally it is difficult for the speedway fraternity to eat well on the road. But Charlie was an excellent cook and prepared a range of pre-packed pasta dishes for us to consume en route.

The motor home had other virtues, too. Like being at a practice when the rain was lashing down and watching other riders, particularly the East Europeans, trying to sort their goggles out under an umbrella – while we were sitting comfortably in the warm. This facility also allowed Simon to be more rested and relaxed when he emerged to get ready for racing.

Julian had really got the message across that it takes as much energy to bodge a job as to get it right first time, so every aspect of Simon's jigsaw became more professional.

However, Simon could also be a nightmare to work for as a mechanic when he suddenly wanted to make changes. I liked to get to a meeting early – for instance, if a meeting began at 7.30pm, we'd get there at 5.30pm and set up. This meant that there was no faffing around and as I knew how much time was required to change a jet or whatever, then I could work to this.

We were at Harsewinkel one day and watching the National Licence riders, having made our customary early appearance. Now the swing arms on a longtrack bike can either be brass or rubber but getting to them is a long job, as you have to take the engine out, drop the gear box, and by the time you have moved the engine plates everything is in bits with only the frame, wheels and handlebar in place.

That day we had a brass swing arm fitted. Simon watched the races and then went over to the winner and had a few words with him. Simon then came back and told me that he wanted to change to a rubber swing arm, which is what the young victor had fitted. So I had an intensive 25 minutes to sort out the requested change. Soon Simon re-appeared and announced that he had changed his mind and wanted the brass swing arm put back in!

At Marmande, practice is at 2pm but the actual event starts at 9pm. Mark Loram had won it the previous year and Simon logged that this was on a speedway engine. So after confirming details with Mark, Simon wanted the engine switched. That day, there were eventually a total of seven engine changes between the start of practice and the end of the meeting proper. I had severe back-strain and didn't see any racing after chasing around like a maniac!

We used to have pretty busy longtrack trips, too, where I would collect a variety of riders *en route* and try to cram everything into the motor home. On one of these trips we had an Australian pal of Simon's whose name was Nick Capper. We were setting off for Estonia on one of Simon's organised events. Nick was full of excitement sitting next to me, with my bloodshot eyes after nearly a month on the road. We collected Simon from Toulouse airport as he had been home and back from a meeting in Italy and was about to contest a World Championship round at Marmande – a meeting that he won with a maximum. Afterwards I had to organise a longtrack bike and three speedway bikes, which were quite dirty by now. We took Simon to an airport in the south-west of Bordeaux and then set off for Hans Zierk's base near Hanover. There, we sorted a few engines out and tested them before going on to collect the late Detlef Conrada (who was killed subsequently at Celle) from Cloppenburg, so that we had another nationality for the promoter in Estonia.

Marvyn Cox and Tony Briggs were next to meet up with us in Hamburg. Tony had no gear but was a New Zealand dimension to the field. We had to lend him everything except leathers. Stockholm in Sweden was our next destination, to rendezvous with Joonas Kylmakorpi. By this time there was no room for any more bikes inside the motorhome with 10 on board already, so Joonas' bike had to go on the bull-bar at the front.

Our next task was more of a mental challenge – crossing the Baltic Sea soon after a ferry had sunk with all lives lost on board. When we saw the 'Neptunis', it was half the size of the normal ferries, as the Estonia line bought old stock off the Scandinavian ferry companies, and in a very rusty condition. After 18 hours of high seas in this old bathtub, I don't think even Nick Capper was finding the journey glamorous. Little did Nick realise what yet lay in store for him!

When we got to Estonia we met up with Simon, who had flown in and looked as if he was on holiday! He had taken the precaution of contacting the promoter to tell him that we had an extra person on board – an Australian called Nick Capper. Just to make sure that Nick had no hassles when he went to spectate. Anyway, once having arrived at the venue, unloading was a nightmare and we also had a repeat problem with a gearbox that had played up at Marmande. When the riders were called for a medical, a programme was produced with Nick Capper listed as a rider representing Australia! We really played along with it and emphasised to him that he had to make a start, otherwise Simon was in deep trouble. Poor old Nick was as white as a sheet. He was scheduled to be in Heat One against Simon and I kept telling him how much I envied him the experience of lining up next to Simon and maybe making the gate on him. Nick was mumbling about lining up and then pulling onto the centre green when the tapes went up. Eventually, we put him out of his misery at breakfast the next morning!

After the meeting, and with this being towards the end of the season, it was an opportunity for Simon to sell some bikes before being the 'first class hero' – as I called him – and taking a flight back home. These trips were slogs but they were very stimulating and thanks to Simon pushing the margins, we also took in Croatia and Russia in our time. I didn't like the latter country at all and was grateful for a military escort on visits there.

Australian passports were 64 pages long and I had to get mine stamped wherever I went in Europe. I got through three passports in a reasonably short period. Such was my schedule that I didn't have time to go and wait around all day in London waiting for a renewal. That's how I ended up being smuggled in and out of the UK hidden in a bunk bed! I had a current passport and visa but just didn't want to collect any more border stamps.

Incidentally, once Simon became a family man, unloading meant also moving the walker, rocker and high chair to get to the bikes on some trips. Abigail was a treat to have around but she always wanted 'Uncle Brett' to read to her when, in reality, it was *my* bedtime! I became a godfather to Ricki and eventually both kids ended up having a game of hiding tools from me in the workshop while I was having lunch, which made life confusing!

Occasionally, when Simon's spirit would go flat in mid-season, I'd remind him of his early days working on a production line and how boring he found it. How excited he was at the prospect of becoming a professional motorcyclist. How he might never have left the UK or even his village. However, now he was a World Champion, which few riders become, with a global racing diary, what on earth was *he* on about?

My little oration always worked wonders and he didn't feel sorry for himself for very long. So as well as that of mechanic, I also ended up with the part-time role of philosopher, sports psychologist and childminder in my spare time!

I had seven seasons with Simon, from 1992 to '98. I had flown home and was in mid-air when he first collapsed. Eventually, I picked up a series of urgent messages from Charlie. When she told me that Simon was on a life-support machine, I couldn't believe it. I am not a doctor, and hindsight is a precise science, but I wonder how long the problem had been lurking – possibly for many years?

Over his career Simon had suffered a range of traumas including a broken neck, a major skin graft and a series of fractures to both collar-bones with plates inserted. He never compromised on safety. Everything he wore was the best quality and any of his helmets involved in crashes were properly disposed of.

By 1998 Simon had been involved in a number of crashes in which he had suffered very severe concussion, including one resulting from a particularly bad crash with Berndt Diener at a Grand Prix longtrack meeting in Holland. Simon went straight through the fence.

I couldn't immediately follow him to hospital as I had to load up and get the motorhome through the car park. When I arrived at the hospital I wasn't impressed by the standard of attention – the medical staff were more absorbed in watching the televised World Cup football from France than their patients, so I discharged him and took him back to England.

When Simon couldn't ride in 1999 because of his fit, I'd decided to take a year off. Then I was approached by both Jason Crump and Tony Rickardsson. In Tony's case, he had spoken to me in past years, so I moved to Sweden to take up his offer.

However, on my free weekends, I'd fly over to see Simon and his family. This was crucial in 2000, when I took some time out to go and give Charlie some help. I would take Abigail to school at 9am and then continue on to see Simon at the hospice.

I was with Simon at the very end and witnessing a mother pre-deceasing her son was very hard to take. The world seemed back to front at that point.

Having said our goodbyes, we threw ourselves into the organisation of an unforgettable funeral. I shall always remember sorting out – with Talon Engineering boss George Sartin – the sprockets he made to be placed at the end of Simon's coffin, inscribed with his lifespan and his World Championship achievements *(see page 248)*.

The funeral wasn't conventional – it was a celebration of Simon's life. Hans Fock came over from Germany and took reams of photos. They provide me with memories today as I look at my baby daughter, Mia, and Charlie's new daughter, Libby, and realise that life does move on.

Simon was like a big brother to me and I'm so pleased that those whose lives were touched by his are still bonded by love and friendship.

THE MEDIA

Richard Clark
Editor, Speedway Star magazine

PRAGUE'S Marketa Stadium, Sunday, July 10, 1994, scene of the World Championship semi-final. This was the final hurdle before what became the last-ever one-off World Final at Vojens in Denmark prior to the FIM introducing a Grand Prix system in 1995.

Before tapes-up, few could resist admiring the immaculate-looking green and white machine, boasting rare-for-the-time spoilers.

It looked like a speedway bike from the future.

Unfortunately for Simon Wigg, the pilot of said machine, it didn't perform like that, and neither did the pilot.

Simon managed just two points that afternoon, and afterwards cursed the meticulous time and patience he'd expended on preparing for the meeting, wishing he'd simply turned up and had a go instead.

His problem, he insisted, was being a grasstrack/longtrack rider first, and a speedway rider second.

So typical of Simon, though, it was a doddle for your attendant hack to get his view of the meeting, ever-willing for an interview, no matter what his result.

Some two to three hours after his disappointment, a group of us gathered at the U Fleku, one of Prague's oldest drinking establishments.

Present were Simon, his pit crew Brett Walton and Steve Brandon, defending World Champion Sam Ermolenko, and *Speedway Star's* John Hipkiss and your's truly.

A couple of U Fleku's home-brewed efforts soon raised the spirits of one and all.

(Sam's hardly needed too much, he'd made the cut for Vojens with 11 points.)

And it was impossible for the bubbly Wiggy to be down too long.

His insatiable appetite for life itself was soon dominating once again, and with that, he dragged us all off to a poky little cellar club across Charles Bridge.

There we encountered a local band giving their Fenders and Marshalls what for, and gallantly doing their best with English lyrics.

And, as one of those magical unplanned nights unfolded, before long, there we all were, with Milo, the group's leader, taking it in turns with Sam and myself to 'serenade' the rest of the party on his trusty acoustic guitar.

Milo was well chuffed to meet up with some Westerners able to converse in music's international language, and chuffed his own efforts had been appreciated.

Milo's considered notes wafted into the Prague evening air, alongside Sam and mine's not-so-considered ones, and a splendid time was had by all.

So what became of our merry group, 11 years on?

Sam's still piling up the points, as classy as ever in his 'old age'.

Brett is happily married and settled back in his native Australia.

Steve is still on the speedway scene as part of the Sky Sports team.

Hippo's still flashing away.

But, on numerous return trips to Prague, I've never found that little cellar bar again.

And I don't know what became of Milo.

Sadly, we do know what became of Simon.

But what remains indelibly in the memory is his love of life, that desire to drag his chosen sport forward, Wiggy's love of racing itself, of communication, of company, of the world as his oyster.

Of life, simply.

Larger than life has become such a cliché, but that's exactly what the 'Big Man' was.

And, I'm no expert, but for a grasstrack/longtrack rider first, he certainly gave speedway a run for its money.

Certainly, speedway misses him to this day.

We all do.

But that evening in downtown Prague is just one of a thousand happy memories of time spent in his company.

If you happen to find yourself in a poky cellar bar in the shadow of Prague Castle one evening, raise a glass to Wiggy.

He's bound to be grinning down at you . . .

John Gaisford

Oxford Mail

SIMON Wigg – the sport of speedway has probably never had or ever will have a man with such a personality. The confidence just oozed from the man whether he was sat on a bike at 90-100mph on a longtrack or mucking about on a moto-cross bike.

To say he was a dream to work with would be an understatement. When Simon and Hans Nielsen were together at Oxford, it was a sheer delight to cover the team that provided no shortage of good copy and headlines to match.

Although he was a different guy when he got astride a bike, there was another side to the man who always had time for the media and fans alike.

No-one at Oxford will forget his gladiator-type arrival by helicopter at Oxford Stadium after he had won his first World Longtrack title, a discipline he was to become a legend in over the years, or the time he tried to glue Troy Butler to the saddle to stop the young Aussie falling off!

But I remember Simon best for his absolute friendship, he never let you down. I recall visiting his newly-purchased, splendid manor house at Middle Claydon, just two days after he had returned from a winter in Australia. He was jet-lagged, of course, but very hospitable. He was stood in front of a blazing fire, his fur coat done up to the neck, sipping coffee, because the pipes had frozen during one of our mildest winters! But was he fazed by it? Was he heck – he was just glad to be home and chatting about his trip. What's more, he had the pasta on the boil for a pleasant lunch to boot.

He always said to me that I ought to take in a longtrack meeting, because the speed he got up to was awesome. To this day I regret missing out on the spectacle.

I also recall a cold winter's afternoon when he invited me along to see his local moto-cross circuit, which he and Hans Nielsen used to dust off some of the cobwebs in a practice session – and did they get up to some spectacular stuff!

Wiggy was magic. Who else would breeze into Oxford Stadium driving a Rolls Royce with a trailer on the back carrying a speedway bike? Or arrive on an off night for a greyhound meeting wearing crocodile boots and a stetson? Not many of today's Grand Prix stars, I hasten to add.

We only had one minor setback – well, in my eyes it was. It came after Simon had a disappointing afternoon in the British Final at Coventry. As reporters tend to do after a meeting, I asked him how he felt. The reply was not for printing but that was a one-off riposte which everyone is entitled to make.

He was the perfect showman – but don't tell that to referee Paul Ackroyd. Wiggy had won his first five rides and was completing what he thought was a fine 18-point maximum for England against the USA in a Test match at Oxford in 1986. As he crossed the finish line, the England skipper celebrated by pulling a wheelie . . . only to be excluded by the official in the name of 'dangerous riding'. Wiggy was incensed at what he called a 'diabolical decision.'

Simon's loss to the sport has been immense, not only in speedway but grasstrack and longtrack, too, and it was a sad day for all of us when he was laid to rest at Milton Keynes.

Peter York

Former Oxford Speedway presenter & BSPA Manager

MANY people may not realise that I rode grasstrack myself in the 70s, in both the 350 and 500 categories. Julian Wigg was a top British rider of the era and I was on nodding terms with him. Then I was at a meeting in the Birmingham area when I heard that Julian's younger brother was taking part in the schoolboy section. I didn't even know of this lad, Simon, at the time.

Well, my first impression of Simon Wigg and speed was not on track, but in the pits, where this 15-year-old was racing up and down – which was an absolute no-no – and then being collared by the officials for a ticking-off. It didn't prevent him from winning his section, however.

Our paths crossed properly in 1983, when I was the announcer at Cradley Heath and Simon had joined the Heathens from Weymouth. We happened to park next to each other for a pre-season social, chatted as we went in and I took to this friendly and bubbly character immediately. At that time, everybody was aware of the image that Bruce Penhall had created and the standards the American World Champion had set. But I thought to myself, in Simon we could have the British equivalent, very presentable and decked out in the latest fashion.

By 1984, I was working for BBC Radio Oxford and had accepted an invitation to become presenter with the new British League set-up at Oxford Speedway. Within a few weeks of my agreeing to be involved at Cowley, both Hans Nielsen and Simon Wigg were unveiled as big-money signings and I knew at that point that the club was definitely going places.

The first season was OK but, by 1985, the team really took off and it was the bond between the riders that helped everything gel – neither Hans nor Simon acted as if they were superstars. Hans would report back to the reserves after Heat One on what to watch out for on track, while Simon would often be down on his hands and knees assisting another team member with a mechanical problem. The other Cheetahs' riders felt that they were being treated with respect by these two senior stars and it made for a good atmosphere in the changing room.

I recall one of the juniors, Phil Roberts, who was later sadly paralysed in a track crash, having great difficulties in getting his engine going, so Simon offered to examine the problem. Back at his workshop, muttering about the number of stickers plastered across the machine, Simon took the engine apart and rebuilt it. When Phil realised this, he was concerned about the cost – to which Simon said: 'I didn't take the engine away to make money from you – don't worry about it.' Now although Simon had a reputation for being more than careful with his cash, this showed another side to him. While I suspect that he played hardball with people who could afford it, Phil Roberts did not come into this category – it was simply an act of kindness.

Not sure his pompous PE teacher would approve.

Simon could, of course, be great fun and I have a clear memory of a supporters' club social evening in the former bar on the first turn at Cowley. We arrived to find the stadium manager, Harry George, showing some Milton Keynes speedway videos on the monitor, when Simon soon picked up that the fans found them pretty underwhelming. Simon told Harry that he had the latest World Longtrack qualifier on a tape in his Mercedes, so he popped out, returned and presented the tape to Harry who wandered off to put it in the machine.

In fact the tape was a hardcore porn movie called *Debbie Does Dallas!* When Harry pressed the play button, there was uproar, which completely confused him at first. He came back into the room to see what all the fuss was about and then stood there ashen-faced when he realised what was being shown on screen!

Harry huffed and puffed his way back to the equipment to eject the tape – this time to be greeted by massive boos from the audience – while Simon stood there grinning from ear to ear!

Simon was a gift for a presenter following any accident that meant a delay in proceedings. You could ask him a question like: 'Tell us the difference between a speedway bike and a longtrack bike?' and point the mike at him for at least five minutes.

He was also strong on trying to promote the sport to a wider local audience and would often complain about Oxford Speedway being 'the best kept secret' despite our media initiatives. Then, with his own efforts and at his own cost, he set up a tour of five schools, finishing at his own former seat of learning in High Wycombe.

Simon roped me in to open proceedings with a question-and-answer session with bike, leathers, helmet and other kit on display. We reached Simon's old school at 2pm and he was looking forward to meeting up again with one of the PE staff whom he disliked intensely for the way he had treated him as a youth. Simon was good at certain sports but he wasn't an all-rounder and hadn't had a happy time with the particular teacher.

We set everything up in the school hall before I introduced Simon as an 'old boy' who had gone on to professional motorcyce sport. I set the audience the task of spotting the difference between a typical road bike and a racing machine. Then Simon asked them if they'd like to hear the bike start up, which was greeted enthusiastically by the 40 or so lads present. We took the bike outside to the playing fields, where the PE master, whom Simon had described, turned up and referred to Simon as 'Wigg' in a very pompous tone. Simon calling him 'Sir' in reply did seem strange but, for both, I suppose old habits died hard.

In a very imperious manner, the PE teacher instructed Simon to keep outside the white boundary line of the sports field at all times.

Having warned the kids to keep a distance because of the back wheel spinning,Simon asked me to warm up the bike while he went and got changed. By this time about 120 pupils had congregated and he asked them if they'd like him to take it for a gentle spin around the outer perimeter of the sports field.

Simon took things gently at first but picked up speed on each circuit and, suddenly, he was inside the perimeter line and going full bore.He threw the bike on full lock in some of the corners, churning clumps of turf into the air, all to the wild cheers of the young spectators.

The PE master reappeared absolutely apoplectic and instructed me to stand in front of Simon and stop him in his tracks! I quickly explained that speedway bikes had no brakes and I had no intention of standing in front of one bearing down on me at more than 60mph! The guy spluttered something about 'no brakes being illegal' and he wouldn't believe me when I tried to explain what speedway was about.

Simon on one of his school visits, spreading the speedway gospel.

He then announced, against my strong advice, that he'd go out and restrain Simon as he passed by. Soon Simon trundled over to his former tormenter and explained that a bump had forced him sideways over the perimeter line and it had taken him a couple of laps to bring the machine under control. Simon apologised for the mess but felt that it would give the groundsman something to occupy his time!

We departed the scene, leaving the PE master contemplating his churned-up field, while a chuckling Simon made it very plain to me that he'd waited many years for payback time.

One other incident when Simon pushed things to the limit – but one that was enjoyed by onlookers – comes to mind from his time at Coventry, where I was again presenter at the club which tracked Simon and Hans. The occasion was the Coventry Dinner and Dance, presided over by promoters Charles and Linda Ochiltree, or Lord and Lady Brandon as I called them.

I was on the top table as the MC, with Charles looking increasingly uncomfortable at the banter between myself and the riders as I called them up for an interview. It was actually quite funny and Linda looked like she wanted to laugh but, of course, Charles would have disapproved.

By the time it was Wiggy's turn, he'd spotted a huge floral display in one corner of the room, so he picked it up, marched over to Linda, presented it to her 'on behalf of her many admirers', and planted a big kiss on her! It brought the house down – even Charles grinned!

Simon made a big impact with the Coventry supporters during his first meeting as a Bees' rider at Brandon in 1993, once I put a mike under that famous nose of his. After a couple of races, I took him out onto the centre green for a chat and he was so enthusiastic about the set-up at Coventry. He said something along the lines of: 'A Saturday night . . . speedway under lights . . . a great track . . . great crowd . . . this is speedway, the rest are just dirt-tracks.'

His words went down a treat with everybody in the crowd.

Although Simon was the life and soul of his many parties, this was when he was truly the centre of attention. However, I've actually witnessed a Simon Wigg that many wouldn't recognise – a more introverted version.

Simon was publicity-mad for himself and his sport and in doing so, he created an image of himself which he tried to live up to, but there was a deeper soul. After he broke his neck at Lonigo, he had a lot more time on his hands and he once invited me over to his home at Middle Claydon for a coffee and a chat – it was before Charlie came into his life and he just needed someone to talk to that day. I was there for about three hours and while I am no psychologist, I got the impression that the fact that his father hadn't given him support and shown interest in his early racing career, was a hurt that he retained, and that he'd created this larger than life image to compensate for that.

There were certainly long periods of silence and introspection and there was no doubt that Julian was Simon's surrogate dad, although Simon's early struggles had developed his maturity at an early stage of his racing career.

To assess Simon as a rider I have to point out that he was basically very good on anything with two wheels. His cycle speedway skills are early proof of that, while his subsequent progress through grasstrack, longtrack and speedway is well chronicled.

However, when I was more closely involved with him through speedway, I observed the consternation that Simon could cause among those around him. He'd score a maximum one week and then take the engine apart to find out why it had gone so well for him, perhaps disturbing something and then scoring far less points the next week. I've witnessed a frustrated Julian having to walk away and count to 10 in the Oxford pits.

My greatest personal impression of Simon was gained immediately following the Munich World Final of 1989. He was a contender for the speedway crown, with his team-mate Hans Nielsen, right to the climax of the meeting and despite having to settle for the silver medal, he was equally magnificent at the press conference afterwards. Simon took questions in German and answered them in the same language, before translating each question and his answer for the benefit of the British press.

That was so professional. That was so Simon.

Glynn Shailes

Former Oxford Speedway Press Officer

THERE was no better all-round motorcyclist, in my opinion, than Simon Antony Wigg. Simon was always a credit to the motorcycling profession and whatever competition it was, he would be well turned out, both before and after he changed into his riding gear.

With the tremendous sense of fun he possessed, he was popular with both opponents and the general public. Yes, Wiggy was a man of whom this country could be justly proud.

I was reminded of something extra special about Simon when I was putting together the souvenir brochure for the recent reunion of the 1985 and 1986 Oxford Cheetahs, and I was discussing with former co-promoter John Payne his article for the brochure. I was reminded that although Simon was a very busy man, often riding in different countries on different days of the week, if there was a sick child, either in hospital or at home, and the promoters had received a letter asking if someone from the Cheetahs team could pop in and see them, then Simon would make time. His visits always cheered up the unfortunate youngster and there can be no doubt about that old saying: 'If you want a job doing, always give it to a busy person, since they will *always* make time'. That old adage fitted Wiggy perfectly.

I always think, too, of the time, in 1985, when Simon arrived by helicopter at the Oxford Stadium having won the World Longtrack Championship in Korskro, Denmark. He was a very proud man – and he had every right to be.

One aspect that always tended to annoy me was the fact that Simon was British and proud of it, and he was a World Champion, but beyond the motorcycling world and speedway, few people seemed to be aware of his successes. This was a great pity since he always did his country proud with his all-out racing style.

I cannot forget the 1989 season at Oxford when, following the World Final at Munich, Oxford not only had the World Champion in Hans Nielsen, but the runner-up and British and Commonwealth Champion in Simon Wigg, while Hans had also won the Nordic Final at Tampere, Finland. What a celebration there was at Oxford – a wonderful moment for all those fans who supported and were associated with the club.

There are one or two funny stories which involve Simon. I recall an Inter-Continental Final where the powers that be had delayed proceedings by arranging for the bikes of the competitors to be weighed. One – I think it was Jeremy Doncaster's – was a little too light, and the meeting presenter was in the pits asking 'what happens now?' Then the crowd was treated to a loud voice over the PA system – it was Oxford co-promoter Bernard Crapper, who boomed out the response: 'Tie Wiggy's wallet to it!'

Always smart, mentally and in appearance – on and off track.

Although the joke was on Wiggy, nobody laughed more than Simon himself.

As a regular competitor on the world stage, Wiggy raced in many far away places and I remember one night at Swindon when he was riding for Exeter. It was known that he'd raced somewhere abroad (it was reported at the time that it took a couple of days to get there, and of course a couple of days to get back), so the start time of the meeting was put back from 7.30pm to 8.00, to assist Wiggy in getting to the Blunsdon track in time.

Sure enough, he'd stepped off an aircraft at Heathrow, got straight into a car for his journey to Swindon, jumped on his bike and went up to the starting gate to race. Jet-lag? I don't think Simon had ever heard of it – and if he had, he certainly didn't show it.

A truly remarkable man who left behind a string of memories – all of them good.

Tony Lethbridge

Exeter PRO and former Falcons team manager

SIMON Wigg nearly didn't join the Exeter Falcons for the 1996 season. At the start of that year Colin Hill was looking to strengthen a side spearheaded by Mark Loram. I had been in Poland in 1990 and seen in action a sensational young Polish rider at Bydgoszcz called Tomasz Gollob, who went on to join Ipswich Witches.

In February 1996, Tomas had been booked to ride at the Telford ice event. Ipswich's Polish co-promoter, Magda Louis, assisted Colin with the negotiations but a lack of availability for away fixtures proved the downfall and the Pole didn't come.

About a week later, Mark had to travel out with Simon to the Jawa factory in the Czech Republic, where he broached the subject of Wiggy riding for Exeter. Simon had briefly been at Long Eaton the previous season but it wasn't very successful, so he was reluctant at first. However, Simon did have a good record at Exeter from his National League days with Weymouth – once Neil Street had instilled in him a positive mental attitude about riding at the County Ground.

Now the south-western corner of England is a strong grasstrack area, so many of the fans were very positive about such a talented rider joining our club, although a few doubters were still banging on about Simon's Long Eaton period.

Simon was immediately impressive in practice and I remember my father, Ted, who looked after track maintenance, commenting on how well Wiggy had ridden the County Ground. He and his colleague, Colin Endicott, were even more impressed when Simon joined them in their shed for a constructive dialogue about track preparation – only Ivan Mauger had actually sat down and chatted to them like this in recent club history.

However, Simon's Exeter career nearly finished before it had even started. He missed both legs of a Spring Gold Cup match over the Easter Bank Holiday – he'd been injured at Poole the previous week – despite having ridden abroad that same day.

Colin Hill was less than happy but at the next match, Wiggy took the mike to make a solid defence of himself against comments that Colin had made, emphasising that there must have been a misunderstanding. Simon certainly won the fans over with his speech but he also impressed Colin. From that point, they got on like a house on fire.

I was handling the PR for Exeter and you won't be surprised that Simon was excellent in this department. He always made the effort to meet my requests and he was particularly keen to meet reporters who knew nothing about speedway, so that he could 'sell' the sport to them.

One of my outstanding memories was when he was invited to be the subject of the equivalent of *Desert Island Discs* by Radio Devon's sports editor Vic Morgan. Simon recorded 45 minutes of fluent conversation in the press box at the County Ground, having just emerged from his post-meeting shower. This was the basis of an impressive one-hour package when it was eventually transmitted.

Simon would often tell me that Rock 'n' Roll was related to speedway in the entertainment sense, although I think he meant more in terms of event promotion. He was always full of ideas of how to take the club and the sport forward and ready to discuss his promotional thoughts.

The trip that he organised for the Exeter team to visit Russia was pure Wiggy, who was actually riding for Togliatti in the Russian League at the time – unbelievable for a westerner but, then again, perhaps not so for Simon, because over there he was a superstar. However, the trip the trip was riddled with unusual incidents, including bits falling off the plane during an internal flight and then, on arrival, finding that the local promoter had been shot dead!

I have many memories of Simon during a happy year for the Falcons, both on and off track. We broke our sequence of away losses, which stretched back to 1992, with a victory at Middlesbrough on the Thursday, before moving on to Belle Vue the next night.

Simon was the first rider to have four helmets ready in the pits and during the match the Belle Vue clerk of the course, Alan Morrey, called Colin Hill over to say that the referee wanted to speak to him. It was pointed out to Colin that Simon had to ride in the traditional yellow-and-black helmet cover, not just the plain yellow of his personalised helmet.

To lighten the mood, Simon got some insulating tape and a pair of scissors, cut out 'Hi Ref!' in large black letters, stuck them on his helmet and proceeded to race on!

What a character.

That season, we had a good run in the Knockout Cup and for our quarter-final at Swindon we were sweating on Wiggy landing at Heathrow from Moscow at 5.45pm. Derek Daly was despatched to collect him while Colin and myself settled down at Bob Radford's place in Swindon to watch Ceefax and confirm the arrival of his flight.

When they rolled into the pits at Blunsdon at 7.15, we realised what speed merchants Derek and Wiggy were! We proceeded to gain a draw with a 'wall of sound' being conducted by myself from our fans. In previous seasons, we would have been lucky to have had a straggle of fans at our away matches, but not with Mark Loram and Simon Wigg in tandem on track.

A couple of other memories come to mind – the first is painful and the second a perspective on Simon's humanity.

I recall Wiggy going down the back straight at Exeter, clipping the fence and heading for the centre green – an inner greyhound circuit was unique to Exeter Speedway at the time. Simon ran spectacularly along the hare rail and injured his left leg, causing him to miss a few matches.

In 1993 I travelled to Muldhorf to support Exeter's Paul Fry in the World Longrack Final. After the victory presentation to Simon, who won his fourth title, our paths crossed as he made his way back to the changing rooms. We shook hands and had a chat – he always seemed to make time for people and I was impressed, especially as he must have had so much going through his mind having just become World Champion again. He was a great ambassador and would have continued to be.

Simon Wigg was a champion – not only as a rider but as a human being.

Martin Neal

Backtrack Magazine

AS a journalist with the weekly *Speedway Mail* newspaper during the 80s, I got to meet Wiggy a number of times, both in speedway stadia around Europe and at social gatherings, too. And on every occasion Wiggy proved himself to be a thoroughly friendly, accommodating and professional bloke.

One of my strongest memories of him was at the end-of-season Speedway Writers and Photographers' Association (SWAPA) dinner, the year that Paul Muchene had been tragically killed in a crash at Hackney.

Paul was riding for Hackney at the time of his accident but was a junior contracted to British League Oxford, where Wiggy was one of the big stars.

It transpired that Paul's fiancé was pregnant at the time of his crash – and the tragic waste of a young life as well as the prospect of a baby growing up without its father, and a young woman cruelly robbed of her partner, clearly affected Wiggy deeply.

The SWAPA dinner was always a well-attended and swanky do, and Wiggy stood up to make a heartfelt appeal for us to support the fund set up to help his fallen colleague's family.

The fact that one was a world star and the other a rider who had been on the junior scene for some time, without managing to make that elusive step up, didn't matter. In Simon's eyes, they were equal.

Such was the emotion he felt that, for once, he struggled to articulate exactly what he wanted to say – but we all understood and admired his efforts.

I also recall arguably his greatest moment on the speedway – as opposed to longtrack – circuit – the Munich World Final of 1989.

Hans Nielsen won the title with a flawless 15-point maximum but Wiggy totalled a highly-impressive 12 and beat England team-mate Jeremy Doncaster in a run-off for second place.

By this time he was pushing 29 – hardly a veteran but he'd been on the scene for some time and was desperate to add a world speedway title to his longtrack crown.

In the media scrum that followed in the bowels of the Olympic Stadium, I managed to grab him for some quotes to go in the World Final edition of *Speedway Mail*.

It was a great evening for British speedway and a fantastic night for Wiggy, yet there was actually an air of disappointment about him.

For all that he was delighted to establish himself as the No.2 speedway rider on the planet, he also knew that being No.1 was what he'd really gone to Munich to do.

He looked at me as he we concluded our interview and said: 'I'll win this b*****d yet...'

I'll remember Wiggy as a fantastic talent and a fantastic bloke.

Thomas Schiffner

Editor-in-Chief, Bahnsport Aktuell magazine (Germany)

WIGGY was different to other speedway and longtrack riders. When I first saw Simon in Germany in the early 80s, of course I first got to know him as a rider. But after a short term I realised there was a human being behind the helmet.

Very quickly I learned about Wiggy's character, as everybody who knew him personally did, whether they were another rider, mechanic, promoter, journalist or just a supporter. As a journalist, I was struck by his kindness and ability to listen and think about everything before he made a statement or gave a simple answer.

Of course, Simon´s death was a big loss for the sport – primary as a rider, but also as an ambassador of the sport, for he was a top marketing manager on two wheels.

Wiggy loved his trips to Germany, where he came nearly every week to his favourite longtrack meetings. And when Simon arrived for a meeting in the home country of longtrack racing, where he had more supporters than most of the native riders, he was always more than simply a fast rider – the smart British guy was an ideal ambassador of track racing in every way.

He did everything to attract the people before, during and after the meetings. He was always present for children, autograph sessions, media people, supporters and whoever.

It was certainly by no coincidence that, when he started his career in Germany in 1979, Simon was a great fan of German superstar Egon Müller, who was a phenomenon at that time.

Wiggy become a phenomenon, too. And he will stay one – forever.

SUPPORTERS

Simon Wigg was universally popular wherever he rode – as this chapter of tributes from fans from all over the world clearly illustrates . . .

My greatest memory of Simon is not for being the ultimate track racer, or for his immaculate presentation, but for having time for the fans no matter how young or old.

Alhough I had followed Simon's career from his first days on the grass, I did not know him personally – yet after an experience in 1990, I felt as though I did.

After his Masters win at Severn Valley, I stood at the presentation with my four-year-old daughter on my shoulders and called out: 'Can my little girl say well done, Simon?'.

Surrounded by well-wishers, Wiggy replied: 'Of course she can', and took my daughter into his arms, gave her a giant kiss and placed her gently back from whence she came.

It was a moment not just my daughter (who is now 19), but my whole family will never forget and is often spoken of today.

Great rider, great sportsman, great bloke.

Mick Nokes (Grasstrack correspondent, Speedway Star magazine)

I only met Simon once – it was at the 1986 BLRC at Belle Vue. He signed my programme board and was happy to chat with us.

A brilliant speedway rider, and an even better bloke.

Graham Kelly, Glasgow.

The best there is, the best there was and the best there ever will be.

Thanks for all the great times.

Jörg

I used to take my son to most of the grasstracks when he was young. We usually camped the night before and he always looked for Simon's van to arrive. I had to take him to see Wiggy, who always had time for him and everyone else, no matter how busy he was.

Simon was still the same even after he'd travelled all night from the Continent in order to support the British grasstrack scene. My son will never, ever forget Simon.

Abi and Ricki – you were very young when I last saw you with your Dad at the grasstrack, but you could tell then how proud he was of you both. I'm sure you know that.

Trevor and Peter Bird, Tadley, Hampshire.

As someone who first saw him ride at Weymouth, and who had the pleasure of working with the legendary Wiggy during his time at both Hackney and King's Lynn, I have so many happy memories of him and it was so, so cruel that he died at such a relatively early age.

I sat by him as we drank a beer each together with the rest of the team in the Coventry dressing room following his last-ever speedway match for the Silver Machine - a memory I'll treasure forever.

The fact that team race-suits and team bike covers, which are now the norm in the speedway world, were both his ideas, is a fitting and lasting tribute to the great man.

Bryn Williams

I first really came across Wiggy when he rode for Hackney in 1987. I always found him to be very approachable and was always willing to sign autographs for my children and I.

However, my best memory of Simon is after we moved from London to High Wycombe following Hackney's closure in 1991. My twin sons passed their exams to go to John Hampden Grammar School in High Wycombe and in our local paper around the same time, there was an article about Wiggy visiting his old school, which happened to be John Hampden.

I wrote to Simon, who was riding for Coventry that year, to tell him about my twins going to his former school and also to tell him about the centenary celebrations that the school were holding.

A few weeks later, Simon very kindly answered my letter and enclosed a couple of signed photographs of himself in action. He said in the letter that he hoped that my sons would do well at the school.

Considering that he had a very busy schedule, I thought this was really nice of him.

I really miss seeing Wiggy around the tracks, as he was always cheerful and smiling – even when he was ill. I have been very ill myself this year but, like Wiggy, I have always tried to keep smiling and stay positive.

A lovely guy who will always be missed.

RIP Simon.

Mrs Linda De Boise
(aka cheetahhawk on the British Speedway Forum)

Simon Wigg – Speedway with a smile!
Brian Longman, Hackney.

Oxford fans have many happy memories of Wiggy's time with the Cheetahs, it was a great period for both club and rider.

One such memory comes from a Bank Holiday meeting at Reading in 1990. The Cheetahs are getting hammered in a Gold Cup clash by their local rivals, when suddenly the lights go out! There has been an explosion at the local electricity substation, plunging the whole Reading area into darkness, and the meeting has to be abandoned.

A damaged hand couldn't stop Simon from signing for his vast legion of fans, world-wide.

Simon about to get pushed on his way by brother Julian at the 1995 World Longtrack Final at Scheessel, Germany, where he was beaten in a run-off by Kelvin Tatum. Picture courtesy of Steve Hone.

But as the fans are waiting for that decision to be made, a light suddenly appears.
It's Wiggy, going around the Smallmead track, holding a green glow stick in his hand!
Simon was always great fun, it was hard not to enjoy speedway when he was around.
Rob Peasley, Woodstock, Oxfordshire.

One of my fondest memories of Wiggy was standing by the pits at Oxford in 1994. Sheffield were the visitors and Jiri Stancl Jnr was riding for the Tigers in one of his first appearances in England.

He was wearing some bright green leathers, very much like Simon wore, and when I commented to Wiggy about the leathers, he quipped: 'Jiri needs to learn to gate, as they help to dazzle the back-markers!'
JD, Reading.

From memory, I think Wiggy rode for Weymouth in 1982, before stepping up into the big league a year later, when he joined Cradley and became a heat leader in the greatest league side ever!

In a brilliant year, he started at reserve and finished on a nine-point average, second only to Erik G.

It wasn't only his brilliant riding ability, but his capacity to want to entertain the fans. I remember he went on Beacon, our local radio station, during that year – on the Pat Foley show – to promote the sport, and he didn't mind all the mickey-taking from Pat.

Simon always had a smile on his face.

He was only sold at the end of '83 because of the points limit.

A brilliant and funny bloke/rider, who is sadly missed.
Mark Cox

When Bruce Penhall walked out on Cradley in 1982, he left a massive hole, both in terms of points-scoring ability and personality.

That Simon Wigg was able to fill that void (in both categories), when he rode full time for the Heathens in 1983, is a testament to the qualities of the man.
He just had one of the best smiles, didn't he?
Salty

My best memory of Wiggy was back in 1983 –part of the deal that brought him to Cradley was that the Heathens had to agree to take a full-strength team to Weymouth for a challenge match.
As per normal, a coach-load of Heathens made their way to Weymouth for a day out, followed by the meeting. When we arrived in Weymouth, who did we bump into on the go-karts, but Wiggy and Phil Collins – probably two of the nicest and funniest guys I've ever had the pleasure of meeting.
Anyway, after wrecking the go-karts and taking the mickey out of the attendant, Wiggy and 'Flyer' (Phil) decided to go into a joke shop and purchase policemen's helmets – and they then proceded to direct the traffic in Weymouth High Street, managing to bring it to a standstill! It's one of the funniest things I've ever seen.
Wiggy – a super, funny guy, and probably the most naturally talented all round motorcyclist this country has ever seen. Greatly missed but very, very fondly remembered.
Rami

You are more than welcome to use the pictures I took at the 1995 World Longtrack Final in Germany. It was a fantastic weekend at Scheessel – with Wiggy and Tatum level on 20 points each, it meant a run-off for the title.
England first and second, in front of all those Germans!
I recently dug out the video of the first ever GP round at Wroclaw, where Simon and Barry Briggs were in the Sky TV studio and Wiggy was pretty vocal and extremely annoyed by the way the qualifiers were sorted for the series that year.
Wonder how he would feel about the situation now!
Steve Hone

Always making time for a smile and a chat with the fans – this time in Germany, with Margit Roessler (second from right) and fellow avid Wiggy followers from her country.

Signing autographs for supporters at Oxford on the occasion of his farewell meeting, March 1999.

I took my log-in name (for the British Speedway Forum website) from a comment made by Simon Wigg.

He was being interviewed by a magazine (can't remember when or for which mag), and was asked something like: 'What's the best way to ride speedway?'

To which Wiggy replied: 'Drop the clutch and keep turning left!'

I thought that was brilliant and never forgot it.

keepturningleft

Wiggy – a true English sportsman, who will never be forgotten. He was a world-wide name on longtack, shale and grass and someone who was not only respected for his racing, but also for who he was and what he stood for.

His distinctive green leathers and white wheels made him so easy to pick out when you were stood on the second bend at a grasstrack.

He always had a smile on his face and seemed at home on the rostrum.

Real sadness was felt when he was taken away from the sport he loved and the people who loved him.

May he be resting in peace, with a smile on his face.

Ruby Tuesday

We sponsored Simon for a number of years and, although not a huge speedway fan, I got to really appreciate his contribution to your sport. And let's not forget what he did for Britain's overall sporting achievements – how many times do we get a five-times World Champ?

But despite his crazy racing schedule all over Europe, he always had time for his sponsors, his fans and young riders learning their trade. His passing is a tremendous loss.

Andy Haddleton, NSK-RHP

In my 20 years' as a referee, I can honestly say that I never came across a nicer man or rider than Simon Wigg. He was a true professional and a true gentleman, although that may sound a little old fashioned today.

He always sought out the referee before a meeting on behalf of his team – he usually asked if he could walk the track with me. He was articulate, intelligent and good company.

Right from the start of his career in the early 80s, he stood out as rider, not least in his behaviour and professional attitude to the sport and the rules and regulations.

I have thought hard and checked a few records, and can honestly say that I never once had to penalise him in any way, either by way of caution over the phone, exclusion or fine. There aren't many top riders who I can say that about – for me, he stands out alongside Dennis Sigalos and Michael Lee in this respect.

I have been out of touch with speedway for some years now, but the sad news about Simon was such a terrific shock. My heart, and that of my wife Val who also knew Simon, goes out to his wife Charline and to his children, Abigail and Ricki

Barry Bowles, North Notts.

Simon was a person who reset the standards in our sport. He was a wonderful influence on all those he came into contact with, both in his attitude and professionalism, and he will be sadly missed.

Rest in peace now, Simon, God bless you.

Andy Sell, Bristol

Since I began grasstrack in 1978, it was always a pleasure to watch The Messiah in action. He will be truly missed by so many people.

Barry Woodruff, Bristol

The Golden Boy of British speedway, gone, and terribly sad that it should end this way. The thoughts of all fans will be with Simon's wife and children. Cradley supporters, my wife and I remember the great days in '83 – 8.8 average and all.

Thanks for then and for everything, Simon. God bless.

Frank Pizzey, Halesowen, West Midlands

I really enjoyed racing and 'drinking' with such a genuine bloke – he will be sadly missed.

Rob Cameron, Nr Brands Hatch

You *were* the best. We will miss you.

Louwe Renkema, Holland

I have seen Simon several times at our grasstrack meeting in Alken. Besides being a great sportsman, he also had a great personality.

Nico Moors, Zolder, Belgium

I would like to thank Simon for bringing myself and many other grasstrack/speedway fans such pleasure over his career. I have raced in the same grasstrack meetings as Simon in the past and remember his first meeting at Peterborough Speedway with Weymouth. Simon will always live on in our memories – a true champion to the end.

Brian Best, Peterborough

The first time I saw Wiggy was back in his Weymouth Speedway days – he was a great bloke then as well as an obvious talent. I was fortunate enough to see him around the world on grass and sandtracks and he was always the most approachable guy you could hope to meet. A true gent who'll be missed all around the world.

Keith Packer, Coventry

I am 16-years-old and have been going to grasstrack all my life. As long as I can remember I have wanted to be the next 'Simon Wigg'. The man was an idol in our humble sport – a true ambassador and he should be tributed as the best grasstrack rider ever.

Gareth Bemister, Bournemouth

For me, Simon Wigg was a real TOPPER. I spoke to him several times, he was such a kind person. May he rest in peace.

Wim Van Den Berg, Rotterdam, Holland

Everybody knew about Simon's illness but nobody thought that the end was so near. We are all very sad. Rest in peace, Simon.
Gerd Hubrich, Bochum, Germany

A unique man who will never be replaced.
Les, Trevor & Ronnie Steward, Basildon, Essex

Sorry to see you leave way too early. I'm sure God has a racejacket for you in Heaven – he can't ask for a better skipper of his team.
Peter Nahlin, Sweden

". . . And all that you take with you is what you leave behind."

Happy memories – that toothy smile – the way he would always recognise you in a crowd and come over and say 'Hello!'.

The fact that although blessed with an abundance of talent, he was never big-headed and never lost touch with his fans, whatever their age group.

The quality of his riding, the affection that he received because of his gentlemanly behaviour.

The courage he showed in the last stages of his tragically shortened life – these are a few of the things that he has left behind and will ensure his name will never be forgotten.

We'll miss you, mate – the world of grasstrack, speedway and longtrack will not be the same again.
Mike Brown, Wiltshire

Truly a great rider, always exciting and a great role model for the kids of today.
Susanna Ferry, Daventry, Northamptonshire

Thanks for the great times you gave us. Many people go through life to be appreciated by so few – you, though, were appreciated by so many.
Deano, Oxford

To one of the most admired and enthusiastic speedway riders who ever donned green leathers, god bless Simon. We, the speedway world, will miss you.
Michael Farrant, Milton Keynes

Thanks for all you have done for speedway. Bye-bye, friend.
Tom Rambousek, Pardubice, Czech Republic

Simon has left us with lasting memories of his amazing talents on a speedway motorcycle.
Adrian & Des West, Adelaide, South Australia

I raced with Simon many years ago – late 70s and early 80s – on grasstrack. I often went to watch him at the Ace of Aces and he always had the time to say hello and remember the old days when we were a lot younger.

I was deeply upset to hear of his death and he will be greatly missed by us ex-grasstrackers – myself, John Cox and Steve Jenkins – up in Cheshire. He was a wonderful person to know.
Roy Dugdale, Cheshire

A man I only knew as Simon Wigg grasstrack racer, an idol of mine from childhood. It won't be the same watching the video tapes of old races any more.
Matt Saggus, Gosford, Australia

Simon has gone to the Great Longtrack in the Sky. May he rest in peace.
Tony F, Kent

It was with a real sense of shock to read in the national newspaper (*The Daily Telegraph*) of the passing of Simon Wigg. I first watched his brother, Julian, ride on the grass, then Simon himself, and admired his rapid progress.

Often he was in a class of his own – others put in the effort but could not match Simon from the gate or during the race period. Occasional machine failures at critical times robbed him of even more victories.

I especially remember him at the Berks Bonanza, at the former riverside track. Once, he was ahead in all of the qualifying races, but had to leave before the finals for a speedway commitment that evening.

Perhaps, because he was so dominant, one was always cheering someone else on to try to beat him. Perhaps, though, this is the biggest compliment he could receive from a fan of grasstrack.

Following the report of his death, a few days later *The Daily Telegraph* also printed an obituary with his photograph – a fitting tribute, indeed, to be in the national press. Thank you, Simon, for some great racing.

Roger Kennell, Hadleigh, Suffolk

So proud to race on the same grasstrack circuit with such a legend. Champion of champions, brilliant, untouchable.

Andy Wedlake, Cornwall

Thanks for all the memories, Simon, you were the greatest track rider of all time – nuff said!

Adrian Pavey, Whitehaven, Cumbria

Simon will be greatly missed – not only by those grasstrack supporters in this country but also by his many fans on the Continent. As members of the 500cc Sidecar Association, racing in the same meetings as Simon, all the members of the club found him to be the most professional and also approachable solo rider. His great skills will never be forgotten but I think the abiding memory of many people will be his broad grin and happy smile.

Gary Southgate, Biggleswade, Beds

Signing off – his last-ever trip to his beloved Germany, at Berghaupton, September, 1999.

Simon – in the words of the song, simply the best, better than all the rest, better than anyone, anyone I've ever met. A diamond geezer!
Alec & Di Wain, GRASA

Simon – you were an inspiration not only for me and my sons, but everyone else that was connected with our great sport. We will all miss you, God bless.
Gary Hiett, Swindon

So sad that Simon lost his battle. My condolenses to all his family, especially Jules, whom I raced against in the 70s. Not only was Simon a great rider, but an all round great bloke. We will always remember his infectious smile.
Lindsay Kier, Perth, Western Australia

We rode in the same team in Sweden, at Kumla, Indianerna, 1990-91. He was a very good rider and a really good and helpful friend to me. I felt sad to hear that he is no longer with us. Rest in peace.
Goran Flood, Sweden

Simon – a great rider and ambassador for the sport. A true champion, you will be missed by speedway, grasstrack and longtrack enthusiasts everywhere.
Alan & Karen Kingswell, Southampton

Having been a grasstrack supporter for over 30 years, I remember my visits to the Western Winner meetings with my Dad and watching a certain Simon Wigg, who was only a boy himself. It was very easy to spot that certain something Simon had that other riders did not. The only word I can use is CLASS.
Nick Dibben, Somerset

I am so sad at losing the greatest-ever grasstracker and smiling friend. Goodbye, Simon.
Rudi Hagen, Germany

The sport will take a long, long time to recover from this tragedy. RIP Simon.
Ian Checketts, Bordeaux, France

Simon used to ride for our club in Sweden, where he was a very popular rider, a real gentlemen and a great ambassador for the sport. It's very sad that he's not with us any more.
Lars B Dicker, Sweden

Well done, Simon – you are The Man.
Daniel Theobald, Ringwood, Hants

I had many dealings with Simon, he was an absolute gentleman with a tremendous thirst for winning. My wife and family join me in this tribute to a truly wonderful friend and fellow sportsman.
Steve Smith, Flamstead, St Albans

Having watched Wiggy ride all over the world, my thoughts go out to his family, and just to say what a great amount of joy, pleasure and entertainment he has given me since the days of Weymouth.
Steve Watkinson, Ringwood, Hants

Once met, always in my mind – R.I.P.
Seppo, Finland

When Wiggy rode for the Bradford Dukes in the early 90s, he was a star – not just on the track, but off it as well. No matter if he was setting off to go abroad that night for a longtrack/grasstrack meeting, he would still sign every autograph and answer all questions. He always gave 100 per cent on the track.

My best memory of Wiggy was in 1991, when we went to Cradley Heath in the second leg of the KO Cup and he basically won the trophy for the Dukes with a near faultless display.

There will never be another.

Gerard Lynch, Halifax

Please let his family know that he has been a fair and friendly (sports)man, who we all will miss.

Thomas Schade, Bonn, Germany

Simon was not only one of the best grasstrack riders I have ever seen, he was undoubtedly the friendliest. He had time and a smile for everyone and I will never forget how he drove all night to take part in the Berks Bonanza, which in all honesty was a small meeting compared to the one he had ridden in the day before in Germany.

He will always be remembered as the last Ace of Aces. It was meant to be.

At every grasstrack I go to he will be sadly missed. Please let there be bike racing in Heaven for him.

Trevor Bird, Newcastle

Thank you for the good times that you brought to Exeter and the way you enthralled the Falcons fans – *From John.*

Simon – Thank you for taking the time to have your photo taken with me at Exeter when you were so ill. It takes pride of place in our living room – *Love Craig Nethercott (age 9), Exeter Aces Cycle Speedway Club.*

John and Craig Nethercott, Exeter

A legend on track, consummate professional and one of life's nice guys.

David, Oxford

This man was simply the best.

Neil Hiscock, Trowbridge, Wilts

You gave me so much pleasure when I saw you ride and things will never be the same without you.

Brian Hiscock, Warminster, Wilts

Everybody will miss him but no-one will forget the man in the green lethers – GOD SPEED!

Stephen Mcnally, Berwick

Dear Simon. In 1987, I took my stepson, Craig, to the Speedway Royale at the Sydney Showground for a 'one off' international race meeting. At the time he was an avid surfer and rugby union footballer with no interest in motorcycle racing.

You won the meeting that night and Craig, who was 13 at the time, asked if he could have a look at some of the bikes up close, so I brought him around to the rear of the pits. While I was explaining some finer points of a speedway bike, you walked out of the pits and I introduced him to you and asked if you'd sign his programme, which you kindly did.

Craig is 27 now and married and has been a keen follower of all forms of motorcycle sport since that night. He currently owns an R1 Yamaha road bike and I know that, from that night, Craig and I became closer as we both had a common interest. He still reminds me of the night he met Simon Wigg.

I just wanted to thank you for making a young boy very happy and an old dirt track rider very proud that a CHAMPION took the time.

Dave & Craig Lewis, Gosford, NSW, Australia

We're just ordinary spectators but Simon will never be forgotten by us for his performances at the Western Winner. Those wonderful long and lazy summer meetings of the 70s were such a wonderful showcase for his unique mastery of the grass. All grasstrack will miss him.
Colin & Sheila Read, Poole, Dorset

I am pleased to have known Simon for many years, through speedway and grasstrack, and send my condolences to his family and relatives.
Simon always had a grin even when things were at a low and lean time in his life. When he rode for Long-Eaton he never seemed the same Simon we knew from passed years, but he always grinned and carried on as only a true racer knows how.
Jeff Boardman, ex-Long-Eaton track staff

We would very much like to thank the following two websites – ***www.speedway-forum.co.uk*** *and* ***www.grasstrack.freeserve.co.uk*** *– for permission to reproduce here many of the supporters" messages that originally appeared as internet postings. We would recommend you visit both sites. The grasstrack one – hosted by Marc – includes more fine tributes to Simon Wigg.*

Honours

World-wide Champion

...R HONOURS

...st all of the 500-plus individual victories Wiggy won in the course of his illustrious ...ernational career would fill another book, but here are his major successes in speedway, grasstrack and longtrack . . .

SPEEDWAY

World Championship runner-up	Munich	1989 (2nd-12pts)
World Championship Finalist	Gothenburg	1985 (6th-9pts)
	Vojens	1988 (6th-9pts)
Grand Prix	Prague	1997 (3pts)
	Landshut	1997 (2pts)
	Wroclaw	1997 (8pts)
Commonwealth Champion	Belle Vue	1989
British Champion	Coventry	1988
	Coventry	1989
World Team Cup winner	Odsal	1989 (11pts)
World Team Cup Finalist	Leszno	1984 (9pts*)
	**Gothenburg/Vojens/Odsal	1986 (24pts*)
	**Fredericia/Prague/Coventry	1987 (29pts*)
	Long Beach	1988 (0pts)
	Pardubice	1990 (8pts)
World Pairs runner-up (with Kelvin Tatum)	Pardubice	1987 (20pts)
World Pairs Finalist (with Jeremy Doncaster)	Pocking	1986 (11pts)
Grand Prix Challenge winner	Prague	1996
Czech Golden Helmet winner	Pardubice	1994
German Golden Helmet winner (twice)		
German Silver Helmet winner (four times)		
Dutch Golden Helmet winner (twice)		
Australian Mr Melbourne winner (five times)		
Series 500 International Masters rounds:	Winner at Perth (twice)	
	Winner at Brisbane (twice)	
	Adelaide, Sydney & Bunbury (once each)	
British League Championship winner	Cradley Heath	1983
	Oxford	1985
		1986
		1989
British League Knockout Cup winner	Cradley Heath	1983
	Oxford	1985
		1986***
	Bradford	1991
	Bradford	1992
League Cup winner	Oxford	1986***

**Simon Wigg top-scored for England in these World Team Cup Finals. **The World Team Cup 'final' was staged over three rounds, with aggregate points counting. ***Trophy shared with Cradley Heath due to postponements.*

LONGTRACK

World Championship winner	Korskro, Denmark	1985 (22pts)
	Marianske Lazne, CZ	1989 (38pts)
	Herxheim, Germany	1990 (37pts)
	Muhldorf, Germany	1993 (22pts)
	Marianske Lazne, CZ	1994 (25pts)
World Championship runner-up	Muhldorf, Germany	1987 (2nd-21pts)
	Scheessel, Germany	1995 (2nd-25pts*)
World Championship Finalist	Korskro, Denmark	1982 (13th-5pts)
	Marianske Lazne, CZ	1983 (8th-11pts)
	Scheessel, Germany	1988 (8th-21pts)
	Marianske Lazne, CZ	1991 (9th-10pts)
	Pfarrkirchen, Germany	1992 (19th-0pts)
	Herxheim, Germany	1996 (7th-11pts)

World Longtrack Grand Prix 1998 (10th-40pts)
Rounds held at: Aduard, Holland; Marmande, France;
Abingdon, England; Scheessel, Germany; Muhldorf, Germany

Australian Longtrack Grand Prix winner (three times)
New Zealand Longtrack Grand Prix winner (three times)
Teterow Golden Helmet winner (five times)
Teterow Bergring Pokal winner (four times)

GRASSTRACK

British Grasstrack Champion 1981, 1982, 1983, 1985, 1989, 1990

Marmande winner (three times)
German Grasstrack Super Cup winner (three times)
Ace of Aces winner (four times)

Wiggy salutes Herxheim after winning the 1990 World Longtrack Final – watched by German supremo Gunther Sorber of the FIM.

Last Words

Messages for Simon

One of the commemorative steel wheel sprockets – made by George Sartin of Talon Engineering and used to decorate Simon's coffin. The inscription reads: 'SIMON WIGG 15 OCT, 1960-15 NOV 2000 – 5 TIMES WORLD LONG TRACK CHAMPION'.

WHEN Simon was admitted to The Willen Hospice, near Milton Keynes, where he spent the last three months of his life, he received many visitors from all corners of the world who came to say their final 'goodbyes'.

Many of those visitors – members of his close family, dear friends and some people he hadn't seen for some considerable time – wrote a simple little message in a book kept in his room. Many of these entries, some heart-rending and others full of humour, summed up their feelings for Simon and just how much he meant to everyone who knew and met him.

Several also reflect Simon's belated craving for chocolate!

On the facing page, we have reproduced just some of the many messages that conveyed such loving thoughts in Simon's last days . . .

DATE	NAME	ADDRESS
15.10.00	Liz	Have a fantastic day! Keep on smiling lots of love Liz xx
HAPPY BIRTHDAY! 15.10.00.	SHARON,	Oh, BLOODY HELL! So glad you've had such a great day Cheers!!
15.10.00	Olli & Paul.	Great Mate. — (I nicked all your sweets) always Smiling always Swearing always a Pleasure
17/10/	Mum (Rosemary)	Very much love, now + always. xxxx
17/10/00	Lynne	What a party!
18/10/00	Johno & Glen.	Welcome to the OLD FARTS CLUB.
19.10.00	Mick & Mom, Phyl Gordon	Super Party. Super People (Bloody Great Venue)
19-10-00	KEV & TRISH	He's seen an advert on the telly & has now taken up singing Tenor — looks like he's going for even more records!!
20.10.00	Chris & Col. HARRISON	STILL a CHARACTER,
24.10.00	Phyl Gordon. GEORGE WATTS	Best wishes from old mate / sponsor.
2.11.00	Johno	*off to Aus mate but thinking of you always
5/11/00	JON SURMAN GLEN ARMSTRONG.	Just a quick visit to top up on Pringles!! All the very Best Jono.

DATE	NAME	ADDRESS
12.11.00	NANNA, NATALIE, BRIAN, ELAINE LOUISE, ANDY, RICKI, CHARLIE, BRETT.	SLEEPING LIKE A BABY.
13.11.00	BRETT + CHARLIE	XXX OOO NO JET SKIING TODAY!
13.11.00	Olli & Sabine	everybody nicking your chocolates while you are asleep...
13.11.2000	STEVE + ELAINE BRANSON	SLEEPING LIKE A BABY AGAIN, BUT IT GAVE US A GOOD CHANCE TO EAT SOME OF YOUR CHOCOLATES! "Simon I like" big hug & kiss from XXXXX. Jack & Amelia.
13.11.2000	Wiggy.	Wiggy my friend & mate!! / xx.
14.11.2000	Crossie	fast asleep, still looking good. family send love.
14.11.2000	Paul x.	Your an inspiration!!
14.11.2000.	BRETT.	I ALWAYS THINK OF YOU AS THE BIG BROTHER I NEVER HAD!!

The Author

This is Gareth Rogers' second speedway title – his first being *Main Dane,* with four times World Champion Hans Nielsen, in 1994.

He is also the author of *Fleet and Free*, the history of the Birchfield Harriers Athletics Club, and *Beyond the Yellow Teapot*, the history of the Renault F1 racing team.

As well as a multi-club announcer since his early days in speedway with his home-town club the Newport Wasps, Gareth has been a promoter at Eastbourne, Milton Keynes and the Isle of Wight, where he introduced the sport onto the island.

Recently he has been involved in the initiative to revive speedway in Middlesbrough.

When it's time to go . . . Simon walking through the pits entrance at Oxford Speedway for the last time, at the end of his spectacular Farewell to British Speedway meeting, March 1999. It was some life!

"Sorry to see you leave way too early. I'm sure God has a racejacket for you in Heaven – he can't ask for a better skipper of His team"

Peter Nahlin, Sweden